Also by America's Test Kitchen

For a full listing of all our books:

CooksIllustrated.com

AmericasTestKitchen.com

Praise for America's Test Kitchen Titles

"This 'very' Chinese cookbook from a father–son duo is a keeper. The book—ATK's first devoted to Chinese cooking—proves that you can teach and entertain in the same volume . . . All in all, it's one of the most charming works I've seen in years, and I already want to get a second copy."

Washington Post on *A Very Chinese Cookbook*

A Best Cookbook of 2023
New York Times on *A Very Chinese Cookbook*

"An exhaustive but approachable primer for those looking for a 'flexible' diet. Chock-full of tips, you can dive into the science of plant-based cooking or just sit back and enjoy the 500 recipes."

Minneapolis Star Tribune on *The Complete Plant-Based Cookbook*

"Here are the words just about any vegan would be happy to read: 'Why This Recipe Works.' Fans of America's Test Kitchen are used to seeing the phrase, and now it applies to the growing collection of plant-based creations in *Vegan for Everybody*."

Washington Post on *Vegan for Everybody*

"This comprehensive guide is packed with delicious recipes and fun menu ideas but its unique draw is the personal narrative and knowledge-sharing of each ATK chef, which will make this a hit."

Booklist on *Gatherings*

"True to its name, this smart and endlessly enlightening cookbook is about as definitive as it's possible to get in the modern vegetarian realm."

Men's Journal on *The Complete Vegetarian Cookbook*

"A mood board for one's food board is served up in this excellent guide . . . This has instant classic written all over it."

Publishers Weekly (starred review) on *Boards: Stylish Spreads for Casual Gatherings*

"Reassuringly hefty and comprehensive, *The Complete Autumn and Winter Cookbook* by America's Test Kitchen has you covered with a seemingly endless array of seasonal fare . . . This overstuffed compendium is guaranteed to warm you from the inside out."

NPR on *The Complete Autumn and Winter Cookbook*

"If you're one of the 30 million Americans with diabetes, *The Complete Diabetes Cookbook* by America's Test Kitchen belongs on your kitchen shelf."

Parade.com on *The Complete Diabetes Cookbook*

"Another flawless entry in the America's Test Kitchen canon, *Bowls* guides readers of all culinary skill levels in composing one-bowl meals from a variety of cuisines."

BuzzFeed Books on *Bowls*

"*The Perfect Cookie* . . . is, in a word, perfect. This is an important and substantial cookbook . . . If you love cookies, but have been a tad shy to bake on your own, all your fears will be dissipated. This is one book you can use for years with magnificently happy results."

HuffPost on *The Perfect Cookie*

"The book offers an impressive education for curious cake makers, new and experienced alike. A summation of 25 years of cake making at ATK, there are cakes for every taste."

Wall Street Journal on *The Perfect Cake*

"The go-to gift book for newlyweds, small families, or empty nesters."

Orlando Sentinel on *The Complete Cooking for Two Cookbook*

"*Five-Ingredient Dinners* is as close to a sure thing to an easy meal as you'll find . . . If you want to get cooking, cut down on takeout, and deliver a ton of flavor, you can't lose with these recipes."

Providence Journal on *Five-Ingredient Dinners*

MOSTLY MEATLESS

GREEN UP YOUR PLATE WITHOUT
totally DITCHING THE MEAT

AMERICA'S TEST KITCHEN

Library of Congress Control Number: 2024925199

ISBN 978-1-954210-72-1

AMERICA'S TEST KITCHEN

21 Drydock Avenue, Boston, MA 02210

Printed in Canada

10 9 8 7 6 5 4 3 2 1

Distributed by Penguin Random House Publisher Services

Tel: 800.733.3000

Pictured on Front Cover: Gochujang Meatballs (page 183) shown as part of a bowl with farro, steamed broccolini and baby bok choy, cucumber, snap peas, purple daikon and watermelon radishes, baby kale, and chopped fresh herbs

Pictured on Back Cover (from top left): Spinach Pesto Pasta Bowl (page 162), Vegetarian Chili (page 112), Bacon and Cheese Black Bean Burgers (page 189)

Featured Photography: Daniel J. van Ackere

Editorial Director, Books: Adam Kowit

Executive Food Editor: Dan Zuccarello

Deputy Food Editor: Stephanie Pixley

Executive Managing Editor: Debra Hudak

Project Editor: Megan Zhang

Senior Editors: Camila Chaparro, Joe Gitter, and Sara Mayer

Test Cooks: Olivia Counter, Laila Ibrahim, and José Maldonado

Assistant Editor: Julia Arwine

Design Director: Lindsey Timko Chandler

Associate Art Director and Designer: Molly Gillespie

Photography Director: Julie Bozzo Cote

Senior Photography Producer: Meredith Mulcahy

Senior Staff Photographers: Steve Klise and Daniel J. van Ackere

Staff Photographer: Kritsada Panichgul

Additional Photography: Joseph Keller and Carl Tremblay

Food Styling: Joy Howard, Sheila Jarnes, Catrine Kelty, Chantal Lambeth, Gina McCreadie, Kendra McNight, Ashley Moore, Christie Morrison, Marie Piraino, Elle Simone Scott, Kendra Smith, and Sally Staub

Project Manager, Books: Kelly Gauthier

Senior Print Production Specialist: Lauren Robbins

Production and Imaging Coordinator: Amanda Yong

Production and Imaging Specialist: Tricia Neumyer

Production and Imaging Assistant: Chloe Petraske

Copy Editor: Cheryl Redmond

Proofreader: Ann-Marie Imbornoni

Indexer: Elizabeth Parson

Chief Executive Officer: Dan Suratt

Chief Content Officer: Dan Souza

Senior Content Adviser: Jack Bishop

Executive Editorial Directors: Julia Collin Davison and Bridget Lancaster

Senior Director, Book Sales: Emily Logan

Contents

Welcome to America's Test Kitchen

This book has been tested, written, and edited by the folks at America's Test Kitchen, where curious home cooks become confident cooks. Located in Boston's Seaport District in the historic Innovation and Design Building, it features 15,000 square feet of kitchen space including multiple photography and video studios. It is the home of *Cook's Illustrated* magazine and *Cook's Country* magazine and is the workday destination for more than 60 test cooks, editors, and cookware specialists. Our mission is to empower and inspire confidence, community, and creativity in the kitchen.

We start the process of testing a recipe with a complete lack of preconceptions, which means that we accept no claim, no technique, and no recipe at face value. We simply assemble as many variations as possible, test a half-dozen of the most promising, and taste the results blind. We then construct our own recipe and continue to test it, varying ingredients, techniques, and cooking times until we reach a consensus. As we like to say in the test kitchen, "We make the mistakes so you don't have to." The result is our best version of every recipe. We use the same rigorous approach when we test equipment and taste ingredients.

All of this would not be possible without a belief that good cooking, much like good music, is based on a foundation of objective technique. Some people like spicy foods and others don't, but there is a right way to sauté, there is a best way to cook a pot roast, and there are measurable scientific principles involved in producing perfectly beaten, stable egg whites. Our ultimate goal is to investigate the fundamental principles of cooking to give you the techniques, tools, and ingredients you need to become a better cook. It is as simple as that.

To see what goes on behind the scenes at America's Test Kitchen, check out our social media channels for kitchen snapshots, exclusive content, video tips, and much more. You can watch us work (in our actual test kitchen) by tuning in to *America's Test Kitchen* or *Cook's Country* on public television or on our websites. Listen to *Proof* (AmericasTestKitchen.com/podcasts) to hear engaging, complex stories about people and food. Want to hone your cooking skills or finally learn how to bake—with an America's Test Kitchen test cook? Enroll in one of our online cooking classes.

However you choose to visit us, we welcome you into our kitchen, where you can stand by our side as we test our way to the best recipes in America.

Join Our Community of Recipe Testers

Our recipe testers provide valuable feedback on recipes under development by ensuring that they are foolproof in home kitchens. Help the America's Test Kitchen book team investigate the how and why behind successful recipes from your home kitchen.

A GUIDE TO MOSTLY MEATLESS EATING

Introduction

We're seeing a shift all around us in the way American eaters think about meat—namely, how much of it we're eating. There are a lot of reasons you might be looking to consume less meat. You may be trying to cut back on saturated fat, or perhaps your doctor has recommended paying attention to your cholesterol. Maybe you're concerned about the environmental impacts of animal farming, and you'd like to play a part in lowering the food system's carbon footprint. Perhaps the rising cost of meat is motivating you to stretch your grocery budget further, as vegetables, legumes, and grains are often more cost-effective than meat. Or, you may simply want to increase your vegetable consumption, without totally giving up meat. After all, there's ever-growing evidence that a plant-forward diet that minimizes animal products can lower the risk of chronic diseases such as heart disease and diabetes. Whatever your motivation for picking up this book, reducing meat intake can have wide-ranging upsides.

Yet, it's undeniable that meat isn't merely a source of protein. It often plays a central role in cultural identity, family traditions, and satiation. While our readers have loved our vegan and vegetarian cookbooks, we also know that an all-or-nothing approach toward meat may dissuade many home cooks from tapping into the myriad benefits that reducing meat consumption can yield. That's why this book is not about cutting out meat entirely. Rather, we wanted to embrace a plant-forward way of eating that makes vegetables the star of the kitchen while still leaving a little room on the plate for meat. Even a small reduction in meat can move the needle toward a significant positive impact. Armed with this book, you'll find balance and deliciousness in eating habits that prioritize plants without entirely forgoing the taste, nutrients, and cultural role of meat—and certainly without sacrificing flavor.

To help you navigate cooking with less meat, we set out to reimagine traditionally meat-heavy dishes—think beef stew, meatballs, and tacos—with a little less meat and a lot more vegetables. This was a challenge at first, as it can be easy to define a dish by the meat component. When we simply cut the amount of meat in a recipe and replaced it with vegetables, we were sometimes disappointed (we sampled many bland burgers). So we shifted to a mindset of reinvention, rather than replication. Experimenting with new techniques, we identified strategies for selecting and cooking meat in ways that extract maximum flavor from a smaller portion. For example, we learned that rendering some meat and then cooking vegetables in the fat left behind made for meals so rich and hearty that we didn't even notice we were eating less meat. To bulk up modest amounts of meat, we used vegetables in innovative ways—turning carrots into noodles, adding jackfruit to pulled-meat sandwiches, and mixing zucchini into burger patties—that not only made the most of each plant's unique traits, but also better enabled them to soak up seasonings. With this shift to seeing plants as the main event and meat as the supporting act, we were able to embrace a mentality of abundance and create some of our most interesting and vibrant recipes to date, from Nopales and Shrimp Tacos to Mushroom Tea Rice with Chicken and Caramel-Braised Shallots.

As we filled this book with flavorful creations, we drew inspiration from cuisines around the world that inherently prioritize plants and tend to use meat in modest amounts. Hopping around the globe in your kitchen is a great way to continuously reset your interest in home cooking, making a plant-forward lifestyle feel exciting and expansive, not at all restrictive. Wherever you might be on your journey to eating less meat, you'll find recipes that support your goals in this diverse book—whether you're looking for meat-light weeknight dinners or vegetarian options that still taste satisfyingly meaty.

By the end of our testing and development process, we'd created recipes that will remain a part of our day-to-day cooking. These are recipes we've already come to crave and that we feel good about eating. Writing this cookbook made us better appreciate the potential of ingredients that had been there all along. Now, you, too, can discover how easy and enjoyable it can be to go meatless—mostly.

The Building Blocks of Satisfying (Mostly) Meatless Meals

When we talk about satisfying meals, we mean more than getting full. A hearty breakfast, lunch, or dinner should be flavorful, substantial, and texturally interesting—satiating your tastebuds as much as your stomach. To achieve this with less meat, it's important to rethink what ingredients you consider kitchen staples.

In developing the mostly meatless recipes in this book, we asked ourselves: What role does meat play in a particular dish? Does it provide richness, smokiness, umami, or succulence? Once we understood that, we could then examine a recipe holistically and determine how to implement less meat or enhance plant-based ingredients to accomplish the same purpose. This often meant finding creative ways to add heartiness through vegetables, grains, legumes, and seasonings, while using smaller amounts of meat to support the dish, rather than dominate it.

The following pages outline some foundational ingredients for mostly meatless meals that don't skimp one bit on satisfaction. We recommend keeping at least a few from each of the following categories on hand for quick and easy meal-building.

A Note on Tags

To help you identify recipes that suit your needs, we've implemented a tagging system:

▲ *fast:* can be made in less than 45 minutes

✦ *vegetarian:* contains no animal meat (and mentions plant-based alternatives for condiments, such as fish sauce, that do contain animal products)

■ *fiber-ful:* one serving contains at least 1.4 grams of fiber for every 100 calories (see more on page 7)

● *one-pan:* comes together in a single cooking vessel

ASSEMBLING A MOSTLY MEATLESS MEAL

As we developed recipes, we drew inspiration from a model followed by the United States Department of Agriculture (USDA) as a starting point to think about how to assemble nutritious meals. According to the MyPlate model, half your meal should come from vegetables (and fruits). The next-largest section is grains. The smallest is protein, be it from plants or animals. From this framework, we created recipes that use meat in moderation, in a smaller role as a sidekick, and in an even smaller role as just a seasoning. These are different ways to balance your meals, with an emphasis on plants.

MEAT IN MODERATION

HERBY ROASTED CAULIFLOWER AND CHICKEN WITH QUINOA PILAF (PAGE 330)

One succulent chicken thigh per serving is enough for a satiating meal when it's roasted together with cauliflower, bulked up with lemony quinoa, and served with a bright, herbaceous sauce.

MEAT AS A SIDEKICK

MÌ XÀO GIÒN (PAGE 386)

A medley of saucy vegetables ladled over a bed of crisp noodles, this Vietnamese favorite utilizes just one pork chop (for four people) and a host of umami-rich pantry staples for maximum flavor.

MEAT AS A SEASONING

CREAMY WHITE BEAN SOUP WITH CHORIZO OIL AND GARLICKY BREAD CRUMBS (PAGE 64)

There's no shortage of savoriness in this velvety, Parmesan-enriched soup drizzled with a smoky chorizo-scented oil.

Hearty Vegetables

When you're reducing meat, hearty vegetables (and fruits) are your best ally. Not only are they filling, nutritious, and often high in fiber, but many also have a knack for absorbing seasonings or mimicking the texture of meat. We turned often to these versatile plant foods to create satisfying meals that deliver big flavor—with less reliance on meat.

JACKFRUIT

Young jackfruit, when cooked and shredded, has a tender, stringy texture remarkably reminiscent of pulled chicken or pork, so it's no surprise that the tropical ingredient—long beloved in many Asian cultures—is becoming a popular meat alternative all over the world. It's widely available in canned form, packed in water or brine. Enjoy it in:

- Pulled Jackfruit and Chicken Sandwiches (page 199)
- Jackfruit and Chickpea Makhani (page 295)

MUSHROOMS

Mushrooms, especially varieties like portobello, shiitake, and cremini, are some of the most potent sources of plant-based umami. They're naturally rich in glutamate, the flavor compound that makes meat savory. They also have a spongy, chewy mouthfeel comparable to animal protein, which makes them great for bulking up a small amount of meat. Enjoy them in:

- Savory Oatmeal with Pancetta, Mushrooms, and Shaved Parmesan (page 35)
- Mushroom-Beef Blended Burgers (page 186)
- Creamy Mushroom and Pink Pickled Cabbage Sandwiches (page 208)
- Sausage-Stuffed Portobello Mushrooms with Cabbage Salad (page 268)
- Rigatoni with Quick Mushroom Bolognese (page 317)
- Mushroom Tea Rice with Chicken and Caramel-Braised Shallots (page 370)

CAULIFLOWER

This cruciferous vegetable is highly versatile and holds up well under a variety of cooking methods, from roasting to grilling to steaming. It's also a superb vehicle for flavor, readily absorbing any sauces or seasonings it's cooked with. Enjoy it in:

- Laksa Cauliflower Rice Bowl with Shrimp (page 181)
- Chipotle Mushroom and Cauliflower Tacos (page 233)
- Herby Roasted Cauliflower and Chicken with Quinoa Pilaf (page 330)
- Cauliflower Biryani (page 369)

EGGPLANT

Eggplant often brings an appetizingly luscious component to dishes, as its dense, spongy texture becomes tender and almost velvety when cooked. Eggplant's porous nature also allows the flesh to drink up marinades, fats, and spices, which perhaps explains why various cuisines turn to it to anchor rich, savory dishes with great depth of flavor. Enjoy it in:

- Ratatouille with Poached Eggs (page 49)
- Soba Noodles with Roasted Eggplant and Sesame (page 325)
- Baharat Cauliflower and Eggplant with Chickpeas (page 354)
- Vegetable Lasagna (page 382)

CELERY ROOT

Celery root's fibrous, crisp flesh adds substantial heft to dishes, making them heartier and more satiating. The vegetable also has a distinctive earthy flavor—slightly reminiscent of potatoes or turnips—as well as celery-like herbal notes that can add complexity to all kinds of dishes. Enjoy it in:

- Celery Root Galette with Blue Cheese and Walnuts (page 388)

CABBAGE

Whether it's sautéed, braised, stir-fried, or roasted, cabbage of all kinds—green, red, napa, and savoy, to name a few—tends to hold up well during cooking. It retains a firm, hearty bite that adds bulk and substance to mostly meatless meals, while its mild taste complements and adapts to all kinds of flavor profiles. Enjoy it in:

- Neorm Sach Moan (page 124)
- Charred Cabbage Salad with Torn Tofu and Plantain Chips (page 135)
- Creamy Mushroom and Pink Pickled Cabbage Sandwiches (page 208)
- Yaki Udon (page 320)
- Brothy Savoy Cabbage with Pancetta, Rye Bread, and Fontina (page 351)
- Cabbage, Kohlrabi, and Lamb Tagine with Prunes (page 352)

SWEET POTATOES

While white potatoes are certainly satisfying and versatile, we found ourselves turning often to the sweet variety. They give dishes a pleasantly nutty dimension, which is intensified when they're roasted to bring out their natural sugars. Sweet potatoes' creamy, somewhat fibrous flesh also makes them especially hearty, ideal for adding substance to a wide range of recipes. Enjoy them in:

- Breakfast Wraps with Sweet Potatoes and Broccolini (page 29)
- Sweet Potato and Lentil Salad with Crispy Shallots (page 151)
- Sweet Potato, Poblano, and Black Bean Tacos (page 234)
- Loaded Sweet Potato Wedges with Tempeh (page 280)

ZUCCHINI

The high water content and spongy texture of zucchini help them readily soak up seasonings. And because of their mild, neutral taste, zucchini integrate seamlessly into a variety of dishes—whether you're spiralizing them for a salad or shredding them for burger patties. Enjoy them in:

- Zucchini Noodle Salad with Tahini-Ginger Dressing (page 143)
- Turkey-Zucchini Burgers with Cranberry Relish (page 192)
- Crispy Chickpea Cakes with Zucchini Ribbon Salad (page 195)

BUTTERNUT SQUASH

The smooth, dense flesh of butternut squash is excellent at flavor absorption. It also takes on different textures depending on how it's prepared: While roasting caramelizes it and draws out its toasty undertones, simmering and pureeing it makes it luscious and velvety. Enjoy it in:

- Creamy Butternut Squash Soup with Sausage Crumbles and Apple (page 77)
- Sweet and Spicy Glazed Tofu with Coconut-Braised Mustard Greens (page 282)

PARSNIPS

This firm, dense root vegetable has a substantial bite that holds up well during cooking, making it a great candidate for roasts and stews. Denser and starchier than their carrot cousins, parsnips have an earthy flavor that makes a clean canvas for bold seasonings—and the vegetables beautifully absorb any fat and spices they're cooked with. Enjoy them in:

- Parsnip and Chicken Shawarma (page 216)

REIMAGINING VEGETABLES

In developing recipes for this book, we didn't only think about how to amp up the ratio of vegetables to meat. We also adopted a mindset of greening up the plate by diversifying the kinds of vegetables we incorporated into recipes and the ways in which we cooked them. Mixing and matching vegetables often naturally dialed down the amount of meat we used, while simultaneously making a meal more texturally interesting and nutritionally well rounded. Because every plant has unique strengths that make it well suited for certain cooking methods, we experimented with different techniques to capitalize on the unique qualities that make each vegetable delicious. The following examples in particular reminded us how easy and fun it can be to eat a larger quantity and variety of plants.

CARROTS

Firm, dense, and subtly sweet, carrots have a sturdy texture that we realized is perfect for cutting into thin, noodle-like ribbons. They made our Carrot Ribbon, Chicken, and Coconut Curry Soup (page 58) both more engaging to eat—the crisp ribbons were snappy, and fun to twirl on a fork—and more flavorful, as the thin slices thoroughly absorbed the soup's curry flavor. We paired the ribbons with snow peas to amp up the crunch factor.

Shaved carrots made an unexpectedly great stand-in for noodles.

SPINACH

Light, quick-cooking spinach has a neutral flavor and wilts down considerably when cooked, which means you can incorporate a large amount into a dish without overwhelming the other ingredients. In our Spinach Pesto Pasta Bowl (page 162), 10 cups (!) of spinach blended up into a vibrantly green pesto that was smooth, savory, and full of fiber.

SWISS CHARD

We cut this sturdy green into pieces and wilted it in our macaroni and cheese (page 313) and enchiladas (page 349) to accent the dishes with a chewy bite. When kept whole and briefly covered with boiling water, however, Swiss chard leaves become soft and pliable. We took advantage of this to create our Hashweh Stuffed Swiss Chard (page 346), in which the tender greens become pockets for a spiced rice-and-meat mixture.

BEETS

Beets, with their sturdiness, absorbent texture, and bright-pink color, turned out to be an apt stand-in for seafood in our poke bowls (page 176). A stint in the microwave to soften the flesh helped the vegetable drink up a savory-sweet poke-inspired marinade.

Beets' satisfyingly dense bite made for hearty poke bowls.

PEAS

Added to dishes whole, peas have a pleasant, mildly sweet pop, their firm outer skin giving way to a tender interior. But we found that the legumes' creamy texture also made them ideal for blitzing up into a buttery sauce. We blended them with pistachios and mint to make a rich, nutty, vividly green pesto that clung pleasingly to our pasta (page 310).

OKRA

With its slightly crunchy exterior and tender interior, okra is highly versatile and adds a great deal of textural interest to dishes. It can complement and bulk up grains and legumes, as in our Red Beans and Rice with Okra and Tomatoes (page 364). It can thicken stews and curries such as our Green Gumbo (page 96) and Madras Okra Curry (page 291). When lightly charred, it makes a snappy, chewy partner to meat in our Blackened Chicken and Okra Tacos (page 230), and soaks up fiery mala seasoning in our Charred Sichuan-Style Okra (page 288).

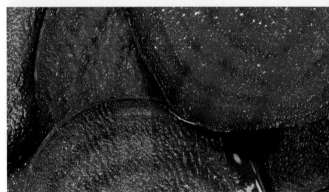

Filling Up on Fiber

Though reducing the amount of meat in a recipe sometimes results in less overall protein, this macronutrient isn't the only path to satiation. Amping up fiber in a dish is a great way to make it more filling. Fiber slows digestion, which in turn prolongs the sensation of fullness and satiety. High fiber content also tends to make foods chewier and more satisfying to eat. Moreover, fiber nurtures gut health by preventing chronic inflammation of the GI tract and keeping you regular. We worked fiber-rich foods—think leafy greens, seeds, and legumes—into many dishes to make them more substantial. Look for the fiber-ful tag to identify recipes that are especially rich in fiber. (Men age 50 or younger should take in 38 grams of fiber per day; women should take in 25 grams. Men age 51 or older should take in 30 grams per day; women, 21 grams.)

The Right Meat for the Job

Choosing the right type or cut of meat for a particular dish can be key to reducing the amount of meat in a dish without sacrificing taste. Often the best choice has a relatively high fat content, which ensures that the savory richness of the protein imbues the other ingredients with maximum flavor. Before you head to the butcher or deli, consult the below chart, which illustrates some of the different animal cuts that appear in this book and why each makes a big flavor impact, even when it's used in smaller quantities.

Storage Smarts

For tips on how to buy and store meat, see page 20.

SOURCE	CUT	WHY IT WORKS	USE IT IN
CHICKEN	Bone-In Thighs	As they cook, bone-in thighs release potently meaty, savory juices; as bones are heated, they expel moisture, salt, and amino acids from the deeply flavored marrow, while the fat and connective tissue around the bones also contribute moisture and flavor. The richness of bone-in thighs lets you use less chicken while maintaining robust chicken flavor. Moreover, bone-in thighs usually come with skin, which crisps up nicely and adds both textural interest and visual appeal.	• Parsnip and Chicken Shawarma (page 216) • Herby Roasted Cauliflower and Chicken with Quinoa Pilaf (page 330) • Chicken and Spiced Freekeh with Cilantro and Preserved Lemon (page 337) • Mushroom Tea Rice with Caramel-Braised Shallots (page 370)
CHICKEN	Boneless, Skinless Thighs	Compared to their bone-in counterparts, boneless, skinless thighs are often more convenient to cook with, especially if the meat needs to be cut into bite-size pieces for stews or other saucy dishes. Distributed throughout a dish, the supple morsels of meat go a long way in promoting richness in a dish, even when used in modest amounts.	• Pulled Jackfruit and Chicken Sandwiches (page 199) • Kare Raisu (page 250) • Green Mole with Chayote and Chicken (page 254) • Arroz Con Pollo (page 334)
BEEF	Skirt Steak	Skirt steak has a strong beefy flavor, so eating even a small portion can feel deeply satisfying. Because it's such a thin cut, skirt steak also offers ample surface area—all the more opportunity for the meat to absorb seasonings.	• Pinto Bean, Ancho, and Beef Salad with Pickled Poblanos (page 127) • Cast Iron Steak and Vegetable Fajitas (page 256)
BEEF	Blade Steaks	A moderate quantity of blade steaks can go a long way in promoting flavor in a recipe. The tough cut turns meltingly tender when simmered in liquid. As nearly all of the fat and connective tissue dissolve into a soft, silky texture, the meat produces an accompanying sauce heady with beefy flavor.	• Almost Beefless Beef Stew (page 91)
BEEF	Ground Beef	You only need a little ground beef to enrich an entire dish with the meat's glutamic flavor. Ground beef blends especially seamlessly with other chewy, crumbly ingredients, so you can easily bulk up a small amount of meat into a larger portion that still drips with beefy flavor.	• Mushroom-Beef Blended Burgers (page 186) • Weeknight Ground Beef and Lentil Tacos (page 241) • Mostly Meatless Meatballs and Marinara (page 378)

SOURCE	CUT	WHY IT WORKS	USE IT IN
PORK	Pork Butt	Pork butt tends to be well marbled with flavorful fat, which imparts juiciness and richness as it cooks. Slowly braising the collagen-rich cut yields tender, succulent meat and a full-bodied broth that oozes porky richness, even when using a moderately sized cut.	• Sancocho (page 106) • Hot Ukrainian Borscht (page 108)
	Ground Pork	Compared to ground beef, pork tends to cook up richer and more tender thanks to its generally higher fat percentage. Spread out across a dish, it readily distributes its wealth of meaty flavor, coating the surrounding ingredients with savoriness.	• Cheesy Black Bean and Pork Skillet Bake (page 260) • Mapo Tofu (page 285) • Bún Chả (page 342)
LAMB	Lamb Shoulder Chops	This well-marbled cut's richness makes it especially suited for braising, stewing, and other slow-cooking methods that break down the connective tissues for fall-apart–tender meat. Even a small cut supplies enough fat and flavor to season a large batch of food	• Cabbage, Kohlrabi, and Lamb Tagine with Prunes (page 352)
	Ground Lamb	A modest quantity of ground lamb is all you need to saturate a dish with the meat's distinctively earthy flavor, which is especially compatible with seasonings like cumin, cardamom, garlic, and mint.	• Hashweh Stuffed Swiss Chard (page 346)
FISH	Salmon Fillets	Fatty salmon fillets offer substantial richness, while their firm, flaky texture lends a meaty mouthfeel that is maximally satisfying even in minimal amounts. It cooks especially beautifully when seared in a skillet, rendering its fat while crisping up the surfaces.	• Salmon, Avocado, Grapefruit, and Watercress Salad (page 139) • Roasted Salmon with White Beans, Fennel, and Tomatoes (page 276) • Sesame Noodles with Pan-Seared Salmon (page 319)
	Smoked Fish	Precooked and ready to eat, smoked fish varieties such as salmon and trout are tender and moist with a luxurious mouthfeel. They have extra depth of savoriness, drawn out by the smoking process, so a little goes a long way.	• Smoked Trout Hash with Eggs (page 51) • Smoked Salmon Niçoise Bowl (page 166)

Anatomy of a Mostly Meatless Meatball

We wanted to create a meatball that consisted of more plants than meat, but was so succulent and flavorful that no one would miss the swapped-out beef. The result (page 378) was a meatball that was 40 percent beef, and 100 percent satisfaction.

40%	*Beef*
60%	*Mushrooms Chickpeas Parmesan Panko*

MEAT AS A SEASONING

When developing this book, our approach to some recipes was to lessen the quantity of meat in a dish by bulking it up with hearty plants. In other recipes, we adopted a different philosophy of treating meat as a seasoning—using it purely for its rich flavor. Many preserved meats in particular contribute tremendous savoriness even in small quantities. Cured meats are often high in fat, but it takes only a minimal amount to significantly enhance a dish. While this entire book aims to treat meat as a supporting character, the processes that produce the following foods intensify their savoriness so much that they squarely prove meat need only be a background actor to make a big impact.

BACON

When its fat is rendered, even a slice or two of bacon brings remarkable richness to dishes. Used to cook vegetables, the bacon distributes its savoriness to the other ingredients. Crisped-up bacon crumbles can make a crackly topping for salads and bowls; stirred into a dish, as in our Breakfast Fried Rice with Spinach and Shiitakes (page 36), the meat studs each bite with smoky flavor.

PANCETTA

This Italian cured pork belly delivers all the savoriness of bacon minus the smokiness. The salt-curing process of making pancetta deepens the meaty flavor, offering clean, buttery richness to any number of pastas and braises, and even our savory oatmeal (page 35).

ANCHOVIES

If you use a large quantity of these tiny, salty fish, they lend a potent seafood flavor to whatever you're cooking. If you use a judicious amount, they dissolve and provide depth and savoriness without tasting like fish. The glutamates in anchovies go a long way in boosting a dish's umami, as in our Almost Beefless Beef Stew (page 91). And the anchovies themselves aren't the only valuable thing in the can or jar: The oil also carries a wonderful flavor that can be great in vinaigrettes, sauces, and soups or stews.

CHORIZO

The blend of smoked paprika, garlic, and chile peppers used to make chorizo is what gives the fatty sausage its intensely savory, mildly spicy flavor profile. When cooked in soups and stews like our Caldo Verde (page 98), the fat melts, enriching a whole dish with smoky richness.

'NDUJA

This soft and spreadable cured sausage that hails from Calabria consists of pork fat, chili peppers, and herbs, which combine to give 'nduja its distinctive creamy texture, mild acidity, and spicy funk. It goes a long way in boosting the richness of the vegetables in our 'Nduja with Beans and Greens (page 264).

DRIED SHRIMP

Shrimp that have been dehydrated are a robust flavor magnifier, as the drying process concentrates their natural briny flavor and enhances their glutamates. Even just a few teaspoons brings unparalleled depth of flavor, as in our Laksa Cauliflower Rice Bowl with Shrimp (page 181).

BONITO FLAKES

Bonito flakes—smoked, fermented skipjack tuna shavings—impart intense savoriness and smokiness that makes this ingredient a potent flavor enhancer. Commonly used in Japanese cuisine, they make a big impact in our Yaki Udon (page 320) and Okonomiyaki (page 270).

Two strips of bacon are all it takes to give our Breakfast Fried Rice with Spinach and Shiitakes (page 36) ample smokiness, not to mention enough fat to scramble a few eggs.

Rendering pancetta produces a salty oil ideal for heightening the umami of mushrooms in our Savory Oatmeal with Pancetta, Mushrooms, and Shaved Parmesan (page 35).

Anchovies punch above their weight, bringing significant savoriness to our Almost Beefless Beef Stew (page 91) that pairs a pound of beef with over 4 pounds of vegetables.

Cooking onion and garlic in the fat of Spanish-style chorizo distributes the sausage's concentrated richness throughout our Caldo Verde (page 98), a soup beloved in Portugal.

Meatless Protein Powerhouses

A well-stocked pantry is a storehouse of tasty meatless proteins that can add flavor and substance to meals. Here, we highlight some of our favorites to stock in the pantry or refrigerator for quick and easy meal assembly.

LEGUMES

Both beans and lentils come in a wide variety of colors, sizes, shapes, and textures. In our Beans Marbella (page 95), the hearty, meaty character of large lima beans makes them a satisfying swap for meat. Earthy, greenish-brown Umbrian lentils hold their shape when cooked as in our Lentil and Escarole Soup (page 71), while subtly sweet red lentils break down into a thick puree as in our Red Lentil Kibbeh (page 228).

NUTS AND NUT BUTTERS

Nuts can lend richness, substance, and crunch to nearly any recipe. Soaked and then blended, they can transform into the base for a rich dairy-free cream sauce (page 314). Nut butters are great for making spreads and dips, as in our Tofu Summer Rolls with Spicy Almond Butter Sauce (page 227), or enriching sauces for bowls and salads, as in our Gado Gado (page 154).

SEEDS

Seeds—such as chia, flax, and hemp, to name just a few—make excellent additions to many meals. They contribute richness, protein, and crunch, and we sprinkled them liberally throughout recipes, from sesame seeds in our fried rice (page 36) to sunflower seeds in a hearty barley bowl (page 175). Toasting seeds can be a low-lift way to intensify their nutty aroma. If you can't decide on a seed garnish, take a maximalist approach with a batch of our Savory Seed Brittle (page 183).

TOFU

Available in many varieties, tofu is made from soymilk that has been coagulated to form curds and then pressed to extract liquid. Its mild taste makes a clean canvas for added flavors. Firm and extra-firm tofu are best when you want the tofu to hold its shape as in our Tofu Katsu Sandwiches (page 203) and Saag Tofu (page 359). Soft and silken tofu tend to break down when cooked as in our Mapo Tofu (page 285) and Kimchi Jjigae (page 100).

TEMPEH

Made from fermented, cooked soybeans (and often other beans, grains, and flavorings), tempeh comes in dense cakes with a nutty, slightly funky flavor. Their crumbly, dense texture gives them a satisfying bite. Originating in Indonesia, the protein stands up especially well to bold seasonings, as in our Crispy Tempeh with Sambal Sauce (page 279).

EGGS

Not only do eggs have an impressive nutritional profile, but they're also highly versatile, becoming runny and creamy or firm and chewy depending on how they're cooked, and for how long. Adding them to a dish is an easy way to boost how filling and satiating it is. Stirring soft-scrambled eggs into sautéed kale and black beans made for a hearty, nutrient-packed breakfast burrito (page 30). And we cracked eggs directly into a skillet of ratatouille (page 49) to start our morning sunny-side up.

CHEESE

Rich in protein, calcium, and savory flavor, cheese comes in widely varying textures and flavor profiles around the world. Halloumi, a firm, spongy variety, brings its meaty chew to our freekeh bowl (page 172). Shaved into shreds, Parmesan makes a punchy garnish for all kinds of grain bowls, salads, and pastas. Milky ricotta is key in our airy, pillowy gnudi (page 376), while blue cheese adds appetizing funk to our celery root galette (page 388).

Kimchi Jjigae
(page 100)

Flavor Boosters

You don't need the raw cuts behind the glass of the deli case to build satisfying flavor. There's a whole world of profoundly savory, zesty ingredients that pack a punch and lend great depth of flavor. We leaned on these high-performing ingredients to ensure that the recipes in this book are so flavorsome and satiating, you won't notice any reduction in meat.

FISH SAUCE

Made from salted, fermented anchovies, this Southeast Asian staple brings complexity and funk to everything from soups (page 58) to salads (page 124). We often use it when we want an umami boost but aren't looking for anchovy flavor, as in our Laksa Cauliflower Rice Bowl with Shrimp (page 181). Vegan and vegetarian options are also available, or make your own with our recipe, below, which provides just the right meaty punch to use as a 1:1 substitute for fish sauce.

1 To make fish sauce substitute, simmer 3 cups water, ¼ ounce dried sliced shiitake mushrooms, 3 tablespoons salt, and 2 tablespoons soy sauce in saucepan over medium heat until reduced by half.

2 Strain, cool, and store in refrigerator for up to 3 weeks.

OYSTER SAUCE

A viscous, salty-sweet seasoning integral to Chinese cuisine, oyster sauce brings salty tang and savory flavor, as in our Stir-Fried Beef and Gai Lan (page 259). Plant-based versions made from mushrooms, such as Lee Kum Kee's Vegan Oyster Flavored Sauce, are also available.

WORCESTERSHIRE SAUCE

Another anchovy derivative, this pungent sauce includes malt vinegar, molasses, and tamarind. It's key in many umami-forward dishes, such as our Kare Raisu (page 250), Yaki Udon (page 320), and Turkey Shepherd's Pie (page 338). For a plant-based version, we like Annie's Organic Vegan Worcestershire Sauce.

MISO

Salty, slightly funky, deeply savory miso paste is made by fermenting soybeans and sometimes grains with a mold called koji. Miso will easily keep for up to a year in the refrigerator (and some sources say it keeps indefinitely).

SOY SAUCE

Made from fermented soybeans, salt, water, and sometimes roasted grains, soy sauce is one of the oldest food products in the world. We use it in a wide range of preparations to add deep savory flavor.

GOCHUJANG

This thick, savory-spicy paste made from gochugaru (Korean chile flakes) flavors soups, stews, marinades, and sauces. We use it to make a bold sauce for fried rice (page 37) and to flavor meatballs (page 183).

CURRY PASTES

These pantry-friendly pastes combine chile heat with potent aromatics such as lemongrass, galangal, and makrut limes. Beyond their use as a base for curries, they're great starting points for soups such as our Carrot Ribbon, Chicken, and Coconut Curry Soup (page 58), and even salad dressings (page 135).

CITRUS ZEST AND JUICE

A splash of acidic citrus juice brightens the flavor of rich dishes. Citrus zest adds less sharp, more floral flavor. Always juice lemons and limes at the last minute and add the juice toward the end of cooking or just before serving, as the flavor mellows quickly.

VINEGAR

Like citrus juice, sharp-tasting vinegar perks up every food it comes in contact with, but it's particularly beneficial in bringing contrast to richer dishes. Vinegars like red wine, white wine, cider, and balsamic each bring a distinct flavor profile to the table, so the type we reach for depends on the recipe. We use unseasoned rice vinegar to add bright punch to our Zucchini Noodle Salad with Tahini-Ginger Dressing (page 143), while sherry vinegar makes an excellent finishing touch for soups (page 77).

TOMATO PASTE AND SUN-DRIED TOMATOES

All tomatoes are full of umami flavor thanks to the glutamates abundantly present in their seeds and pulp. Due to their low moisture, tomato paste and sun-dried tomatoes possess ultraconcentrated umami. Tomato paste is key in many of our soups and stews, while sun-dried tomatoes bring a rich hit of acid to our Farro and Broccoli Rabe Gratin (page 375).

DRIED MUSHROOMS

Drying mushrooms concentrates their flavor, so we turn to dried versions often. In our Bacon and Cheese Black Bean Burgers (page 189), dried porcinis bring potent umami to our bean-based patties. With a little bacon to echo those savory notes, these burgers are superbly satisfying.

CHILI PEPPERS

There is a whole world of chiles to try. Serranos are fiery, as in our Palak Dal (page 105), while Sichuan chili powder, which we use in our Dan Dan Mian with Shiitake Mushrooms (page 384) offers milder, more aromatic heat. Aleppo pepper conveys a gentle heat and raisin-like sweetness. Red pepper flakes and cayenne are standbys for turning up the heat and flavor in everything from soups and sauces to stews and sandwiches. Don't be afraid to experiment with different kinds.

TAMARIND JUICE CONCENTRATE

Tamarind's sweet-tangy flavor profile instantly makes any dish more complex. The concentrated juice is easily stirred into sauces and seasoning pastes, as in our Laksa Soup (page 84). In this book, we call for Thai/Indonesian-style tamarind concentrate labeled "nuoc me chua" (do not use Indian-style tamarind concentrates). Look for it at Asian grocery stores; you might also find it at some well-stocked supermarkets. If you can only find tamarind pulp (which comes as a block of paste with or without seeds), you can use it in place of concentrate.

1 Place 1 tablespoon tamarind pulp in bowl, add ¼ cup of hot water, and mash with fork to break paste up as much as possible. Let steep 10 minutes.

2 Strain mixture through fine-mesh strainer into small bowl, pressing on solids; discard pulp. Season liquid with salt to taste.

BROTHS

Broths (page 114) can be the cooking liquid for grains, paste, and noodles; a flavorful medium for cooking vegetables; and the base for a savory sauce. Because it's such an efficient way to add flavor to dishes without using any meat, we love cooking big batches of it—which has the added bonus of letting you tailor the sodium to your taste—and storing it in the freezer. Concentrated bouillon is a reliable alternative; simply mix it with water to make only as much broth as you need.

WAKE UP FLAVOR

Successful mostly meatless cooking isn't just about stocking a range of ingredients; it's also about getting the maximum mileage (read: savoriness) from what you've got. As test cooks, we're always experimenting with different ways to make a recipe more flavorful while also being approachable. Often, a simple cooking technique—employed at the right stage, in the right way—can transform a basic pantry staple into a catalyst for flavor. Every one of these simple but effective tips will help you enliven the plant-based stars of your plate—with support from a modest amount of meat when it counts the most.

BROWN YOUR TOMATO PASTE

Tomato paste, which is full of glutamates, is a versatile, inexpensive flavor powerhouse that's great for adding concentrated tomato flavor and umami to sauces, soups, and pastas. Browning the tomato paste in oil or fat helps the paste caramelize, heightening its natural sweetness and developing complex smokiness. Cook tomato paste with aromatics for even more depth of flavor.

GIVE IT A RUB (OR A TOSS)

Sear chicken pieces and the heat will kiss them with flavor; but rub the chicken with a zesty spice blend before it hits the skillet, and it'll form an irresistible crust on the rich, crisp skin and elevate the flavor of the juicy meat, as in our Herby Roasted Cauliflower and Chicken with Quinoa Pilaf (page 330). Don't just rely on condiments to punch up vegetables; tossing them with a lively mix of spices prior to cooking, as in our Baharat Cauliflower and Eggplant with Chickpeas (page 354), locks in the seasonings' flavor.

TOAST PANKO

Crisp, airy panko bread crumbs elevate dishes with their light crunch. Season and toast them until they're deep golden brown and then sprinkle them on mac and cheese (page 313), casseroles (page 375), roasted vegetables, or just about any other savory favorite you can think of.

SALT FOOD EARLY AND LATE

We season with salt at different times during the cooking process so it blends in properly. Applying salt to meat in advance of cooking helps the crystals thoroughly penetrate the protein, improving its texture and flavor while allowing you to use less salt overall. Seasoning fattier foods, such as marbled meat, more aggressively than lean ones is smart because fat has a dulling effect on taste. Sprinkling salt on vegetables before roasting gives it time to penetrate the plants' rigid cell walls. Salting stews before braising ensures well-rounded seasoning, as salt's rate of diffusion increases with heat. A final scattering of finishing salt, on the contrary, isn't meant to provide even seasoning, but rather heighten the flavors and bring out dimension.

GRIND DRIED MUSHROOMS

Dried shiitake and other mushrooms are glutamate-rich umami powerhouses. We often rehydrate them to use in recipes, but you can also grind them to a powder that gives a quick earthy, meaty flavor boost to all kinds of dishes, such as our Bean Bourguignon (page 93). Grind dried mushrooms to a fine powder in a spice grinder and store it in a clean spice jar out of direct sunlight. Add to dishes before or during cooking so that the powder can hydrate; otherwise, it will taste dry and dusty. Use in stews, chilis, ground beef, or risotto, or make spice rubs to coat steaks or fish before sautéing. Start with a teaspoon and add more to taste.

CHAR VEGETABLES

An easy way to intensify the savory flavor of almost any sturdy vegetable is to char it. A little oil and a lot of heat is all it takes to add dramatic color, toasty notes, and a delightfully soft-chewy exterior to humble everyday vegetables, as in our Roasted Radicchio, Fennel, and Root Vegetables with Sausage and Herbs (page 267) and Charred Sichuan-Style Okra (page 288).

Charring okra gives it a crisp-tender bite and smoky aroma.

USE SOAKING LIQUID

The soaking liquid from rehydrating dried ingredients, such as mushrooms, is a valuable byproduct that definitely shouldn't be poured down the drain. It's an excellent way to boost umami in a dish. Reserve soaking liquid to cook lentils or grains, as in our Mushroom Tea Rice with Caramel-Braised Shallots (page 370), in which the entire dish is redolent with the savoriness of shiitake mushrooms. Or use the leftover liquid to make stews, sauces, and marinades.

BLOOM YOUR SPICES IN FAT

Heating spices in oil or butter is called blooming. This process changes the fat-soluble flavor molecules in spices from a solid state to a liquid one where they mix and interact, thereby producing more complexity. In less than a minute, blooming magnifies a spice's flavor, making dishes taste bolder and more well rounded. We often turn to this technique after rendering the fat from a small amount of meat: In our Parsnip and Chicken Shawarma (page 216), blooming awakens the aromas of the turmeric, cardamom, and other spices and disseminates the chicken thighs' richness into the parsnips.

Pasta, Noodles, and Grains

Many of this book's recipes start with a can of beans, a scoop of rice, or a package of dried noodles. These starches are as pantry-friendly as they are versatile. They can be the focal point of the meal or a supportive partner to a mostly meatless main. Carbohydrates are also satiating—not only because they're our bodies' primary source of energy, but also because, with their often dense and springy bite, they're pleasing to our palates.

Choosing Whole Grains

Whole grains are "whole" because the bran, germ, and endosperm are present in the same proportions as when the grain was growing. Refining grains diminishes their nutritional quality: Processing can strip away much of the vitamins and fiber. Opting for whole-grain foods over their more refined counterparts (such as choosing whole-wheat wraps over white-wheat) can be an easy tweak to make a meal more nutrient-rich and satiating.

BARLEY

This high-fiber, high-protein cereal grain has a nutty flavor akin to that of brown rice. Boiled until tender but still distinct, the grains make a mild canvas for vibrant seasonings, as in our Beet Barley Risotto (page 372).

Use in: Soups and stews, grain salads, risotto

BULGUR

Made from parboiled or steamed wheat kernels/berries that are dried, partially stripped of their outer bran layer, and coarsely ground, bulgur should be rinsed before use to remove excess starch that can turn it gluey. Then, simply boil the nutty grains until tender. They readily soak up seasonings, whether in savory turkey sausage (page 165) or a smoked paprika–spiced, honey-sweetened vinaigrette (page 147).

Use in: Pilafs, soups and stews, grain salads, filling for stuffed vegetables

DRIED PASTA AND NOODLES

This wide category, which includes everything from rigatoni and fregula to rice vermicelli and udon, cooks in minutes and can be combined with just about any permutation of sauce, vegetable, and topping to make a quick, tasty meal. Orecchiette is thick and springy, pairing well with robust add-ins like navy beans and brussels sprouts (page 309). Buckwheat-based soba noodles are earthy and chewy, and are great served cold as in our Beet Poke Bowl (page 176).

FARRO

These hulled whole-wheat kernels have a subtly sweet flavor and delicately chewy texture. They can add heft to stews and salads or bake into a comforting casserole, as in our Farro and Broccoli Rabe Gratin (page 375). Farro is also one of the fastest whole grains to make, cooking in just 20 minutes in salted water.

Use in: Soups and stews, grain salads, gratins

FONIO

An ancient variety of millet from West Africa, fonio has a mildly nutty flavor and cooks up quickly to a light, fluffy texture, swiftly absorbing seasonings along the way, as in our Joloff-Inspired Fonio (page 305).

Use in: Soups and stews, grain salads, simple sides

FREEKEH

Beloved across the Mediterranean, freekeh is made from roasted durum wheat harvested while the grains are still young and green. Through simmering, freekeh retains its pleasantly chewy texture while imparting a distinctive smokiness. It absorbs seasoning nicely as in our Chicken and Spiced Freekeh with Cilantro and Preserved Lemon (page 337), and makes an excellent base for salads and bowls (page 172).

Use in: Soups and stews, grain salads, bowls

OATS

This fiber-rich cereal grain comes in a number of varieties, including old-fashioned and steel-cut. Not just for sweet applications, oats can form the basis for warm and comforting savory meals (page 35).

Use in: Oatmeal, grain salads, muesli and granola

RICE

There are many rice varieties to choose from, but we especially leaned on brown rice in this book for its fiber-rich, satisfyingly chewy nature. It can be the bedrock of dishes such as our Garlic-Chicken and Wild Rice Soup (page 57), or a neutral side to saucy, well-seasoned mains such as our Green Gumbo (page 96) or Kimchi Jjigae (page 100).

Use in: Grain bowls, pilafs, simple sides, fried rice, curries, filling for stuffed vegetables

QUINOA

This seed (not technically a grain) has a pleasingly crunchy texture and mild nutty taste that make it a great canvas for bold seasonings, as in our Quinoa Taco Salad (page 148). Unless labeled "prewashed," quinoa should be rinsed before cooking to remove its bitter protective layer (called saponin).

Use in: Pilafs, grain salads, soups and stews, chilis

Storage Smarts

A mostly meatless mindset asks you to rethink how you buy and store meat. Most raw animal proteins last only a few days in the fridge. Luckily, your freezer is a great way to extend the life of meat and ensure that you always have some different types around for easy meals. Here are some tips for maintaining the freshness and quality of meat, and for sourcing and storing smaller portion sizes.

FREEZER FUNDAMENTALS

☑ MAXIMIZE AIRFLOW

To help cold air circulate, keep food away from freezer vents. For more efficiency and to maintain colder temps, vacuum the filters and coils of your refrigerator and freezer periodically (unplug the appliance before doing so).

☑ OPTIMIZE SHELF SPACE

The quicker foods freeze, and the fewer fluctuations in temperature once frozen, the less they suffer when defrosted. Clearing shelf space will maximize airflow for a quicker freeze. Increase shelf space with portable wire cabinet shelving.

☑ KEEP YOUR FREEZER COLD

Your freezer should register zero degrees Fahrenheit or colder (you can use a thermometer to check). Make sure your freezer is at the coldest possible setting (unlike your fridge, where the coldest setting is normally too cold), and store meat in the coldest part of your freezer (this is usually the rear center).

☑ FIRST IN, FIRST OUT

Take care to place older items at the front of your freezer so that you use them first. Be mindful of expiration dates, and the rest will take care of itself.

MAKING MEAT LAST

☑ DIVIDE BULK PORTIONS

Even a single 1-pound package of ground meat can be divided into smaller portions before freezing. When cooking, thaw only the amount you need.

☑ WRAP IT TIGHT

To discourage the formation of large ice crystals, which can impair meat's ability to hold on to juices, remove protein from its packaging, wrap tightly in plastic wrap, place the portion in a zipper-lock bag, and squeeze out excess air before sealing. Label the bag with the purchase date and contents for easy identification. Meat can remain frozen for up to one month before cooking.

☑ FOR SMALL CUTS

For smaller cuts of meat, like steaks or chops, we like to first freeze them uncovered, overnight, on a parchment-lined baking sheet. This dries out the meat's surface and freezes the protein as quickly as possible, which discourages large ice crystals from developing. We then proceed with wrapping the meat in plastic wrap and placing it in a zipper-lock bag as above.

☑ THAW FROZEN MEAT SAFELY

To prevent the growth of harmful bacteria, defrost cuts that are at least 1 inch thick in the refrigerator. Place cuts that are less than 1 inch thick on a heavy cast-iron or steel pan at room temperature; the metal's rapid heat transfer safely thaws the meat in about an hour.

PARED-DOWN PORTIONS

To eliminate the need for freezer optimization, look for meats sold in small portions. While certain meats are readily available in smaller quantities, sourcing others may require some strategizing. Try these tips when looking for petite portions of protein.

☑ GO TO THE BUTCHER COUNTER

When you talk directly to the butcher, you can specify exact portions of meat, whether that's a few slices of bacon or a pair of chicken thighs. This way, you only pick up the amount of meat you need, and you won't have to worry about freezing any unused odds and ends.

☑ BUY PREPACKAGED PORTIONS

Many kinds of meats, such as filet mignon, chicken breasts, sausages, smoked salmon, and fish fillets, are often sold in small, prepackaged portions. Look for a weight label that matches the quantity you're looking for, and you'll have just what you need—no more and no less.

☑ ORDER FROM FARMS OR ONLINE SUPPLIERS

Many farms and online meat suppliers that distribute directly to consumers may offer customizable options, so you can select the exact quantity you want, or a close approximate.

Use It Up

Looking for recipes to use up that last portion of meat? The following dishes utilize less than a traditionally sized package of animal protein and can help you use up any leftover bits in your freezer.

BONELESS, SKINLESS CHICKEN THIGHS

- Spiced Chicken Soup with Squash and Navy Beans (page 54)
- Tortilla Soup with Black Beans and Spinach (page 61)
- Red Curry Chicken and Sweet Potatoes (page 248)

BONELESS, SKINLESS CHICKEN BREASTS

- Garlic-Chicken and Wild Rice Soup (page 57)
- Laksa Soup (page 84)
- Neorm Sach Moan (page 124)

GROUND BEEF

- Madzoon ov Kofte (page 88)
- Weeknight Ground Beef and Lentil Tacos (page 241)
- Spiced Stuffed Peppers (page 345)
- Mostly Meatless Meatballs and Marinara (page 378)

GROUND PORK

- Cheesy Black Bean and Pork Skillet Bake (page 260)
- Mapo Tofu (page 285)
- Dan Dan Mian with Shiitake Mushrooms (page 384)

Helpful Tools for Mostly Meatless Cooking

Cooking more vegetables and less meat doesn't mean having to spend more time preparing your meals. We continuously found ourselves turning to these useful pieces of equipment to save us time. All the products recommended on this page are winners of our Reviews team's extensive testing.

FOOD PROCESSOR

We used this kitchen must-have to blend meats and vegetables for our Mushroom-Beef Blended Burgers (page 186) and Mostly Meatless Meatballs and Marinara (page 378), to make dips and sauces supersmooth, and to create chunkiness and textural variation in bean- and tuber-based mashes. The **Cuisinart Custom 14 Cup Food Processor** is powerful, precise, and compact, while also taking up less space than most food processors—despite having one of the largest capacities.

VEGETABLE SPIRALIZER

Using a spiralizer allowed us to get perfectly thin vegetable noodles for "pastas," soups, salads, and side dishes. The **OXO Good Grips 3-Blade Tabletop Spiralizer** creates long, unbroken noodles and generates little waste; it also accommodates vegetables of different sizes, shapes, and densities with ease.

VEGETABLE PEELER

A great peeler makes short work of prepping vegetables and fruit. The **Kuhn Rikon Original Swiss Peeler**, a straight option, and **OXO Good Grips Swivel Peeler**, a Y-shaped peeler, are light and ergonomic, with sharp, maneuverable blades that neatly shave off skin without waste and keep their edge. It's up to you whether a Y-shaped peeler or a straight peeler feels more comfortable to use.

SALAD SPINNER

If you're trying to eat plenty of greens, there's no better tool than a salad spinner to make short work of cleaning and drying the leaves. The **OXO Good Grips Salad Spinner** is roomy enough to prep large quantities in the fewest possible batches. You can also operate it with one hand to effectively remove water from a variety of greens.

MANUAL CITRUS JUICER

A press-style juicer quickly traps seeds and extracts the most juice with minimal effort. The **Chef'n FreshForce Citrus Juicer** accommodated even large lemons, and could even fit medium-size oranges with ease. Distinct from citrus presses that have small holes, this juicer features a star-like arrangement of large draining slots, which directs juice in a steady stream while avoiding any splattering or overflowing.

Mushroom-Beef Blended Burgers

(page 186)

Breakfast All Day

▲ fast   *✦ vegetarian*   *■ fiber-ful*   *● one-pan*

Fried Egg Sandwiches with Hummus and Sprouts

Why This Recipe Works   While there's certainly a place for a classic bacon-egg-and-cheese sandwich in your rotation, we wanted to build a satisfying, texturally dynamic egg sandwich that tasted fresher and lighter—and that you might especially crave in warmer months. We started by smearing sandwich bread (multigrain, for extra fiber and heartiness) with creamy, garlicky hummus and tart, spicy sambal oelek. The nuttiness of the hummus and heat of the sambal oelek harmonized nicely with the richness of the oozy eggs. We layered the sandwiches with cucumber, red onion, tomato, and alfalfa sprouts for their refreshing crunch, while a sprinkle of crumbly feta injected each bite with briny tang. With a breakfast sandwich this substantial and wholesome, you won't miss the meat. If you can't find sambal oelek, you can substitute chili-garlic sauce or sriracha.

- 2   teaspoons extra-virgin olive oil
- ½   cup garlic hummus
- 8   slices hearty sandwich bread, lightly toasted
- 2   Persian cucumbers, sliced thin on bias
- 4   teaspoons sambal oelek
- 4   large eggs
- ¼   teaspoon table salt, divided
- ¼   teaspoon pepper, divided
- 2   ounces feta cheese, crumbled (½ cup)
  Thinly sliced tomato
  Thinly sliced red onion
- 2   ounces (2 cups) alfalfa sprouts

1   Heat oil in 12-inch nonstick skillet over low heat for 5 minutes. While pan heats, spread hummus on 1 side of 4 slices bread, then arrange cucumber slices on top of hummus. Spread sambal on one side of remaining 4 slices bread.

2   Crack 2 eggs into small bowl and season with ⅛ teaspoon salt and ⅛ teaspoon pepper. Repeat with remaining 2 eggs, remaining ⅛ teaspoon salt, and remaining ⅛ teaspoon pepper in second small bowl.

3   Increase heat to medium-high and heat until oil shimmers. Working quickly, pour 1 bowl of eggs on 1 side of pan and second bowl of eggs on other side. Cover and cook for 1 minute. Remove skillet from burner and let stand, covered, 15 to 45 seconds for runny yolks (white around edge of yolk will be barely opaque), 45 to 60 seconds for soft but set yolks, and about 2 minutes for medium-set yolks.

4   Using spatula, place eggs on top of cucumbers. Top each egg with feta, tomato slices, onion slices, and sprouts. Top with remaining bread slices and serve.

Breakfast Wraps with Sweet Potatoes and Broccolini

Why This Recipe Works We love the heartiness, portability, and customizable nature of a morning wrap. We set out to develop one guaranteed to keep you full until lunch, so we leaned on fiber-rich vegetables that are sturdy enough to stay intact in a wrap: creamy sweet potatoes, crunchy broccolini, and peppery shallots. To simplify the process of cooking the vegetables to just one skillet, we steamed them all together until the broccolini was tender; we then removed the broccolini and continued to cook the sweet potatoes and shallots until the tubers were nicely browned, which drew out their warm caramel notes. We then made a savory spread by mixing tangy goat cheese with thyme and lemon zest, thinning it into a spreadable consistency with some water. Finally, we scrambled a few eggs, one for each wrap—because this is breakfast, after all. We smeared lavash wraps with the goat cheese spread, spooned on the vegetables and eggs, and rolled it all up into a compact, on-the-go meal.

2 ounces goat cheese, softened (½ cup)

1½ teaspoons minced fresh thyme

1 teaspoon grated lemon zest plus 1 tablespoon juice

2 tablespoons plus ⅓ cup water, divided

6 ounces broccolini, trimmed

1 small sweet potato (8 ounces), peeled, halved lengthwise and sliced crosswise ¼ inch thick

1 shallot, sliced thin

3 tablespoons extra-virgin olive oil, divided

½ teaspoon table salt, divided

1 teaspoon ground coriander

4 large eggs

⅛ teaspoon pepper

4 (12- by 9-inch) lavash breads

1 Stir goat cheese, thyme, lemon zest, and 2 tablespoons water in bowl until well combined; set aside until ready to serve. Cut broccolini stalks measuring more than ½ inch in diameter at base in half lengthwise. Cut stalks measuring ¼ to ½ inch in diameter at base in half lengthwise, starting below where florets begin and keeping florets intact. Leave stalks measuring less than ¼ inch in diameter at base whole.

2 Arrange broccolini in even layer in 12-inch nonstick skillet, then scatter sweet potato and shallot over top. Add 2 tablespoons oil and remaining ⅓ cup water, then sprinkle with ¼ teaspoon salt. Bring to boil; cover; reduce heat to medium-low; and cook until broccolini is bright green and crisp-tender, 5 to 6 minutes, tossing gently with tongs halfway through cooking.

3 Uncover and continue to cook until any remaining liquid has evaporated, 1 to 3 minutes. Use tongs to transfer broccolini to bowl. Sprinkle coriander over remaining vegetables in skillet, increase heat to medium, and cook until sweet potatoes are browned and tender, 3 to 6 minutes, flipping slices gently as needed. Transfer to bowl with broccolini then sprinkle with lemon juice and toss to combine. Wipe out skillet with paper towels.

4 Beat eggs, pepper, and remaining ¼ teaspoon salt with fork in bowl until eggs are thoroughly combined and color is pure yellow.

5 Heat remaining 1 tablespoon oil in now-empty skillet over medium heat until shimmering. Add egg mixture to skillet and, using rubber spatula, constantly and firmly scrape along bottom and sides of skillet until eggs begin to clump and spatula just leaves trail on bottom of skillet, 30 to 60 seconds. Reduce heat to low and gently but constantly fold eggs until clumped and just slightly wet, 30 to 60 seconds.

6 Working with 1 lavash at a time, place on counter with short side parallel to edge of counter. Spread one-quarter of reserved cheese mixture on bottom quarter of lavash, leaving 2-inch border along bottom and 1-inch border along sides. Top with one-quarter broccolini, one-quarter sweet potato mixture, and one-quarter eggs. Fold bottom of lavash up and over filling, then fold in sides and roll tightly away from you around filling. Cut wraps in half and serve.

Kale and Black Bean Breakfast Burritos

Why This Recipe Works Breakfast burritos often rely on meat for bulk and flavor. We wanted to develop a breakfast burrito that had all the heft and satisfaction you would expect, but without leaning on meat. To do this, we turned to hearty black beans, fiber-ful kale, and fluffy scrambled eggs. For a flavorful base, we sautéed onion, garlic, and poblano with cumin to imbue our aromatics with some warmth. We stirred in our beans, mashing half to create a creamier consistency while retaining some textural variation in each bite. Next, we quickly braised baby kale until it was tender but still had some pleasant chew. We then scrambled the eggs, taking care to remove them from the heat when just beginning to clump. Stirring the kale into the eggs off the heat sufficiently wilted the greens while ensuring that the eggs preserved their fluffiness and didn't overcook. We spread the bean mixture onto whole-grain tortillas, added the kale-egg scramble, and finished with sweet-tart chopped tomato for a hearty and dynamic handheld breakfast. Softening the tortillas in the microwave made them easier to roll. We like to serve these burritos with hot sauce.

1 Heat 2 teaspoons oil in 12-inch nonstick skillet over medium-high heat until shimmering. Add onion, poblano, and ¼ teaspoon salt and cook until softened, about 5 minutes. Stir in garlic and cumin and cook until fragrant, about 30 seconds. Stir in beans and water and cook until beans are warmed through, 3 to 4 minutes. Off heat, mash half of beans to chunky paste; transfer to bowl, season with salt and pepper to taste, and cover to keep warm. Wipe out skillet with paper towels.

2 In now-empty skillet, heat 2 teaspoons oil over medium-high heat until shimmering. Add kale and ⅛ teaspoon salt and cook until kale wilts, 3 to 4 minutes; transfer to second bowl. Wipe out skillet with paper towels.

3 Beat eggs, milk, pepper, and remaining pinch salt with fork in bowl until eggs are thoroughly combined and color is pure yellow.

4 Heat remaining 1 teaspoon oil in again-empty skillet over medium-high heat until shimmering. Add egg mixture and, using rubber spatula, constantly and firmly scrape along bottom and sides of skillet until eggs begin to clump and spatula leaves trail on bottom of pan, 1½ to 2½ minutes. Off heat, gently stir in kale and constantly fold eggs and kale until eggs have finished cooking, 30 to 60 seconds. Cover to keep warm.

5 Wrap tortillas in damp dish towel and microwave until warm and pliable, about 1 minute. Lay warm tortillas on counter and spread bean mixture evenly across center of each tortilla, close to bottom edge. Top with kale-egg mixture, then sprinkle with tomato and drizzle with oil to taste. Working with 1 tortilla at a time, fold sides and then bottom of tortilla over filling, then continue to roll tightly into wrap. Serve immediately.

5 teaspoons extra-virgin olive oil, divided, plus extra for serving

1 small onion, chopped fine

1 poblano, stemmed, seeded, and chopped fine

¼ teaspoon plus ⅛ teaspoon plus pinch table salt, divided

2 garlic cloves, minced

½ teaspoon ground cumin

1 cup canned black beans, rinsed

½ cup water

5 ounces baby kale, chopped coarse

4 large eggs

1 tablespoon milk

   Pinch pepper

4 (10-inch) flour tortillas

1 plum tomato, cored and chopped fine

Avocado and Bean Toast

Why This Recipe Works Avocado toast is one of our favorite snacks, but we wanted to create a more substantial meal. We turned to canned black beans, as they're easy to keep around for breakfast emergencies, not to mention extra hearty and packed with protein. We seasoned the legumes with lime zest and juice and mashed them with hot water and oil, which gave us a bright, flavorsome, well-textured base. A quick trip to the broiler turned slices of rustic bread golden and crisp—a sturdy foundation for toppings. We smeared the bread with the black bean mixture, then adorned it with avocado slices, lightly seasoned tomatoes, and fresh cilantro. The end result delivered all the creamy satisfaction of avocado toast, but the added flavor and textural components made for a more filling, well-rounded meal. We like to top this with our Quick Sweet and Spicy Pickled Red Onion, but you can use a pinch of red pepper flakes for heat if you prefer. For an accurate measure of boiling water, bring a full kettle of water to boil and then measure out the desired amount.

- 4 ounces cherry tomatoes, quartered
- 4 teaspoons extra-virgin olive oil, divided
- Pinch plus ½ teaspoon table salt, divided
- ⅛ teaspoon pepper, divided
- 1 (15-ounce) can black beans, rinsed
- ¼ cup boiling water
- ½ teaspoon grated lime zest plus 1 tablespoon juice
- 4 (½-inch-thick) slices rustic bread
- 1 ripe avocado, halved, pitted, and sliced thin
- ¼ cup Quick Sweet and Spicy Pickled Red Onion (recipe follows)
- ¼ cup fresh cilantro leaves

1 Combine tomatoes, 1 teaspoon oil, pinch salt, and pinch pepper in bowl; set aside. Mash beans; boiling water; lime zest and juice; and remaining 1 tablespoon oil, ½ teaspoon salt, and pinch pepper with potato masher to coarse puree in second bowl, leaving some whole beans intact. Season with salt and pepper to taste.

2 Adjust oven rack 4 inches from broiler element and heat broiler. Place bread on aluminum foil–lined baking sheet and broil until golden, 1 to 2 minutes per side.

3 Spread mashed bean mixture evenly on toasts, then top with avocado slices. Top with pickled onions, if using; cilantro; and reserved tomatoes. Serve.

Quick Sweet and Spicy Pickled Red Onion

Makes 1 cup
Total time: 5 minutes, plus 45 minutes pickling

- 1 cup red wine vinegar
- ⅓ cup sugar
- ¼ teaspoon table salt
- 1 red onion, halved and sliced thin
- 2 jalapeño chiles, stemmed, seeded, and cut into thin rings

Microwave vinegar, sugar, and salt in bowl until steaming, 1 to 2 minutes. Stir in onion and jalapeño and let sit, stirring occasionally, for 45 minutes. Drain vegetables in colander. Serve. (Drained pickled onion can be refrigerated for up to 1 week.)

Savory Oatmeal with Pancetta, Mushrooms, and Shaved Parmesan

Why This Recipe Works Oatmeal makes a great canvas for savory flavors—especially when the oats are cooked in a mushroom-enriched liquid and showered with rich garnishes. Steel-cut oats have a more satisfying bite than old-fashioned or instant, but take longer to cook. To shorten the pot-watching, we presoaked them in a savory liquid: After sautéing a leek in oil, we added water and brought it to a boil. Off the heat, we stirred in the oats along with dried porcini mushrooms and let them sit for 2 hours (or up to 10) before simmering until thickened. For added savoriness, we crisped up pancetta and almonds and then used the rendered fat to cook more mushrooms. Lemon zest and parsley, added to the pancetta and almonds, yielded a gremolata-like topping. Use a single variety of mushroom or a combination. Stem and halve portobello mushrooms and cut into ½-inch pieces. Trim white or cremini mushrooms; quarter them if large or medium or halve them if small. Tear trimmed oyster mushrooms into 1- to 1½-inch pieces. Stem shiitake mushrooms; quarter large caps and halve small caps. Cut trimmed maitake (hen-of-the-woods) mushrooms into 1- to 1½-inch pieces. The oatmeal will thicken as it cools; thin it out with boiling water for a looser consistency.

  2 tablespoons extra virgin olive oil, divided, plus extra for drizzling

  1 small leek, trimmed, halved lengthwise, sliced thin, and washed and dried thoroughly

4¼ cups water, divided, plus extra hot water as needed

  1 cup steel-cut oats

  ¼ ounce dried porcini mushrooms, rinsed and minced

  ½ teaspoon table salt, divided

  2 ounces pancetta, cut into ¼-inch pieces

  ¼ cup sliced almonds

  1 pound mushrooms

  1 teaspoon minced fresh thyme

  ½ cup chopped fresh parsley

  1 teaspoon grated lemon zest plus 1 tablespoon juice, plus lemon wedges for serving

  2 ounces Parmesan cheese, shredded (1 cup), plus extra shaved for serving

1 Heat 1 tablespoon oil in large saucepan over medium-high heat until shimmering. Add leek and cook, stirring often, until softened, 3 to 5 minutes. Add 3 cups water and bring to boil over high heat. Off heat, stir in oats, porcini, and ¼ teaspoon salt. Cover saucepan and let sit for at least 2 hours or up to 10 hours.

2 Stir 1 cup water into oats and bring to boil. Reduce heat to medium and cook, stirring occasionally, until oats are softened but still retain some chew and mixture thickens and resembles warm pudding, 4 to 6 minutes. Remove from heat and cover to keep warm while preparing topping.

3 Cook pancetta in 12-inch nonstick skillet over medium-high heat until fat begins to render, about 2 minutes. Add almonds and cook until pancetta is crisp and almonds are toasted, about 2 minutes. Using slotted spoon, transfer pancetta and almonds to small bowl; set aside.

4 Add mushrooms, remaining ¼ cup water, and remaining ¼ teaspoon salt to fat left in skillet. Cook over high heat, stirring occasionally, until skillet is almost dry and mushrooms begin to sizzle, 4 to 6 minutes. Reduce heat to medium-high and continue to cook, stirring occasionally, until mushrooms are well browned, 4 to 6 minutes. Add thyme and cook, stirring frequently, until fragrant, about 30 seconds.

5 Stir parsley and lemon zest into pancetta-almond mixture. Stir shredded Parmesan, remaining 1 tablespoon oil, and lemon juice into oatmeal, stirring vigorously until oatmeal becomes creamy. Adjust consistency with extra hot water as needed. Season with salt and pepper to taste.

6 Divide oatmeal among individual serving bowls. Top with mushrooms, pancetta-almond mixture, and extra Parmesan. Drizzle with extra oil and serve.

Breakfast Fried Rice with Spinach and Shiitakes

Why This Recipe Works In many cultures for which rice is a staple, it's common to enjoy the versatile grains leftover alongside some eggs and vegetables, beans, or meat for a quick, filling breakfast (or anytime meal). We took a cue from the one-pan simplicity and endless customizability of fried rice—perfect for pulling together with precooked rice when you need a meal fast—to create a vegetable-forward take. For the grains, we chose brown rice; not only did it add a fiber boost, but the grains also broke apart easily with little clumping. Just two strips of bacon gave us plenty of smoky flavor; using its fat to quickly scramble a few eggs helped distribute the meat's irresistible aroma throughout the dish. After cooking the shiitakes, which brought more savoriness and chew, we added fistfuls of spinach so the greens could absorb the umami of the mushrooms. We embellished each portion with avocado slices for a cool, creamy element. We like to make this with long-grain brown rice, but you can use long-grain white rice if you prefer; day-old grains are preferable because they're drier than freshly cooked. All rice should be roughly room temperature before stir-frying. We like to serve this with our Gochujang Maple Sauce, but you can use sriracha if you prefer.

- 3 large eggs
- ¾ teaspoon table salt, divided
- 2 slices bacon, chopped
- 4 teaspoons vegetable oil, divided
- 4 ounces shiitake mushrooms, trimmed and sliced thin
- 4 cups (4 ounces) baby spinach
- 4 scallions, white and green parts separated and sliced thin
- 3 cups cooked long-grain brown rice (page 326), room temperature
- 1 recipe Gochujang Maple Sauce (recipe follows)
- 1 avocado, halved, pitted, and sliced thin
- 1 tablespoon sesame seeds, toasted

1 Beat eggs and ⅛ teaspoon salt in bowl until well combined; set aside. Cook bacon in 14-inch flat-bottomed wok or 12-inch nonstick skillet over medium heat, stirring constantly until well browned and crispy, 5 to 7 minutes. Using slotted spoon, transfer bacon to medium bowl. Increase heat to medium-high; add eggs to fat left in wok; and cook, stirring frequently, until very little liquid egg remains, 30 to 60 seconds. Transfer eggs to bowl with bacon.

2 Add 1 teaspoon oil to now-empty wok and reduce heat to medium. Add mushrooms and ⅛ teaspoon salt and cook, stirring frequently, until mushrooms are tender and light golden, about 4 minutes. Add spinach and cook until just wilted, 1 to 2 minutes. Transfer mushrooms and spinach to bowl with bacon mixture.

3 Add scallion whites and remaining 1 tablespoon oil to again-empty wok. Cook, stirring constantly, until fragrant, 30 seconds to 1 minute. Add rice and stir until combined, then spread into even layer. Sprinkle remaining ½ teaspoon salt evenly over rice. Continue to cook, stirring frequently and pressing on rice with spatula to break up any clumps, until grains are separate and heated through, 2 to 5 minutes longer. Add scallion greens and bacon mixture, and cook, stirring frequently and using edge of spatula to break eggs into small pieces, until vegetables and eggs are heated through, and mixture is well combined, about 2 minutes.

4 Divide fried rice evenly among bowls. Drizzle with gochujang maple sauce, top with avocado, and sprinkle with sesame seeds. Serve.

Gochujang Maple Sauce

Makes about ⅓ cup | Total time: 10 minutes

2   teaspoons vegetable oil

2   garlic cloves, minced

2   tablespoons gochujang

2   tablespoons water

1   tablespoon maple syrup

2   teaspoons unseasoned rice vinegar

1   teaspoon sesame oil

Microwave vegetable oil and garlic in small bowl until bubbly and fragrant, about 30 seconds. Stir in gochujang, water, maple syrup, vinegar, and sesame oil, then micro-wave until bubbly and fragrant, 1 to 2 minutes. (Sauce can be refrigerated for up to 3 days.)

Mangú

Why This Recipe Works In the Dominican Republic, many start the day with mangú, a starchy, stick-to-your-ribs dish of mashed plantains. The popular breakfast is often served with tres golpes, or "three hits" of savory flavor: salame dominicano (smoky sausage seasoned with black pepper and oregano), queso de freír (a salty and chewy cheese), and eggs or avocado. For a mostly meatless take on mangú, we paired a little meat and cheese with an entire avocado. To prepare the plantains, we followed the method favored by Dominican cooks: boiling the unripe fruit until softened, then mashing it with a bit of oil, a little minced garlic, and some of the cooking water (to double down on plantain flavor and add more starchiness to the mash). Because the plantains can get stickier as they cool, we found that it was handy to save extra cooking water for adjusting the mash to our preferred consistency. Finally, we quickly seared salame dominicano and queso de freír to deepen their richness, introduce some smokiness, and lightly melt the cheese; the two salty, chewy ingredients alongside the buttery avocado made a harmonious trio. For a tart component, we like to serve this with our Quick Sweet and Spicy Pickled Red Onion. Look for unripe plantains that are green and firm. To peel the fruit, cut off both ends before slicing the skin lengthwise, from end to end; pull the skin apart and remove the starchy flesh. If you can't find salame dominicano or queso de freír, you can substitute summer sausage and halloumi, respectively.

1 Place plantains and salt in large saucepan, add 4 cups cold water, and bring to boil over high heat. Reduce heat to medium–high and cook until plantains are very tender, 15 to 20 minutes. Reserve 1½ cups cooking water, then drain plantains and return to now–empty saucepan.

2 Add 1 teaspoon oil, garlic, and ¾ cup reserved cooking water to plantains in saucepan and mash with potato masher until mostly smooth (mash should be scoopable with some chunks remaining). Season with salt and pepper to taste and cover to keep warm. (Adjust plantain consistency with remaining ¾ cup cooking liquid as necessary just before serving.)

3 Heat remaining 1 teaspoon oil in 12-inch nonstick skillet over medium heat until shimmering. Arrange salame dominicano and queso de freír in skillet and cook until golden brown, 1 to 2 minutes. Flip salame and queso de freír and cook until golden brown on second side and edges of cheese start to melt, 1 to 2 minutes.

4 Serve mangú with salame, cheese, avocado, and pickled onions.

- 2 pounds green (unripe) plantains, trimmed, peeled, and cut into 2-inch lengths

- ½ teaspoon table salt

- 2 teaspoons extra-virgin olive oil, divided

- 2 garlic cloves, minced

- 4 ounces salame dominicano, sliced ¼ inch thick

- 2 ounces queso de freír or halloumi cheese, sliced ¼ inch thick, halved crosswise

- 1 ripe avocado, halved, pitted, and sliced ¼ inch thick

- ½ cup Quick Sweet and Spicy Pickled Red Onion (page 33)

Peeling Plantains

1 To peel, cut off both ends of plantain, then make 1 cut lengthwise through skin, but not into fruit.

2 Pull away skin from side of plantain.

Huevos Rancheros with Beans

Why This Recipe Works Huevos rancheros—Mexican "ranch-style" eggs flavored with onions, tomatoes, and chiles and often served with tortillas—is just the hearty, flavor-packed breakfast to lure you out of bed. To give the dish a savory backbone, we sautéed onions until well browned and then added aromatics: chipotle chile in adobo for smokiness, tomato paste for concentrated sweetness and umami, and garlic and cumin for earthy complexity. In a food processor, we pulsed the seasoned onions with fire-roasted tomatoes into a chunky salsa, which we simmered in a skillet to deepen the flavors. Beans, a popular addition to huevos rancheros, thickened the salsa, while also upping the protein and fiber. We made small wells in the simmering bean-salsa mixture and cracked eggs into the indentations, where they gently poached while absorbing the surrounding bright flavors. Use a 12-inch nonstick skillet with a tight-fitting lid for this recipe. We like to serve this with diced avocados and chopped scallions, but you can omit if you prefer.

1 tablespoon vegetable oil

1 small onion, chopped

1 tablespoon tomato paste

2 teaspoons minced canned chipotle chile in adobo sauce

2 garlic cloves, minced

1½ teaspoons ground cumin

1 (28-ounce) can diced fire-roasted tomatoes, undrained

1½ teaspoons packed brown sugar

½ teaspoon plus pinch table salt, divided

5 coarsely chopped cilantro sprigs, plus 3 tablespoons minced fresh cilantro, divided

1 (15-ounce) can pinto or black beans, rinsed

½ cup water

1 tablespoon lime juice, plus lime wedges for serving

4 large eggs

Pinch pepper

8 (6-inch) corn tortillas, warmed

1 Heat oil in 12-inch nonstick skillet over medium heat until shimmering. Add onion and cook, stirring often, until well browned, 6 to 8 minutes. Stir in tomato paste, chipotle, garlic, and cumin, and cook until fragrant, about 30 seconds. Transfer onion mixture to food processor.

2 Pulse onion mixture, tomatoes and their juices, sugar, ½ teaspoon salt, and cilantro sprigs in food processor until coarsely chopped, 10 to 15 pulses.

3 Stir tomato mixture, beans, and water together in now-empty skillet. Bring to simmer over medium heat and cook, stirring occasionally, until thickened slightly, about 15 minutes. Off heat, stir in 2 tablespoons minced cilantro and lime juice. Season with salt and pepper to taste.

4 Using back of large spoon, make 4 shallow indentations (about 2 inches wide) in salsa. Crack 1 egg into each indentation and sprinkle with pepper and remaining pinch salt. Bring to simmer over medium heat (there should be small bubbles across entire surface). Reduce heat to medium-low to maintain simmer. Cover and cook, 4 to 5 minutes for runny yolks (white around edge of yolk will be barely opaque), 5 to 6 minutes for soft but set yolks, or 6 to 7 minutes for medium-set yolks. Sprinkle with remaining 1 tablespoon minced cilantro. Serve with lime wedges and tortillas.

Ful Medames

Why This Recipe Works Fava beans are hugely popular in Egypt, so it's no surprise that ful medames, a chunky mash of favas flavored with cumin and garlic and topped with an array of fresh ingredients, is one of the nation's most beloved breakfast dishes. It also makes regular appearances on Egyptian tables as a side at lunch or dinner, and as a dip with pita. While various versions now exist across the Mediterranean region, this simple recipe is loyal to this comforting dish's ancient roots. Traditionally it's made by cooking dried fava beans in a pear-shaped pot for hours until the beans are soft enough to be mashed; many modern recipes opt for canned beans, which not only eliminate the need for specialty cookware but also get the dish on the table in less than half an hour. Blooming cumin in oil before stirring in the beans helped saturate the beans with warm, peppery flavor. Lemon juice not only helped thin out the coarse bean mixture but also introduced a tart quality that married well with the earthiness of the beans. Tomato, onion, parsley, and serrano made crisp, fresh toppings. Our Easy-Peel Hard-Cooked Eggs, which we arranged on top of the ful medames, brought more protein and heartiness to the meal, but you can omit if you prefer.

3 tablespoons extra-virgin olive oil, divided, plus extra for drizzling

4 garlic cloves, minced

2 teaspoons ground cumin

2 (15-ounce) cans fava beans, undrained

3 tablespoons lemon juice

3 tablespoons tahini

1 tomato, cored and cut into ½-inch pieces

¼ cup finely chopped onion

2 tablespoons minced fresh parsley

1 serrano chile, stemmed, seeded, and minced

2 Easy-Peel Hard-Cooked Eggs, quartered (recipe follows) (optional)

4–6 (8-inch) pitas

1 Combine 1 tablespoon oil and cumin in medium saucepan and cook over medium heat until fragrant, about 2 minutes. Stir in beans and their liquid. Bring to simmer and cook until liquid thickens slightly, 8 to 10 minutes.

2 Off heat, mash beans to coarse consistency using potato masher. Stir in lemon juice, garlic, and remaining 2 tablespoons oil and season with salt to taste. Transfer to serving dish. Drizzle with tahini, then top with tomato; onion; parsley; serrano; and eggs, if using. Drizzle with extra oil and serve with pitas.

Easy-Peel Hard-Cooked Eggs

Makes 2 to 6 eggs
Total time: 35 minutes

Use large eggs that have no cracks and are cold from the refrigerator.

2–6 large eggs

1 Bring 1 inch water to rolling boil in medium saucepan over high heat. Place eggs in steamer basket. Transfer basket to saucepan. Cover, reduce heat to medium-low, and cook eggs for 13 minutes.

2 When eggs are almost finished cooking, combine 2 cups ice cubes and 2 cups cold water in medium bowl. Using tongs or spoon, transfer eggs to ice bath; let sit for 15 minutes. Peel before serving. (Eggs can be refrigerated in their shells in airtight container for up to 5 days.)

Chilaquiles Verdes with Sheet-Pan Fried Eggs

Why This Recipe Works Chilaquiles, the Mexican dish of fried tortilla wedges tossed in chile sauce and adorned with cheese, is a symphony of flavors and textures. Red chile sauce is a classic choice, but this rendition goes green with onion, poblano, serrano, and garlic. We also used canned tomatillos, which can be easier to find than fresh. We broiled the aromatics to char them, enhancing their sweet-peppery flavors, then blitzed them in a blender with cilantro leaves for a silky sauce. Baking the eggs gave us set whites and tender yolks. For toppings, we maximized textural diversity with creamy avocado, crunchy radishes and onion, briny queso fresco, and zesty cilantro. Use thicker tortilla chips for this recipe. Proper timing is crucial to ensure the sauced chips don't become soggy: Have all your garnishes ready to go, coat the chips in the sauce just as the eggs finish cooking, and serve immediately. If you can't find Mexican crema, you can substitute sour cream.

1 (26-ounce) can whole tomatillos, drained

1 small white onion (half peeled and quartered, half sliced thin)

1 poblano chile, halved, stemmed, seeded, and pressed flat

1 serrano chile, stemmed and seeded

3 garlic cloves, peeled

2 teaspoons plus ¼ cup vegetable oil, divided

1 cup coarsely chopped fresh cilantro leaves and tender stems, plus ½ cup coarsely chopped fresh cilantro

1½ cups vegetable or chicken broth

½ teaspoon table salt, divided

6 large eggs

½ teaspoon pepper

10 ounces tortilla chips

1 avocado, pitted, and cut into ½-inch pieces

4 ounces queso fresco, crumbled (1 cup)

2 radishes, trimmed and sliced thin

2 tablespoons Mexican crema

1 Adjust oven rack to upper-middle position and heat broiler. Line rimmed baking sheet with aluminum foil. Gently toss tomatillos, quartered onion half, poblano, serrano, and garlic with 2 teaspoons oil on prepared sheet. Arrange vegetables in even layer, placing chiles skin side up. Broil until tomatillos and chiles are spotty brown and tomatillo skins begin to burst, 7 to 10 minutes. Let cool for 10 minutes, then remove and discard charred skins from poblanos (leave skins on tomatillos and serrano intact). Transfer vegetables along with any accumulated juices to blender. Add chopped cilantro leaves and stems to blender and process until smooth, about 30 seconds, scraping down sides of blender jar as needed.

2 Discard foil from baking sheet and wipe sheet clean with paper towels; set aside. Adjust oven temperature to 425 degrees. Heat 2 tablespoons oil in Dutch oven over medium-high heat until shimmering. Carefully add tomatillo sauce (sauce will splatter), broth, and ¼ teaspoon salt. Bring to simmer and cook, stirring occasionally, until sauce thickens slightly and darkens in color, about 5 minutes. Off heat, season with salt to taste.

3 Place now-empty sheet in oven and heat for 15 minutes. Meanwhile, crack eggs into large measuring cup or pitcher. Carefully remove hot sheet from oven and drizzle with remaining 2 tablespoons oil, tilting sheet to coat evenly. Quickly pour eggs onto hot sheet and sprinkle with pepper and remaining ¼ teaspoon salt. Transfer sheet to oven (eggs will slide around a bit) and bake for 3 to 4 minutes (for set whites and runny yolks) or 5 to 6 minutes (for set whites and jammy yolks).

4 While eggs finish cooking, return sauce to brief simmer over medium-high heat. Off heat, stir in chips and toss gently to coat, taking care not to break up chips. Transfer chilaquiles to large serving platter, continuing to toss chips gently in sauce as needed to coat remaining chips. Working quickly, slide eggs on top, then sprinkle with avocado, queso fresco, radishes, remaining sliced onion, and chopped cilantro. Drizzle with crema and serve immediately.

• *fast* • *vegetarian* • *fiber-ful* • *one-pan* •

Gallo Pinto

Why This Recipe Works Gallo pinto, the national dish of Costa Rica, is made from leftover rice and beans cooked anew with spices, onions, garlic, peppers, and cilantro. Compared to fresh-cooked rice, day-old grains more readily absorb the bean liquid and seasonings. We chose brown rice to up the fiber, and canned beans to shorten the cook time. We used bell peppers in two ways: First we cooked a generous amount until soft and juicy so they would infuse the rice and beans with their vegetal aroma. Then, off the heat, we showered the whole mixture with chopped raw peppers for a fresh crunch. For added protein, we scrambled a few eggs, the traditional partner to gallo pinto. For a final flourish, a few dashes of the bottled Costa Rican condiment Salsa Lizano offered a bracingly acidic contrast to the savory flavors. Day-old rice works best here; in a pinch, cook the rice 2 hours ahead, spread it on a rimmed baking sheet, and let it cool before chilling for 30 minutes. If you can't find Salsa Lizano, you can substitute Worcestershire sauce. Serve with warmed corn tortillas and sliced avocado.

1 tablespoon plus 2 teaspoons vegetable oil, divided

1 white onion, chopped fine

1 red bell pepper, stemmed, seeded, and cut into ¼-inch pieces (about 1 cup), divided

1 yellow bell pepper, stemmed, seeded, and cut into ¼-inch pieces (about 1 cup), divided

½ teaspoon table salt, divided

4 garlic cloves, minced, divided

¾ teaspoon chili powder

½ teaspoon ground coriander

½ teaspoon ground cumin

½ teaspoon minced fresh thyme or ⅛ teaspoon dried

¼ teaspoon plus ⅛ teaspoon pepper, divided

2 cups cooked long-grain brown rice (page 326), cold

1 (15-ounce) can black beans, drained, with ¼ cup liquid reserved

2 tablespoons Salsa Lizano, plus extra for serving

½ cup chopped fresh cilantro

4 large eggs

Hot sauce

1 Heat 1 tablespoon oil in 12-inch nonstick skillet over medium heat until shimmering. Add onion, ¾ cup red bell pepper, ¾ cup yellow bell pepper, and ¼ teaspoon salt and cook, stirring occasionally, until softened and lightly browned, 8 to 10 minutes. Stir in garlic, chili powder, coriander, cumin, thyme, and ¼ teaspoon pepper and cook until fragrant, about 1 minute.

2 Add rice and beans and cook, stirring constantly and breaking up rice clumps until mixture is warmed through, about 2 minutes. Gently stir in Salsa Lizano and reserved bean canning liquid until thoroughly combined. Off heat, stir in chopped cilantro and remaining bell peppers. Season with salt and pepper to taste. Transfer to serving dish and cover to keep warm. Wipe skillet clean with paper towels.

3 Beat eggs, remaining ¼ teaspoon salt, and remaining ⅛ teaspoon pepper in bowl with fork until eggs are thoroughly combined and color is pure yellow. Heat remaining 2 teaspoons oil in now-empty skillet over medium-high heat until shimmering. Add egg mixture and, using rubber spatula, constantly and firmly scrape along bottom and sides of skillet until eggs begin to clump and spatula just leaves trail on bottom of pan, 30 to 60 seconds. Reduce heat to low and gently but constantly fold eggs until clumped and just slightly wet, 30 to 60 seconds. Serve eggs with rice and beans, passing hot sauce and extra Salsa Lizano separately.

Ratatouille with Poached Eggs

Why This Recipe Works Ratatouille is a sunny salute to summer vegetables—specifically zucchini, eggplant, and tomatoes. This icon of classic French cookery celebrates the plants' abundance and sweet, earthy flavors by cooking them together into a deeply savory stew. Though ratatouille makes an excellent side or entrée, we reimagined it as a morning meal by cooking it in a skillet and poaching eggs directly in the stew. This not only boosted the protein but also introduced a satisfyingly creamy dimension. Browning the vegetables was essential for deepening their flavors, extracting their natural savory sweetness, and infusing them with a complex smokiness. To avoid overcooking the zucchini, we browned it first and removed it from the pan before cooking the eggplant. We found that leaving the skin on the eggplant helped prevent its texture from becoming mushy. Poaching the eggs right in the ratatouille worked like a charm; the eggs cooked up tender, coating the surrounding vegetables with velvetiness. You will need a 12-inch nonstick skillet with a tight-fitting lid for this recipe.

¼ cup extra-virgin olive oil, divided, plus extra for drizzling

1¼ pounds zucchini, cut into ¾-inch pieces

1¼ pounds eggplant, cut into ¾-inch pieces

¾ teaspoon plus pinch table salt, divided

¼ teaspoon plus pinch pepper, divided

1 onion, chopped fine

4 garlic cloves, minced

1 pound plum tomatoes, cored and cut into ½-inch pieces

¾ cup water

1 teaspoon herbes de Provence

1 teaspoon red wine vinegar

4 large eggs

¼ cup chopped fresh basil

1 Heat 1 tablespoon oil in 12-inch nonstick skillet over medium-high heat until just smoking. Add zucchini and cook, stirring occasionally, until well browned, 5 to 8 minutes; transfer to bowl.

2 Add eggplant, 2 tablespoons oil, ½ teaspoon salt, and ⅛ teaspoon pepper to now-empty skillet (skillet will be quite full) and cook over medium-high heat until eggplant is well browned, 6 to 9 minutes, stirring occasionally. Stir in onion and remaining 1 tablespoon oil and cook until onion is softened, about 5 minutes. Stir in garlic and cook until fragrant, about 30 seconds. Stir in tomatoes, water, herbes de Provence, ¼ teaspoon salt, and ⅛ teaspoon pepper. Simmer until eggplant and tomatoes are softened, 7 to 10 minutes. Stir in zucchini along with any accumulated juices and vinegar.

3 Using back of large spoon, make 4 shallow indentations (about 2 inches wide) in ratatouille. Crack 1 egg into each indentation and sprinkle with remaining pinch salt and remaining pinch pepper. Bring to simmer over medium heat (there should be small bubbles across entire surface). Reduce heat to medium-low to maintain simmer. Cover and cook, 4 to 5 minutes for runny yolks (white around edge of yolk will be barely opaque), 5 to 6 minutes for soft but set yolks, or 6 to 7 minutes for medium-set yolks. Sprinkle with basil and drizzle with extra oil. Serve.

Smoked Trout Hash with Eggs

Why This Recipe Works We put a protein-rich twist on breakfast hash by choosing an unusual star ingredient: smoked trout. The tender, buttery fish packs a flavor punch with its intense smokiness and briny finish. Because the rich fish is often paired with mustard or horseradish, we echoed that flavor with mustard greens, a nutritional powerhouse with a horseradish-like edge. For convenience, we used the microwave to soften the greens, as well as some potatoes, to shorten the time they would need on the stovetop. The greens' slightly bitter spiciness contrasted nicely with the fish, while giving the dish a fibrous chew and crisp, lacy edges. For a saucy element to further tame the strong flavor of the fish, we cooked four eggs right in the hash. The runny yolks gave us the satisfyingly velvety component and mild flavor we were after, while the whites brought additional protein to the mix. A squeeze of lemon brightened everything up and pulled the whole dish together. You will need a 12-inch nonstick skillet with a tight-fitting lid for this recipe.

1 pound russet potatoes, peeled and cut into ¼-inch pieces

2 tablespoons extra-virgin olive oil, divided

½ teaspoon plus pinch table salt, divided

¼ teaspoon plus pinch pepper, divided

1½ pounds mustard greens, stemmed and cut into 1-inch pieces

1 onion, chopped fine

1 garlic clove, minced

4 ounces smoked trout, flaked

4 large eggs

1 tablespoon minced fresh dill

Lemon wedges

1 Microwave potatoes, 1 tablespoon oil, ½ teaspoon salt, and ¼ teaspoon pepper in covered bowl until potatoes are translucent around edges, 5 to 8 minutes, stirring halfway through microwaving.

2 Microwave mustard greens in second large covered bowl until wilted, 8 to 10 minutes, stirring halfway through microwaving. Transfer to colander, drain well, then add to bowl with potatoes; set aside.

3 Heat remaining 1 tablespoon oil in 12-inch nonstick skillet over medium-high heat until shimmering. Add onion and cook until softened and lightly browned, 5 to 7 minutes.

4 Stir in garlic and cook until fragrant, about 30 seconds. Stir in reserved potatoes and mustard greens, breaking up any clumps. Using back of spatula, firmly pack potato mixture into skillet and cook undisturbed for 2 minutes. Flip hash, one portion at a time, and repack into skillet. Repeat flipping process every few minutes until potatoes are well browned and mustard greens are tender, 6 to 8 minutes.

5 Off heat, sprinkle trout evenly over hash. Using back of large spoon, make 4 shallow indentations (about 2 inches wide) in surface of hash. Crack 1 egg into each indentation and sprinkle with remaining pinch salt and remaining pinch pepper. Cover and cook over medium-low heat, 4 to 5 minutes for runny yolks (white around edge of yolk will be barely opaque), 5 to 6 minutes for soft but set yolks, or 6 to 7 minutes for medium-set yolks. Sprinkle with dill and serve with lemon wedges.

Soups, Stews, & Chilis

Spiced Chicken Soup with Squash and Navy Beans

Why This Recipe Works When we set out to develop a richly seasoned chicken soup with some heat, we were immediately drawn to the flavors of hararat, the earthy, slightly spicy North African seasoning blend featuring flavors such as coriander, cardamom, and allspice. (Hararat is also often referred to as bzaar, or Libyan five-spice blend.) For the star vegetable, we chose butternut squash, which softened to a tender texture as it simmered, while beautifully absorbing the savoriness of the succulent chicken thighs. For added fiber and protein, we stirred in canned navy beans along with their liquid, which helped thicken the broth. Lightly mashing a portion of the squash and beans also made the soup creamier, while creating some textural contrast. A scattering of chopped cilantro, plus a few lemon wedges served on the side, made fresh, bright finishing touches.

1 tablespoon extra-virgin olive oil

2 tablespoons tomato paste

4 garlic cloves, minced

2 teaspoons ground coriander

1 teaspoon ground cardamom

½ teaspoon ground allspice

¼ teaspoon cayenne pepper

3½ cups water

1 pound butternut squash, peeled, seeded, and cut into 1-inch pieces

12 ounces boneless, skinless chicken thighs, trimmed, and cut into 1-inch strips

1 onion, sliced thin

1¾ teaspoons table salt

1 (15-ounce) can navy beans, undrained

½ cup chopped fresh cilantro

Lemon wedges

1 Heat oil in Dutch oven over medium-high heat until shimmering. Stir in tomato paste, garlic, coriander, cardamom, allspice, and cayenne and cook until fragrant, about 30 seconds. Stir in water, squash, chicken, onion, and salt, scraping up any browned bits, and bring to simmer. Reduce heat to medium-low and cook, partially covered, for 15 minutes. Stir in beans and their liquid and cook until squash and chicken are tender, about 10 minutes.

2 Use back of spoon to mash portion of squash and beans to thicken soup to desired consistency. Stir in cilantro and season with salt and pepper to taste. Serve with lemon wedges.

Garlic-Chicken and Wild Rice Soup

Why This Recipe Works   There are few comforts in the world like a bowl of steaming soup, especially when you're feeling under the weather. Both chicken soup and garlic soup have been lauded as powerful home remedies for cold and flu infections and as restorative tonics. Our goal was to combine these powerhouse soups by super-charging chicken broth with a megadose of garlic, before adding tender morsels of chicken. Don't be alarmed by the number of cloves called for—they're the key to the soup's intensely savory, bright yet balanced character. For extra-potent flavor, we added aromatic vegetables, thyme, bay leaves, and tomato paste to the broth. We opted to cook wild rice directly in the soup to infuse the chewy grains with garlicky aroma. To keep our chicken tender, we simmered it during the last few minutes of cooking. Finally, baby spinach and chopped fresh parsley gave our soup a vegetal, fibrous boost.

1   Heat oil and garlic in Dutch oven over medium–low heat, stirring occasionally, until garlic is light golden, 3 to 5 minutes. Add carrots, onion, celery, and salt; increase heat to medium; and cook, stirring occasion-ally, until vegetables are just beginning to brown, 10 to 12 minutes.

2   Stir in thyme and tomato paste and cook until fragrant, about 30 seconds. Stir in broth and bay leaves, scraping up any browned bits, and bring to simmer. Stir in rice; return to simmer; cover; and cook over medium–low heat until rice is tender, 40 to 50 minutes.

3   Discard bay leaves. Stir in chicken and spinach and cook over low heat, stirring occasionally, until chicken is cooked through and spinach is wilted, 3 to 5 minutes. Off heat, stir in parsley and season with salt and pepper to taste. Serve.

- 3   tablespoons extra-virgin olive oil
- ½   cup minced garlic (about 25 cloves)
- 2   carrots, peeled and sliced ¼ inch thick
- 1   onion, chopped fine
- 1   celery rib, minced
- ¼   teaspoon table salt
- 2   teaspoons minced fresh thyme or ½ teaspoon dried
- 1   teaspoon tomato paste
- 6   cups chicken broth
- 2   bay leaves
- ⅔   cup wild rice, rinsed
- 8   ounces boneless, skinless chicken breasts, trimmed and cut into ¾-inch pieces
- 3   ounces (3 cups) baby spinach
- ¼   cup chopped fresh parsley

Carrot Ribbon, Chicken, and Coconut Curry Soup

Why This Recipe Works We wanted to develop a weeknight-friendly, plant-forward dish that drew inspiration from the many fragrant noodle soups enjoyed across Southeast Asia. In place of rice or wheat noodles, we used a vegetable peeler to create long ribbons of carrot. Shaving the carrots thin maximized their surface area for soaking up the flavors of the soup, and also made them pleasingly light and crisp. Thai curry paste, which we first bloomed in oil so its many aromatics could thoroughly suffuse the dish, gave our soup a delectably spicy-sweet foundation. We then added some ground chicken, simmering it in coconut milk to make a quick, savory broth in which to cook our carrot noodles and snow peas. We finished this off with a mound of fresh herbs and scallions. It's worth seeking out Thai yellow curry paste for its sweet complexity; however, you can substitute red curry paste. Thai curry paste can range from mild to spicy; taste yours and, if it's very spicy, use the lower amount.

1 Shave carrots into thin ribbons lengthwise with vegetable peeler; set aside. Combine oil and curry paste in Dutch oven and cook over medium heat until fragrant, about 3 minutes, stirring occasionally. Add chicken and cook, breaking up meat into small pieces with wooden spoon, until chicken is no longer pink, 3 to 4 minutes.

2 Add water, coconut milk, fish sauce, sugar, and reserved carrot ribbons. Bring to simmer, then add snow peas and simmer until vegetables are crisp-tender, 3 to 5 minutes.

3 Divide evenly among individual serving bowls. Sprinkle with scallions, basil, and cilantro. Serve with lime wedges, sriracha, and extra fish sauce to taste.

- 1 pound carrots, peeled
- 2 tablespoons vegetable oil
- 2–4 tablespoons Thai yellow curry paste
- 1 pound ground chicken
- 2 cups water
- 1 cup canned coconut milk
- 2 tablespoons fish sauce, plus extra for serving
- 1 tablespoon sugar
- 6 ounces snow peas, trimmed and sliced ½-inch-thick on bias
- 4 scallions, sliced thin on bias
- 1 cup fresh Thai basil, torn
- 1 cup fresh cilantro leaves and tender stems, torn
-    Lime wedges
-    Sriracha

SERVES 4 TO 6 | TOTAL TIME 50 MINUTES • *fiber-ful* •

Tortilla Soup with Black Beans and Spinach

Why This Recipe Works Sopa Azteca, a tortilla soup beloved in Mexico, is light yet deeply flavorful. The broth usually gets its potency from poaching a whole chicken. To lessen the amount of meat while maintaining the dish's heartiness, we added black beans for extra protein and bite, as well as spinach for more fiber, and we also employed savoriness-boosting techniques throughout the cooking process. Typically, the vegetables are charred on a comal, a griddle commonly used in Mexico, before they're pureed and fried. To simplify this, we made a smoky puree from chipotles in adobo, tomatoes, onion, and garlic and then fried the mixture to intensify the flavors. We added broth and oregano (the latter stood in for the more traditional but harder-to-find Mexican herb epazote) before scraping the brown bits from the bottom of the pot. For the garnish, we oven-toasted tortilla strips—simpler than frying, with equally crunchy results.

8 (6-inch) corn tortillas, cut into ½-inch-wide strips

3 tablespoons vegetable oil, divided

  Pinch plus ¾ teaspoon table salt, divided

2 tomatoes, cored and quartered

1 large white onion, quartered

8 sprigs fresh cilantro, leaves and stems separated

4 garlic cloves, peeled

1 tablespoon minced canned chipotle chile in adobo sauce

¼ teaspoon dried oregano

4 cups chicken broth

2 cups water

1 (15-ounce) can black beans, rinsed

12 ounces boneless, skinless chicken thighs, trimmed

5 ounces (5 cups) baby spinach

  Lime wedges

1 Adjust oven rack to middle position and heat oven to 400 degrees. Toss tortilla strips with 1 tablespoon oil; spread over rimmed baking sheet; and bake, stirring occasionally, until golden brown and crisp, 8 to 12 minutes. Sprinkle with pinch salt and transfer to paper towel–lined plate.

2 Meanwhile, process tomatoes, onion, cilantro stems, garlic, chipotle, oregano, and remaining ¾ teaspoon salt in food processor until smooth, about 30 seconds, scraping down sides of bowl as needed. Heat remaining 2 tablespoons oil in Dutch oven over medium-high heat until shimmering. Add pureed tomato mixture and cook, stirring frequently, until mixture has darkened in color and liquid has evaporated, about 10 minutes.

3 Stir in broth, water, beans, and chicken, scraping up any browned bits, and bring to simmer. Cook until chicken registers 195 degrees and easily shreds with fork, 14 to 18 minutes.

4 Transfer chicken to cutting board and let cool slightly. Once cool enough to handle, shred chicken into bite-size pieces using 2 forks. Stir chicken and baby spinach into soup. Season with salt and pepper to taste. Place some tortilla strips in bottom of individual bowls, ladle soup over top, and sprinkle with cilantro leaves. Serve with lime wedges, passing remaining tortilla strips separately.

• *fast* • *vegetarian* • *fiber-ful* • *one-pan* •

Chickpea Noodle Soup

Why This Recipe Works Chicken noodle soup is often thought of as the ultimate comfort food, so we welcomed the challenge of creating a hearty meatless version that anyone would be excited to eat. To replace the chicken, we chose chickpeas for their creamy texture, neutral flavor, and hearty bite (and the fun phonetic similarity wasn't lost on us). We sautéed onion, carrots, and celery to infuse our broth with aroma, but it still lacked the soul-satisfying comfort of chicken noodle soup. We tested various flavor boosters before settling on a unanimous favorite: Umami-packed nutritional yeast turned our soup from ordinary to extraordinary. Simmering the chickpeas, sautéed aromatics, and broth together gave the soup a chance to develop its flavor while also softening the beans. At the end, we cooked the pasta directly in the soup until just tender and stirred in fresh parsley for an herbaceous accent.

2 tablespoons vegetable oil

1 onion, chopped fine

3 carrots, peeled and sliced ¼ inch thick

2 celery ribs, sliced ¼ inch thick

¼ teaspoon pepper

3 tablespoons nutritional yeast

2 teaspoons minced fresh thyme or
   ¾ teaspoon dried

2 bay leaves

6 cups vegetable or chicken broth

2 (15-ounce) cans chickpeas, rinsed

2 ounces (½ cup) ditalini pasta

2 tablespoons minced fresh parsley

1 Heat oil in Dutch oven over medium heat until shimmering. Add onion, carrots, celery, and pepper and cook, stirring occasionally, until softened, 5 to 7 minutes. Stir in nutritional yeast, thyme, and bay leaves and cook until fragrant, about 30 seconds.

2 Stir in broth and chickpeas and bring to boil. Reduce heat to medium-low and simmer, partially covered, until flavors meld, about 10 minutes.

3 Stir in pasta, increase heat to medium-high, and boil until just tender, about 10 minutes. Off heat, discard bay leaves and stir in parsley. Season with salt and pepper to taste, and serve.

Creamy White Bean Soup with Chorizo Oil and Garlicky Bread Crumbs

Why This Recipe Works

A humble can of white beans can become a luxuriously silky, deeply savory soup without any special equipment. To start, we simmered great northern beans and their canning liquid with softened aromatic vegetables and herbs. Heating the beans caused their starches to hydrate, which made the soup especially creamy. Blending the bean mixture with some broth helped their skins break down so the puree was completely smooth, while adding Parmesan cheese and butter boosted the soup's richness. For an extra umami garnish, we heated olive oil with chorizo, which imbued the oil with the meat's smoky flavor. The chorizo-infused oil, plus a sprinkle of toasted, garlic-scented bread crumbs, gave the mild soup base added complexity, not to mention vibrant color. Use a conventional blender here; an immersion blender will not produce as smooth a soup.

Chorizo Oil and Garlicky Bread Crumbs

5 tablespoons extra-virgin olive oil, divided

¼ cup panko bread crumbs

1 garlic clove, minced

Pinch table salt

2½ ounces Spanish-style chorizo sausage, chopped fine

Soup

2 tablespoons extra-virgin olive oil

½ cup chopped onion

⅓ cup minced celery

3 sprigs fresh thyme

2 garlic cloves, sliced thin

Pinch cayenne pepper

2 (15-ounce) cans great northern beans, undrained

2 tablespoons grated Parmesan cheese

2 cups chicken broth, divided

2 tablespoons unsalted butter

½ teaspoon lemon juice, plus extra for seasoning

1 For the chorizo oil and garlicky bread crumbs Cook 1 tablespoon oil and panko in 8-inch skillet over medium heat until golden brown, 3 to 5 minutes, stirring frequently. Add garlic and cook until fragrant, about 30 seconds. Transfer to bowl and stir in salt. Heat remaining ¼ cup oil and chorizo in now-empty skillet over medium heat until chorizo is crispy, about 2 minutes, stirring frequently. Using slotted spoon, transfer chorizo to paper towel–lined plate and cover skillet to keep oil warm.

2 For the soup Heat oil in large saucepan over medium heat until shimmering. Add onion and celery and cook, stirring frequently, until softened but not browned, 6 to 8 minutes. Add thyme sprigs, garlic, and cayenne and cook, stirring constantly, until fragrant, about 1 minute. Add beans and their liquid and stir to combine. Reduce heat to medium-low, cover, and cook, stirring occasionally, until beans are warmed through and just starting to break down, 6 to 8 minutes. Remove saucepan from heat and discard thyme sprigs.

3 Process bean mixture and Parmesan in blender on low speed until thick, smooth puree forms, about 2 minutes. With blender running, add 1 cup broth and butter. Increase speed to high and continue to process until butter is incorporated and mixture is pourable, about 1 minute.

4 Return soup to clean saucepan and whisk in remaining 1 cup broth. Cover and bring to simmer over medium heat, adjusting consistency with up to 1 cup hot water as needed. Off heat, stir in lemon juice. Season with salt and extra lemon juice to taste. Drizzle each portion of soup with chorizo oil and sprinkle with chorizo and bread crumbs. Serve.

Black Bean Soup with Chipotle Chiles

Why This Recipe Works This hearty black bean soup is a prime example of how even a little meat can go a long way in boosting a dish's savoriness. Here, we made the most of 4 ounces of ham steak by cooking it in a simmering pot of dried beans. As the beans softened, they absorbed the rich flavor released by the ham. Adding baking soda raised the pH and contributed sodium ions, both of which made the pectin holding the beans' cell walls together break down faster; the result was extra-creamy beans. Smoky chipotle chiles in adobo sauce gave the hearty soup spicy character and smoky depth, all with the crack of a can. For a satisfyingly chunky texture, we coarsely mashed a portion of the beans before adding them back to the soup. Garnishes are essential for this dish, as they add not only flavor but texture and color as well. Serve with lime wedges, minced fresh cilantro, finely diced red onion, diced avocado, and sour cream. For a spicier soup, use the larger amount of chipotle.

Beans

- 1 pound (2½ cups) dried black beans, picked over and rinsed
- 5 cups water, plus extra as needed
- 4 ounces ham steak, trimmed
- 2 bay leaves
- 1 teaspoon table salt
- ⅛ teaspoon baking soda

Soup

- 3 tablespoons extra-virgin olive oil
- 2 large onions, chopped fine
- 3 celery ribs, chopped fine
- 1 large carrot, peeled and chopped fine
- ⅛ teaspoon table salt
- 5 garlic cloves, minced
- 1½ tablespoons ground cumin
- 6 cups chicken broth
- 1–2 tablespoons minced canned chipotle chile in adobo sauce
- 2 tablespoons cornstarch
- 2 tablespoons water
- 2 tablespoons lime juice

1 For the beans Combine beans, water, ham, bay leaves, salt, and baking soda in large saucepan. Bring to boil, skimming any impurities that rise to surface. Cover; reduce heat to low; and simmer gently until beans are tender, 1¼ to 1½ hours. (If after 1½ hours beans are not tender, add 1 cup more water and continue to simmer until beans are tender.) Discard bay leaves. Transfer ham steak to cutting board and cut into ¼-inch pieces; set aside. (Do not drain beans.)

2 For the soup Heat oil in Dutch oven over medium heat until shimmering. Add onions, celery, carrot, and salt and cook until vegetables are softened and lightly browned, 12 to 15 minutes.

3 Stir in garlic and cumin and cook until fragrant, about 1 minute. Stir in broth, chipotle, and cooked beans with their cooking liquid, and bring to boil. Reduce heat to medium-low and cook, uncovered and stirring occasionally, until flavors have blended, about 30 minutes.

4 Puree 1½ cups of beans and 2 cups of liquid in blender until smooth, then return to pot. Whisk cornstarch and water together in small bowl, then bring soup to simmer. Stir half of cornstarch mixture into soup and simmer, stirring occasionally, until slightly thickened, 3 to 5 minutes. (If at this point soup is thinner than desired, repeat with remaining cornstarch mixture.) Off heat, stir in lime juice and reserved ham, season with salt and pepper to taste, and serve.

Soupe au Pistou

Why This Recipe Works Provençal soupe au pistou is a light soup of pasta, beans, and vegetables. White beans beans; their delicate nuttiness echoed our earthy aromatics: leek, celery, and carrot. To give the soup more body, we made use of the viscous seasoned liquid left over from cooking the dried beans. A bounty of plants—green beans, zucchini, and tomato—bulked up our soup. For a rich finish, we dolloped the dish with fragrant pistou, a pesto-like condiment made by blitzing fresh basil, Parmesan, olive oil, and garlic. If you can find flageolet beans, they are especially earthy and you can swap them in for the cannellinis. You can also substitute two undrained 15-ounce cans of cannellini beans for the dried beans if you prefer; skip steps 2 and 3.

Pistou

- 1   cup fresh basil leaves
- 1   ounce Parmesan cheese, grated (½ cup)
- ⅓   cup extra-virgin olive oil
- 1   garlic clove, minced

Soup

- 1½   tablespoons table salt for brining
- 8   ounces (1¼ cups) dried cannellini or flageolet beans, picked over and rinsed
- 1   tablespoon extra-virgin olive oil
- 1   leek, white and light green parts only, halved lengthwise, sliced ½ inch thick, and washed thoroughly
- 1   celery rib, cut into ½-inch pieces
- 1   carrot, peeled and sliced ¼ inch thick
- 1½   teaspoons table salt, plus salt for cooking beans
- 2   garlic cloves, minced
- ½   cup tubetti or ditalini
- 8   ounces green beans, trimmed and cut into ½-inch lengths
- 1   small zucchini, halved lengthwise, seeded, and cut into ¼-inch pieces
- 1   large tomato, cored, seeded, and cut into ¼-inch pieces

1 For the pistou Process all ingredients in food processor until smooth, scraping down sides of bowl as needed, about 15 seconds, set aside until ready to serve.

2 For the soup Dissolve 1½ tablespoons salt in 2 quarts cold water in large container. Add beans and soak at room temperature for at least 8 hours or up to 24 hours. Drain and rinse well. (If you're pressed for time, see page 69 for information on quick-brining your beans.)

3 Bring soaked beans and 7 cups water to simmer in Dutch oven. Simmer, partially covered, over medium-low heat until beans are tender, 30 to 40 minutes. Remove from heat; stir in 1½ teaspoons salt; cover; and let sit until completely tender, about 15 minutes. Drain beans, reserving 3 cups cooking liquid, adding water if necessary to reach volume. Reserve beans and measured cooking liquid.

4 Heat oil in now-empty Dutch oven over medium heat until shimmering. Add leek, celery, carrot, and salt and cook until vegetables are softened, 8 to 10 minutes. Stir in garlic and cook until fragrant, about 30 seconds. Stir in reserved bean cooking liquid and 4 cups water and bring to simmer.

5 Stir in pasta and simmer until slightly softened, about 5 minutes. Stir in green beans and simmer until bright green but still crunchy, 3 to 5 minutes. Stir in reserved beans, zucchini, and tomato and simmer until pasta and vegetables are tender, about 3 minutes. Season with salt and pepper to taste. Serve, topping individual portions with pistou.

Quick-Brining Beans

If you are pressed for time, do a quick brine (water plus salt) for an hour. Note that we strongly recommend over-night brining, as longer brining results in superior texture and the creamiest beans. Quick-brined dried beans will be less creamy and may take longer to cook.

To quick-brine beans: Combine 8 to 16 ounces dried beans with 1½ tablespoons salt in 2 quarts cold water in large Dutch oven and bring to boil. Remove from heat, cover, and let sit for 1 hour. Drain and rinse well under cold water before continuing with recipe.

Lentil and Escarole Soup

Why This Recipe Works This warming, main-course-worthy dish is inspired by the aromatic soups of Umbria, in which chewy, sturdy lentils often play a starring role. We started by browning our aromatics before stirring in broth, which gave us a deeply savory liquid in which to cook the lentils. We opted for Umbrian lentils or lentilles du Puy, as these varieties hold their shape particularly well during cooking; they retained their bite, while the soup stayed brothy, rather than thick and creamy. Supporting ingredients in lentil soup vary throughout Umbria, but we particularly liked escarole, a popular and hearty choice; adding the leafy green toward the end of cooking helped the vegetable hold on to its fibrous bite and nutty taste. We also included canned diced tomatoes—a classic addition—and a couple bay leaves for warmth. A rind of Parmesan, if you have one, adds a complex note to the soup as it simmers.

¼ cup extra-virgin olive oil, plus extra for drizzling

1 onion, chopped fine

1 carrot, peeled and chopped fine

1 celery rib, chopped fine

½ teaspoon table salt

6 garlic cloves, sliced thin

2 tablespoons minced fresh parsley

4 cups chicken or vegetable broth, plus extra as needed

3 cups water

8 ounces (1¼ cups) Umbrian lentils or lentilles du Puy, picked over and rinsed

1 (14.5-ounce) can diced tomatoes

1 Parmesan cheese rind (optional), plus grated Parmesan for serving

2 bay leaves

½ head escarole (8 ounces), trimmed and cut into ½-inch pieces

1 Heat oil in Dutch oven over medium heat until shimmering. Add onion, carrot, celery, and salt and cook until softened and lightly browned, 8 to 10 minutes. Stir in garlic and parsley and cook until fragrant, about 30 seconds. Stir in broth; water; lentils; tomatoes and their juice; Parmesan rind, if using; and bay leaves and bring to simmer. Reduce heat to medium-low, partially cover, and simmer until lentils are tender, 1 to 1¼ hours.

2 Discard Parmesan rind, if using, and bay leaves. Stir in escarole, 1 handful at a time, and cook until wilted, about 5 minutes. Adjust consistency with extra hot broth as needed. Season with salt and pepper to taste. Drizzle individual portions with extra oil and serve, passing grated Parmesan separately.

• *fast* • *vegetarian* • *fiber-ful* • *one-pan* •

Turkish Bulgur and Lentil Soup

Why This Recipe Works The lore surrounding ezogelin çorbasi, a beloved Anatolian bridal soup, is that a woman named Ezo could not impress her mother-in-law, so resourcefully created this recipe to win her over. Over time, the dish became associated with brides and evolved into a cultural symbol of sustenance and good fortune. But you definitely don't need to be planning a wedding to win anyone over with this one-pot dish. Heady with warming spices and brimming with fiber-rich lentils and bulgur, it makes a hearty, convenient dinner for any average night. To build a flavorful base for the dish, we cooked onion and tomato paste and enhanced them with the subtle sweetness of paprika and the heat of Aleppo pepper. We then stirred in the lentils and bulgur so they could toast in the saucepan, a step that drew out their nutty, earthy aroma. Chicken broth gave the dish savory underpinnings. A shower of fresh mint and a dollop of yogurt offered a cooling contrast to the soup, while lemon wedges brought a burst of brightness.

2 tablespoons extra-virgin olive oil, plus extra for drizzling

1 small onion, chopped fine

4 teaspoons paprika

1 tablespoon tomato paste

1 teaspoon ground dried Aleppo pepper

1 cup dried red lentils, picked over and rinsed

½ cup medium-grind bulgur, rinsed

5 cups vegetable or chicken broth

2½ cups water

¼ cup torn fresh mint

Greek yogurt

Lemon wedges

1 Heat oil in large saucepan over medium-high heat until shimmering. Add onion and cook until softened and beginning to brown, 5 to 7 minutes. Stir in paprika, tomato paste, and Aleppo pepper and cook until fragrant, about 30 seconds.

2 Stir in lentils and bulgur and toast, stirring constantly, for 1 minute. Add broth and water and bring to boil. Reduce heat to medium-low and cook, partially covered, until lentils are broken down and bulgur is tender, 20 to 25 minutes.

3 Sprinkle individual portions with mint and drizzle with extra oil. Serve with yogurt and lemon wedges.

Chorba Frik

Why This Recipe Works Stews and soups are a universal starter on Ramadan iftar dinner tables worldwide, as they hydrate the body and prepare it for digestion after fasting. Chorba, meaning soup, is widely consumed in different variations across Algeria, Tunisia, Morocco, and Libya. Chorba frik is one version starring freekeh; the chewy grains brim in a tomato-based broth with cilantro, morsels of meat, and sometimes chickpeas. For our take, we made the most of two bone-in chicken thighs by cooking them on the stovetop to render their fat, which was a flavorful foundation on which to build the rest of our dish. We used it to cook our aromatics and bloom an assortment of warm spices, before adding tomatoes, chickpeas, and cracked freekeh. We nestled the chicken into the pot, where the meat could further disperse its richness throughout the dish. As the freekeh simmered, it retained its chew while imparting its distinctly smoky, nutty flavor. Do not use whole freekeh in this recipe.

1 (14.5-ounce) can whole peeled tomatoes

2 (5- to 7-ounce) bone-in chicken thighs, trimmed

1¼ teaspoons table salt, divided

2 tablespoons extra-virgin olive oil

1 onion, chopped fine

1 celery rib, minced

1 cup minced fresh cilantro, plus ¼ cup leaves for serving

2 tablespoons tomato paste

3 garlic cloves, minced

1 tablespoon ground coriander

1 tablespoon paprika

2 teaspoons ground cumin

½ teaspoon pepper

¼ teaspoon ground cinnamon

¼ teaspoon cayenne pepper

6 cups water

1 (15-ounce) can chickpeas, undrained

½ cup cracked freekeh, rinsed

1 teaspoon dried mint

Lemon wedges

1 Pulse tomatoes and their juice in food processor until pureed, about 30 seconds. Pat chicken dry with paper towels and sprinkle with ¼ teaspoon salt. Heat oil in Dutch oven over medium-high heat until just smoking. Cook chicken skin side down until well browned, about 5 minutes; transfer chicken to plate. Pour off all but 2 tablespoons fat from pot.

2 Add onion, celery, and remaining 1 teaspoon salt to fat in pot and cook over medium heat until softened, about 5 minutes. Stir in minced cilantro, tomato paste, garlic, coriander, paprika, cumin, pepper, cinnamon, and cayenne and cook until fragrant, about 1 minute. Stir in pureed tomatoes, water, chickpeas and their liquid, and freekeh, scraping up any browned bits. Nestle chicken and any accumulated juices into pot and bring to simmer. Adjust heat as needed to maintain simmer and cook until freekeh is tender and chicken registers 195 degrees and easily shreds with fork, 35 to 45 minutes.

3 Transfer chicken to cutting board and let cool slightly. Once cool enough to handle, shred chicken into bite-size pieces using 2 forks, and discard skin and bones. Stir shredded chicken and any accumulated juices back into pot and season with salt and pepper to taste. Sprinkle individual portions with cilantro leaves and dried mint. Serve with lemon wedges.

Creamy Butternut Squash Soup with Sausage Crumbles and Apple

Why This Recipe Works Butternut squash blends up into a lusciously smooth consistency, which makes the vegetable a wonderful soup base. Here, we took the concept a step further by crisping Italian sausage in a bit of oil and using the rendered fat to cook and soften the squash and leeks, which infused the vegetables with the meat's richness. We cut the squash into 1-inch pieces to ensure they would cook evenly. Seasoning the squash with garlic and red pepper flakes deepened its flavor by imparting nuttiness and heat. We deglazed the pan with chicken broth and water to make the most of that flavorful fond and then blitzed the whole mixture into a creamy, comforting soup. Leaning into the warm, autumnal vibe of the dish, we garnished it with apple matchsticks and the reserved sausage; the crunch and sweetness of the fruit made a delightful contrast to the meaty topping.

1 tablespoon extra-virgin olive oil, plus extra for drizzling

8 ounces sweet Italian sausage, casings removed

3 pounds butternut squash, peeled, seeded, and cut into 1-inch pieces (8 cups)

1 leek, white and light green parts only, quartered lengthwise, sliced thin, and washed thoroughly

2 garlic cloves, smashed and peeled

½ teaspoon red pepper flakes

3 cups chicken broth

1½ cups water

2 sprigs fresh thyme

¼ teaspoon table salt

1 apple, cored and cut into 2-inch-long matchsticks

Sherry vinegar

1 Heat oil in large saucepan over medium-high heat until shimmering. Add sausage and cook, breaking up meat into pieces no larger than ½ inch, until lightly browned, about 10 minutes. Using slotted spoon, transfer sausage to bowl; cover to keep warm and set aside.

2 Add squash and leek to fat left in saucepan, and cook over medium heat until leek is softened, about 5 minutes. Stir in garlic and pepper flakes and cook until fragrant, about 30 seconds. Stir in broth, water, thyme, and salt and bring to simmer, scraping up any browned bits. Reduce heat to medium-low; cover; and cook until squash is very tender, about 25 minutes.

3 Discard thyme sprigs. Working in batches, process soup in blender until smooth, about 1 minute. Return soup to clean saucepan and bring to brief simmer, adjusting consistency with hot water as needed and season with salt and pepper to taste. Top each soup portion with reserved sausage and apple and drizzle with vinegar and extra oil. Serve.

Hot and Sour Soup

Why This Recipe Works A staple in Chinese restaurants around the world, this spicy, tangy soup is beloved for its bold and contrasting flavors. To get deep, complex heat, the "hot" side of the soup calls for two heat sources—a full teaspoon of distinctive, penetrating white pepper, and a little chili oil. To create the "sour" side, we turned to 5 tablespoons of bracing Chinese black vinegar. We started by cutting a single boneless pork chop into thin strips, a useful technique for stretching a little meat and dispersing its flavor throughout a whole dish. We then simmered the pork—along with bamboo shoots, shiitake mushrooms, and tofu, for textural complexity and plant-powered bulk—in an umami-rich concoction of chicken broth and soy sauce. To achieve a thick, luxuriously slurpable texture, we stirred in a cornstarch slurry. At the end, we whisked in an egg—combined with a little more cornstarch—while stirring the soup to create tender ribbons, for a delicate finishing touch. Use more or less chili oil depending on your desired level of spiciness. Serve with extra chili oil, black vinegar, and white pepper. For a spicier dish, use the larger amount of chili oil.

- 7 ounces extra-firm tofu, cut into ½-inch cubes
- 1 (6-ounce) boneless pork chop, trimmed
- 6 cups chicken broth
- 3 tablespoons soy sauce, plus extra for seasoning
- 1 (5-ounce) can bamboo shoots, sliced thin lengthwise
- 4 ounces shiitake mushrooms, stemmed and sliced ¼ inch thick
- 3 tablespoons plus 1 teaspoon water, divided
- 3 tablespoons plus ½ teaspoon cornstarch, divided
- 5 tablespoons Chinese black vinegar
- 1 teaspoon white pepper
- 1 teaspoon toasted sesame oil
- 1–3 teaspoons chili oil
- 1 large egg
- 3 scallions, sliced thin

1 Spread tofu over paper towel–lined plate and let drain for 20 minutes, then gently press dry with paper towels. Place pork chop on separate plate and freeze until firm, about 15 minutes. Transfer pork chop to cutting board and, holding knife parallel to cutting board, carefully slice into 2 thin cutlets. Slice each cutlet crosswise into thin strips.

2 Bring broth and soy sauce to simmer in large saucepan over medium heat. Add bamboo shoots and mushrooms and cook until mushrooms are just tender, about 2 minutes. Stir in tofu and pork and cook until pork is no longer pink, about 2 minutes.

3 Whisk 3 tablespoons water, 3 tablespoons cornstarch, vinegar, and pepper together in bowl, then stir mixture into soup. Increase heat to medium-high and cook, stirring occasionally, until soup thickens and turns translucent, about 1 minute. Remove soup from heat and cover to keep warm. Stir in sesame oil and chili oil and season with extra soy sauce to taste.

4 Whisk remaining 1 teaspoon water and remaining ½ teaspoon cornstarch together in 2-cup liquid measuring cup, then whisk in egg until combined. Off heat, use fork or chopsticks to stir soup; while stirring, pour egg mixture in slow, steady stream into swirling soup. Continue stirring soup until cooked thin egg ribbons appear, about 1 minute. Sprinkle individual portions with scallions before serving.

Miso Dashi Soup with Udon and Halibut

Why This Recipe Works The salty, umami-rich flavor of miso soup—the Japanese dish often made with tofu and wakame seaweed—can be a tasty foundation for myriad ingredients. We bulked up the dish with tender and buttery halibut, chewy udon noodles, crisp-tender carrots, and quickly wilted spinach. We began by making a dashi base, Japan's versatile stock made by extracting the umami-rich compounds found in kombu (dried kelp) and katsuobushi (dried, smoked, fermented, and shaved skip-jack tuna flakes). We steeped the kombu in cold water and then gently heated the kombu and its soaking liquid to extract the seaweed's savory compounds (too-high temperatures can turn the kombu bitter). Finally, we removed the kombu, further heated the infused liquid, and added katsuobushi to give the liquid a delicate smoky quality. Slurpable udon noodles cooked quickly while absorbing the soup's briny flavors. Scallion whites, garlic, and ginger complemented the oceanic dashi with fresh peppery notes, carrots delivered extra fiber, and halibut packed in the protein.

Dashi

- 2 quarts cold water
- 1½ ounces kombu
- 1½ ounces katsuobushi

Soup

- 1 pound fresh or frozen udon noodles
- 1 tablespoon vegetable oil
- 3 scallions, white and green parts separated and sliced thin
- 3 garlic cloves, minced
- 1 tablespoon grated fresh ginger
- 3 carrots, peeled, halved lengthwise, and sliced thin on bias
- 1 (12-ounce) skinless halibut fillet, 1½ inches thick, cut into 2-inch pieces
- ⅓ cup white miso
- 5 ounces (5 cups) baby spinach
- 1 tablespoon sesame seeds, toasted

1 For the dashi Combine water and kombu in large saucepan and let sit for at least 1 hour or up to 8 hours. Meanwhile, line large fine-mesh strainer with double layer of cheesecloth, letting excess hang over sides. Set strainer over large bowl or 8-cup liquid measuring cup and set aside. After kombu has soaked, place saucepan over medium-low heat and cook until kombu-water reaches 150 degrees (water should be steaming with bubbles forming and clinging to bottom and sides of saucepan but not rising to surface), about 10 minutes. Using tongs or spider skimmer, discard kombu (or reserve for another use).

2 Increase heat to high and cook until water reaches 200 degrees (bubbles should break surface just at edges of saucepan; do not let boil), about 3 minutes. Remove saucepan from heat, add katsuobushi, and let steep for 3 minutes. Strain dashi through prepared strainer. Gather sides of cheesecloth to form bundle and lightly pinch with tongs to release any liquid into bowl. Discard bundle. (Dashi can be refrigerated for up to 2 days or frozen for up to 1 month.)

3 For the soup Bring 2 quarts water to boil in now-empty saucepan. Add noodles and cook, stirring often, until almost tender (center should still be firm with slightly opaque dot), 2 to 4 minutes (cooking times will vary). Drain noodles and set aside.

4 Wipe pot dry, then heat oil in again-empty saucepan over medium heat until shimmering. Stir in scallion whites, garlic, and ginger and cook until fragrant, about 30 seconds. Add carrots and dashi and bring to simmer. Submerge halibut in dashi and return to simmer. Reduce heat to medium-low, cover, and gently simmer until fish flakes apart when gently prodded with paring knife and registers 130 degrees, 6 to 8 minutes.

5 Stir miso into soup to dissolve. Add spinach and cook until wilted, about 30 seconds. Divide reserved noodles among bowls, then spoon soup over top. Sprinkle with scallion greens and sesame seeds and serve.

Shiitake, Tofu, and Mustard Greens Soup

Why This Recipe Works We wanted a nourishing soup comprised of hearty, meaty vegetables bobbing in a light, clean-tasting broth. To build an aromatic foundation, we started by infusing chicken broth with generous amounts of ginger and garlic. Then we added dried shiitake mushrooms, fresh shiitake stems, and just enough soy sauce to contribute savory character. Shiitakes have a dense, pleasantly spongy chew, and they're also particularly rich in glutamates. After simmering and straining the liquid, we had an aromatic broth, but it still needed more vibrancy; a splash of rice vinegar did the trick, giving the soup subtle sweetness and tang. Sliced shiitake mushroom caps reinforced the umami-rich flavor of the broth, while a hefty amount of mustard greens brought a wonderful wasabi-like back note that perked up the soup. In lieu of noodles, we added tofu cubes for a dose of protein and some meaty bite. A sprinkle of sliced scallions was the perfect fresh finish. Some tasters enjoyed a drizzle of chili oil to ramp up the spicy flavor, but it is completely optional.

1　tablespoon vegetable oil

1　onion, chopped

½　teaspoon table salt

1　(4-inch) piece ginger, peeled and sliced thin

5　garlic cloves, smashed

4　cups vegetable or chicken broth

4　cups water

8　ounces shiitake mushrooms, stemmed and sliced thin, stems reserved

½　ounce dried shiitake mushrooms, rinsed

2　tablespoons soy sauce

14　ounces firm tofu, cut into ½-inch pieces

8　ounces mustard greens, stemmed and cut into 2-inch pieces

2　tablespoons unseasoned rice vinegar

3　scallions, sliced thin

　　Chili oil (optional)

1　Heat oil in large saucepan over medium-high heat until shimmering. Stir in onion and salt and cook until softened and lightly browned, 5 to 7 minutes. Stir in ginger and garlic and cook until lightly browned, about 2 minutes.

2　Stir in broth, water, mushroom stems, dried mushrooms, and soy sauce and bring to boil. Reduce heat to low; cover; and simmer until flavors meld, about 1 hour.

3　Strain broth through fine-mesh strainer set over large bowl, pressing on solids to extract as much liquid as possible; discard solids. Wipe saucepan clean with paper towels and return strained broth to saucepan.

4　Stir in sliced mushrooms, tofu, mustard greens, and vinegar and cook until mushrooms and tofu are warmed through and greens are wilted, about 3 minutes. Sprinkle individual portions with scallions and drizzle with chili oil, if using. Serve.

Laksa Soup

Why This Recipe Works An extremely vibrant, iconic dish beloved in Southeast Asia, laksa soup features noodles; proteins such as shrimp, chicken, or cockles; and vegetables such as bean sprouts and cilantro—all swimming in a deeply aromatic coconut–milk broth. The soup's namesake is laksa paste, a seasoning base used in dishes across Malaysia, Singapore, and Indonesia. Many variations of the profoundly fragrant, spicy-savory condiment exist, but most contain peppery galangal, floral lemongrass, and umami-rich dried shrimp. We based our recipe on versions that also include citrusy makrut lime leaves and sweet-tangy tamarind, which take the laksa to even more complex and flavorful heights. Many iterations also call for fruity cabeh merah peppers, which deliver heat in addition to brightness, but these can be difficult to source; after some testing, we found that arbol chiles made a suitable substitute. Blitzing all these aromatic ingredients in a food processor brought the paste together quickly. To start cooking our soup, we heated laksa paste with garlic and sugar, which deepened all the flavors and gave us a wonderfully potent base. We thinned this out with chicken broth, making sure to scrape up and make full use of the browned bits at the bottom of the pan. We then stirred in our protein, 12 ounces each of chicken and shrimp, cooking both directly in the soup so they could drink up the vibrant seasonings in the broth. Enhancing the broth with coconut cream made it delectably rich, while lime juice and fish sauce introduced tang and more savoriness, respectively. For the noodles, we opted for tender, chewy rice vermicelli, a popular choice for laksa soup. Don't hold back on the garnishes, as they are an integral part of the soup; their grassy and herbaceous flavors balance out the richness of the coconut cream in the broth. Look for Thai/Indonesian-style tamarind concentrate labeled "nuoc me chua"; do not use Indian-style tamarind concentrates (see page 15 for more information). We strongly recommend sourcing galangal for its distinctive sharp, citrusy flavor, but if you can't find it, you can substitute ginger. We like to make our laksa paste from scratch, but you can substitute 1 cup store-bought paste if you prefer (keep in mind that different brands vary in flavor and intensity). Be sure to use coconut cream, not sweetened cream of coconut, in this recipe. This soup is often also garnished with crispy shallots and tofu puffs. We like to use our own Crispy Shallots (recipe follows), but you can use store-bought if you prefer. We recommend buying the tofu puffs.

Laksa Paste

4 dried arbol chiles, stemmed

2½ tablespoons dried shrimp

½ cup tamarind juice concentrate

1 onion, chopped

6 makrut lime leaves, middle vein removed and sliced thin crosswise

¼ cup raw cashews, chopped

4 stalks lemongrass, trimmed to bottom 6 inches, tough outer leaves discarded, halved lengthwise, and minced

2½ tablespoons vegetable oil

1 (5-inch) piece fresh galangal, chopped

5 garlic cloves, peeled

1 tablespoon packed dark brown sugar

1 tablespoon ground coriander

2 teaspoons ground cumin

1½ teaspoons paprika

1½ teaspoons ground turmeric

1½ teaspoons table salt

Soup

- 8 ounces rice vermicelli
- 1 tablespoon vegetable oil
- 4 garlic cloves, minced
- 1 tablespoon packed dark brown sugar
- 4 cups chicken broth
- 12 ounces boneless, skinless chicken breasts, trimmed and cut into 1-inch pieces
- 12 ounces large shrimp (26 to 30 per pound), peeled, deveined, and tails removed
- 1 (13.5-ounce) can coconut cream
- 1 tablespoon lime juice, plus lime wedges for serving
- 1 tablespoon fish sauce
- 4 ounces (2 cups) bean sprouts
- ½ cup fresh cilantro leaves and tender stems
- 4 scallions, sliced thin
- Sambal oelek

1 **For the laksa paste** Soak arbols and dried shrimp in warm water for 20 minutes, then drain well. Process soaked arbols and dried shrimp, tamarind, onion, lime leaves, cashews, lemongrass, oil, 2½ tablespoons water, galangal, garlic, sugar, coriander, cumin, paprika, turmeric, and salt in food processor until smooth, about 5 minutes, scraping down sides of bowl as needed; set aside.

2 **For the soup** Bring 4 quarts water to boil in large pot. Remove from heat; add vermicelli; and let sit, stirring occasionally, until vermicelli are fully tender, 10 to 15 minutes. Drain, rinse with cold water, drain again, and distribute evenly among large soup bowls.

3 Meanwhile, heat oil in large saucepan over medium heat until shimmering. Add laksa paste, garlic, and sugar and cook, stirring occasionally, until fragrant and mixture starts to brown, about 2 minutes.

4 Whisk in broth and ½ cup water, scraping up any browned bits, and bring to boil. Stir in chicken and return to simmer. Cook, adjusting heat as needed to maintain simmer, until chicken is tender, 4 to 6 minutes. Stir in shrimp and coconut cream and cook until shrimp is just opaque, 1 to 2 minutes.

5 Off heat, stir in lime juice and fish sauce and season with salt to taste. Ladle soup over noodles in bowls and sprinkle with bean sprouts, cilantro, and scallions. Serve with lime wedges and sambal.

Crispy Shallots

Makes ½ cup | Total time: 20 minutes

- 3 shallots, sliced thin
- ½ cup vegetable oil for frying

1 Combine shallots and oil in medium bowl. Microwave for 5 minutes. Stir and continue to microwave for 2 minutes. Repeat stirring and microwaving in 2-minute increments until beginning to brown (4 to 6 minutes).

2 Repeat stirring and microwaving in 30-second increments until deep golden brown (30 seconds to 2 minutes). Using slotted spoon, transfer shallots to paper towel–lined plate; season with salt to taste. Let drain and crisp for about 5 minutes. Save oil for another use. (Shallots can be stored at room temperature for up to 1 month; shallot oil can be stored in refrigerator for up to 1 month.)

Laksa Soup
(page 84)

Madzoon ov Kofte

Why This Recipe Works Bulgur, a popular grain across the Middle East, adds satiating heft and pleasant chew to the meatballs in this creamy, comforting Armenian yogurt soup. Though the dish traditionally calls for stuffed, spiced meatballs, we combined ground beef with quick-cooking bulgur for a less time-consuming version. We added baking soda to the mixture, a technique that made the meatballs light and airy. Cooking onion and mint in some butter gave us a rich base for our soup. We added chicken broth to this mixture and then cooked chickpeas and our meatballs in this earthy concoction. Some pasta shells bulked up the dish with a starchy component. Whisking Greek yogurt and an egg yolk into the soup lent creaminess and thickening power, with just the right amount of tartness. For garnishes, we used fresh cilantro and Aleppo pepper–infused butter to echo the soup's earthy flavors. If you can't find dried mint, it's better to omit it than to substitute fresh (their flavors are quite different). You can substitute small elbow macaroni for the pasta shells if you prefer.

    8 ounces 85 percent lean ground beef

    3 tablespoons water

1¾ teaspoons table salt, divided

    ¼ teaspoon baking soda, divided

    ½ cup medium-grind bulgur, rinsed

    ¼ cup chopped fresh cilantro, divided

    2 teaspoons ground dried Aleppo pepper, divided

    1 teaspoon ground coriander

    ½ teaspoon pepper, divided

    4 tablespoons unsalted butter, divided

    1 onion, chopped fine

    1 teaspoon dried mint

    4 cups chicken broth

    1 (15-ounce) can chickpeas, undrained

    4 ounces (1 cup) small pasta shells

1½ cups plain Greek yogurt

    1 large egg yolk

1 Toss beef with water, 1 teaspoon salt, and ⅛ teaspoon baking soda in bowl until thoroughly combined. Add bulgur, 1 tablespoon cilantro, 1 teaspoon Aleppo pepper, coriander, and ¼ teaspoon pepper and mix by hand until uniform. Transfer meat mixture to cutting board and press into 6-inch square. Using bench scraper or sharp knife, divide mixture into 36 squares (6 rows by 6 rows). Using your lightly moistened hands, roll each square into smooth ball and leave on cutting board.

2 Melt 2 tablespoons butter in large saucepan over medium heat. Add onion, mint, remaining ¾ teaspoon salt, remaining ⅛ teaspoon baking soda, and remaining ¼ teaspoon pepper and cook, stirring occasionally, until onion has broken down into soft paste and is just starting to stick to saucepan, 6 to 8 minutes.

3 Stir in broth, chickpeas and their liquid, and meatballs and bring to boil. Simmer over medium-low heat for 5 minutes, stirring occasionally. Add pasta and continue to cook until pasta is tender. While pasta cooks, whisk yogurt and egg yolk together in large bowl.

4 Remove saucepan from heat. Using ladle, transfer 1½ cups broth to liquid measuring cup (try to avoid meatballs, pasta, and chickpeas). Whisking vigorously, gradually add broth to yogurt mixture. Add half of yogurt-broth mixture back to saucepan and stir to combine. Stir in remaining yogurt-broth mixture. Cover and let sit for 10 minutes to thicken.

5 Heat soup over medium heat, stirring occasionally, until temperature registers between 180 and 185 degrees (do not allow soup to boil or yogurt will curdle). Remove from heat, stir in 1 tablespoon cilantro, and season with salt to taste. (Broth should have consistency of buttermilk; if thicker, adjust by adding hot water, 2 tablespoons at a time.)

6 Melt remaining 2 tablespoons butter in small skillet over medium-high heat. Off heat, stir in remaining 1 teaspoon Aleppo pepper. Ladle soup into bowls, drizzle each portion with 1 teaspoon spiced butter, sprinkle with remaining 2 tablespoons cilantro, and serve.

Almost Beefless Beef Stew

Why This Recipe Works   The hallmark of an excellent beef stew is exceedingly tender meat swimming in a deeply savory broth. This is usually achieved by using a large cut of meat, so we wondered if there could, or should, be space for such a dish in a book that aims to reduce meat consumption. Early tests seemed to confirm our skepticism—until we tried blade steaks, which consistently turned tender and were convenient to buy in small amounts. The chunks distributed plenty of richness to our medley of vegetables: potatoes, carrots, peas, and pearl onions. However, our glossy sauce seriously lacked beefiness. To rectify this, we turned to ingredients adept at building up tasty browning. Garlic, anchovies, and tomato paste created a flavor-rich base for our stew. We also added a pound of mushrooms, taking care to drive away moisture to concentrate their flavor. Our final recipe had over 4 pounds of veggies and under a pound of meat, yet every bite brimmed with beefy flavor. Use extra small Yukon Gold or red potatoes measuring less than 1 inch in diameter. You can substitute Yukon Gold or red potatoes that are 1 to 2 inches in diameter; just be sure to halve them before adding to the stew in step 4.

2 (6- to 8-ounce) blade steaks, ¾ to 1 inch thick, trimmed and cut into 1½-inch pieces

3 tablespoons vegetable oil, divided

1 pound cremini mushrooms, trimmed and halved if small or quartered if large or medium

¾ teaspoon table salt, divided

1 large onion, halved and sliced thin

6 garlic cloves, minced

2 tablespoons tomato paste

6 anchovy fillets, minced

¼ cup all-purpose flour

1 cup plus 2 tablespoons red wine, divided

2½ cups chicken or beef broth

1 pound extra-small potatoes

4 carrots, peeled and sliced ¼ inch thick on bias

1½ cups frozen pearl onions, thawed

1 cup frozen peas, thawed

¼ teaspoon pepper

1 Adjust oven rack to lower-middle position and heat oven to 325 degrees. Pat beef dry with paper towels. Heat 1 tablespoon oil in Dutch oven over medium-high heat until just smoking. Add beef and cook until well browned on all sides, 5 to 8 minutes; transfer to bowl.

2 Add mushrooms, 1 tablespoon oil, and ¼ teaspoon salt to fat left in pot and cook, covered, over medium-high heat until mushrooms have released their liquid, 3 to 5 minutes. Uncover and cook until mushrooms are well browned, 7 to 10 minutes, stirring occasionally. Transfer mushrooms to bowl with beef.

3 Add onion, remaining 1 tablespoon oil, and remaining ½ teaspoon salt to now-empty pot and cook until golden brown, 7 to 10 minutes. Add garlic, tomato paste, and anchovies and cook, stirring constantly, until tomato paste is slightly darkened, about 2 minutes. Stir in flour and cook until no dry flour remains, about 30 seconds.

4 Slowly add 1 cup wine, scraping up any browned bits. Stir in broth, potatoes, and beef-mushroom mixture and any accumulated juices. Bring to simmer, cover, and transfer to oven. Cook for 1 hour.

5 Remove pot from oven. Stir in carrots and pearl onions and bring to simmer over medium heat. Cook, stirring occasionally and scraping bottom of pot, until carrots are tender, 8 to 12 minutes.

6 Stir in peas and cook until heated through, about 2 minutes. Stir in pepper and remaining 2 tablespoons wine and season with salt and pepper to taste. Serve. (Stew can be refrigerated for up to 2 days.)

Bean Bourguignon

Why This Recipe Works Creamy, chestnut-like Christmas lima beans marry chewy, earthy portobello mushrooms in this vegan version of the French classic that's as luxurious and satisfying as the original. Mushrooms' ability to create fond—coupled with umami boosters like miso, soy sauce, and tomato paste—created a supremely savory sauce. Simmering beans in this slightly acidic sauce lengthened their cook time, leading to uneven results, so we cooked them separately and added them to the sauce for the last 15 minutes to imbue them with the stew's umami. You can substitute dried shiitake mushrooms for the porcini; yellow or red miso for the white; and dried large lima beans for the Christmas lima beans, if you prefer. Leave the mushroom gills intact; they enhance the stew's color and flavor. Serve over Creamy Parmesan Polenta (page 327).

1½   tablespoons table salt for brining

8   ounces (1⅓ cups) dried Christmas lima beans, picked over and rinsed

½   teaspoon table salt, plus salt for cooking beans

¼   cup extra-virgin olive oil, divided

1½   pounds portobello mushroom caps, cut into 1-inch pieces

¼   teaspoon pepper

2   carrots, peeled and chopped fine

1   large shallot, minced

½   ounce dried porcini mushrooms, rinsed and minced

4   garlic cloves, minced

2   teaspoons minced fresh thyme or ¾ teaspoon dried

3   tablespoons all-purpose flour

1   cup plus 2 tablespoons dry red wine, divided

2   tablespoons white miso

2   tablespoons soy sauce

1   tablespoon tomato paste

2   bay leaves

1   cup frozen pearl onions, thawed

¼   cup minced fresh parsley

1 Dissolve 1½ tablespoons table salt in 2 quarts cold water in large container. Add beans and soak at room temperature for at least 8 hours or up to 24 hours. Drain and rinse well. (If you're pressed for time, see page 69 for information on quick-brining your beans.)

2 Bring soaked beans and 7 cups water to simmer in large saucepan. Simmer, partially covered, over medium-low heat until beans are tender, 20 to 30 minutes. Remove from heat, stir in 1½ teaspoons salt, cover, and let sit for 15 minutes. Drain beans and set aside.

3 While beans cook, add ¼ cup water and 2 tablespoons oil to Dutch oven and bring to simmer over medium-high heat. Add portobello mushrooms, remaining ½ teaspoon salt, and pepper. Cover and cook for 5 minutes, stirring occasionally (mushrooms will release liquid).

4 Uncover and continue to cook, stirring occasionally, until pot is dry and dark fond forms, 6 to 8 minutes longer. Add carrots, shallot, and remaining 2 tablespoons oil to pot and cook, stirring frequently, until vegetables start to brown, 3 to 4 minutes. Add porcini mushrooms, garlic, and thyme and cook until fragrant, about 30 seconds. Stir in flour and cook for 30 seconds. Whisk in 1 cup wine, scraping up any browned bits.

5 Whisk in miso, soy sauce, and tomato paste, then stir in 5 cups water and bay leaves. Bring to boil over high heat. Reduce heat to maintain vigorous simmer and cook, stirring occasionally and scraping bottom of pot to loosen any browned bits, until sauce is reduced and has consistency of heavy cream, 20 to 25 minutes.

6 Stir in cooked beans, pearl onions, and remaining 2 tablespoons wine. Cover and cook over low heat, stirring occasionally, until pearl onions are tender, about 15 minutes. Discard bay leaves and stir in parsley. Serve.

Beans Marbella

Why This Recipe Works   This enticing stew is a bean-ified version of a timeless classic: Chicken Marbella from *The Silver Palate Cookbook*. The combination of sweet prunes and briny olives marries nicely with large lima beans, which cook up tender and creamy, with a hearty, meat-like character. We added pancetta and anchovies for savory depth and umami; cooking the two with garlic and red pepper flakes allowed all the flavors to intermingle, giving us an incredibly flavorful base. Due to their size, large lima beans have a longer than average cook time, so rather than cook them separately, we simmered the beans and sauce together, saturating the legumes with glutamic depth. We also removed wine from the sauce, as it can impede bean cook time; instead, red wine vinegar, added just before serving, gave us a bright hit of acidity. If you can find Royal Corona beans, they are particularly buttery and you can swap them in for the lima beans; Royal Coronas will take closer to 3 hours to cook in step 2. Serve with crusty bread.

1½ tablespoons table salt for brining

  1 pound (2½ cups) large dried lima beans, picked over and rinsed

  1 tablespoon extra-virgin olive oil

  4 ounces pancetta, cut into 1-inch-long by ¼-inch-wide lardons

  4 garlic cloves, minced

  4 anchovy fillets, rinsed, patted dry, and minced

  ¼ teaspoon red pepper flakes

  2 tablespoons all-purpose flour

  3 tablespoons packed brown sugar

  1 cup pitted prunes, halved, divided

  ¾ cup pitted green olives, halved, divided

  ¼ cup capers, divided

  2 bay leaves

  ½ teaspoon dried oregano

1½ teaspoons table salt

  ½ teaspoon pepper

  2 tablespoons red wine vinegar

  ¼ cup chopped fresh parsley

1 Dissolve 1½ tablespoons table salt in 2 quarts cold water in large container. Add beans and soak at room temperature for at least 8 hours or up to 24 hours. Drain and rinse well. (If you're pressed for time, see page 69 for information on quick-brining your beans.)

2 Adjust oven rack to middle position and heat oven to 325 degrees. Heat oil in Dutch oven over medium heat until shimmering. Add pancetta and cook until browned, 5 to 7 minutes. Add garlic, anchovies, and pepper flakes and cook until fragrant, about 30 seconds. Stir in flour and cook for 30 seconds. Slowly whisk in 7 cups water and sugar, scraping up any browned bits and smoothing out any lumps. Stir in beans, ½ cup prunes, 6 tablespoons olives, 2 tablespoons capers, bay leaves, oregano, salt, and pepper. Bring to simmer, then cover pot and transfer to oven. Cook until beans are tender, 2 to 3 hours, stirring every 30 minutes.

3 Stir remaining prunes, remaining olives, remaining capers, and vinegar into pot. Cover pot and let rest off heat until prunes have softened, about 10 minutes. Discard bay leaves. Stir in parsley and season with salt and pepper to taste. Serve.

Green Gumbo

Why This Recipe Works Green gumbo, or gumbo z'herbes, was originally a Louisiana Lenten dish signifying abstinence (from meat). It's now served year round, with and without meat; this take offers the quick gratification of the meatless version. Like most gumbo, it starts with a dark oil-flour roux, which provides thickening power and nutty richness. What sets this gumbo apart from its cousins is lots of greens. Some recipes have more than a dozen kinds; to streamline things, we chose one chewier variety (collards, mustard greens, or kale) and one softer one (spinach or Swiss chard) for a balance of fibrousness and silkiness. (Do experiment with whatever greens you have on hand.) Cayenne and smoked paprika echoed the smokiness of meaty gumbos. Though not traditional, the addition of other plants—okra, green beans, and black-eyed peas—made for a heartier and more delicious stew. Don't use fresh okra here, though you can substitute frozen spinach for fresh, if you prefer. Serve over rice.

½ cup vegetable oil

½ cup all-purpose flour

1 large onion, chopped fine

2 celery ribs, chopped fine

1 green bell pepper, stemmed, seeded, and chopped fine

3 garlic cloves, minced

1 tablespoon minced fresh thyme or 1 teaspoon dried

2¼ teaspoons table salt, divided

2 teaspoons smoked paprika

1 teaspoon cayenne pepper

5 cups water

12 ounces collard greens, mustard greens, or kale, stemmed and cut into 1-inch pieces

1 cup frozen cut okra

1 (15-ounce) can black-eyed peas, rinsed

12 ounces curly-leaf spinach or Swiss chard, stemmed and cut into 1-inch pieces

6 ounces green beans, trimmed and cut into 1-inch lengths

1 tablespoon cider vinegar, plus extra for seasoning

2 scallions, sliced thin (optional)

1 Heat oil in Dutch oven over medium-high heat until just smoking. Using rubber spatula, stir in flour and cook, stirring constantly, until mixture is color of peanut butter, 2 to 5 minutes. Reduce heat to medium-low and continue to cook, stirring constantly, until roux has darkened to color of milk chocolate, 5 to 10 minutes longer.

2 Stir in onion, celery, bell pepper, garlic, thyme, 1 teaspoon salt, paprika, and cayenne. Cover and cook, stirring frequently, until vegetables have softened, 8 to 10 minutes.

3 Stir in water, scraping up any browned bits, and bring to boil over high heat. Stir in collard greens, 1 handful at a time; okra; and remaining 1¼ teaspoons salt. Cover; reduce heat to low; and simmer until greens are just tender, 5 to 7 minutes. Stir in black-eyed peas; spinach, 1 handful at a time; and green beans and simmer until green beans and spinach are tender, about 5 minutes. Stir in vinegar and season with salt, pepper, and extra vinegar to taste. Sprinkle with scallions, if using. Serve.

Caldo Verde

Why This Recipe Works This rich and hearty soup of potatoes, greens, and often sausage is a beloved staple in many Portuguese households. The sausage is usually linguiça, a smoky, garlicky Portuguese-style variety, which can be hard to find, but widely available Spanish-style chorizo boasts a similar flavor profile. Either option is so flavorful, with spicy and complex warmth, that we found 12 ounces was all we needed to build a deeply savory soup. After cooking the sausage, we sautéed onion and garlic in the same pot so the aromatics could soak up the rendered fat. Next, we added cubed potatoes and a mixture of broth and water to simmer until the tubers turned tender. Blitzing some of the solids and broth with olive oil in a blender and stirring the mixture back into the pot gave the soup silky-smooth body; while not a traditional step, this transformed a simple soup into a filling, seriously satisfying full meal. Traditionally, shredded couve tronchuda (a kale relative) is stirred in during the last few minutes of cooking, studding the soup with green—and giving the dish its name. Collards, with their delicate sweetness and fibrous bite, not to mention wider availability, made a fitting substitute for the couve tronchuda. A final splash of white wine vinegar gave our soup a subtle hit of tartness.

¼ cup extra-virgin olive oil, divided

12 ounces Spanish-style chorizo sausage or linguiça, cut into ½-inch pieces

1 onion, chopped fine

4 garlic cloves, minced

1¼ teaspoons table salt

¼ teaspoon red pepper flakes

2 pounds Yukon Gold potatoes, peeled and cut into ¾-inch pieces

4 cups chicken broth

4 cups water

1 pound collard greens, stemmed and cut into 1-inch pieces

2 teaspoons white wine vinegar

1 Heat 1 tablespoon oil in Dutch oven over medium-high heat until shimmering. Add chorizo and cook, stirring occasionally, until lightly browned, 4 to 5 minutes. Using slotted spoon, transfer chorizo to bowl and set aside. Add onion, garlic, salt, and pepper flakes to fat left in pot and cook, stirring frequently, over medium heat until onion is translucent, 2 to 3 minutes. Add potatoes, broth, and water and bring to boil. Reduce heat to medium-low and simmer, uncovered, until potatoes are just tender, 8 to 10 minutes.

2 Transfer ¾ cup solids and ¾ cup broth to blender. Add collard greens to pot and simmer for 10 minutes. Stir in chorizo and continue to simmer until greens are tender, 8 to 10 minutes longer.

3 Add remaining 3 tablespoons oil to soup in blender and process until very smooth and homogeneous, about 1 minute. Off heat, stir pureed soup mixture and vinegar into soup in pot. Season with salt and pepper to taste, and serve.

Kimchi Jjigae

Why This Recipe Works   Korean cuisine is well celebrated for its supremely comforting stews, and spicy-savory kimchi jjigae may be the most famous one of all. For the base of the broth, most Korean cooks use well-aged cabbage kimchi, first cooking it in oil to intensify its briny-tart fermented flavor. If you have access to aged kimchi, you should use it, but here we bolstered our kimchi's savoriness with an extra dose of fish sauce, as well as sugar to balance out the other intense aromas. Kimchi jjigae typically includes a lot of stewed pork; to lessen the meat, we used a modest amount of pork shoulder. We cut it into slivers to maximize the surface area for browning, which enhanced the meaty flavor of the dish. This cut braised beautifully, turning fall-apart tender after a short simmer while imparting plenty of richness. A dash of gochugaru, Korean chile flakes, offered mild heat and subtle sweetness. Tofu is a popular add-in; we opted for a soft kind, which contrasted well with the crunch of scallions and the kimchi. Pork shoulder steaks are steaks cut from the shoulder. You can substitute 8 ounces boneless pork butt roast if you prefer; pork butt roast is often labeled Boston butt in the supermarket. Serve with rice.

1   Heat 1 tablespoon oil in Dutch oven over medium-high heat until shimmering. Add pork and salt and cook until light golden brown, 4 to 6 minutes. Add kimchi and cook until edges of white cabbage turn translucent, 5 to 7 minutes. Add garlic, gochugaru, and remaining 1 tablespoon oil and cook, stirring constantly, until fragrant, about 1 minute.

2   Stir in broth, water, fish sauce, sugar, and reserved kimchi juice. Bring to simmer; reduce heat to low; and cook, covered, until pork is tender, about 30 minutes.

3   Stir in scallions and nestle tofu into stew. Return to simmer and cook, uncovered, until scallions have softened, about 10 minutes. Season with extra fish sauce to taste. Serve.

- 2 tablespoons vegetable oil, divided
- 8 ounces pork shoulder steaks, trimmed, cut into 1-inch strips, and sliced crosswise ¼ inch thick
- ¼ teaspoon table salt
- 1 pound cabbage kimchi, drained with ¼ cup juice reserved, cut into 2-inch pieces
- 6 garlic cloves, minced
- 1 tablespoon gochugaru
- 2 cups chicken broth
- 1 cup water
- 2 teaspoons fish sauce, plus extra for seasoning
- 1 teaspoon sugar
- 6 scallions, cut into 2-inch lengths
- 14 ounces soft or medium-firm tofu, cut into 1½-inch-wide, ½-inch-thick squares

Misir Wot

Why This Recipe Works One of Ethiopia's most famous vegetarian dishes, misir wot is a deeply flavored lentil dish traditionally seasoned with the spice blend berbere, which delivers intense warmth alongside sweet and citrusy notes. Since it's not always easy to find, we made it ourselves. Premade berbere often contains powdered ginger, which has a strong peppery aroma; we wanted to bring out the floral sweetness of fresh ginger. To start, we cooked our aromatics—red onion, umami-rich tomato paste, and fresh ginger and garlic—before adding our berbere blend of paprika, coriander, cardamom, cumin, and cayenne to bloom. Next came quick-cooking red lentils, as well as some plum tomatoes, which brought a necessary freshness and almost cooling effect to this complex dish. We finished with a drizzle of red wine vinegar, the acidity of which helped to cut through the many layers of delicious heat. Do not substitute other types of lentils for the red lentils here; they have a very different texture. Adjust the amount of cayenne according to your preference. Be sure to bloom the spices for the full minute; otherwise, you'll be left with a raw, dusty texture in the dish. Serve with injera.

1 Heat oil in large saucepan over medium-high heat until shimmering. Add onion and cook, stirring occasionally, until softened and lightly browned, 5 to 7 minutes. Add tomato paste, ginger, garlic, paprika, coriander, cardamom, cumin, and cayenne and cook until fragrant, about 1 minute.

2 Stir in water, lentils, tomatoes, and salt and bring to simmer. Reduce heat to low and simmer, stirring occasionally, until lentils are tender and beginning to break down, 15 to 25 minutes. Season with salt, pepper, and vinegar to taste. Serve.

3 tablespoons extra-virgin olive oil

1 red onion, chopped fine

2 tablespoons tomato paste

4 teaspoons grated fresh ginger

3 garlic cloves, minced

2½ teaspoons paprika

1¼ teaspoons ground coriander

¾ teaspoon ground cardamom

¾ teaspoon ground cumin

½–1 teaspoon cayenne pepper

2 cups water

1 cup dried red lentils, picked over and rinsed

4 plum tomatoes, cored and chopped fine

1 teaspoon table salt

Red wine vinegar

Palak Dal

Why This Recipe Works   In India, both raw lentils and the stews made with them are called "dal." The legumes are a staple of the vegetarian Indian meal: quick, affordable, flavorful, and packed with protein. For a take that's ideal for busy weeknights, we used quick-cooking red lentils. Once they had simmered to a soft texture, a vigorous whisk transformed them into a porridge-like puree, no blender or food processor needed. We also added spinach, which bulked up the dish with plant-powered nutrients. Seasoning the lentils with the Indian tadka technique—frying whole spices in a few tablespoons of fat before using the fragrant mixture as a gorgeous garnish—gave the dish complexity, a stunning appearance, and an enticing aroma. A final squeeze of lemon juice infused each bite with subtle tang that perfectly complemented the stew's earthy flavors. If you can't find brown mustard seeds, you can substitute yellow. Monitor the spices and aromatics carefully during frying and reduce the heat if needed to prevent them from scorching. Serve with naan and/or rice.

4½   cups water

1½   cups (10½ ounces) dried red lentils, picked over and rinsed

1   tablespoon grated fresh ginger

¾   teaspoon ground turmeric

6   ounces (6 cups) baby spinach

1½   teaspoons table salt

3   tablespoons ghee

1½   teaspoons brown mustard seeds

1½   teaspoons cumin seeds

1   large onion, chopped

15   curry leaves, coarsely torn (optional)

6   garlic cloves, sliced

4   whole dried arbol chiles

1   serrano chile, halved lengthwise

1½   teaspoons lemon juice, plus extra for seasoning

⅓   cup chopped fresh cilantro

1   Bring water, lentils, ginger, and turmeric to boil in large saucepan over medium-high heat. Reduce heat to maintain vigorous simmer. Cook, uncovered, stirring occasionally, until lentils are soft and starting to break down, 18 to 20 minutes.

2   Whisk lentils vigorously until coarsely pureed, about 30 seconds. Continue to cook until lentils have consistency of loose polenta or oatmeal, up to 5 minutes. Stir in spinach and salt and continue to cook until spinach is fully wilted, 30 to 60 seconds. Cover and set aside off heat.

3   Melt ghee in 10-inch skillet over medium-high heat. Add mustard seeds and cumin seeds and cook, stirring constantly, until seeds sizzle and pop, about 30 seconds. Add onion and cook, stirring frequently, until onion is just starting to brown, about 5 minutes. Add curry leaves, if using; garlic; arbols; and serrano and cook, stirring frequently, until onion and garlic are golden brown, 3 to 4 minutes.

4   Add lemon juice to lentils and stir to incorporate. (Dal should have consistency of loose polenta. If too thick, loosen with hot water, adding 1 tablespoon at a time.) Season with salt and extra lemon juice to taste. Transfer dal to individual serving bowls and spoon onion mixture on top. Sprinkle with cilantro and serve.

Sancocho

Why This Recipe Works Hearty, comforting sancocho—derived from the Spanish word "sancochar," which means to parboil—is a popular stew in several Latin American and Caribbean cuisines. The ingredients vary by region, but the common denominators are root vegetables, plantains, corn, a variety of proteins, and seasonings such as culantro and sazón, the warm spice blend widely used in Latin American homes. The dish is usually meat-centric, but developing a version with less meat proved simple: One pound of pork butt, a fatty cut with a longer cook time, went a long way in flavoring the dish; we cut it into 1-inch pieces to increase the surface area through which the pork could disperse its richness. So as not to overcook our vegetables, we added them only after giving the pork a head start in the pot. We chose yuca (also called cassava) and kabocha squash along with green plantains and corn: four hearty, firm choices that beautifully absorbed the broth's savory flavors. All the ingredients united into a texturally varied dish, each ingredient dense and satisfying. Pork butt roast is often labeled Boston butt. We like to use fresh yuca in this recipe, but you can use thawed frozen yuca if you prefer. Be sure to use sazón with achiote (often labeled "con culantro y achiote"). Eat the corn right off the cob with your hands and serve with rice, avocado, lime wedges, and hot sauce.

1 tablespoon vegetable oil

1 onion, chopped fine

1 tablespoon sazón with achiote

2 garlic cloves, minced

1 pound boneless pork butt roast, trimmed and cut into 1-inch pieces

4 cups water

4 cups chicken broth

1 pound yuca root

1 pound kabocha squash, cut into 1-inch pieces

2 green plantains, peeled, halved lengthwise and sliced ½ inch thick

2 ears corn, husks and silk removed, cobs quartered

2 cups chopped fresh culantro or cilantro, divided

½ teaspoon table salt

1 Heat oil in Dutch over medium heat until shimmering. Add onion and cook until beginning to brown, 5 to 7 minutes. Stir in sazón and garlic and cook until fragrant, about 1 minute. Stir in pork, water, and broth and bring to boil. Reduce heat to low, cover, and simmer for 45 minutes, occasionally skimming foam off surface.

2 Meanwhile, trim ends of yuca, then cut into 2-inch lengths. Working with 1 length at a time, stand on cutting board and use sharp knife to cut off outer peel. Cut each length into quarters, then remove center woody core.

3 Stir yuca, squash, plantains, corn, 1 cup culantro, and salt into pot with pork. Cook over medium-low heat until pork and vegetables are tender, about 45 minutes.

4 Stir in remaining 1 cup culantro and cook until wilted, about 1 minute. Season with salt and pepper to taste, and serve.

Prepping Yuca Root

1 After trimming the ends and cutting the yuca into manageable lengths, use a sharp knife to cut off the tough skin of the yuca.

2 After peeling the yuca, quarter the root lengthwise. Using a sharp knife, remove the center woody core of the yuca.

Hot Ukrainian Borscht

Why This Recipe Works There are a few markers of a classic Ukrainian borscht: beets, for their earthy sweetness and vivid hue, as well as green cabbage, carrots, onions, and potatoes, staple crops that grow abundantly in Ukraine. Two pounds of collagen-rich pork butt (a particularly fatty, flavorful cut well suited to slow cooking) yielded a large batch of full-bodied broth with tender, succulent meat; further bulked up with a medley of vegetables, this amount was enough for six to eight generous servings. Skimming fat from the surface of the liquid ensured the dish wouldn't be overly rich and mask the earthy, tangy flavors. Shredding the beets and carrots not only helped the hard roots cook efficiently but also varied their texture from that of the potato chunks. Tomato paste and a shot of lemon juice brightened the savory broth with tart notes. Resting the soup before serving gave the flavors time to meld, while a sprinkle of dill made a refreshing, grassy finish. Pork butt roast is often labeled Boston butt in the supermarket. For efficiency, prep the vegetables while the broth cooks, or make the broth ahead. This soup benefits from being made in advance—at least a few hours before eating and up to three days. Serve with bread and sour cream.

Broth

- 10 cups water
- 2 pounds boneless pork butt roast, well trimmed and cut in half
- 1 onion, halved
- 1 large carrot, sliced 1 inch thick
- 2 bay leaves
- ½ teaspoon table salt

Soup

- 1 pound Yukon Gold potatoes, peeled and cut into 1-inch pieces
- ½ small head green cabbage, halved, cored, and sliced thin crosswise (5 cups)
- 1½ teaspoons table salt, divided
- ¼ cup vegetable oil
- 1 onion, chopped fine
- 8 ounces beets, trimmed, peeled, and shredded (2 cups)
- 2 carrots, peeled and shredded (1½ cups)
- 1 (6-ounce) can tomato paste
- ⅓ cup chopped fresh dill, plus more for garnish
- 1 tablespoon lemon juice, plus more for serving

1 For the broth Combine all ingredients in Dutch oven and bring to boil over high heat. Adjust heat to simmer and cook, covered, until pork is tender, about 2 hours, occasionally skimming foam off surface.

2 Transfer pork to large plate or cutting board. Discard onion, carrot, and bay leaves. When pork is cool enough to handle, cut into bite-size pieces (it's OK if meat starts to shred). Skim fat from surface of broth. (Alternatively, let broth cool completely and refrigerate overnight. Refrigerate pork separately.)

3 For the soup Set aside ½ cup broth. In Dutch oven, bring remaining broth to boil over high heat. Add potatoes, cabbage, and ½ teaspoon salt. Adjust heat to maintain gentle simmer and cook, covered, until potatoes are just tender, 8 to 10 minutes.

4 Meanwhile, heat oil in 12-inch skillet over medium heat until shimmering. Add onion and cook, stirring frequently, until softened, about 5 minutes. Add beets, carrots, and ½ teaspoon salt and cook, stirring frequently, until softened, 3 to 5 minutes. Stir in tomato paste (mixture will be thick) and cook until fragrant and tomato paste is slightly darkened in color, 1 to 2 minutes. Slowly add reserved ½ cup broth, scraping bottom of pan to loosen any browned bits.

5 Add beet mixture to Dutch oven and stir gently to combine. Cover and simmer for 5 minutes. Stir in pork, dill, lemon juice, and remaining ½ teaspoon salt. Season with salt, pepper, and lemon juice to taste. Portion borscht into bowls and garnish each serving with more dill. Serve. (Borscht can be refrigerated for up to 3 days.)

Simple Beef Chili with Kidney Beans

Why This Recipe Works   Some beef chilis are all about the meat, but we wanted one that gives the same prominence to beans, while still delivering on the promise of heartiness and comfort. With the goal of developing a no-fuss recipe that would be greater than the sum of its pantry-staple parts, we found that adding spices to the pan with the aromatics significantly boosted their potency. We then added the beef to this flavorful mixture; browning the meat maximized its meaty flavor, giving our chili an exceptionally savory foundation. We added the beans with the tomatoes so that they cooked enough to absorb flavor, but not so much that they fell apart. Cooking the chili with the lid on for half the cooking time gave it an appealingly chunky yet velvety consistency. Lime wedges are a must in this earthy stew, but you can also top with any of your favorite chili toppings, such as sour cream, diced avocado, chopped red onion, cilantro, and shredded Monterey Jack or cheddar cheese. The flavor of the chili improves with age; if possible, make it the day before you plan to serve it.

1   Heat oil in Dutch oven over medium heat until shimmering. Add onions, bell pepper, garlic, chili powder, cumin, coriander, pepper flakes, oregano, and cayenne and cook, stirring occasionally, until vegetables are softened and beginning to brown, about 10 minutes. Increase heat to medium-high and add half of beef. Cook, breaking up pieces with spoon, until no longer pink and just beginning to brown, 3 to 4 minutes. Add remaining beef and cook, breaking up pieces with spoon, until no longer pink, 3 to 4 minutes.

2   Add beans, tomatoes and their juice, tomato puree, and salt; bring to boil, then reduce heat to low and simmer gently, covered, stirring occasionally, for 1 hour. Remove cover and continue to simmer 1 hour longer, stirring occasionally (if chili begins to stick to bottom of pot, stir in ½ cup water and continue to simmer), until beef is tender and chili is dark, rich, and slightly thickened. Season with salt to taste. Serve with lime wedges. (Chili can be refrigerated for up to 2 days.)

   2   tablespoons vegetable oil

   2   onions, chopped fine

   1   red bell pepper, stemmed, seeded, and cut into ½-inch pieces

   6   garlic cloves, minced

   ¼   cup chili powder

   1   tablespoon ground cumin

   2   teaspoons ground coriander

   1   teaspoon red pepper flakes

   1   teaspoon dried oregano

   ½   teaspoon cayenne pepper

   1½   pounds 85 percent lean ground beef, divided

   2   (15-ounce) cans red kidney beans, rinsed

   1   (28-ounce) can diced tomatoes

   1   (28-ounce) can tomato puree

   ¼   teaspoon table salt

      Lime wedges

Vegetarian Chili

Why This Recipe Works To make a rich and flavorful vegetarian chili, we extracted maximum umami from many savory ingredients. We started with a base of onion and fresh poblano chile, which we sautéed in plenty of olive oil until lightly browned; the oil unlocked the vegetables' aroma. We then added tomato paste and plenty of garlic, along with dried oregano and a heap of warm, earthy ground cumin. We let it all sizzle until the tomato paste began to darken and the sugars caramelized, intensifying all the ingredients' flavors. Many recipes call for store-bought chili powder, but we toasted torn dried ancho and guajillo chiles, reconstituted them in water, and then blitzed them in a blender with tomatoes and canned chipotle chile to create a significantly more complex dish. To make up for the lack of meat, we added soy sauce and dried porcini mushrooms for umami depth. To make this an especially hearty chili, we also added barley and a medley of canned beans—black, pinto, and kidney—for an appealing mosaic of colors, flavors, and textures. One ounce of ancho chiles is approximately two or three chiles; ½ ounce of guajillo chiles is about three or four chiles. Use more or fewer chipotle chiles depending on your desired level of spiciness. We like using a mix of pinto, black, and red kidney beans here, but you can use all of one type or any combination of the three. Do not substitute hulled, hull-less, quick-cooking, or presteamed barley in this recipe (read the ingredient list on the package to determine this). Top the chili with any of your favorite chili toppings: lime wedges, sour cream, diced avocado, chopped red onion, and/or shredded Monterey Jack or cheddar cheese.

- 1 ounce dried ancho chiles, stemmed, seeded, and torn into 1-inch pieces
- ½ ounce dried guajillo chiles, stemmed, seeded, and torn into 1-inch pieces
- 1 (28-ounce) can whole peeled tomatoes
- 1–3 canned chipotle chiles in adobo sauce
- 3 tablespoons soy sauce
- 1½ teaspoons table salt, divided
- ¼ cup extra-virgin olive oil
- 1 onion, chopped
- 1 poblano chile, stemmed, seeded, and chopped
- 3 tablespoons tomato paste
- 6 garlic cloves, minced
- 2 tablespoons ground cumin
- 1 tablespoon dried oregano
- 1 (15-ounce) can pinto beans, rinsed
- 1 (15-ounce) can black beans, rinsed
- 1 (15-ounce) can red kidney beans, rinsed
- ¾ cup pearl barley
- ½ ounce dried porcini mushrooms, rinsed and chopped fine
- ½ cup chopped fresh cilantro

1 Place anchos and guajillos in Dutch oven and toast over medium heat, stirring often, until fragrant and darkened slightly but not smoking, 3 to 5 minutes. Immediately transfer to bowl and cover with hot water. Let sit until chiles are soft and pliable, about 5 minutes.

2 Drain chiles and combine with tomatoes and their juice, 1 cup water, chipotle(s), soy sauce, and 1 teaspoon salt in blender. Process until smooth, 1 to 2 minutes; set aside.

3 Heat oil in now-empty Dutch oven over medium-high heat until shimmering. Add onion, poblano, and remaining ½ teaspoon salt. Cook, stirring occasionally, until onion begins to brown, 3 to 5 minutes. Stir in tomato paste, garlic, cumin, and oregano and cook until tomato paste darkens, 1 to 2 minutes.

4 Stir in pinto, black, and kidney beans; barley; mushrooms; reserved chile puree; and 2½ cups water. Bring to boil then reduce heat to medium-low and simmer, stirring occasionally, until barley is tender, 35 to 45 minutes. Let sit off heat for 10 minutes (chili will continue to thicken as it sits). Season with salt to taste. Stir in cilantro and serve.

Building-Block Broths

Chicken Broth

Makes 2 quarts
Total time: 4¾ hours

- 1 tablespoon extra-virgin olive oil
- 3 pounds whole chicken legs, backs, and/or wings, hacked into 2-inch pieces, divided
- 1 onion, chopped
- 8 cups water, divided
- 3 bay leaves
- ½ teaspoon table salt

1 Heat oil in Dutch oven over medium-high heat until just smoking. Pat chicken dry with paper towels. Brown half of chicken, about 5 minutes; transfer to large bowl. Repeat with remaining chicken; transfer to bowl.

2 Add onion to fat left in pot and cook over medium heat until softened, about 5 minutes. Stir in 2 cups water, bay leaves, and salt, scraping up any browned bits.

3 Stir remaining 6 cups water into pot, then return browned chicken and any accumulated juices to pot and bring to simmer. Reduce heat to low; cover; and simmer gently until broth is rich and flavorful, about 4 hours.

4 Remove large bones from pot, then strain broth through fine-mesh strainer into large container; discard solids. Let broth settle for 5 to 10 minutes, then defat using wide, shallow spoon or fat separator. (Broth can be refrigerated for up to 4 days or frozen for up to 1 month.)

Vegetable Broth

Makes 2 quarts
Total time: 2½ hours

- 3 onions, chopped
- 2 celery ribs, chopped
- 2 carrots, peeled and chopped
- 8 scallions, chopped
- 15 garlic cloves, peeled and smashed
- 1 teaspoon vegetable oil
- 1 teaspoon table salt
- 12 cups water
- 1 head cauliflower (2 pounds), cored and cut into 1-inch florets
- 1 plum tomato, cored and chopped
- 8 sprigs fresh thyme
- 3 bay leaves
- 1 teaspoon black peppercorns

1 Combine onions, celery, carrots, scallions, garlic, oil, and salt in large Dutch oven or stockpot. Cover and cook over medium-low heat, stirring often, until golden brown fond has formed on bottom of pot, 20 to 30 minutes.

2 Stir in water, cauliflower, tomato, thyme sprigs, bay leaves, and peppercorns, scraping up any browned bits, and bring to simmer. Partially cover pot, reduce heat to gentle simmer, and cook until broth tastes rich and flavorful, about 1½ hours.

3 Strain broth gently through fine-mesh strainer (do not press on solids). (Broth can be refrigerated for up to 4 days or frozen for up to 1 month.)

Cheater Beef Broth

Makes 2 quarts
Total time: 1 hour

This broth is a great stand-in when there isn't time to make one entirely from scratch. Since store-bought beef broth contains almost no beef, we added real beef to amp up the flavor. Use this broth in our Almost Beefless Beef Stew (page 91), or swap it into any recipe that calls for chicken or vegetable broth to give it a beefy boost.

- 1 teaspoon vegetable oil
- 1 pound 85 percent ground beef
- 8 cups beef broth
- 8 teaspoons unflavored gelatin

1 Heat oil in large saucepan over medium-high heat until shimmering. Add beef to pot, breaking into rough 1-inch chunks. Cook, stirring occasionally, until beef is browned and fond develops on pan bottom, 6 to 8 minutes.

2 Add broth and gelatin and bring to simmer, scraping up any browned bits. Reduce heat to medium-low and gently simmer, covered, for 30 minutes. Strain broth through fine-mesh strainer into large pot or container, pressing on solids to extract as much liquid as possible. Let broth settle for about 5 minutes, then skim off fat. (Broth can be refrigerated for up to 4 days or frozen for up to 1 month.)

Umami Broth

Makes 2 quarts
Total time: 40 minutes

This vegan broth rivals the flavor of meat-based stocks. Look for fermented black beans at Asian grocery stores; if you can't find them, omit them. Do not substitute black bean paste or canned black beans. Straining the broth through a double layer of cheesecloth yields a clearer broth, though some sediment will remain. Swap this broth into any recipe that calls for chicken or vegetable broth for more savoriness.

- 8 cups water
- ¼ cup nutritional yeast
- 2 tablespoons fermented black beans
- 1½ tablespoons soy sauce
- 1 tablespoon white miso
- 1½ teaspoons onion powder
- 1½ teaspoons garlic powder
- ½ ounce dried shiitake mushrooms, rinsed and chopped coarse

1 Combine all ingredients in large pot. Bring to boil, then cover, reduce heat to low, and simmer for 30 minutes.

2 Strain broth through fine-mesh strainer lined with double layer of cheesecloth. (Broth can be refrigerated for up to 4 days or frozen for up to 1 month.)

The key to a great soup, stew, or chili is varying textures and flavors.
The recipes in this chapter have these variables in spades, but sometimes
whipping up a fun garnish to pass at the table kicks dinner up a notch.

Great Garnishes

Classic Croutons

Makes 3 cups
Total time: 30 minutes

6   slices hearty white sandwich
    bread, crusts removed, cut into
    ½-inch cubes (3 cups)

3   tablespoons unsalted butter,
    melted, or extra-virgin olive oil

Adjust oven rack to middle position
and heat oven to 350 degrees. Toss
bread with melted butter, season
with salt and pepper to taste, and
spread onto rimmed baking sheet.
Bake until golden brown and crisp,
20 to 25 minutes, stirring halfway
through baking. Let cool before
serving. (Croutons can be stored in
airtight container at room temperature for up to 3 days.)

Variation

Garlic Croutons

Whisk 1 minced garlic clove into
melted butter before tossing
with bread.

Umami Croutons

Makes 5 cups
Total time: 30 minutes

¼   cup extra-virgin olive oil

3   tablespoons nutritional yeast

1   teaspoon white miso

1   teaspoon Dijon mustard

¼   teaspoon distilled white vinegar

⅛   teaspoon table salt

6   ounces baguette, cut into 1-inch
    pieces (5 cups)

Adjust oven rack to middle position
and heat oven to 400 degrees.
Whisk oil, nutritional yeast, miso,
mustard, vinegar, and salt together
in large bowl. Add baguette pieces
and, using your hands, massage oil
mixture into bread. Transfer to
rimmed baking sheet and bake until
golden brown and crisp, 13 to
15 minutes. Let cool and serve.
(Croutons can be stored in airtight
container at room temperature for
up to 3 days.)

Herbed Croutons

Makes 2 cups
Total time: 10 minutes

1   tablespoon unsalted butter

1   teaspoon minced fresh parsley

½   teaspoon minced fresh thyme

4   slices hearty white sandwich
    bread, cut into ½-inch cubes

Melt butter in 10-inch skillet over
medium heat. Add parsley and
thyme; cook, stirring constantly, for
20 seconds. Add bread and cook,
stirring frequently, until light golden
brown, 5 to 10 minutes. Transfer
croutons to paper towel–lined plate
and season with salt and pepper to
taste. Let cool before serving.
(Croutons can be stored in airtight
container at room temperature for
up to 3 days.)

Pita Crumble

Makes 2 cups
Total time: 30 minutes

---

1 (8-inch) pita bread

4 teaspoons extra-virgin olive oil

⅛ teaspoon table salt

⅛ teaspoon pepper

1 Adjust oven rack to middle position and heat oven to 375 degrees. Using kitchen shears, cut around perimeter of pita and separate into 2 thin rounds. Cut each round in half.

2 Place pitas smooth side down on wire rack set in rimmed baking sheet. Brush surface of pitas with oil, then sprinkle with salt and pepper. Bake until pitas are crisp and pale golden, 10 to 14 minutes. Let cool to room temperature, then crumble into bite-size pieces. (Pita crumble can be stored in airtight container at room temperature for up to 3 days.)

Crispy Leeks

Makes about ½ cup
Total time: 25 minutes

---

1 leek, white and light green part only

2 tablespoons all-purpose flour

½ cup vegetable oil for frying

1 Halve leek lengthwise, then slice into very thin 2-inch-long strips. Wash and dry thoroughly. Toss with flour in medium bowl. Add oil and stir to combine. Microwave for 5 minutes. Stir and continue to microwave 2 minutes longer. Repeat stirring and microwaving in 2-minute increments until leek begins to brown (4 to 6 minutes total), then repeat stirring and microwaving in 30-second increments until strips are deep golden (30 seconds to 2 minutes total).

2 Using slotted spoon, transfer leek to paper towel–lined plate; discard oil. Let leek drain and turn crispy, about 5 minutes, then season with salt to taste. (Leek can be stored in airtight container for up to 1 month.)

Chili Oil

Makes about 1½ cups
Total time: 40 minutes, plus 12 hours resting

½ cup Sichuan chili flakes

2 tablespoons sesame seeds

2 tablespoons Sichuan peppercorns, ground coarse, divided

½ teaspoon table salt

1 cup vegetable oil

1 (1-inch) piece ginger, sliced into ¼-inch-thick rounds and smashed

3 star anise pods

5 cardamom pods, crushed

2 bay leaves

1 Combine chili flakes, sesame seeds, half of peppercorns, and salt in heatproof bowl. Cook oil, ginger, star anise, cardamom, bay leaves, and remaining peppercorns in small saucepan over low heat, stirring occasionally, until spices have darkened and mixture is very fragrant, 25 to 30 minutes.

2 Strain mixture through fine-mesh strainer into bowl with chili flake mixture (mixture may bubble slightly); discard solids. Stir well to combine. Let sit at room temperature until flavors meld, about 12 hours, before using. (Oil can be stored at room temperature in airtight container for up to 1 week or refrigerated for up to 3 months; flavor will mature over time.)

Salads & Bowls

Charred Broccoli Salad with Avocado, Grapefruit, and Ginger-Lime Dressing

Why This Recipe Works The union of charred broccoli and a pungent Thai-inspired dressing, plus meaty wedges of avocado and grapefruit, makes for a hearty salad with many layers of texture and flavor. We charred the broccoli wedges to a smoky brown and then tossed them with a delectably zesty blend of tamarind, lime, and ginger. Crispy shallots and peanuts gave the meal wonderful richness and crunch. Look for Thai/Indonesian-style tamarind concentrate labeled "nuoc me chua"; do not use Indian-style tamarind concentrates (see page 15 for more information). In this recipe, if you can't find tamarind juice concentrate, you can increase the amount of lime juice to ¼ cup. You will need a 12-inch skillet with a tight-fitting lid for this recipe. We prefer to use our own Crispy Shallots here, but you can substitute store-bought. If using our recipe, use the reserved shallot oil instead of the vegetable oil for extra flavor.

1¼ pounds broccoli crowns

1 tablespoon tamarind juice concentrate

1 tablespoon grated fresh ginger

1 tablespoon honey

1 teaspoon grated lime zest plus
   3 tablespoons juice (2 limes)

1 red Thai chile, stemmed and sliced thin

¾ teaspoon table salt, divided

5 tablespoons vegetable oil

2 tablespoons water

2 grapefruits

1 avocado, halved, pitted, and cut into 1-inch wedges

1½ cups fresh Thai basil, cilantro, and/or mint
   leaves, divided

½ cup Crispy Shallots (page 85), divided

3 tablespoons roasted salted peanuts, chopped

1 Cut broccoli crowns into 4 wedges if 3 to 4 inches in diameter, or 6 wedges if 4 to 5 inches in diameter. Whisk tamarind, ginger, honey, lime zest and juice, Thai chile, and ½ teaspoon salt in large bowl until emulsified; set aside.

2 Add oil to 12-inch nonstick skillet. Add broccoli, cut side down (pieces will fit snugly; if a few pieces don't fit in bottom layer, place on top), and drizzle with water. Cover and cook over medium-high heat, without moving broccoli, until it is bright green, about 4 minutes.

3 Sprinkle broccoli with remaining ¼ teaspoon salt and press gently into skillet with back of spatula. Cover and cook until undersides of broccoli are deeply charred and stems are crisp-tender, 4 to 6 minutes. Uncover and turn broccoli so second cut side is touching skillet. Move any pieces that were on top so they are flush with skillet surface. Continue to cook, uncovered, pressing gently on broccoli with back of spatula, until second cut side is deeply browned, 3 to 5 minutes. Transfer broccoli to bowl with dressing.

4 Cut away peel and pith from grapefruits. Quarter grapefruits, then slice crosswise into 1-inch-thick pieces. Add three-quarters grapefruit, avocado, 1 cup herbs, and half of crispy shallots to bowl with broccoli and gently toss to coat. Arrange broccoli mixture attractively in serving bowl and top with peanuts, remaining grapefruit, remaining ½ cup herbs, and remaining shallots. Serve.

Chicken and Arugula Salad with Figs and Warm Spices

Why This Recipe Works We wanted a chicken salad that channeled the healthful fare of the Mediterranean, while being a hearty, well-rounded meal all on its own. High in fiber and beautifully purple, fresh figs made the perfect partner; the fruit's dense, fleshy chew stood up to the meaty chicken breast. To cook the meat, we gently poached it in salted water and then turned off the heat and let the chicken sit, covered, until it registered 165 degrees. This ensured that the meat didn't overcook, instead staying tender and juicy. To enhance the figs' natural floral quality, we turned to coriander for its citrus notes, along with smoked paprika and cinnamon for depth. We microwaved the spices to bloom their flavor, then whisked in lemon juice and honey to make a balanced, flavorful dressing. For textural interest, we shredded the chicken, forming craggy surfaces for the dressing to settle into. We also added creamy chickpeas, which brought protein, fiber, and hearty bite. A bed of peppery baby arugula complemented our bright dressing, while toasted and chopped almonds made the perfect crunchy garnish. You can substitute dried figs for fresh if you prefer.

1 Dissolve 1 tablespoon salt in 6 cups cold water in Dutch oven. Submerge chicken in water. Heat pot over medium heat until water registers 170 degrees. Turn off heat; cover pot; and let stand until chicken registers 165 degrees, 15 to 17 minutes. Transfer chicken to cutting board and let cool slightly. Using 2 forks, shred chicken into bite-size pieces.

2 Meanwhile, microwave 1 tablespoon oil, coriander, paprika, and cinnamon in large bowl until fragrant, about 30 seconds. Whisk lemon juice, honey, pepper, and salt into spice mixture. Whisking constantly, slowly drizzle in remaining 5 tablespoons oil.

3 Add shredded chicken, chickpeas, arugula, parsley, and shallot to dressing in bowl and gently toss to combine. Transfer salad to serving platter, arrange figs over top, and sprinkle with almonds. Serve.

½ teaspoon table salt, plus salt for cooking chicken

2 (6- to 8-ounce) boneless, skinless chicken breasts, no more than 1 inch thick, trimmed

6 tablespoons extra-virgin olive oil, divided

1 teaspoon ground coriander

½ teaspoon smoked paprika

¼ teaspoon ground cinnamon

3 tablespoons lemon juice

1 teaspoon honey

¼ teaspoon pepper

1 (15-ounce) can chickpeas, rinsed

5 ounces (5 cups) baby arugula

½ cup fresh parsley leaves

1 shallot, sliced thin

8 fresh figs, stemmed and quartered

½ cup whole almonds, toasted and chopped

Neorm Sach Moan

Why This Recipe Works This layered chicken salad with cabbage and fish sauce—based on a recipe from Nite Yun, chef and owner of Nyum Bai, a Cambodian restaurant in Oakland, California—makes the most of just one chicken breast by cooking and seasoning it in a way that maximizes its impact. To ensure that the lean breast meat didn't dry out during cooking, we poached it gently in just-simmering salted water. After pulling the chicken into shreds, we tossed it with thinly sliced cabbage and an umami-forward dressing made up of Thai chile, garlic, sugar, rice vinegar, and fish sauce. Right before serving, we tossed in plenty of fresh mint, cilantro, and Thai basil to give this salad an aromatic boost. If you can't find Persian cucumber, use 1 cup thinly sliced English cucumber. A mandoline makes quick work of evenly shredding the cabbage and slicing the radishes and cucumber.

1 Combine chicken, 4 cups water, and 2 teaspoons salt in large saucepan. Cook over medium heat until water just begins to simmer, about 10 minutes. Cover pot; reduce heat to low; and gently simmer until chicken registers 160 degrees, 12 to 17 minutes.

2 Transfer chicken to plate or cutting board and let cool for 15 minutes. Shred into thin, bite-size strips.

3 Whisk fish sauce, sugar, vinegar, Thai chile, garlic, and salt in large bowl until sugar is dissolved. Add green cabbage, mizuna, red cabbage, bell pepper, cucumber, radishes, chopped cilantro, Thai basil, mint, and shredded chicken and toss thoroughly to combine. Top with cilantro leaves and peanuts. Serve.

1 (6- to 8-ounce) boneless, skinless chicken breast, trimmed

¼ teaspoon table salt, plus salt for poaching chicken

6 tablespoons fish sauce

¼ cup sugar

¼ cup unseasoned rice vinegar

1 Thai chile, minced

1 garlic clove, minced

4 cups shredded green cabbage

2 ounces (2 cups) baby mizuna or baby arugula, chopped coarse

1 cup shredded red cabbage

1 red bell pepper, stemmed, seeded, and sliced thin

1 Persian cucumber, halved crosswise and sliced thin lengthwise

4 radishes, trimmed and sliced thin

¼ cup chopped fresh cilantro, plus 2 tablespoons leaves

¼ cup chopped fresh Thai basil

¼ cup chopped fresh mint

¼ cup salted dry-roasted peanuts, chopped

Pinto Bean, Ancho, and Beef Salad with Pickled Poblanos

Why This Recipe Works For this well-seasoned salad, we combined the impactful flavors of several Mexican ingredients. Ancho chiles, frequently used in Mexican cuisine, are dried poblanos; we employed both fresh and dried forms by quick-pickling poblanos for sweet-sour spiciness and using ancho chile powder as a steak rub. We chose skirt steak; the thin cuts are richly beefy with lots of surface area, and hence potential for flavorful browning. Crunchy jicama contrasted nicely with creamy pinto beans in our salad, which we tossed with refreshing onion, cilantro, and lime juice. Crumbled cotija studded the salad with milky brininess. We sprinkled everything with finely chopped unsweetened chocolate, which rounded out the dish with a complex, slightly bitter earthiness (but you can omit if you prefer). It is important to chop the chocolate fine, as bigger pieces of chocolate will be overpoweringly bitter. Be sure to slice the steak thin against the grain or it will be very chewy.

1 cup red wine vinegar

⅓ cup sugar

1¼ teaspoons table salt, divided

4 ounces poblano chiles, stemmed, seeded, and sliced ⅛ inch thick

1 (1-pound) skirt steak, trimmed and cut into thirds

2 teaspoons ancho chile powder

¾ teaspoon pepper, divided

2 tablespoons vegetable oil, divided

2 (15-ounce) cans pinto beans, rinsed

12 ounces jicama, peeled and grated (1½ cups)

½ cup finely chopped red onion

¼ cup chopped fresh cilantro leaves and stems, plus extra for serving

3 tablespoons lime juice (2 limes)

1½ ounces cotija cheese, crumbled (⅓ cup)

½ ounce unsweetened chocolate, chopped fine (optional)

1 Microwave vinegar, sugar, and ¼ teaspoon salt in medium bowl until simmering, 3 to 4 minutes. Whisk to dissolve any residual sugar and salt, then stir in poblanos. Let sit, stirring occasionally, for 30 minutes. Drain and set aside.

2 Meanwhile, pat steak dry with paper towels, then sprinkle with chile powder, ¼ teaspoon pepper, and ½ teaspoon salt. Heat 1 tablespoon oil in 12-inch skillet over medium-high heat until just smoking. Add steak and cook until well browned and meat registers 120 to 125 degrees (for medium-rare), about 2 minutes per side. Transfer steak to cutting board, tent with aluminum foil, and let rest for 5 minutes.

3 Gently toss beans; jicama; onion; cilantro; lime juice; and remaining ½ teaspoon salt, ½ teaspoon pepper, and 1 tablespoon oil to combine, then transfer to serving platter. Slice steak thin against grain and arrange over top of salad. Sprinkle with cotija; chocolate, if using; poblanos; and extra cilantro. Serve.

Bitter Greens and Chickpea Salad with Warm Vinaigrette

Why This Recipe Works In this lightly wilted salad dressed in a warm vinaigrette, an assortment of bitter greens—such as curly frisée, ruffled escarole, and frilly chicory—makes a texturally interesting canvas for hearty chickpeas and satisfyingly crunchy vegetables. We sautéed the colorful mix-ins (carrots, raisins, and almonds); cooled them slightly; and then added the greens, some mint, and a citrusy vinaigrette off the heat. The residual heat wilted the greens to just the right slightly softened, yet still pleasurably chewy and fibrous, texture. The nutty chickpeas plus some salty feta made delicious accents that injected each mouthful with savory notes. This salad is highly adaptable; it would be just as flavorsome with white beans, dried cranberries, hazelnuts, cilantro, or goat cheese. The volume measurement of the greens may vary depending on the variety or combination used.

1 Whisk lemon zest and juice, mustard, shallot, cumin, coriander, paprika, cayenne, ¼ teaspoon salt, and pepper together in medium bowl. Whisking constantly, slowly drizzle in 2 tablespoons oil until emulsified.

2 Toss chickpeas with 1 tablespoon vinaigrette and remaining pinch salt in bowl; set aside. Heat remaining 1 tablespoon oil in Dutch oven over medium heat until shimmering. Add carrots, raisins, and almonds and cook, stirring frequently, until carrots are wilted, 4 to 5 minutes. Let cool for 5 minutes.

3 Add half of remaining vinaigrette to pot, then add half of greens and toss for 1 minute to warm and wilt. Add mint and remaining greens, followed by remaining vinaigrette, and continue to toss until greens are evenly coated and warmed through, about 2 minutes. Season with salt and pepper to taste. Transfer greens to serving platter, top with feta and reserved chickpeas, and serve.

- 1 tablespoon grated lemon zest plus 6 tablespoons juice (2 lemons)
- 1 tablespoon Dijon mustard
- 1 tablespoon minced shallot
- ½ teaspoon ground cumin
- ½ teaspoon ground coriander
- ¼ teaspoon smoked paprika
- ¼ teaspoon cayenne pepper
- ¼ teaspoon plus pinch table salt, divided
- ¼ teaspoon pepper
- 3 tablespoons extra-virgin olive oil, divided
- 1 (15-ounce) can chickpeas or white beans, rinsed
- 3 carrots, peeled and shredded
- ¾ cup raisins or dried cranberries, chopped
- ½ cup slivered almonds or chopped hazelnuts
- 12 ounces (10–12 cups) bitter greens, such as escarole, chicory, and/or frisée, torn into bite-size pieces
- ⅓ cup chopped fresh mint or cilantro
- 1½ ounces feta or goat cheese, crumbled (⅓ cup)

Shrimp and White Bean Salad

Why This Recipe Works Northern Italian cooks combine their beloved cannellini beans with all sorts of ingredients. We channeled the region's adoration for the beans by making them the foundation of this salad studded with tender shrimp. We wanted to utilize a cooking method that boosted the oceanic flavor of the shrimp while preserving the snappy meatiness of their flesh, and our tests confirmed that searing on the stovetop worked best. We lightly cooked the beans, as well as bell peppers and onions, to make sure the ingredients didn't become too soft and instead retained some hearty bite. The mildly sweet beans made the perfect foil for the delicate, subtly briny shrimp. A couple fistfuls of arugula provided the salad with an aromatic, peppery underpinning.

12 ounces extra-large shrimp (21 to 25 per pound), peeled, deveined, and tails removed

¾ teaspoon table salt, divided

¼ teaspoon pepper

5 tablespoons extra-virgin olive oil, divided

1 red, orange, or yellow bell pepper, stemmed, seeded, and chopped fine

1 small red onion, chopped fine

2 garlic cloves, minced

¼ teaspoon red pepper flakes

2 (15-ounce) cans cannellini or small white beans, rinsed

2 ounces (2 cups) baby arugula or baby spinach

2 tablespoons lemon juice

1 Pat shrimp dry with paper towels and sprinkle with ¼ teaspoon salt and pepper. Heat 1 tablespoon oil in 12-inch nonstick skillet over medium-high heat until just smoking. Add shrimp in single layer and cook, without stirring, until spotty brown and edges turn pink on bottom, about 1 minute. Flip shrimp and continue to cook until all but very center is opaque, about 30 seconds; transfer shrimp to plate and let cool while making salad.

2 Heat remaining ¼ cup oil in now-empty skillet over medium heat until shimmering. Add bell pepper, onion, and remaining ½ teaspoon salt and cook until softened, about 5 minutes. Stir in garlic and pepper flakes and cook until fragrant, about 30 seconds. Stir in beans and cook until heated through, about 5 minutes.

3 Add arugula and shrimp along with any accumulated juices and toss gently until arugula is wilted, about 1 minute. Stir in lemon juice and season with salt and pepper to taste. Serve.

Chopped Salad with Spiced Skillet-Roasted Chickpeas

Why This Recipe Works We wanted a hearty chopped salad that could be a satisfying meal on its own. So we turned to protein-rich chickpeas, seasoning them with paprika and crisping them in a skillet for irresistible heat and crunch. To start, we nuked the legumes to dry their interiors and rupture their exteriors. Pan-frying these dehydrated chickpeas blistered their skins, which crackled into crisp shells. We scattered them atop arugula, cucumber, tomatoes, Peppadew peppers, and feta and finished the salad with an invigorating tangy-sweet vinaigrette. If you can't find Peppadews, substitute pepperoncini. We like to use our Spiced Skillet-Roasted Chickpeas, but you can substitute 1½ cups store-bought crispy spiced chickpeas if you prefer.

Spiced Skillet-Roasted Chickpeas

   2 (15-ounce) cans chickpeas, rinsed and patted dry

  ½ teaspoon smoked paprika

  ¼ teaspoon table salt

  ¼ teaspoon pepper

  ¼ cup extra-virgin olive oil, plus extra as needed

Salad

   2 tablespoons sherry vinegar

   1 teaspoon honey

  ¾ teaspoon Dijon mustard

  ½ teaspoon minced fresh thyme

  ⅛ teaspoon table salt

  ⅛ teaspoon pepper

   4 tablespoons extra-virgin olive oil

   1 English cucumber, quartered lengthwise and cut into ½-inch pieces

   8 ounces cherry tomatoes, quartered

   2 ounces (2 cups) baby arugula, chopped coarse

   2 ounces feta cheese, crumbled (½ cup), divided

  ⅓ cup jarred hot Peppadew peppers, sliced thin

1 For the spiced skillet-roasted chickpeas Line large plate with double layer of paper towels. Spread chickpeas over plate in even layer. Microwave until exteriors of chickpeas are dry and many have ruptured, 8 to 12 minutes. Meanwhile, combine paprika, salt, and pepper in bowl.

2 Line rimmed baking sheet with single layer of paper towels. Heat oil in 12-inch nonstick skillet over medium-high heat until shimmering. Transfer chickpeas to skillet, spreading into single layer. Cook, stirring occasionally, until chickpeas are golden brown and make rustling sound when stirred, 4 to 8 minutes.

3 Using slotted spoon, transfer chickpeas to large bowl and toss with paprika mixture to coat. Transfer chickpeas to prepared sheet to cool slightly; discard oil. (Chickpeas can be stored in airtight container at room temperature for up to 1 week.)

4 For the salad Whisk vinegar, honey, mustard, thyme, salt, pepper, and oil in small bowl until emulsified. Combine cucumber, tomatoes, arugula, ¼ cup feta, Peppadews, and half of chickpeas in large bowl. Drizzle with three-quarters of vinaigrette and toss to evenly coat. Season with salt and pepper to taste. Sprinkle remaining ¼ cup feta and remaining half of chickpeas over top and serve, passing extra vinaigrette separately.

Charred Cabbage Salad with Torn Tofu and Plantain Chips

Why This Recipe Works This showstopping salad seasons cabbage and tofu with beloved Southeast Asian flavors for a flavor-packed meatless meal. We first cut a whole head of red cabbage into eight substantial wedges, then coated them in oil, Thai red curry paste, and turmeric before roasting. The oven time tenderized the cabbage while charring the edges, giving us textural variation and imbuing the leaves with potent flavor. Like cabbage, tofu is also adept at absorbing seasonings; tearing the protein gave us lots of craggy surfaces for a marinade—a sweet-savory concoction of vinegar, lime juice, ginger, honey, and fish sauce—to sink into. For a warm dressing, we bloomed more curry paste, turmeric, and ginger in the microwave, then added rice vinegar. Crushed plantain chips made a perfect sweet-salty garnish. The tofu can be marinated for up to 24 hours. Note that this recipe uses seasoned rice vinegar; we don't recommend using unseasoned rice vinegar in its place. If you don't have plantain chips or banana chips, you can substitute chopped macadamia nuts or cashews. For a fully meatless version, make our vegan fish sauce (page 14).

14 ounces firm tofu, torn into bite-size pieces

3 tablespoons seasoned rice vinegar, divided

2 tablespoons lime juice

4 teaspoons grated fresh ginger, divided

1 tablespoon honey

1 tablespoon fish sauce or vegan fish sauce

1 head red cabbage (2 pounds)

7 tablespoons vegetable oil, divided

4 teaspoons Thai red curry paste, divided

1 tablespoon ground turmeric, divided

½ teaspoon table salt

1 tablespoon water

1 cup bean sprouts

¼ cup chopped fresh basil

2 scallions, sliced thin on bias

¼ cup plantain or banana chips, crushed

1 Adjust oven rack to lowest position and heat oven to 500 degrees. Gently press tofu dry with paper towels. Whisk 1 tablespoon vinegar, lime juice, 2 teaspoons ginger, honey, and fish sauce together in medium bowl. Add tofu and toss gently to coat; set aside for 20 minutes.

2 Halve cabbage through core and cut each half into 4 approximately 2-inch-wide wedges, leaving core intact (you will have 8 wedges). Whisk ¼ cup oil, 1 teaspoon curry paste, 2 teaspoons turmeric, and salt together in bowl. Arrange cabbage wedges in single layer on aluminum foil–lined rimmed baking sheet, then brush cabbage all over with oil mixture. Cover tightly with foil and roast for 10 minutes. Remove foil and drizzle 2 tablespoons oil evenly over wedges. Return sheet to oven and roast, uncovered, until cabbage is tender and sides touching sheet are well browned, 10 to 15 minutes. Let cool slightly, about 15 minutes.

3 Whisk remaining 2 teaspoons ginger, remaining 1 tablespoon oil, remaining 1 tablespoon curry paste, and remaining 1 teaspoon turmeric together in bowl. Microwave until fragrant, about 30 seconds. Whisk water and remaining 2 tablespoons vinegar into ginger mixture.

4 Chop cabbage coarse and spread over serving platter, then top with bean sprouts, basil, scallions, and reserved tofu. Drizzle with vinaigrette and sprinkle with plantain chips. Serve.

SERVES 4 | TOTAL TIME 45 MINUTES • *fast* • *fiber-ful* • *one-pan* •

Beet and Carrot Noodle Salad with Chicken

Why This Recipe Works This colorful dish stars spiralized beets and carrots, evoking the appeal of a hearty bowl of cold noodles while celebrating the freshness and lightness of raw vegetables. With their firm, dense texture, beets made excellent "noodles," as spiralizing rendered them delicate enough to eat raw. Pairing them with carrots made for a visually stunning, pleasingly crisp salad. For a protein boost, we seasoned, pan-seared, and sliced up chicken cutlets—a quick, fuss-free way to up the satiation factor of the meal. The noodles, with their crisp-tender texture, were an ideal canvas for a creamy, sweet-savory dressing enriched with peanut butter and tahini. You will need a spiralizer to make the beet and carrot noodles; if you don't have one, use pre-cut store-bought vegetable noodles. You'll need about 12 ounces of each. Generously sized vegetables spiralize more easily, so use beets that are at least 1½ inches in diameter and carrots that are at least ¾ inch across at the thinner end and 1½ inches across at the thicker end.

¼ cup smooth or chunky peanut butter

3 tablespoons tahini

2 tablespoons lime juice, plus lime wedges for serving

1 tablespoon soy sauce

1 tablespoon honey

1 tablespoon grated fresh ginger

2 garlic cloves, minced

½ teaspoon toasted sesame oil

½ teaspoon plus ⅛ teaspoon table salt, divided

1–6 tablespoons hot water

1 pound beets, trimmed and peeled

1 pound carrots, trimmed and peeled

5 scallions, sliced thin on bias

4 (3- to 4-ounce) chicken cutlets, ½ inch thick, trimmed

¼ teaspoon pepper

1 tablespoon vegetable oil

¼ cup fresh cilantro leaves

1 Whisk peanut butter, tahini, lime juice, soy sauce, honey, ginger, garlic, sesame oil, and ½ teaspoon salt in large bowl until well combined. Whisking constantly, add hot water, 1 tablespoon at a time (up to 6 tablespoons), until dressing has consistency of heavy cream.

2 Using spiralizer, cut beets and carrots into ⅛-inch-thick noodles, cutting noodles into 6- to 8-inch lengths with kitchen shears as you spiralize (about every 2 to 3 revolutions). Add beet and carrot noodles and scallions to dressing and toss well to combine.

3 Pat chicken dry with paper towels and sprinkle with remaining ⅛ teaspoon salt and pepper. Heat oil in 12-inch nonstick skillet over medium-high heat until just smoking. Add chicken and cook until golden brown and registers 160 degrees, about 3 minutes per side. Transfer chicken to cutting board and let cool for about 10 minutes.

4 Divide noodles among individual serving plates. Slice chicken thin and arrange over salads. Sprinkle with cilantro and serve with lime wedges.

Salmon, Avocado, Grapefruit, and Watercress Salad

Why This Recipe Works
This colorful salad of contrasting flavors and textures is dinner-worthy thanks to a medley of filling, nutrient-dense ingredients. To start, we roasted salmon just until it was medium-rare before flaking it into substantial chunks. For a bright, light contrast to the rich fish, we cut up two sweet-tart red grapefruits and reserved some of the grapefruit juice to whisk together a simple vinaigrette accented with white wine vinegar and Dijon mustard. Slices of buttery avocado gave the dish a cooling, creamy component. Sturdy watercress, with its pleasant bitterness and peppery punch, made an ideal base for the rich toppings. We crowned the salad with a sprinkling of toasted hazelnuts and torn mint leaves, for crisp crunch and complexity.

1 pound skin-on salmon, 1 inch thick

1 teaspoon plus 3 tablespoons extra-virgin olive oil, divided

¾ teaspoon table salt, divided

¼ teaspoon pepper

2 red grapefruits

1 tablespoon minced shallot

1 teaspoon white wine vinegar

1 teaspoon Dijon mustard

4 ounces (4 cups) watercress, torn into bite-size pieces

1 ripe avocado, halved, pitted, and sliced ¼ inch thick

¼ cup fresh mint leaves, torn

¼ cup blanched hazelnuts, toasted and chopped

1 Adjust oven rack to lowest position, place aluminum foil-lined rimmed baking sheet on rack, and heat oven to 500 degrees. Pat salmon dry with paper towels, rub with 1 teaspoon oil, and sprinkle with ¼ teaspoon salt and pepper. Reduce oven to 275 degrees. Carefully place salmon skin side down on prepared sheet. Roast until center is still translucent when checked with tip of paring knife and registers 125 degrees (for medium-rare), 6 to 8 minutes. Let salmon cool to room temperature, about 20 minutes. Flake salmon into 2-inch pieces.

2 While salmon cools, cut away peel and pith from grapefruits. Holding fruit over bowl, use paring knife to slice between membranes to release segments. Measure out 2 tablespoons grapefruit juice and transfer to separate bowl.

3 Whisk shallot, vinegar, mustard, and remaining ½ teaspoon salt into grapefruit juice. Whisking constantly, slowly drizzle in remaining 3 tablespoons oil. Arrange watercress in even layer on platter. Arrange salmon pieces, grapefruit segments, and avocado on top of watercress. Drizzle dressing over top, then sprinkle with mint and hazelnuts. Serve.

• *fast* • *fiber-ful* • *one-pan* •

Shaved Salad with Pan-Seared Scallops

Why This Recipe Works Mexican flavors inspired this refreshing salad that combines sweet mango, crisp cucumber, jicama, peppery radish, and spicy jalapeño. We shaved or sliced all of them thin; the tossed vegetable ribbons made a pleasantly crunchy bed for meaty scallops. We seared the scallops quickly in a skillet to keep their interior juicy and tender. A dressing of honey, lime zest and juice, and olive oil coated the vegetables with sweet-tangy flavor. For garnishes, we turned to the herbaceous freshness of cilantro and the nutty crunch of toasted pepitas. We recommend buying "dry" scallops, which don't have chemical additives and taste better than "wet." Dry scallops will look ivory or pinkish; wet scallops are bright white. Persian cucumbers (also called "mini cucumbers") are similar to seedless cucumbers in flavor and texture. Use a sharp "Y-shaped" vegetable peeler or mandoline to shave the jicama and cucumbers. For more spice, reserve, mince, and add the ribs and seeds from the jalapeño.

1 pound large sea scallops, tendons removed

1 pound jicama, peeled and shaved into ribbons

1 mango, peeled, pitted, and sliced thin

3 Persian cucumbers, shaved lengthwise into ribbons

4 ounces (4 cups) mesclun

2 radishes, trimmed and sliced thin

1 shallot, sliced thin

1 jalapeño or serrano chile, stemmed, halved, seeded, and sliced thin crosswise

1 teaspoon table salt, divided

¼ teaspoon pepper

6 tablespoons extra-virgin olive oil, divided

1 tablespoon honey

2 teaspoons grated lime zest plus ¼ cup juice (2 limes)

¼ cup fresh cilantro or parsley leaves

3 tablespoons roasted, unsalted pepitas or roasted sunflower seeds

1 Place scallops on clean dish towel, then top with second clean dish towel and gently press to dry. Let scallops sit between towels at room temperature for 10 minutes.

2 Meanwhile, gently toss jicama, mango, cucumbers, mesclun, radishes, shallot, and jalapeño in large bowl, then arrange attractively on individual plates.

3 Line large plate with double layer of paper towels. Sprinkle scallops with ½ teaspoon salt and pepper. Heat 1 tablespoon oil in 12-inch nonstick skillet over medium-high heat until just smoking. Add half of scallops in single layer, flat side down, and cook, without moving them, until well browned, 1½ to 2 minutes. Using tongs, flip scallops and continue to cook until sides of scallops are firm and centers are opaque, 30 to 90 seconds. Transfer scallops to prepared plate. Wipe out skillet with paper towels and repeat with 1 tablespoon oil and remaining scallops.

4 Divide scallops evenly among salad on prepared plates. Whisk honey, lime zest and juice, and remaining ½ teaspoon salt together in bowl. Whisking constantly, slowly drizzle in remaining ¼ cup oil until emulsified. Drizzle salad and scallops with dressing, then sprinkle with cilantro and pepitas. Serve.

Zucchini Noodle Salad with Tahini-Ginger Dressing

Why This Recipe Works There's a reason zucchini noodles are so popular. The squash is easy to work with and produces long, slurpable noodles that have a bouncy bite and neutral flavor—perfect for being drenched in sauce. We made these noodles the canvas for a boldly flavored, East Asian–inspired salad. After testing both boiled and stir-fried noodles, we realized that leaving the zucchini raw gave us the crispest texture and retained the vegetable's sweet, fresh flavor. We also incorporated plenty of other vegetables for color and crunch: red bell pepper, shredded carrot, and sautéed broccoli. Tahini, soy sauce, ginger, rice vinegar, and garlic united to make a creamy, salty-sweet dressing that clung satisfyingly to our vegetables. If possible, use smaller, in-season zucchini, which have thinner skins and fewer seeds. We prefer to spiralize our zucchini at home for the best flavor, but you can use store-bought zucchini noodles if you prefer. You will need 3 pounds of zucchini to get 2½ pounds of zucchini noodles. Note that this recipe uses unseasoned rice vinegar; we don't recommend using seasoned rice vinegar in its place.

½ cup tahini

¼ cup soy sauce

2 tablespoons unseasoned rice vinegar

4 teaspoons grated fresh ginger

1 tablespoon honey

2 teaspoons hot sauce

1 garlic clove, minced

¼ teaspoon table salt

2 tablespoons toasted sesame oil

12 ounces broccoli florets, cut into ½-inch pieces

2½ pounds zucchini noodles, cut into 12-inch lengths

1 red, orange, or yellow bell pepper, stemmed, seeded, and cut into ¼-inch-wide strips

1 carrot, peeled and shredded

4 scallions, sliced thin on bias

1 tablespoon sesame seeds, toasted

1 Process tahini, soy sauce, vinegar, ginger, honey, hot sauce, garlic, and salt in blender until smooth and emulsified, about 30 seconds. Transfer to large serving bowl.

2 Heat oil in 12-inch nonstick skillet over medium-high heat until shimmering. Add broccoli and cook until softened and spotty brown, about 5 minutes. Transfer to plate and let cool slightly.

3 Add zucchini, bell pepper, carrot, scallions, and broccoli to bowl with dressing and toss to combine. Season with salt and pepper to taste. Sprinkle with sesame seeds. Serve.

Farro and Kale Salad with Fennel, Olives, and Pecorino

Why This Recipe Works This salad tastes fantastic warm, at room temperature, or chilled, which makes it a versatile dish that can slide easily onto the menu for any occasion. Farro's chewiness makes it particularly enjoyable to eat, so we paired the grain with an equally hearty vegetable: lacinato kale. The earthy quality of the farro married beautifully with the slightly bitter edge of the greens, which we massaged to help make them more tender. We also tossed in fennel, which accented the dish with a faint licorice aroma. For a tart contrast, we drizzled our salad with a sharp lemon-shallot vinaigrette and added briny olives. Tearing the olives, rather than chopping them, gave them craggy edges that upped the textural interest. Salty shreds of Pecorino Romano underpinned all the flavors with a satisfying umami funk. It's best to use whole-grain farro here. You can use pearled farro, but cooking times vary, so start checking for doneness after 10 minutes. Don't substitute quick-cooking farro. Lacinato kale (also known as dinosaur or Tuscan kale) is more tender than curly-leaf or red kale, but you can substitute curly-leaf or red kale; if you do, increase the massaging time to 5 minutes. Do not use baby kale. You can use any type of brined olives, but we love the meatiness of Castelvetrano olives.

1½ cups whole farro, rinsed

½ teaspoon table salt, plus salt for cooking farro

5 ounces lacinato kale, stemmed and sliced crosswise ¼ inch thick

3 tablespoons extra-virgin olive oil

2 tablespoons lemon juice

1 small shallot, minced

¼ teaspoon pepper

1 fennel bulb, fronds minced, stalks discarded, bulb halved, cored, and sliced thin

⅓ cup pitted Castelvetrano olives, torn in half

¼ cup slivered almonds, toasted, divided

1 ounce Pecorino Romano cheese, shaved thin

1 Bring 2 quarts water to boil in large saucepan. Stir in farro and 1 tablespoon salt and simmer until tender, 15 to 20 minutes. Drain well. Spread farro on rimmed baking sheet and let cool for 15 minutes.

2 Vigorously squeeze and massage kale with your hands until leaves are uniformly darkened and slightly wilted, about 1 minute. Whisk oil, lemon juice, shallot, salt, and pepper together in large bowl. Add cooled farro and kale, fennel bulb, olives, and 2 tablespoons almonds and toss to combine. Season with salt and pepper to taste. Sprinkle with Pecorino Romano, fennel fronds, and remaining 2 tablespoons almonds. Serve.

Bulgur Salad with Spinach, Chickpeas, and Apples

Why This Recipe Works Bulgur does a superb job of enhancing the heartiness of any salad, as the grain offers nutty notes and a satisfyingly chewy bite. As we often do with grains, we spread the bulgur on a rimmed baking sheet after cooking so it could cool without clumping. We tossed the bulgur with spinach and chickpeas for even more plant-powered heft, as well as chopped apples to punctuate the salad's earthy flavor profile with welcome pops of sweetness. Toasted walnuts dotted the dish with their rich crunch and slightly bitter edge. We dressed the grains and vegetables in a lemony, smoked paprika–spiced vinaigrette; the microwave not only made quick work of pulling together this sweet, peppery condiment, but also helped bloom the flavor of the smoked paprika.

1 Bring 2 quarts water to boil in large pot. Stir in bulgur and 1 teaspoon salt and cook until tender, about 5 minutes. Drain well, spread over rimmed baking sheet, and set aside to cool, about 15 minutes.

2 Meanwhile, whisk oil, shallot, paprika, and lemon zest together in large bowl, then microwave until bubbling and fragrant, about 30 seconds. Whisk in lemon juice, honey, and salt.

3 Add cooled bulgur, chickpeas, spinach, apples, and walnuts to vinaigrette and toss to combine. Season with salt and pepper to taste. Serve.

1½ cups medium-grind bulgur, rinsed

½ teaspoon table salt, plus salt for cooking bulgur

5 tablespoons extra-virgin olive oil

1 shallot, minced

1 teaspoon smoked paprika

½ teaspoon grated lemon zest, plus ¼ cup juice (2 lemons)

1 tablespoon honey

1 (15-ounce) can chickpeas, rinsed

5 ounces (5 cups) baby spinach, chopped

2 apples, cored and cut into ½-inch pieces

½ cup walnuts, toasted and chopped

Quinoa Taco Salad

Why This Recipe Works For a spin on taco salad that ups the fiber content, we turned to hearty quinoa as our base. The chewy texture of the grain made it a surprisingly superb stand-in for ground beef; toasted and simmered in broth with chipotles in adobo, tomato paste, anchovy paste, and cumin, the quinoa acquired a deeply savory flavor. In place of lettuce, we used escarole for a hint of bitterness, which contrasted pleasantly with the rich, briny queso fresco. Black beans, avocado, cherry tomatoes, and scallions completed our multitextured salad. This recipe is so substantial, with plenty of bite, that you won't miss the tortilla chips, but if you like, you can serve it with tortilla chips or multigrain chips. We like the convenience of prewashed quinoa; rinsing removes the quinoa's bitter protective coating (called saponin). If you buy unwashed quinoa, rinse it and then spread it out on a clean dish towel to dry for 15 minutes.

- ¾ cup prewashed white quinoa
- 3 tablespoons extra-virgin olive oil, divided
- 1 small onion, chopped fine
- ½ teaspoon table salt, divided
- 2 teaspoons minced canned chipotle chile in adobo sauce
- 2 teaspoons tomato paste
- 1 teaspoon anchovy paste (optional)
- ½ teaspoon ground cumin
- 1 cup vegetable or chicken broth
- 2 tablespoons lime juice
- ¼ teaspoon pepper
- 1 head escarole (1 pound) or frisée, trimmed and sliced thin
- 2 scallions, sliced thin
- ½ cup chopped fresh cilantro or parsley, divided
- 1 (15-ounce) can black beans, rinsed
- 8 ounces cherry or grape tomatoes, quartered
- 1 ripe avocado, halved, pitted, and chopped
- 2 ounces queso fresco or feta cheese, crumbled (½ cup)

1 Toast quinoa in large saucepan over medium-high heat, stirring often, until very fragrant and quinoa makes continuous popping sound, 5 to 7 minutes; transfer to bowl.

2 Heat 1 tablespoon oil in now-empty saucepan over medium heat until shimmering. Add onion and ¼ teaspoon salt and cook until onion is softened and lightly browned, 5 to 7 minutes.

3 Stir in chipotle; tomato paste; anchovy paste, if using; and cumin and cook until fragrant, about 30 seconds. Stir in broth and quinoa, increase heat to medium-high, and bring to simmer. Cover; reduce heat to low; and simmer until quinoa is tender and liquid has been absorbed, 18 to 22 minutes, stirring halfway through cooking. Let sit off heat, covered, for 10 minutes. Spread quinoa onto rimmed baking sheet and let cool completely, about 20 minutes.

4 Whisk lime juice, pepper, remaining 2 tablespoons oil, and remaining ¼ teaspoon salt together in large bowl. Add escarole, scallions, and ¼ cup cilantro and toss to combine. Gently fold in beans, tomatoes, and avocado. Transfer to serving platter and top with quinoa, queso fresco, and remaining ¼ cup cilantro. Serve.

Sweet Potato and Lentil Salad with Crispy Shallots

Why This Recipe Works Hearty, protein-rich black lentils have a slightly spicy earthiness that marries beautifully with autumnal flavors. We found that a quick brine in warm salted water helped to season them and soften their skins, leading to very few blowouts when cooking. Creamy chunks of roasted sweet potatoes and chewy bites of lacinato kale made for a texturally varied salad. Fried shallots made an appealingly crisp topping that imbued each bite with subtly sweet, nutty aroma. Crumbled goat cheese scattered over the salad studded the meal with milky funk and briny savoriness. If you can't find black lentils, you can substitute two 15-ounce cans of lentils, rinsed, and skip steps 1 and 3. We like to use our own Crispy Shallots in this recipe, but you can substitute store-bought if you prefer. If using our recipe, use the reserved shallot oil instead of the vegetable oil for extra flavor.

1½ teaspoons table salt for brining

1½ cups black lentils, picked over and rinsed

1½ pounds sweet potatoes, peeled and cut into ½-inch pieces

½ cup vegetable oil, divided

¾ teaspoon table salt, divided

¼ teaspoon pepper

2 tablespoons sherry vinegar

1 teaspoon mayonnaise

1 teaspoon Dijon mustard

8 ounces lacinato kale, stemmed and sliced crosswise ¼ inch thick

4 ounces goat cheese, crumbled (1 cup)

½ cup Crispy Shallots (page 85)

1 Dissolve 1½ teaspoons salt in 1 quart warm water in bowl. Add lentils and let brine at room temperature for at least 1 hour or up to 24 hours. Drain well.

2 Meanwhile, adjust oven rack to lower-middle position and heat oven to 400 degrees. Toss sweet potatoes with 2 tablespoons oil, ½ teaspoon salt, and pepper. Spread sweet potatoes on rimmed baking sheet and roast until well browned and tender, 20 to 25 minutes, stirring halfway through roasting. Let cool slightly, about 5 minutes.

3 Bring lentils and 6 cups water to boil in medium saucepan over high heat. Reduce heat to medium-low and simmer gently until lentils are just tender, 20 to 25 minutes. Drain.

4 Combine vinegar, mayonnaise, mustard, and remaining ¼ teaspoon salt in large bowl and season with pepper to taste. Whisk until mixture is milky in appearance and no lumps of mayonnaise remain. Whisking constantly, slowly drizzle remaining 6 tablespoons oil into vinegar mixture until emulsified.

5 Add kale, sweet potatoes, and lentils to dressing and toss to combine. Season with salt and pepper to taste. Transfer to serving platter and sprinkle with goat cheese and crispy shallots. Serve.

Roasted Vegetable and Black Chickpea Salad

Why This Recipe Works We love the dense, creamy bite of chickpeas, so we married them with equally hearty roasted vegetables in this extra-satisfying salad worthy of a main course. We opted for black chickpeas, an heirloom variety especially common in India and Italy that boasts a firm texture and earthy, nutty, almost smoky character. Not only did roasted golden beets and delicata squash stand up to the legumes' dense texture, but the bright vegetables' natural sweetness also tempered the earthiness of the chickpeas. The vividly yellow beets and squash also offered a pleasing visual contrast to the dark legumes. A creamy bed of herbed yogurt anchored the whole dish, while a drizzle of fiery harissa ensured that the flavors didn't lean too sweet. We like to use our own Harissa in this recipe, but you can use store-bought if you prefer. We prefer golden beets because they don't discolor the rest of the salad. If you can't find black chickpeas, you can substitute dried common chickpeas.

1½   tablespoons table salt for brining

8   ounces dried black chickpeas, picked over and rinsed

½   teaspoon table salt, divided, plus salt for cooking chickpeas

1   pound golden beets, trimmed

1   delicata squash (12 to 16 ounces), ends trimmed, halved lengthwise, seeded, and sliced crosswise ½ inch thick

3   tablespoons extra-virgin olive oil, divided, plus extra for drizzling

1   cup plain Greek yogurt

¼   cup chopped fresh cilantro, divided

¾   teaspoon grated lemon zest, divided, plus 1½ tablespoons juice

¼   cup Harissa (recipe follows)

½   cup pomegranate seeds

¼   cup shelled pistachios, toasted and chopped

1   Dissolve 1½ tablespoons salt in 2 quarts cold water in large container. Add chickpeas and brine at room temperature for at least 8 hours or up to 24 hours. Drain and rinse well. (If you're pressed for time, see page 69 for information on quick-brining your beans.)

2   Adjust oven rack to middle position and heat oven to 425 degrees. Bring soaked chickpeas and 7 cups water to simmer in large saucepan. Simmer, partially covered, over medium-low heat until chickpeas are tender, 30 to 40 minutes. Remove from heat, stir in 1½ teaspoons salt, cover, and let sit for 15 minutes. Drain well and set aside.

3   Meanwhile, wrap beets individually in aluminum foil and place on aluminum foil–lined rimmed baking sheet. Roast for 30 minutes.

4   Toss squash with 1 tablespoon oil and ¼ teaspoon salt in bowl. Remove sheet with beets from oven and arrange beets on 1 half of sheet. Spread squash in even layer on other side of sheet, then return to oven and roast until beets and squash are tender (you will need to unwrap beets to test them), about 15 minutes.

5   Remove beets and squash from oven and carefully open beet foil packets. Once beets are cool enough to handle, carefully rub off skins using paper towels. Slice beets into ½-inch-thick wedges, and, if large, cut in half crosswise.

6   Whisk yogurt, 1 tablespoon oil, 1 tablespoon cilantro, ¼ teaspoon lemon zest, and ⅛ teaspoon salt together in bowl; set aside. Whisk remaining 1 tablespoon oil, remaining ½ teaspoon lemon zest, lemon juice, and remaining ⅛ teaspoon salt together in large bowl. Add reserved drained chickpeas, beets, and squash and toss to combine. Season with salt and pepper to taste.

7   Spread yogurt mixture over wide serving platter. Arrange chickpea-vegetable mixture over top, then drizzle with harissa and sprinkle with pomegranate seeds, pistachios, and remaining 3 tablespoons cilantro. Drizzle with extra oil and serve.

Harissa

Makes ½ cup | Total time: 10 minutes

---

6 tablespoons extra-virgin olive oil

6 garlic cloves, minced

2 tablespoons paprika

1 tablespoon ground coriander

1 tablespoon ground dried Aleppo pepper

1 teaspoon ground cumin

¾ teaspoon caraway seeds

½ teaspoon table salt

Combine all ingredients in bowl and microwave until bubbling and very fragrant, about 1 minute, stirring halfway through microwaving. Let cool completely. (Harissa can be refrigerated for up to 4 days. Bring to room temperature before serving.)

Gado Gado

Why This Recipe Works We love this Indonesian salad of vegetables and proteins drizzled in a flavor-rich peanut sauce. For our take, we chose hearty vegetables ranging from tender (potatoes) to crunchy (napa cabbage). The irresistible sauce highlights Indonesian staples: citrusy makrut lime leaves, tamarind for sweet tang, terasi (shrimp paste) for pleasant funk, and kecap manis (Indonesian sweet soy sauce) for umami depth. All-natural chunky peanut butter stood in for the typical fried, ground peanuts. Look for palm sugar, terasi, and kecap manis at Asian grocery stores; you might also find them at some well-stocked supermarkets. If you prefer a less pronounced flavor, use the smaller amount of terasi. If you can't find terasi, you can substitute another shrimp paste; otherwise, omit it. If you can't find kecap manis, increase the sugar to 3 tablespoons and add 2 teaspoons each of soy sauce and molasses to the peanut sauce. Look for Thai/Indonesian-style tamarind concentrate labeled "nuoc me chua" at Asian grocery stores (do not use Indian-style tamarind concentrates); you might also find it at some well-stocked supermarkets. (See page 15 for more information.) Use extra-small potatoes measuring less than 1 inch in diameter. We like to top this with our Crispy Shallots, but you can substitute store-bought if you prefer. Serve with emping (Indonesian seed-based crackers) or kerupuk (shrimp crackers). All ingredients, including the peanut sauce, can be cooked and then stored, allowing you to make the dish entirely ahead.

Sambal Kacang (Peanut Sauce)

   5 Thai chiles, stemmed and chopped

   5 makrut lime leaves, middle vein removed, chopped fine

   2 tablespoons palm sugar or brown sugar

   4 garlic cloves, chopped

2–4 teaspoons terasi

   ¾ teaspoon table salt

   ¾ cup chunky natural no-sugar-added peanut butter

   ¾ cup canned coconut milk

   ¼ cup lime juice (2 limes)

   ¼ cup tamarind juice concentrate

   2 tablespoons kecap manis

Salad

  12 ounces extra-small potatoes, unpeeled

      Table salt for cooking vegetables

  12 ounces green beans, trimmed

   4 cups shredded napa cabbage

   8 ounces (4 cups) bean sprouts

   ¼ cup vegetable oil

   8 ounces tempeh or firm tofu, halved lengthwise and cut crosswise into ¼-inch-wide pieces

   6 Easy-Peel Hard-Cooked Eggs (page 42), quartered

   8 ounces cherry tomatoes, halved

   ½ English cucumber, halved lengthwise and sliced thin

   1 recipe Crispy Shallots (page 85)

1 For the sambal kacang Process chiles, lime leaves, sugar, garlic, terasi, and salt in food processor until coarse paste forms, about 10 seconds. Scrape down sides of bowl and add peanut butter, coconut milk, lime juice, tamarind, and kecap manis. Process until thick, fluid sauce forms, about 15 seconds, scraping down sides of bowl after 10 seconds. Transfer to 2-cup liquid measuring cup and set aside.

2 For the salad Line 2 rimmed baking sheets with double layer of paper towels and set aside. Bring 2 quarts water to boil in large pot over high heat. Add potatoes and 1½ teaspoons salt and cook until potatoes are easily pierced with paring knife, about 15 minutes. While potatoes cook, fill large bowl halfway with ice and water. Transfer potatoes to bowl to cool.

3 Return water to boil. Add green beans and cook until crisp-tender, 3 to 5 minutes. Transfer beans to ice water. Let beans cool, about 5 minutes. Transfer beans to 1 prepared sheet and pat dry.

4 Return water to boil. Add cabbage and bean sprouts and cook for 30 seconds. Drain in colander and rinse with cold water until cool enough to handle. Transfer to second prepared sheet and pat dry.

5 Line large plate with double layer of paper towels. Heat oil in 12-inch nonstick skillet over medium heat until shimmering. Add tempeh and cook until deep golden brown on both sides, 6 to 8 minutes. Transfer to prepared plate.

6 Halve potatoes and cut green beans into bite-size pieces. Piling them into separate mounds, arrange potatoes, green beans, cabbage and bean sprouts, tempeh, eggs, tomatoes, and cucumber in large salad bowl. Microwave reserved peanut sauce until warm and pourable, 1 to 2 minutes, stirring halfway through heating. Pour 1½ cups of peanut sauce over salad and toss until ingredients are well coated. Garnish with crispy shallots. Serve, passing remaining peanut sauce separately.

Indian-Spiced Carrot and Coconut Salad with Tilapia

Why This Recipe Works Sweet, spicy, and acidic, this salad takes cues from gajarachi koshimbir, a dish from the state of Maharashtra in India that combines carrots with coconut, peanuts, cilantro, and a spiced oil. To start, we salted and sugared carrots to heighten their sweetness. We then made a spiced oil using the technique of tadka—meaning tempering or blooming—a method for releasing maximum flavor from spices. This gave us a potent oil heady with the aromas of peppery black mustard seeds, onion-scented asafetida, and musky curry leaves. Crisp, nutty pigeon peas bulked up the salad. For extra protein, we lightly seasoned two tilapia fillets, which made a mild counterpoint for the more intense flavors. Halving each fillet gave us four pieces; we gave the thicker halves a head start in the skillet to ensure that all the fish cooked up tender on the inside and golden brown on the outside. We prefer to shred fresh coconut on the large holes of a box grater, but you can also use frozen unsweetened, shredded coconut. Look for it, as well as asafetida and curry leaves, at Indian or Asian grocery stores; you might also find them at some well-stocked supermarkets. If you can't find the asafetida or curry leaves, you can omit. Curry leaves are best used fresh but can be refrigerated for longer storage. Blooming spices progresses very quickly so it's important to have the ingredients measured out before you start. Mustard seeds jump out of the pan when added to hot oil; covering the pan with a splatter screen or lid can be helpful to keep them contained. If you prefer, you can add ¼ teaspoon of cayenne pepper to the carrot mixture with the lime juice in step 1 in place of the Thai chile used in step 2.

Salad

- 1 pound carrots, peeled and shredded
- 3 tablespoons sugar
- 1 teaspoon table salt, divided
- ½ onion, chopped fine (optional)
- 1 (15-ounce) can pigeon peas, rinsed
- 2 tablespoons lime juice
- 2 (5- to 6-ounce) skinless tilapia fillets
- 1 tablespoon vegetable oil
- 3 tablespoons dry-roasted peanuts, chopped
- ¼ cup fresh cilantro leaves and tender stems, cut into 1-inch lengths
- ¼ cup shredded fresh coconut

Spiced Seasoning Oil

- 2 tablespoons vegetable oil
- 4 teaspoons black mustard seeds
- 1 Thai chile, trimmed and halved lengthwise
- ¼ teaspoon ground turmeric
- ¼ teaspoon ground asafetida (optional)
- 20 fresh curry leaves (optional)

1 **For the salad** Toss carrots with sugar and ¾ teaspoon salt in salad spinner and let sit until partially wilted and reduced in volume by one third, about 15 minutes. Spin carrots until excess liquid is removed, 10 to 20 seconds. Transfer carrots to large bowl and toss with onion, if using; pigeon peas; and lime juice.

2 **For the spiced seasoning oil** Heat oil in small saucepan or seasoning wok over medium-high heat until just smoking. (Test temperature of oil by adding 1 mustard seed; mustard seed should sizzle and pop immediately; if it does not, continue to heat oil and repeat testing.) Carefully add mustard seeds, then reduce heat to low. Stir in Thai chile, turmeric, and asafetida, if using, and cook until fragrant, about 5 seconds. Off heat, carefully stir in curry leaves, if using, and cook until leaves sizzle and are translucent in spots, 5 to 10 seconds.

3 Pour hot oil mixture over carrot mixture, toss to coat, and let sit for at least 15 minutes. (Carrot mixture can be refrigerated for up to 6 hours. Bring to room temperature before serving.)

4 Place tilapia on cutting board and sprinkle both sides with remaining ¼ teaspoon salt. Let sit at room temperature for 15 minutes. Pat tilapia dry with paper towels. Using seam that runs down middle of fillet as guide, cut each fillet in half lengthwise to create 1 thick half and 1 thin half. Cut each piece in half crosswise to create 4 thick pieces and 4 thin pieces.

5 Heat oil in 12-inch nonstick skillet over high heat until just smoking. Add thick pieces of tilapia to skillet and cook, tilting and gently shaking skillet occasionally to distribute oil, until undersides are golden brown, 2 to 3 minutes. Using thin spatula, flip pieces. Add thin pieces of tilapia to skillet with thick pieces and cook until all pieces are golden brown on both sides and register 130 to 135 degrees, 2 to 3 minutes, flipping thin pieces halfway through. Transfer tilapia to plate.

6 Transfer carrot mixture to platter; top with tilapia; and sprinkle with peanuts, cilantro, and coconut. Serve.

Prepping Tilapia

1 Using seam that runs down middle of fillet as guide, cut each fillet in half lengthwise to create 1 thick half and 1 thin half.

2 Cut each piece in half crosswise to create 4 thick pieces and 4 thin pieces.

Indian-Spiced
Carrot and Coconut
Salad with Tilapia
(page 156)

Green Goodness Bowl with Chicken

Why This Recipe Works The anchor of any great green goddess salad is creamy, herbaceous green goddess dressing, which gets its fresh flavor and appealing hue from a medley of herbs. We took the concept further with this green "goodness" chicken salad filled with an abundance of green foods, including baby spinach, edamame, and pistachios. We used just one chicken breast, simmering it gently to keep the meat juicy. Sautéing the broccoli gave it nice char, introducing smokiness while accentuating its vibrant green color. Since the classic dressing can be a bit heavy, we lightened ours by replacing mayonnaise with buttermilk and yogurt. Three herbs (chives, parsley, and dried tarragon) gave the dressing plenty of color, and an anchovy added savory depth.

   1 tablespoon lemon juice

   1 tablespoon water

   2 teaspoons dried tarragon

   ½ cup buttermilk

   ¼ cup plain yogurt

   ¼ cup sour cream

   ¼ cup minced fresh parsley

   1 garlic clove, minced

   1 anchovy fillet, minced (optional)

   ¼ cup minced fresh chives

   ¼ plus ⅛ teaspoon table salt, plus salt for poaching chicken

   ¼ teaspoon pepper

   2 (6- to 8-ounce) boneless, skinless chicken breasts, no more than 1 inch thick, trimmed

1½ tablespoons extra-virgin olive oil, divided

   8 ounces broccoli florets, cut into 1-inch pieces

   1 garlic clove, minced

   ¼ teaspoon minced fresh thyme or pinch dried

   8 ounces (8 cups) baby spinach

   1 ripe avocado, halved, pitted, and sliced thin

   ½ cup frozen shelled edamame beans, thawed and patted dry

   ¼ cup shelled pistachios, toasted and chopped

1 Combine lemon juice, water, and tarragon in small bowl and let sit for 15 minutes.

2 Process tarragon mixture; buttermilk; yogurt; sour cream; parsley; garlic; and anchovy, if using, in blender until smooth, scraping down sides of blender jar as needed; transfer dressing to clean bowl. Stir in chives, ¼ teaspoon salt, and pepper. Cover and refrigerate until flavors meld, about 1 hour. Season with salt and pepper to taste.

3 Dissolve 1 tablespoon salt in 6 cups cold water in Dutch oven. Submerge chicken in water. Heat pot over medium heat until water registers 170 degrees. Turn off heat, cover pot, and let stand until chicken registers 165 degrees, 15 to 17 minutes. Transfer chicken to cutting board and let cool slightly. Using 2 forks, shred chicken into bite-size pieces.

4 Heat 1 tablespoon oil in 12-inch skillet over medium-high heat until just smoking. Add broccoli and remaining ⅛ teaspoon salt and cook, without stirring, until beginning to brown, about 2 minutes. Add 1½ tablespoons water; cover; and cook until broccoli is bright green but still crisp, about 2 minutes. Uncover and continue to cook until water has evaporated and broccoli is crisp-tender, about 2 minutes.

5 Clear center of pan; add remaining 1½ teaspoons oil, garlic, and thyme; and cook, mashing garlic into skillet, until fragrant, about 30 seconds. Stir garlic mixture into broccoli. Transfer broccoli to bowl and season with salt and pepper to taste.

6 Toss spinach with half of dressing to coat, then season with salt and pepper to taste. Divide among individual serving bowls, then top with chicken, broccoli, avocado, and edamame. Drizzle with remaining dressing and sprinkle with pistachios. Serve.

Spinach Pesto Pasta Bowl

Why This Recipe Works Pesto is often associated with basil, but you can make one with almost any combination of vegetables, herbs, cheeses, nuts, or seasonings. In this recipe, we left out the nuts and used spinach instead for a fiber-ful boost. We sautéed onion, garlic, and red pepper flakes for a nutty-spicy base and then added the spinach to wilt it. We blitzed this aromatic mixture in a food processor with Parmesan, lemon juice, and pasta water to a spreadable, grainy consistency. Dense artichoke hearts gave the bowl rich, meaty appeal while beautifully absorbing our flavorful pesto. Sautéed cherry tomatoes added gorgeous pops of red and sweet-savory flavor. We garnished the bowl with chopped fresh basil for a sweetly herbaceous finish. We like to top this salad with ricotta, but you can omit if you prefer. If your tomatoes are sweet, you may want to reduce or omit the sugar.

2½ tablespoons extra-virgin olive oil, divided

1 pound cherry or grape tomatoes, halved

1½ teaspoons sugar

3 garlic cloves, minced, divided

4 teaspoons plus 2 tablespoons chopped fresh basil, divided

1 large onion, chopped fine

⅛ teaspoon red pepper flakes

10 ounces (10 cups) baby spinach

1 teaspoon table salt, plus salt for cooking pasta

12 ounces spaghetti

1 ounce Parmesan or Pecorino Romano cheese, grated (½ cup)

2 teaspoons lemon juice

2 cups drained jarred whole baby artichoke hearts packed in water or thawed frozen artichoke hearts, quartered

2 ounces (¼ cup) whole-milk ricotta cheese (optional)

1 Heat 1½ teaspoons oil in 12-inch nonstick skillet over medium-high heat until just smoking. Add tomatoes and sugar and cook, tossing often, until tomatoes begin to soften, about 1 minute. Stir in 1 teaspoon garlic and cook until fragrant, about 30 seconds. Transfer tomatoes to bowl, stir in 4 teaspoons basil, and season with salt and pepper to taste.

2 Heat remaining 2 tablespoons oil in now-empty 12-inch skillet over medium heat until shimmering. Add onion and cook until softened and lightly browned, 5 to 7 minutes. Stir in pepper flakes and remaining garlic and cook until fragrant, about 30 seconds. Add spinach, 1 handful at a time, and salt and cook until spinach is wilted, about 2 minutes.

3 Meanwhile, bring 4 quarts water to boil in large pot. Add pasta and 1 tablespoon salt and cook, stirring often, until tender. Reserve 1 cup cooking water, then drain pasta and return it to pot.

4 Transfer spinach mixture to food processor with Parmesan, lemon juice, and ½ cup reserved cooking water. Process until smooth, about 1 minute, scraping down sides of bowl as needed. Add spinach pesto and artichokes to pot with pasta and stir to coat. Adjust consistency of sauce with remaining ½ cup reserved cooking water as needed and season with salt and pepper to taste. Divide among individual plates. Serve, topping individual portions with tomatoes; remaining 2 tablespoons basil; and ricotta, if desired.

Saffron Bulgur with Fennel and Sausage Bowl

Why This Recipe Works Golden saffron brings both fragrant aroma and vivid color to this bright, bold bulgur bowl. We browned just a pound of turkey sausage on the stovetop to release its flavorful fat, which was perfect for enriching fennel and dried apricots and distributing the meat's flavor throughout the dish. Fennel's grassy edge amplified the rich savoriness of the sausage, while the apricots complemented the meat's richness with bursts of sweetness; a splash of water helped the fruit plump up in the skillet. For the dressing, we whisked up a delicately floral saffron-infused pomegranate vinaigrette. Finally, we adorned the bowl with shaved Manchego for a nutty, buttery finish. When shopping, don't confuse bulgur with cracked wheat, which has a much longer cooking time and will not work in this recipe.

1½ cups medium-grind bulgur

¼ teaspoon table salt, divided, plus salt for cooking bulgur

3 tablespoons extra-virgin olive oil, divided

1 pound Italian turkey sausage

2 fennel bulbs, ¼ cup fronds minced, stalks discarded, bulbs halved, cored, and sliced ¼ inch thick

½ cup dried apricots, chopped

½ teaspoon pepper, divided

¼ teaspoon saffron threads, crumbled

2 tablespoons pomegranate molasses

1 teaspoon grated lemon zest

2 ounces Manchego cheese, shaved

1 Bring 2 quarts water to boil in large pot. Stir in bulgur and 1 teaspoon salt and cook until tender, about 5 minutes. Drain well and set aside.

2 Heat 1 tablespoon oil in 12-inch nonstick skillet over medium heat until shimmering. Add sausages and cook until browned on all sides and register 160 degrees, 6 to 8 minutes. Transfer to cutting board, cover with aluminum foil, and let rest. Slice sausages ½ inch thick on bias just before serving.

3 Pour off all but 2 teaspoons fat from skillet (or add oil to equal 2 teaspoons). Add sliced fennel, apricots, ½ cup water, ⅛ teaspoon salt, and ¼ teaspoon pepper, cover, and cook over medium heat for 1 minute. Uncover and continue to cook, stirring occasionally, until fennel is spotty brown, 3 to 5 minutes; set aside until ready to serve.

4 Combine saffron with 2 teaspoons water in large bowl and let sit for 5 minutes. Whisk in pomegranate molasses; lemon zest; and remaining 2 tablespoons oil, ⅛ teaspoon salt, and ¼ teaspoon pepper, then stir in bulgur to coat. Season with salt and pepper to taste. Divide among individual bowls, then top with fennel mixture and sausage. Sprinkle with fennel fronds and Manchego. Serve.

Smoked Salmon Niçoise Bowl

Why This Recipe Works We love a classic French niçoise salad, a dish that typically includes canned tuna. For a different take, we swapped out the tuna for briny smoked salmon. For the dressing, we found that sour cream and dill—ingredients often paired with smoked salmon—made tasty inclusions; we thinned it out with water and lemon juice, which enhanced the dressing with a tart dimension. We married these nontraditional variations with customary salade niçoise ingredients: hard-cooked eggs, green beans, potatoes, and olives. We cooked the vegetables in the same pot, starting with the potatoes and adding the green beans later to ensure that both finished cooking at the same time. The dense vegetables turned tender while retaining their satisfying bite. For even cooking, use small red potatoes measuring 1 to 2 inches in diameter.

Salad

- 1 pound small red potatoes, unpeeled, halved

   Table salt for cooking vegetables
- 8 ounces green beans, trimmed
- 10 ounces (10 cups) mesclun greens
- 4 Easy-Peel Hard-Cooked Eggs (page 42), halved
- 8 ounces sliced smoked salmon
- ½ cup pitted olives, halved

Dressing

- ⅔ cup sour cream
- 2 tablespoons lemon juice
- 2 tablespoons water
- 1 tablespoon chopped fresh dill or parsley
- ¼ teaspoon table salt
- ⅛ teaspoon pepper

1 For the salad Bring 2 quarts water to boil in large saucepan over medium-high heat. Add potatoes and 1½ tablespoons salt; return to boil and cook for 10 minutes. Add green beans and continue to cook until both vegetables are tender, about 4 minutes. Drain vegetables well and set aside to cool slightly.

2 For the dressing Combine all ingredients in small bowl; set aside.

3 Toss mesclun and ¼ cup dressing together in large bowl. Divide mesclun, potatoes, green beans, and eggs evenly among individual plates. Top each portion with salmon and olives. Drizzle salads with remaining dressing. Serve.

Spiced Vegetable Couscous Bowl

Why This Recipe Works To create this easy, filling vegetable bowl, we leaned on aromatic North African ingredients: the warming spice blend ras el hanout, as well as one of the region's most-loved starches, couscous. Not only is couscous adept at soaking up spice and flavor, the grain's firm, chewy texture also makes for a satisfying eating experience. To complement the couscous, we chose a colorful combination of cauliflower, zucchini, and bell pepper. To encourage deep caramelization on our cauliflower, we cut it into small, even florets to maximize their surface area and potential for flavorful browning. We started the florets in a cold pan, which ensured that the interiors cooked through before the outsides developed toasty goldenness; this gave us crisp-tender cauliflower with dense bite. We then quickly sautéed the zucchini and bell pepper with garlic, lemon zest, and ras el hanout. A dash of marjoram gave the salad some minty freshness. We like to use our Ras el Hanout, but you can substitute store-bought if you prefer (keep in mind flavor and spiciness can vary greatly by brand). You will need a 12-inch nonstick skillet with a tight-fitting lid for this recipe.

- 1 head cauliflower (2 pounds), cored and cut into 1-inch florets
- 6 tablespoons extra-virgin olive oil, divided, plus extra for drizzling
- 1¼ teaspoons table salt, divided
- ½ teaspoon pepper
- 1½ cups couscous
- 1 zucchini or summer squash, cut into ½-inch pieces
- 1 red, orange, or yellow bell pepper, stemmed, seeded, and cut into ½-inch pieces
- 4 garlic cloves, minced
- 2 teaspoons Ras el Hanout (recipe follows)
- 1 teaspoon grated lemon zest, plus lemon wedges for serving
- 1¾ cups chicken or vegetable broth
- 1 tablespoon minced fresh marjoram or oregano

1 Toss cauliflower, 2 tablespoons oil, ¾ teaspoon salt, and pepper together in 12-inch nonstick skillet. Cover and cook over medium-high heat until florets begin to brown and edges just start to become translucent (do not lift lid), about 5 minutes.

2 Remove lid and continue to cook, stirring every 2 minutes, until florets turn golden brown in several spots, about 10 minutes. Transfer to bowl and wipe skillet clean with paper towels.

3 Heat 2 tablespoons oil in now-empty skillet over medium-high heat until shimmering. Add couscous and cook, stirring frequently, until grains are just beginning to brown, 3 to 5 minutes. Transfer to separate bowl and wipe skillet clean with paper towels.

4 Heat remaining 2 tablespoons oil in again-empty skillet over medium-high heat until just smoking. Add zucchini, bell pepper, and remaining ½ teaspoon salt and cook until tender, 6 to 8 minutes. Stir in garlic, ras el hanout, and lemon zest and cook until fragrant, about 30 seconds. Stir in broth and bring to simmer.

5 Stir in couscous. Remove from heat; cover; and let sit until couscous is tender, about 7 minutes. Add marjoram and cauliflower to couscous and fluff gently with fork to combine. Season with salt and pepper to taste, and drizzle with extra oil. Serve with lemon wedges.

Ras el Hanout

Makes ½ cup | Total time: 15 minutes

If you can't find Aleppo pepper, you can substitute
½ teaspoon paprika and ½ teaspoon red pepper flakes.

- 16 cardamom pods
- 4 teaspoons coriander seeds
- 4 teaspoons cumin seeds
- 2 teaspoons anise seeds
- ½ teaspoon allspice berries
- ¼ teaspoon black peppercorns
- 4 teaspoons ground ginger
- 2 teaspoons ground nutmeg
- 2 teaspoons ground dried Aleppo pepper
- 2 teaspoons ground cinnamon

1 Toast cardamom, coriander, cumin, anise, allspice,
and peppercorns in small skillet over medium heat until
fragrant, shaking skillet occasionally to prevent scorching, about 2 minutes. Let cool completely.

2 Transfer toasted spices, ginger, nutmeg, Aleppo
pepper, and cinnamon to spice grinder and process
to fine powder. (Ras el hanout can be stored at room
temperature in airtight container for up to 1 year.)

Quinoa, Black Bean, and Mango Bowl

Why This Recipe Works Delicate, nutty quinoa is often called a supergrain because it's a nutritionally complete protein. We wanted to make this nutrient-dense ingredient the star of a vibrant salad hearty and filling enough to be a main course. We toasted the quinoa to accentuate its flavor, then added liquid to the pan and simmered the grains until they were nearly tender. We spread the quinoa on a rimmed baking sheet to cool, and the residual heat finished cooking the grains, giving them a light, fluffy texture while maintaining their chewy appeal. Black beans gave our bowl more plant-powered bulk and heartiness; mango and bell peppers offered sweetness and textural variation, not to mention vivid color. Scallions studded the salad with fresh crunch, and avocado introduced a cool, creamy component. We like the convenience of prewashed quinoa; rinsing removes the quinoa's bitter protective coating (called saponin). If you buy unwashed quinoa, rinse it and then spread it out on a clean dish towel to dry for 15 minutes.

1 Process lime juice, jalapeño, 1 teaspoon salt, and cumin in blender until jalapeño is finely chopped, about 15 seconds. With blender running, add oil and cilantro; continue to process until smooth and emulsified, about 20 seconds.

2 Toast quinoa in large saucepan over medium-high heat, stirring often, until very fragrant and quinoa makes continuous popping sound, 5 to 7 minutes. Stir in water and remaining ½ teaspoon salt and bring to simmer. Cover; reduce heat to low; and simmer gently until most of water has been absorbed and quinoa is nearly tender, about 15 minutes. Spread quinoa onto rimmed baking sheet and let cool for 20 minutes; transfer to large bowl.

3 Add bell pepper, mango, beans, scallions, and dressing to quinoa and toss to combine. Season with salt and pepper to taste. Divide among individual plates and top with avocado. Serve.

  5 tablespoons lime juice (3 limes)

  ½ jalapeño or serrano chile, seeded and chopped

1½ teaspoons table salt, divided

  ¾ teaspoon ground cumin

  ½ cup extra-virgin olive oil

  ⅓ cup fresh cilantro or parsley leaves

1½ cups prewashed white quinoa

2¼ cups water

  1 red, orange, or yellow bell pepper, stemmed, seeded, and chopped

  1 mango, peeled, pitted, and cut into ¼-inch pieces

  1 (15-ounce) can black beans, rinsed

  2 scallions, sliced thin

  1 avocado, halved, pitted, and sliced thin

Spring Halloumi and Freekeh Bowl

Why This Recipe Works Halloumi cheese has a briny, savory flavor and springy, meaty mouthfeel that make it very satisfying to eat. We made it the star of this flavorful bowl in which carrots, asparagus, peas, and fresh herbs evoke the sweetness of spring. To complement the dense, subtly sweet vegetables, we turned to chewy, smoky freekeh. We chose to use the cracked variety because it cooks faster than whole freekeh, and also has a sturdy yet tender bite that further enhanced the heartiness of this bowl. The grain is also a flavor sponge, readily absorbing the warmth of allspice and cinnamon. We seared cubes of halloumi cheese to crisp the exteriors and amplify the ingredient's richly milky flavor. We drizzled the bowl with our creamy, tangy Tahini-Garlic Sauce and then, for a fresh crunch, we strewed pea tendrils across the top. A final drizzle of pomegranate molasses added a zesty element that pulled all the flavors together. Do not substitute whole freekeh for the cracked freekeh in this recipe.

  7 teaspoons extra-virgin olive oil, divided

  3 onions, cut into ¾-inch-thick pieces

  2 teaspoons ground allspice

  2 teaspoons ground cinnamon

  ¾ teaspoon pepper

  2 cups cracked freekeh, rinsed

2¼ cups chicken or vegetable broth

  3 carrots, peeled and cut ½ inch thick on bias

  1 pound asparagus, trimmed and sliced ½ inch thick

  ½ cup frozen peas

  2 tablespoons lemon juice

  8 ounces halloumi, cut into ¾-inch pieces

  1 recipe Tahini-Garlic Sauce (recipe follows)

  3 tablespoons torn fresh dill, chervil, and/or mint

     Pea tendrils (optional)

     Pomegranate molasses

1 Heat 2 tablespoons oil in large saucepan over medium heat until shimmering. Add onions and cook until golden brown, about 10 minutes, stirring occasionally. Stir in allspice, cinnamon, and pepper and cook until fragrant, about 30 seconds. Add freekeh and toast until fragrant and nutty, about 3 minutes, stirring often. Stir in broth and bring to simmer. Reduce heat to medium-low; cover; and cook, stirring occasionally and scraping bottom of saucepan with wooden spoon, about 15 minutes (freekeh will not be fully cooked).

2 Stir in carrots; cover; and cook until freekeh is almost tender, about 10 minutes. Stir in asparagus; cover; and cook until asparagus is vibrant green and crisp-tender, about 5 minutes. Stir in peas and lemon juice and season with salt to taste. Cover and let sit off heat while cooking halloumi.

3 Pat halloumi dry with paper towels. Heat remaining 1 teaspoon oil in 10-inch skillet over medium-high heat until shimmering. Add halloumi and cook, turning as needed, until halloumi is deep golden brown on multiple sides, about 4 minutes.

4 Divide freekeh among individual serving bowls. Top with seared halloumi; drizzle with tahini sauce; and sprinkle with herbs and pea tendrils, if using. Drizzle with pomegranate molasses to taste, and serve.

Tahini-Garlic Sauce

Makes ¼ cup | Total time: 10 minutes

1/3 cup tahini

3 tablespoons plain yogurt

2 tablespoons lemon juice

2 tablespoons water

2 teaspoons pomegranate molasses

1 garlic clove, minced

1/2 teaspoon table salt

Whisk all ingredients in bowl until well combined. Season with salt and pepper to taste. (Sauce can be refrigerated for up to 3 days. Thin with extra water as needed before serving.)

California Barley Bowl with Avocado, Snow Peas, and Lemon-Mint Yogurt Sauce

Why This Recipe Works For a fresh, California-style take on a rice bowl, we opted for hearty barley as our grain. We paired the sturdy kernels with sweet, crisp snow peas, chunks of creamy avocado, and toasted spiced sunflower seeds—giving us a bowl that brimmed with textural variety and heartiness. While the barley cooked, we sautéed the snow peas with some coriander and toasted the sunflower seeds with warm spices such as cumin and cardamom for layers of appealing flavor. For drizzling over the bowl, we whisked up a tangy lemon-yogurt sauce, seasoning it simply with mint for the herb's cooling freshness. Do not substitute hulled or hull-less barley in this recipe. If using quick-cooking or presteamed barley (read the ingredient list on the package carefully to determine this), you will need to alter the barley cooking time in step 1.

- ¾ cup plain yogurt

- 2 teaspoons grated lemon zest, divided, plus 2 tablespoons juice, divided

- 2 tablespoons minced fresh mint, divided

- 1 teaspoon table salt, divided, plus salt for cooking barley

- ¼ teaspoon pepper

- 1 cup pearl barley

- 2 tablespoons plus 2 teaspoons extra-virgin olive oil, divided

- 8 ounces snow peas, strings removed and halved lengthwise

- 1 teaspoon ground coriander, divided

- ⅔ cup raw sunflower seeds

- ½ teaspoon ground cumin

- ⅛ teaspoon ground cardamom

- 1 avocado, halved, pitted, and cut into ½-inch pieces

1 Whisk yogurt, 1 teaspoon lemon zest and 1 tablespoon juice, 1 tablespoon mint, ½ teaspoon salt, and pepper together in small bowl; cover and refrigerate until ready to serve.

2 Bring 4 quarts water to boil in large pot. Add barley and 1 tablespoon salt and cook until tender, 20 to 25 minutes. Drain barley well. Meanwhile, whisk 2 tablespoons oil, remaining 1 teaspoon lemon zest and 1 tablespoon juice, and remaining 1 tablespoon mint together in large bowl and season with salt and pepper to taste. Stir in barley and toss to coat. Cover to keep warm.

3 While barley cooks, heat 1 teaspoon oil in 12-inch skillet over medium-high heat until just smoking. Add snow peas and ½ teaspoon coriander and cook until peas are spotty brown, about 3 minutes; add to bowl with barley and toss to combine.

4 Add remaining 1 teaspoon oil to now-empty skillet and heat over medium heat until shimmering. Stir in sunflower seeds, cumin, cardamom, remaining ½ teaspoon coriander, and remaining ½ teaspoon salt. Cook, stirring constantly, until seeds are toasted, about 2 minutes; let cool slightly off heat.

5 Portion barley into individual serving bowls, top with avocado and spiced sunflower seeds, and drizzle with yogurt sauce. Serve.

Beet Poke Bowl

Why This Recipe Works

When we set out to create a poke-inspired bowl using only plants, we tested all different vegetables to find out which one was up to the task. We found that beets, with their sturdy density, absorbent nature, and bright-pink color, made an apt stand-in for the typical seafood, like tuna or salmon. To start, we chopped the beets into bite-size pieces and softened them in the microwave. We then tossed the vegetable in a potent savory-sweet marinade flavored with classic poke seasonings such as rice vinegar, toasted sesame oil, and fresh ginger. We found that the beets must sit in the liquid for at least 30 minutes for the flavors to thoroughly infuse (you can marinate for up to 24 hours ahead). The end result was remarkably flavorful and well-seasoned beets that could give any seafood-based poke a run for its money. Rather than the more typical rice, we served the vegetable over chewy, resilient soba noodles, which we tossed in a bit of sesame oil to boost their flavor and slurpability. For a texturally dynamic bowl, we embellished it with carrots, cucumber, avocado, macadamia nuts, scallions, and a sprinkle of furikake. There are many different kinds of the Japanese seasoning blend furikake; we recommend using one that has dried seaweed (nori and/or kombu), bonito flakes, and sesame seeds. Look for it at Japanese or Asian grocery stores; you might also find it at some well-stocked supermarkets.

3 scallions, white and green parts separated and sliced thin on bias

2 tablespoons soy sauce

2 tablespoons vegetable oil

1 tablespoon unseasoned rice vinegar

4 teaspoons toasted sesame oil, divided

2 teaspoons grated fresh ginger

1 garlic clove, minced

¾ teaspoon red pepper flakes

2 pounds beets, trimmed, peeled, and cut into ¾-inch pieces

½ teaspoon table salt

12 ounces dried soba noodles

2 carrots, peeled and cut into 2-inch-long matchsticks

½ seedless English cucumber, halved lengthwise and sliced thin crosswise

1 ripe but firm avocado, halved, pitted, and sliced ¼ inch thick

⅓ cup finely chopped salted dry-roasted macadamia nuts or peanuts

Furikake (optional)

1 Combine scallion whites, soy sauce, vegetable oil, rice vinegar, 2 teaspoons sesame oil, ginger, garlic, and pepper flakes in large bowl; set aside. In separate bowl toss beets with ⅓ cup water and salt. Cover bowl and microwave until beets can be easily pierced with paring knife, 25 to 30 minutes, stirring halfway through microwaving. Drain beets in colander and transfer to bowl with reserved marinade. Refrigerate for at least 30 minutes or up to 24 hours.

2 Meanwhile, bring 4 quarts water to boil in large pot. Stir in noodles and cook according to package directions, stirring occasionally, until noodles are cooked through but still retain some chew. Drain noodles and rinse under cold water until chilled. Drain well.

3 Toss noodles with remaining 2 teaspoons sesame oil and divide among individual serving bowls. Top with marinated beets; carrots; cucumber; avocado; macadamia nuts; scallion greens; and furikake, if using. Serve.

Herby Grain Bowl with Fried Eggs and Pickled Edamame

Why This Recipe Works For a vibrantly green take on a grain bowl, we made the most of several jade-hued vegetables. To anchor the bowl, we used equal parts brown rice and farro for a chewy, fiber-rich base. To dress the grains, we made an herb paste from zesty cilantro, nutty garlic, and a serrano chile, which we blitzed with spinach to further boost the mixture's fiber and color. We bloomed this grass-green mixture in oil to amplify its flavors before coating the grains with it. Fried eggs with jammy yolks boosted the protein in this bowl while adding a rich, luscious component. The finishing touch was edamame, which we quickly pickled in a solution of vinegar, salt, and sugar; the legumes accented the bowl with bright tang and pleasantly dense bite. A food processor did a better job of crushing the herb paste than we could do by hand, but in a pinch you can mince the toasted garlic, cilantro, spinach, and serrano. Do not use quick-cooking farro or pearled farro in this recipe.

⅓ cup white wine vinegar

1 tablespoon sugar for pickling

½ teaspoon table salt for pickling

½ cup frozen edamame, thawed

¾ cup long-grain brown rice

¾ cup whole farro

1⅛ teaspoons table salt, divided, plus salt for cooking grains

10 ounces (10 cups) baby spinach, divided

1½ cups fresh cilantro, basil, and/or parsley

4 garlic cloves, minced, divided

1–2 serrano chiles, stemmed, seeded, and chopped coarse

3 tablespoons plus 2 teaspoons extra-virgin olive oil, divided, plus extra for drizzling

8 ounces green beans, trimmed and cut into 2-inch pieces

1 tablespoon lime juice, plus lime wedges for serving

4 large eggs

⅛ teaspoon pepper

1 Microwave vinegar, sugar, and ½ teaspoon salt in medium bowl until simmering, 1 to 2 minutes. Stir in edamame and let sit, stirring occasionally, for 45 minutes. Drain edamame in colander. (Drained pickled edamame can be refrigerated for up to 1 week.)

2 Meanwhile, bring 2 quarts water to boil in large saucepan over medium-high heat. Add rice, farro, and ½ teaspoon salt and cook, stirring occasionally, until rice and farro are tender, 20 to 25 minutes. Drain well and set aside.

3 Process 2 cups spinach, cilantro, half of garlic, serrano, and ¼ teaspoon salt in food processor until finely chopped, about 15 seconds, scraping down sides of bowl as needed; set aside.

4 Heat 1 tablespoon oil in skillet over medium-high heat until shimmering. Add green beans and ¼ teaspoon salt and cook until green beans are spotty brown, 1 to 2 minutes. Add 4 cups spinach, cover, and cook, stirring occasionally, until just wilted, 2 to 3 minutes. Add remaining 4 cups spinach and cook, covered, stirring occasionally, until all spinach is wilted but still bright green, 2 to 3 minutes. Add remaining half of garlic and cook until fragrant, about 30 seconds. Transfer to large bowl. Wipe skillet clean with paper towels.

5 Heat 2 tablespoons oil in now-empty skillet over medium-high heat until shimmering. Add reserved herb mixture and cook until fragrant, about 30 seconds. Add reserved drained grains and ½ teaspoon salt and stir to thoroughly combine. Cook until grains are warmed through, about 5 minutes. Transfer to bowl with vegetables, toss with lime juice, and season with salt and pepper to taste. Wipe skillet clean with paper towels.

6 Heat remaining 2 teaspoons oil in again-empty skillet over medium-high heat until shimmering. Meanwhile, crack 2 eggs into small bowl. Repeat with remaining 2 eggs and second small bowl. Sprinkle eggs with remaining ⅛ teaspoon salt and pepper. Working quickly, pour 1 bowl of eggs into 1 side of pan and second bowl of eggs into other side. Cover and cook for 1 minute. Remove skillet from heat and let sit, covered, 15 to 45 seconds for runny yolks (white around edge of yolk will be barely opaque), 45 to 60 seconds for soft but set yolks, and about 2 minutes for medium-set yolks.

7 Divide grain mixture among individual serving bowls then top with fried eggs and reserved pickled edamame. Drizzle with extra oil and serve with lime wedges.

Laksa Cauliflower Rice Bowl with Shrimp

Why This Recipe Works This spirited bowl gets its dynamic flavor profile from a homemade laksa paste—a popular building block for dishes across Southeast Asia (especially Malaysia, Singapore, and Indonesia). The versatile condiment can add an umami punch to all sorts of concoctions: soups, marinades, stir-fries, and grain bowls—like this easy one made with cauliflower rice. Many variations of the fragrant, spicy-savory seasoning exist, but most contain peppery galangal, floral lemongrass, and umami-rich dried shrimp. We also added citrusy makrut lime leaves and sweet-tangy tamarind for more complexity. Blitzing everything in a food processor made quick work of making the paste. To give the mixture its heat, we turned to arbol chiles. To streamline things, we cooked the cauliflower rice, green beans, and shrimp in the same skillet, adding the ingredients successively so they all finished cooking at the same time. Look for Thai/Indonesian-style tamarind concentrate labeled "nuoc me chua"; do not use Indian-style tamarind concentrates (see page 15 for more information). We like to make our laksa paste from scratch, but you can substitute ½ cup store-bought paste if you prefer (keep in mind that different brands vary in flavor and intensity). We strongly recommend sourcing galangal for its distinctive sharp, citrusy flavor, but if you can't find it, you can substitute ginger. We kept things simple when garnishing this bowl, but you can add thinly sliced Thai bird chiles, Thai basil leaves, cilantro leaves, thinly sliced scallions, and even Crispy Shallots (page 85).

Laksa Paste

- 2 dried arbol chiles, stemmed
- 4 teaspoons dried shrimp
- ¼ cup tamarind juice concentrate
- ½ onion, chopped
- 3 makrut lime leaves, middle vein removed and sliced thin crosswise
- 2 tablespoons raw cashews, chopped
- 2 stalks lemongrass, trimmed to bottom 6 inches, tough outer leaves discarded, halved lengthwise, and minced
- 1 tablespoon vegetable oil
- 1 (3-inch) piece galangal, chopped
- 3 garlic cloves, peeled
- 1 tablespoon packed dark brown sugar
- 1½ teaspoons ground coriander
- 1 teaspoon ground cumin
- ¾ teaspoon paprika
- ¾ teaspoon ground turmeric
- ¾ teaspoon table salt

Cauliflower Rice

- 1¼ cups water
- 20 ounces frozen cauliflower rice (6 cups)
- 8 ounces green beans, trimmed and halved crosswise into 2-inch lengths
- 8 ounces medium shrimp (41 to 50 per pound), peeled, deveined, and tails removed, split in half lengthwise
- 2 teaspoons fish sauce
- ¼ cup unsweetened coconut flakes, toasted
  Lime wedges

1 For the laksa paste Soak arbols and dried shrimp in warm water for 20 minutes, then drain well. Process soaked arbols and dried shrimp, tamarind, onion, lime leaves, cashews, lemongrass, oil, 2 tablespoons water, galangal, garlic, sugar, coriander, cumin, paprika, turmeric, and salt until mixture forms a mostly smooth paste, about 5 minutes, scraping down sides of bowl as needed; set aside.

2 For the cauliflower rice Heat 12-inch skillet over medium heat for 1 minute. Add laksa paste and water and cook until fragrant, about 1 minute, stirring constantly. Stir in frozen cauliflower rice and green beans; cover; and cook, stirring occasionally, until cauliflower rice is warmed through, about 6 minutes. Stir in shrimp; cover; and cook until shrimp is cooked through, 4 to 6 minutes.

3 Off heat, stir in fish sauce and season with salt to taste. Divide among individual serving bowls and sprinkle with coconut. Serve with lime wedges.

Sometimes it only takes one standout topping to make any ordinary bowl much more satisfying. Whether you want a satiation boost from some spicy-savory meatballs, or the irresistible crunch of a nutty, protein-rich topping, take one of these components for a spin in your next bowl.

Top Up Your Bowl

Crispy Tempeh

Makes 2 cups (enough for 4 to 6 bowls)
Total time: 30 minutes

- ⅓ cup soy sauce
- 1 pound tempeh, crumbled into ¼-inch pieces
- 1½ cups peanut or vegetable oil for frying

1 Bring 8 cups water and soy sauce to boil in large saucepan. Add tempeh, return to boil, and cook for 10 minutes. Drain tempeh well and wipe saucepan dry with paper towels.

2 Set wire rack in rimmed baking sheet and line with triple layer paper towels. Heat oil in now-empty dry saucepan over medium-high heat until shimmering. Add tempeh and cook until golden brown and crisp, about 12 minutes, adjusting heat as needed if tempeh begins to scorch. Using wire skimmer or slotted spoon, transfer tempeh to prepared sheet to drain, then season with salt and pepper to taste. Serve immediately.

Chipotle Shrimp

Makes 2¼ cups (enough for 4 to 6 bowls)
Total time: 15 minutes

- 1 pound extra-large shrimp (21 to 25 per pound), peeled, deveined, and tails removed
- ½ teaspoon chipotle chile powder
- ¼ teaspoon table salt
- ¼ teaspoon pepper
- 1 tablespoon extra-virgin olive oil or vegetable oil

Pat shrimp dry with paper towels and sprinkle with chipotle chili powder, salt, and pepper. Heat oil in 12-inch nonstick skillet over medium-high heat until just smoking. Add the shrimp in single layer and cook, without stirring, until spotty brown and edges turn pink on bottom side, about 1 minute. Flip shrimp and continue to cook until all but very center is opaque, about 30 seconds; transfer shrimp to plate. (Shrimp can be refrigerated for up to 2 days.)

Variation

Lemony Shrimp

Substitute 1½ teaspoons grated lemon zest for chipotle chile powder.

Gochujang Meatballs

Makes 16 meatballs (enough for 4 to 6 bowls)
Total time: 40 minutes

Even after thorough cooking, the meatballs may retain some pink color; use an instant-read thermometer to ensure that they're cooked to temperature before serving.

- ¼ cup water
- 3 tablespoons gochujang
- 3 tablespoons soy sauce
- 2 tablespoons toasted sesame oil
- 2 tablespoons honey
- 1 tablespoon unseasoned rice vinegar
- 3 garlic cloves, minced, divided
- 1¼ teaspoons grated fresh ginger, divided
- 1 pound 85 percent lean ground beef
- ½ cup panko bread crumbs
- 2 large eggs, lightly beaten
- 3 scallions, white parts minced, green parts sliced thin on bias
- ¾ teaspoon table salt
- ¼ teaspoon pepper
- 1 teaspoon vegetable oil
- 2 tablespoons sesame seeds, toasted

1 Adjust oven rack to upper-middle position and heat oven to 400 degrees. Whisk water, gochujang, soy sauce, sesame oil, honey, rice vinegar, one-third of garlic, and ¼ teaspoon ginger together in bowl; set aside.

2 Spray rimmed baking sheet with vegetable oil spray. Combine beef, panko, eggs, scallion whites, salt, pepper, remaining garlic, and remaining 1 teaspoon ginger and mix with your hands until thoroughly combined. Divide mixture into 16 portions. Roll portions between your wet hands to form meatballs and arrange on prepared sheet. Transfer to oven and roast until meatballs register 160 degrees, 16 to 20 minutes.

3 Heat vegetable oil in 12-inch nonstick skillet over medium-high heat until just smoking. Add meatballs and reserved gochujang mixture and cook until sauce thickens, about 2 minutes, gently turning meatballs to coat. (Meatballs and sauce can be refrigerated for up to 2 days. Sprinkle with scallion greens and sesame seeds just before serving.)

Savory Seed Brittle

Makes 2 cups
Total time: 1¼ hours, plus 1 hour cooling

Do not substitute quick or instant oats in this recipe.

- 2 tablespoons maple syrup
- 1 large egg white
- 1 tablespoon extra-virgin olive oil or vegetable oil
- 1 tablespoon soy sauce
- 1 tablespoon caraway seeds, crushed
- ½ teaspoon table salt
- ¼ teaspoon pepper
- ½ cup old-fashioned rolled oats
- ⅓ cup raw sunflower seeds
- ⅓ cup raw, unsalted pepitas
- 2 tablespoons sesame seeds
- 2 tablespoons nigella seeds

1 Adjust oven rack to upper-middle position and heat oven to 300 degrees. Line 8-inch square baking pan with parchment paper and spray parchment with vegetable oil spray. Whisk maple syrup, egg white, oil, soy sauce, caraway seeds, salt, and pepper together in large bowl. Stir in oats, sunflower seeds, pepitas, sesame seeds, and nigella seeds until well combined.

2 Transfer oat mixture to prepared pan and spread into even layer. Using stiff metal spatula, press oat mixture until very compact. Bake until golden brown and fragrant, 45 to 55 minutes, rotating pan halfway through baking.

3 Transfer pan to wire rack and let brittle cool completely, about 1 hour. Break cooled brittle into pieces of desired size, discarding parchment. (Brittle can be stored in airtight container at room temperature for up to 1 month.)

Burgers, Sandwiches, Tacos & More

Mushroom-Beef Blended Burgers

Why This Recipe Works Our blended burger, which replaces a portion of the meat with mushrooms, is a great option for those who want to eat less beef but still crave the experience of eating a deeply savory, succulent patty. Mushrooms are brimming with glutamates that complement the nucleotides in beef, creating a deeply umami taste. We started by processing white mushrooms to a paste before microwaving them to remove some excess moisture; this ensured that the patties would cook up juicy but not wet. Using a food processor, we combined the paste with 80 percent lean ground beef. A high fat content helped these burgers taste meaty, as beef fat contains the aromatic compounds that give the meat its characteristic flavor. Adding salt to the beef before blitzing it with the mushrooms developed a sturdy myosin network that held the patties together. To ensure that the patties cooked up to the best texture, we heated them to at least 135 degrees; any lower, and they turned out too wet to mimic a standard all-beef patty. The final result was a burger so succulent that we forgot we weren't eating an all-beef version. In step 4, if all of the patties do not fit in the skillet, start by cooking three patties until they shrink slightly, about 2 minutes, before adding the remaining patty. To achieve the tender, cohesive texture of an all-beef burger at your preferred level of doneness, cook these to 10 degrees higher than you would an all-beef patty. We like to serve these with cheese, but you can omit if you prefer. Top with your favorite burger toppings; we like tomato, lettuce, and onion.

12 ounces white mushrooms, trimmed

1 pound 80 percent lean ground beef, broken into rough 1½-inch pieces

1¼ teaspoons kosher salt

½–2 teaspoons pepper

1½ teaspoons vegetable oil

4 slices American, Swiss, or cheddar cheese (optional)

4 hamburger buns, toasted

1 Process mushrooms in food processor until smooth paste forms (paste will resemble thick oatmeal), scraping down sides of bowl as needed, about 1 minute. Transfer to large bowl and cover. (Do not wash out processor bowl.)

2 Microwave mushrooms until liquid released begins to boil, about 3 minutes, stirring halfway through. (Do not walk away during final minute; mushrooms could boil over.) Transfer mushrooms to large fine-mesh strainer set over bowl. Using spatula, press on mushrooms to extract ½ cup liquid (if more than ½ cup is removed, stir extra liquid back into mushrooms). Discard liquid and return mushrooms to bowl. Refrigerate mushrooms until room temperature, about 20 minutes.

3 Return mushrooms to processor bowl. Add beef and salt and process until mixture is uniform and begins to pull away from sides of bowl, about 20 seconds. Divide mixture into 4 equal portions and shape into patties that are 4½ inches in diameter. Sprinkle both sides of each patty with pepper. (Patties can be refrigerated overnight or tightly wrapped and frozen for up to 1 month; if frozen, thaw before cooking.)

4 Heat oil in 12-inch skillet over medium-high heat until shimmering. Transfer patties to skillet and cook until well browned on both sides and burgers register 135 degrees (for medium-rare) or 155 degrees (for medium-well), 6 to 10 minutes. If using cheese, place 1 slice on each burger 1 minute before burgers finish cooking. Transfer burgers to plate and let rest for 5 minutes, then transfer to buns and serve.

Bacon and Cheese Black Bean Burgers

Why This Recipe Works Just because a burger patty is vegetarian doesn't mean it can't use a savory boost from a little meat. Here, we topped bean patties with slices of bacon for a small but impactful dose of smokiness. Starchy black beans are a superb candidate for patties, but many versions turn out crumbly. To help them keep their shape while packing all the flavor one expects from a crave-worthy burger, we pulsed the beans with tortilla chips, a binder with just the right amount of absorbency and saltiness. We then added egg and flour and chilled this mixture, which gave the starches time to soak up the eggs' moisture and further improved the patties' cohesiveness. To evoke the richness of their beefier cousins, we seasoned the patties with porcini powder, a secret weapon for more savoriness. To echo the experience of a classic bacon cheeseburger, we topped the patties with American cheese and spread our Classic Burger Sauce on the buns. Use a spice grinder to grind the porcini mushrooms; alternatively, you can use ⅓ cup porcini powder. These patties freeze well, so you can save any extra for future burger hankerings. Top with your favorite burger toppings; we like tomato, shredded lettuce, onion, and dill pickles.

- 2 (15-ounce) cans black beans, rinsed
- 2 large eggs
- 2 tablespoons all-purpose flour
- ½ ounce dried porcini mushrooms, ground to fine powder
- 2 garlic cloves, minced
- 1 teaspoon onion powder
- ¼ teaspoon pepper
- ⅛ teaspoon table salt
- 1 ounce tortilla chips, crushed coarse (½ cup)
- 8 teaspoons vegetable oil, divided
- 6 slices American cheese (4½ ounces)
- 6 slices bacon, halved crosswise
- 6 tablespoons Classic Burger Sauce (page 244)
- 6 hamburger buns

1 Line rimmed baking sheet with triple layer of paper towels and spread beans over paper towels; let stand for 15 minutes. Meanwhile, whisk eggs and flour in large bowl until well combined. Stir in porcini powder, garlic, onion powder, pepper, and salt until well combined.

2 Process tortilla chips in food processor until finely ground, about 30 seconds. Add drained black beans and pulse until beans are roughly broken down, about 5 pulses. Transfer black bean mixture to bowl with egg mixture and mix until well combined. Cover and refrigerate for at least 1 hour or up to 24 hours.

3 Adjust oven rack to middle position and heat oven to 200 degrees. Divide bean mixture into 6 equal portions. Firmly pack each portion into tight ball, then flatten to 3½-inch-wide patty. (Patties can be wrapped individually in plastic wrap, placed in a zipper-lock bag, and frozen for up to 1 month. Thaw patties before cooking.)

4 Heat 2 teaspoons oil in 10-inch nonstick skillet over medium heat until shimmering. Carefully place 3 patties in skillet and cook until bottoms are well browned and crisp, about 5 minutes. Flip patties, add 2 teaspoons oil to center of skillet, top each burger with cheese, and cook until second side is well browned and crisp, 3 to 5 minutes. Transfer burgers to wire rack set in rimmed baking sheet and place in oven to keep warm. Repeat with remaining 3 patties, 3 slices cheese, and 4 teaspoons oil.

5 Place 6 half slices bacon in single layer in now-empty skillet. Increase heat to medium-high and cook until crispy, about 6 minutes, flipping as needed. Transfer to paper towel–lined plate. Repeat with remaining bacon.

6 Spread burger sauce evenly over bun bottoms then top with burgers, bacon, and bun tops. Serve.

Black Bean Mole Burgers

Why This Recipe Works These sturdy black bean patties are extra-flavorful and sure to satisfy your burger cravings. Drawing inspiration from the complex and assertive heat in Oaxacan moles, we layered three forms of chile peppers: ancho chile powder for its earthy aroma, smoked paprika for a whisper of sweetness, and canned chipotles in adobo sauce for smokiness. This gave us well-seasoned, deeply aromatic patties. To ensure the patties held their shape, we found a ratio of panko bread crumbs, pepitas, and sesame seeds that did an excellent job at binding the mixture. Briefly chilling the patties further improved their cohesiveness. To build a gratifyingly crispy crust while keeping the inside tender, we browned them over low heat. Top with your favorite burger toppings; we like our Quick Sweet and Spicy Pickled Red Onion (page 33) and Avocado Crema (page 244).

½ cup panko bread crumbs

2 tablespoons raw, unsalted pepitas

¾ teaspoon ground cumin

¾ teaspoon ancho chile powder

½ teaspoon smoked paprika

¼ teaspoon ground allspice

⅛ teaspoon ground cinnamon

1 (15-ounce) can black beans, rinsed, divided

⅓ cup finely chopped onion

1 large egg, lightly beaten

2 tablespoons sesame seeds, toasted

2 tablespoons golden raisins

2 tablespoons chopped fresh cilantro

2 garlic cloves, minced

1½ teaspoons minced canned chipotle chile in adobo sauce, plus ½ teaspoon adobo sauce

1 teaspoon table salt

¼ teaspoon grated lime zest plus 1½ teaspoons juice

1 tablespoon extra-virgin olive oil, divided

4 hamburger buns, toasted if desired

1 Line rimmed baking sheet with parchment paper. Process panko in food processor until finely ground, about 30 seconds. Add pepitas and process until finely chopped, about 15 seconds; transfer to large bowl. Toast cumin, ancho chile powder, paprika, allspice, and cinnamon in 10-inch nonstick skillet over medium heat, stirring occasionally, until spices are fragrant and begin to darken slightly, about 1 minute; add to bowl with panko mixture.

2 Add half of beans, onion, egg, sesame seeds, raisins, cilantro, garlic, chipotle and adobo sauce, salt, and lime zest and juice to now-empty processor and process until coarsely ground, about 20 seconds, scraping down sides of bowl as needed; add to bowl with panko mixture.

3 Stir remaining beans into bean-panko mixture, then divide into 4 equal portions. Using your lightly moistened hands, firmly pack each portion into 3½-inch-wide patty and place on prepared sheet. Cover and refrigerate until chilled and firm, at least 30 minutes or up to 24 hours.

4 Heat ½ tablespoon oil in 12-inch nonstick skillet over medium heat until shimmering. Reduce heat to low and carefully place patties in skillet. Cook until burgers are crisp and deep golden brown on first side, about 7 minutes. Gently flip patties, add remaining ½ tablespoon oil to center of skillet, and cook until crisp and golden brown on second side, 5 to 7 minutes. Transfer burgers to buns and serve.

Turkey-Zucchini Burgers with Cranberry Relish

Why This Recipe Works

This turkey burger is tender and juicy, thanks in large part to the loads of shredded zucchini mixed in with the meat. The zucchini didn't require any precooking; simply squeezing it dry to eliminate excess moisture before kneading it into the ground turkey gave us the most succulent results. Poultry seasoning—which usually includes herbs like sage, thyme, marjoram, and rosemary—boosted the patties' savory flavor, which contrasted nicely with the subtle sweetness of the zucchini. Before cooking the patties, we pressed down on the center of each one with our fingertips; this divot prevented the center from bulging up when cooked. A dollop of sweet-tart cranberry relish—cooked quickly on the stovetop with sugar and cider vinegar until the berries burst and thickened—plus a scattering of peppery baby arugula made bright finishing touches. Use the large holes of a box grater to shred the zucchini. Be sure to use ground turkey, not ground turkey breast (also labeled 99 percent fat-free), in this recipe, as the latter will result in dry, less flavorful burgers.

Cranberry Relish

- 1 cup fresh or frozen cranberries
- ¼ cup sugar
- 2 tablespoons cider vinegar
- ⅛ teaspoon table salt

Burgers

- 1 pound ground turkey
- 12 ounces zucchini, shredded (3 cups)
- 1½ teaspoons poultry seasoning
- ¾ teaspoon table salt
- ½ teaspoon pepper
- 1 tablespoon vegetable oil
- 4 thin slices sharp cheddar cheese or smoked gouda cheese
- 4 hamburger buns, toasted
- 2 ounces baby arugula or 4 leaves Boston or bibb lettuce

1 For the cranberry relish Bring all ingredients to boil in 12-inch nonstick skillet over medium-high heat. Cook until cranberries burst and mixture starts to thicken, stirring and mashing cranberries slightly, 2 to 4 minutes. Transfer to bowl and set aside to cool while making burgers.

2 For the burgers Break ground turkey into small pieces in large bowl. Place shredded zucchini in dish towel. Gather dish towel ends together and twist tightly over sink to drain as much liquid as possible from zucchini. Add drained zucchini, poultry seasoning, salt, and pepper to turkey in bowl and knead gently with your hands until well combined. Divide turkey mixture into 4 equal portions, then gently shape each portion into ¾-inch-thick patty. Using your fingertips, press center of each patty down until about ½ inch thick, creating slight divot.

3 Heat oil in clean, dry, now-empty skillet over medium-low heat until shimmering. Transfer patties to skillet, divot side up, and cook until well browned on first side, 4 to 7 minutes. Flip patties and continue to cook until browned on second side and burgers register 160 degrees, 4 to 7 minutes; 1 minute before burgers finish cooking, top each burger with 1 slice cheese. Transfer burgers to plate and let rest for 5 minutes. Transfer burgers to buns, top with reserved cranberry relish and arugula, and serve.

Variation

Turkey-Zucchini Burgers with Smashed Ranch Avocado

Omit cranberry relish and arugula. Substitute Monterey jack cheese for sharp cheddar cheese. Roughly mash one ripe, halved, and pitted avocado with 1 tablespoon chopped fresh cilantro or dill, 1 teaspoon lime juice, ¼ teaspoon table salt, and ¼ teaspoon pepper in bowl. Before serving, top each burger with avocado mixture, 1 thin slice tomato, and 1 thin slice red onion.

Crispy Chickpea Cakes with Zucchini Ribbon Salad

Why This Recipe Works We love the crisp-tender texture and nutty, earthy flavor of our popular falafel recipe, but it takes time and elbow grease to make. For a similar eating experience with less work, we streamlined the chickpea mixture from that recipe and turned it into crispy cakes. By pulsing chickpeas, aromatics, and spices in a food processor, we created a cohesive blend ideal for shaping and pan-frying. To make a complete meal, we paired the cakes with a bright zucchini ribbon salad. Use a vegetable peeler or a mandoline to shave the zucchini. We like to serve these with our Tahini-Yogurt Sauce, but you can use Avocado Crema (page 244) or, in a pinch, simply seasoned Greek yogurt if you prefer.

Zucchini Salad

- ¼   cup minced fresh mint
- 3   tablespoons extra-virgin olive oil
- 2   tablespoons lemon juice
- 1   tablespoon plain Greek yogurt
- ½   teaspoon honey
- 3   small zucchini (6 ounces each), shaved lengthwise into ribbons
- 2   tablespoons finely chopped pitted kalamata olives

Chickpea Cakes

- 1½   cups fresh cilantro leaves and stems
- ½   onion, chopped
- 1½   teaspoons ground coriander
- 1   teaspoon ground cumin
- 1   teaspoon table salt
- ½   teaspoon baking powder
- ¼   teaspoon cayenne pepper
- 1   large egg
- 2   (15-ounce) cans chickpeas, rinsed and patted dry
- ¼   cup all-purpose flour
- 3   tablespoons extra-virgin olive oil
- 1   recipe Tahini-Yogurt Sauce (page 244)

1 For the zucchini salad Whisk mint, oil, lemon juice, yogurt, and honey together in medium bowl. Add zucchini ribbons and toss gently to coat. Sprinkle with olives and refrigerate until ready to serve.

2 For the chickpea cakes Process cilantro, onion, coriander, cumin, salt, baking powder, and cayenne in food processor for 5 seconds. Scrape down sides of bowl. Continue to process until mixture resembles pesto, about 5 seconds longer. Add egg and process for 5 seconds. Add chickpeas and flour and pulse 4 times. Scrape down sides of bowl. Continue to pulse until chickpeas are coarsely chopped and flour is fully incorporated, about 4 more pulses.

3 Spray rimmed baking sheet with vegetable oil spray. Remove food processor blade and, using ½ cup measure, drop 6 even portions (about scant ½ cup each) onto prepared sheet. Gently shape into patties about 3 inches in diameter.

4 Line cutting board with single layer of paper towels. Heat oil in 12-inch nonstick skillet over medium-high heat until shimmering. Using thin spatula, carefully transfer patties to skillet. Cook for 4 minutes, then reduce heat to medium-low; cover; and continue to cook until tops are firm to touch and patties register 185 degrees, 7 to 9 minutes. Transfer patties to prepared board, browned side down. Invert cakes to browned side up and serve with tahini-yogurt sauce and zucchini salad.

Curried Millet Burgers with Peach-Ginger Chutney

Why This Recipe Works Millet releases a sticky starch as it cooks, so the grain is ideal for making patties. We combined it with spinach and carrot for vegetal flavor, as well as minced shallot for subtle sweetness and depth. Yogurt and an egg, as binding agents, added moisture and richness. Curry powder gave us a warmly spiced flavor profile that paired well with a sweet-savory peach chutney; frozen peaches made the condiment easy to whip up. Pan-frying the patties was key for a crackly crust and soft interior. These burgers are dense, so we ditched the buns in favor of crunchy lettuce leaves.

Peach-Ginger Chutney

- 1 shallot, minced
- 1 tablespoon vegetable oil
- 1 teaspoon grated fresh ginger
- ⅛ teaspoon table salt
-    Pinch red pepper flakes
- 1½ cups thawed frozen peaches, cut into ½-inch pieces
- 2 tablespoons packed light brown sugar
- 2 tablespoons cider vinegar

Burgers

- 1 cup millet, rinsed
- 2 cups water
- 1 teaspoon table salt, divided
- 3 tablespoons vegetable oil, divided
- 1 shallot, minced
- 6 ounces (6 cups) baby spinach, chopped
- 2 carrots, peeled and shredded
- 2 teaspoons curry powder
- ¼ teaspoon pepper
- ½ cup plain yogurt, divided
- 1 large egg, lightly beaten
- 2 tablespoons minced fresh cilantro
- 8 large leaves iceberg lettuce

1 For the chutney Microwave shallot, oil, ginger, salt, and pepper flakes in small bowl, stirring occasionally, until shallot has softened, about 1 minute. Stir in peaches, sugar, and vinegar and microwave until peaches have softened and mixture has thickened, 6 to 8 minutes, stirring once halfway through microwaving. Set aside to cool to room temperature. (Chutney can be refrigerated for up to 3 days; let come to room temperature before serving.)

2 For the burgers Line rimmed baking sheet with parchment paper. Combine millet, water, and ½ teaspoon salt in medium saucepan and bring to simmer over medium-high heat. Reduce heat to low, cover, and simmer gently until millet is tender, 15 to 20 minutes. Off heat, let millet sit, covered, until liquid is fully absorbed, about 10 minutes. Transfer millet to large bowl and let cool for 15 minutes.

3 Heat 1 tablespoon oil in 12-inch nonstick skillet over medium heat until shimmering. Add shallot and cook until softened, about 3 minutes. Stir in spinach and carrots and cook until spinach is wilted, about 2 minutes. Stir in curry powder, pepper, and remaining ½ teaspoon salt and cook until fragrant, about 30 seconds; transfer to bowl with millet. Wipe skillet clean with paper towels.

4 Stir ¼ cup yogurt, egg, and cilantro into millet mixture until well combined. Divide mixture into 4 equal portions. Using your lightly moistened hands, firmly pack each portion into ¾-inch-thick patty and place on prepared sheet. Reshape patties as needed. Cover and refrigerate until chilled and firm, at least 30 minutes or up to 24 hours.

5 Heat remaining 2 tablespoons oil in now-empty skillet over medium-low heat until shimmering. Place patties in skillet and cook until golden brown and crisp on first side, 5 to 7 minutes. Using 2 spatulas, gently flip patties and cook until browned and crisp on second side, 5 to 7 minutes.

6 Stack lettuce leaves together to create 4 lettuce cups. Serve burgers on lettuce wraps, topped with remaining ¼ cup yogurt and peach chutney.

Pulled Jackfruit and Chicken Sandwiches

Why This Recipe Works   Ripe jackfruit may taste like a combination of papaya, pineapple, and mango, but immature jackfruit is entirely different: dense, vegetal, and fibrous. The latter, when cooked and shredded, has a tender, stringy texture remarkably reminiscent of pulled chicken or pork, so it's no surprise that the tropical ingredient—long beloved in many Asian cultures—is becoming a popular meat alternative all over the world. The fruit has a knack for soaking up seasoning, so tossing it with shredded chicken smothered in a smoky-sweet sauce boosted the fiber content of these sandwiches without sacrificing flavor. To prepare the jackfruit, we simmered it to slightly soften the texture. In true pulled-meat-sandwich fashion, we soaked cabbage and carrot in an oil-vinegar solution to make a tangy slaw. We layered the jackfruit-chicken mixture and slaw onto hamburger buns for a satisfyingly juicy handheld meal. Be sure to use young (unripe) jackfruit packed in brine or water; do not use mature jackfruit packed in syrup. Jackfruit seeds are tender and edible; there is no need to remove them. To minimize added sugar and salt, we like to use our Easy Barbecue Sauce, but you can use store-bought if you prefer. You can also substitute 1¾ cups shredded cole-slaw mix for the red cabbage and carrot.

1   (20-ounce) can young green jackfruit packed in brine or water, drained

2   slices bacon, chopped fine

4   scallions, white and green parts separated and sliced thin

2   garlic cloves, minced

¾   cup Easy Barbecue Sauce (page 245)

12   ounces boneless skinless chicken thighs, trimmed

2   tablespoons cider vinegar

1   tablespoon extra-virgin olive oil

¼   teaspoon table salt

⅛   teaspoon pepper

1½   cups shredded red cabbage

1   carrot, peeled and shredded

4   hamburger buns, toasted

   Dill pickle chips (optional)

1   Place jackfruit in large saucepan, cover with water, and bring to boil over high heat. Reduce heat to medium and simmer for 10 minutes. Drain jackfruit in strainer, rinse well, and shake strainer to drain thoroughly. Transfer jackfruit to cutting board. Using potato masher, 2 forks, or your hands, shred jackfruit into bite-size pieces, then chop coarse with knife. Set aside.

2   Add bacon to now-empty saucepan and cook over medium-low heat until crispy, 4 to 7 minutes. Add scallion whites and garlic and cook, stirring occasionally, until scallions soften, about 2 minutes. Stir in barbecue sauce and 2 tablespoons water, scraping up any browned bits. Nestle chicken into sauce; cover; and simmer until chicken registers 175 degrees, 8 to 12 minutes, flipping chicken halfway through cooking.

3   Remove saucepan from heat. Transfer chicken to plate and let cool slightly. Using 2 forks, shred chicken fine. Return shredded chicken and reserved shredded jackfruit to saucepan and stir to coat evenly in sauce. Cook over medium-low heat until chicken and jackfruit are heated through, 2 to 4 minutes, stirring occasionally.

4   Whisk cider vinegar, oil, salt, and pepper together in medium bowl. Add cabbage, carrot, and scallion greens and toss to coat. Divide chicken and jackfruit mixture among bun bottoms; top with slaw and bun tops. Top with pickles, if using, and serve.

Philly-Style Sausage and Broccoli Rabe Subs with Portobello

Why This Recipe Works A sub roll stuffed with juicy roasted pork, garlicky greens, melty provolone, and vinegary hot peppers is a superbly satisfying Philadelphia icon. To reimagine the sandwich with less meat, we first swapped in Italian sausage, which has more intense flavor packed into a smaller amount of meat—just 8 ounces for 4 substantial sandwiches. Using sausage also made the recipe simpler and quicker. We browned the sausage to render its fat and then cooked portobellos in the meat's flavorful juices. Mushrooms are excellent sponges, so we amped up the fat's flavor with fennel seeds and rosemary, plus soy sauce for extra umami. Instead of melting cheese on top, we stirred it into our mushroom-meat mixture as both a binder and seasoning. As it melted, the cheese oozed delightfully throughout our filling. These subs should be fully stuffed, so we removed much of the rolls' interior crumb to ensure that the fillings wouldn't spill out. To crack fennel, use a mortar and pestle or place the seeds on a cutting board and rock the bottom edge of a skillet over them until they crack. You will need a 12-inch nonstick skillet with a tight-fitting lid for this recipe.

4 (8-inch) Italian sub rolls

3 tablespoons extra-virgin oil, divided

3 garlic cloves, sliced thin

1 pound broccoli rabe, trimmed and cut into ½-inch pieces

¼ plus ⅛ teaspoon table salt, divided

8 ounces Italian sausage, casings removed

1 pound portobello mushroom caps, sliced ¼ inch thick

1 teaspoon fennel seeds, cracked

1 teaspoon minced fresh rosemary

1 teaspoon soy sauce

4 ounces shredded fontina or sharp provolone cheese

2 tablespoons sliced jarred hot cherry peppers (optional)

1 Adjust oven rack to middle position and heat oven to 450 degrees. If needed, slice rolls to make them easier to open (without slicing all the way through). Use spoon to scrape inside of roll and remove all but ¼ inch of interior crumb; discard removed crumb. Set rolls aside.

2 Heat 1 tablespoon oil and sliced garlic in 12-inch nonstick skillet over medium heat until garlic is light golden, 3 to 5 minutes. Add broccoli rabe and ¼ teaspoon salt and cook, stirring occasionally, until tender, 4 to 6 minutes. Transfer to bowl and cover to keep warm.

3 Heat 1 teaspoon oil in now-empty skillet over medium-high heat until just smoking. Add sausage and cook, breaking up meat into small pieces with wooden spoon, until lightly browned, about 5 minutes. Transfer to clean bowl.

4 Add 1 tablespoon oil to fat left in skillet and heat over medium-high heat until shimmering. Add mushrooms and remaining ⅛ teaspoon salt. Cover and cook, stirring occasionally, until mushrooms have released their liquid, 3 to 5 minutes. Uncover and continue to cook, stirring occasionally, until well browned, 5 to 7 minutes. Reduce heat to low. Clear center of skillet and add remaining 2 teaspoons oil, fennel seeds, and rosemary. Stir in soy sauce and cooked sausage, then stir in cheese until melted. Remove from heat and cover to keep warm.

5 Arrange reserved rolls on rimmed baking sheet and bake until lightly toasted, about 3 minutes. Divide mushroom mixture and broccoli rabe evenly among rolls. Top with cherry peppers, if using, and serve.

Scooping Sub Rolls

1 If needed, use bread knife to slice sub rolls, making them easier to fold open.

2 Use spoon to scrap inside of roll and remove all but ¼ inch of interior crumb.

Tofu Katsu Sandwiches

Why This Recipe Works Katsu, the breaded and deep-fried Japanese specialty usually made with pork or chicken cutlets, is prime comfort food. The sandwiches of the same name take the meat a step further, layering it with shredded cabbage between slices of fluffy Japanese milk bread. Here, to develop a no-less-rewarding version that skips the meat, we swapped in slabs of tofu. The ingredient added nutty flavor and allowed us to retain the dish's signature crackly shell and tender interior—while packing a protein punch. To help the panko crust adhere, we skipped the traditional three-stage breading and instead dredged slabs of tofu in an egg-flour mixture, which created a glue-like paste to lock in the panko. To make the savory-sweet tonkatsu sauce, we simply whisked together ketchup, Worcestershire, soy sauce, garlic powder, and a pinch of sugar. Last but not least, the crunchy cabbage needed nothing more than a quick toss with rice vinegar, toasted sesame oil, and a little more sugar before it was ready to be piled atop bread and katsu and drizzled with sauce. If you can find it, use milk bread, which is typical of katsu sandwiches; the fluffy slices contrast delightfully with the crisp tofu. You can substitute coleslaw mix for the shredded cabbage, and bottled tonkatsu sauce for our homemade recipe, if you prefer.

Tonkatsu Sauce

- ¼ cup ketchup
- 4 teaspoons Worcestershire sauce or vegan Worcestershire sauce
- 2 teaspoons soy sauce
- 1 teaspoon garlic powder
- ½ teaspoon sugar

Sandwiches

- 2 large eggs
- 2 tablespoons soy sauce
- 1 tablespoon all-purpose flour
- 1½ cups panko bread crumbs
- 14 ounces extra-firm tofu, cut crosswise into 8 slabs
- ½ cup vegetable oil, for frying
- 1¼ teaspoons unseasoned rice vinegar
- ¾ teaspoon toasted sesame oil
- ¼ teaspoon sugar
- 1½ cups shredded red or green cabbage
- 8 slices soft white sandwich bread

1 For the tonkatsu sauce Whisk all ingredients together in bowl; set aside.

2 For the sandwiches Set wire rack in rimmed baking sheet and line half of rack with triple layer of paper towels. Whisk eggs, soy sauce, and flour together in shallow dish. Place panko in large zipper-lock bag and lightly crush with rolling pin; transfer to second shallow dish. Pat tofu dry with paper towels. Working with 1 tofu slab at a time, dredge in egg mixture, allowing excess to drip off, then coat all sides with panko, pressing gently to adhere. Transfer to unlined side of wire rack.

3 Heat vegetable oil in 12-inch nonstick skillet over medium-high heat until shimmering. Add half of tofu and cook until deep golden brown, 2 to 3 minutes per side. Transfer to lined side of wire rack and repeat with remaining tofu.

4 Combine vinegar, sesame oil, and sugar in small bowl. Add cabbage and toss to coat. Season with salt and pepper to taste. Arrange cabbage and tofu on 4 slices of bread. Drizzle with reserved sauce and top with remaining bread slices. Serve.

Bánh Xèo

Why This Recipe Works Bánh xèo is a Vietnamese dish of spectacularly varied flavors, colors, and textures. The centerpiece is a sizzling, turmeric-dyed crepe made with rice flour and coconut milk, often filled with small shrimp and pork belly. Eaters tuck the crisp-tender crepes into lettuce leaves with Thai basil and cilantro; the fresh vegetables make wonderful foils to the rich crepes. To develop a version that cuts down on meat while being just as craveable, we opted for more readily available medium-large shrimp while omitting the pork and swapping in daikon; the fibrous texture of the vegetable lent the filling a meaty quality and also upped the fiber in the recipe. The crepe came together in one skillet: We stir-fried the daikon, onion, and shrimp and then pushed the mixture to one side of the pan and poured in the batter. When the batter hit the hot skillet, it sizzled audibly, a good indication that a shatteringly crispy exterior was developing. After adding a portion of the shrimp-daikon filling, we placed a handful of bean sprouts on the filled side of the crepe, then cooked the crepe until the bottom turned crisp. Finally, we folded the crepe in half to cover the filling. Using hot water in the batter helped minimize the gritty texture that rice flour can have, while cornstarch absorbed extra moisture so that the crepe could crisp up on the stovetop. (Be sure not to use boiling water, which can cause the cornstarch to overly thicken the batter.) To serve on the side, we whipped up a batch of tangy, crunchy đồ chua, the pickled carrot-daikon dish popular in Vietnam. And no bánh xèo meal is complete without its traditional dipping sauce: nuoc cham, the sweet, spicy, tangy, and umami condiment made from sugar, chiles, garlic, fish sauce, and lime juice. Use hot tap water, not boiling water, in the crepe batter. We prefer the flavor of regular coconut milk, but you can substitute light coconut milk if you prefer. Make sure to thoroughly stir the coconut milk before measuring.

Nuoc Cham

3 tablespoons sugar, divided

1 small Thai chile, stemmed and minced

1 garlic clove, minced

2/3 cup hot water

3 tablespoons fish sauce

¼ cup lime juice (2 limes)

Crepes

1 head Boston lettuce (8 ounces), leaves separated and left whole

1 cup fresh Thai basil leaves

1 cup fresh cilantro leaves and thin stems

1 cup hot water (120 to 130 degrees)

½ cup (3 ounces) white rice flour

3 tablespoons cornstarch

½ teaspoon ground turmeric

⅛ teaspoon table salt

3 tablespoons vegetable oil, divided

6 ounces daikon radish, peeled and cut into ½-inch pieces

1 small red onion, halved and sliced thin

8 ounces medium-large shrimp (31 to 40 per pound), peeled, deveined, and tails removed, halved crosswise then halved lengthwise

⅓ cup canned coconut milk

6 ounces (3 cups) bean sprouts, divided

1 recipe Đồ Chua (recipe follows)

1 **For the nuoc cham** Using mortar and pestle (or using flat side of chef's knife on cutting board), mash 1 tablespoon sugar, Thai chile, and garlic to fine paste. Transfer to medium bowl and add hot water and remaining 2 tablespoons sugar. Stir until sugar is dissolved. Stir in fish sauce and lime juice. Divide sauce among 4 individual small serving bowls; set aside.

2 **For the crepes** Adjust oven rack to middle position and heat oven to 275 degrees. Set wire rack in rimmed baking sheet, spray rack with vegetable oil spray, and set aside. Arrange lettuce, basil, and cilantro on serving platter; set aside. Whisk hot water, rice flour, cornstarch, turmeric, and salt in bowl until smooth.

3 Heat 1 teaspoon oil in 12-inch nonstick skillet over medium-high heat until shimmering. Add daikon and onion and cook, stirring occasionally, until lightly browned and just softened, 5 to 7 minutes. Add shrimp and continue to cook, stirring occasionally, until shrimp just begins to turn pink, about 2 minutes. Transfer to second bowl. Wipe skillet clean with paper towels. Whisk coconut milk and 2 teaspoons oil into rice flour mixture.

4 Heat 2 teaspoons oil in now-empty skillet over medium-high heat until just smoking. Add one-third of daikon mixture and cook until sizzling, about 30 seconds. Push daikon mixture to one half of skillet, then pour ½ cup batter evenly over entire skillet, tilting skillet as needed to distribute batter evenly. Scatter 1 cup bean sprouts over side with daikon mixture, then reduce heat to medium-low and cook until crepe loosens from skillet and underside is golden brown, 4 to 7 minutes.

5 Gently fold unfilled side of crepe over sprouts. Slide crepe onto prepared wire rack and transfer to oven to keep warm. Repeat 2 more times with remaining oil, daikon mixture, batter, and bean sprouts. When final crepe is cooked, use 2 spatulas to transfer all 3 crepes to cutting board and cut each crosswise into 1¼-inch-wide strips.

6 Place crepes and reserved platter with greens in center of table and give each diner 1 bowl of sauce. To eat, wrap individual strip of crepe and several leaves of basil and cilantro in lettuce leaf and dip into sauce.

Đồ Chua

Serves 4
Total time: 10 minutes, plus 1 hour resting

- 8 ounces daikon radish, peeled and shredded (about 2½ cups)
- 2 carrots, peeled and shredded (about 1½ cups)
- 3 tablespoons plus 2 teaspoons sugar, plus sugar for salting vegetables
- ¼ teaspoon table salt, plus salt for salting vegetables
- ½ cup distilled white vinegar
- ⅓ cup water

1 Combine daikon, carrots, 1 teaspoon sugar, and ½ teaspoon salt in large bowl and let sit until vegetables are partially wilted and reduced in volume by half, about 30 minutes. Meanwhile, in second bowl, whisk vinegar, water, remaining sugar, and ¼ teaspoon salt until sugar and salt are dissolved.

2 Transfer daikon mixture to colander and drain, pressing on solids to remove excess moisture. Add daikon mixture to vinegar mixture and toss to combine. Let sit for 30 minutes at room temperature, then serve. (Pickle can be refrigerated for up to 1 week.)

Bánh Xèo
(page 204)

Creamy Mushroom and Pink Pickled Cabbage Sandwiches

Why This Recipe Works This mouthwatering, texturally varied sandwich is a loving vegetarian tribute to acclaimed Cambridge-based bakery Bagelsaurus's hot smoked salmon bagel, which is served with pickled red cabbage, red onion, and fresh dill. Pickles and herbs usually function as a sidekick to the fish in a salmon bagel, but the pickled cabbage is arguably our favorite component of Bagelsaurus's beloved bagel—so we decided to make the bright-fuchsia ingredient the star of this sandwich. We soaked nutrient-dense, fiber-packed red cabbage in rice vinegar with a little sugar, which gave us sturdy, chewy pickles with a balanced taste that wasn't overly acidic; caraway seeds further deepened the flavor profile. Atop this satisfyingly crisp mound of veggies, we added a lot of dill, treating the fragrant herb as more of a salad green than a garnish. Searing some oyster or maitake mushrooms—particularly fleshy, meaty varieties—intensified their umami, making this sandwich even more satisfying. We mixed the mushrooms with some sour cream (being careful to let the mushrooms cool first so the cream's emulsion wouldn't break) and scallions to create a creamy filling with pops of zesty freshness. We like using up to ½ cup torn fresh dill, but you can use less if you prefer.

1 Microwave vinegar, sugar, caraway seeds, and ¼ teaspoon salt in medium bowl until simmering, 1 to 2 minutes; whisk to dissolve sugar. Add cabbage; press to submerge; and let sit, stirring occasionally, for 30 minutes. Drain cabbage and set aside.

2 Heat oil in 12-inch nonstick skillet over medium-high heat until shimmering. Add mushrooms and ¼ teaspoon salt. Cover and cook, stirring occasionally, until mushrooms have released their liquid, 3 to 5 minutes. Uncover and cook, stirring occasionally, until mushrooms are well browned, 5 to 10 minutes.

3 Transfer mushrooms to bowl and let cool for 5 minutes. Add sour cream, scallions, and remaining ¼ teaspoon salt to mushrooms and toss to combine. Divide mushroom mixture among bun bottoms and top with pickled cabbage, dill, and bun tops. Serve.

½ cup unseasoned rice vinegar

2 teaspoons sugar

1 teaspoon caraway seeds

¼ teaspoon table salt for pickling

2 cups shredded red cabbage

1 tablespoon vegetable oil

1 pound maitake or oyster mushrooms, trimmed and torn into 1- to 1½-inch pieces

½ teaspoon table salt, divided

⅓ cup sour cream

3 scallions, sliced thin

4 hamburger buns, toasted

Torn fresh dill

Mushroom, Lettuce, and Tomato Sandwiches

Why This Recipe Works A classic BLT appeals because it splendidly balances a few simple ingredients: salty-crisp bacon, sweet-juicy tomatoes, and refreshing lettuce, all tied together with a slick of mayonnaise. Well, BLT lovers, meet the famous sandwich's equally mouth-watering cousin: the MLT. To create a flavor-packed plant-based version that's just as appealing as the porky variety, we used strips of portobello mushrooms, which made an excellent stand-in for bacon. When sautéed and seasoned with smoked paprika and a little salt, they developed meaty texture, umami character, and even some smokiness. Using a full 1½ pounds of mushrooms provided plenty of substance without causing the sandwich to fall apart. We kept the juicy tomatoes but swapped the usual romaine for arugula, as its peppery bite perked up the other flavors. Finally, for a creamy, tangy spread, we mixed avocado and yogurt and happily slathered it on toasted rustic bread to complete the sandwich.

1 Heat oil in 12-inch nonstick skillet over medium heat until shimmering. Add shallot and cook until softened, about 2 minutes. Add mushrooms and ½ teaspoon salt. Cover and cook, stirring occasionally, until mushrooms have released their liquid, 10 to 12 minutes.

2 Uncover; increase heat to medium-high; and cook, stirring occasionally, until mushrooms are browned, about 10 minutes. Stir in garlic and smoked paprika and cook until fragrant, about 30 seconds. Remove pan from heat and let mushrooms cool slightly, about 10 minutes.

3 Just before serving, combine avocado, yogurt, and remaining ⅛ teaspoon salt in small bowl and mash until smooth. Spread avocado mixture evenly over 4 toast slices. Layer mushrooms, tomatoes, and then arugula over avocado mixture. Top with remaining 4 toast slices. Serve.

1   tablespoon extra-virgin olive oil

1   shallot, minced

1½ pounds portobello mushroom caps, gills removed, sliced ½ inch thick

½   teaspoon plus ⅛ teaspoon table salt, divided

1   garlic clove, minced

½   teaspoon smoked paprika

1   ripe avocado, halved and pitted

2   tablespoons plain yogurt

8   slices rustic bread, toasted

2   tomatoes, cored and sliced thin

2   ounces (2 cups) baby arugula

Chickpea Salad Sandwiches with Quick Pickles

Why This Recipe Works: Chicken and tuna salad sandwiches are old standbys, but we wanted to put a plant-focused spin on the category by using protein-packed chickpeas—while retaining the creamy, practically saucy texture of a deli salad. Mayonnaise lent a smooth richness, but using too much of it masked the legumes' earthiness. To ensure more pronounced chickpea flavor in every bite, we blitzed a portion of the legumes in a food processor with mayo, water, and lemon juice to make a binder reminiscent of hummus. We then added the remaining chickpeas and, to maintain some textural contrast, pulsed the mixture just briefly. This gave us a chunky, extra-satisfying sandwich filling. Dill brought a refreshing grassiness that complemented the cool, creamy chickpeas. For a tart dimension, we quickly pickled some cucumber slices by simply tossing them with onion and vinegar. We also added a layer of thinly sliced boiled eggs to up the protein and heartiness of the meal. Loaded onto chewy pumpernickel bread, this chickpea salad makes a luscious sandwich sure to satisfy any lunchtime craving.

½ English cucumber, sliced thin

½ small red onion, sliced thin

¼ cup cider vinegar

½ teaspoon table salt for brining

2 (15-ounce) cans chickpeas, rinsed, divided

½ cup mayonnaise

1 tablespoon lemon juice

½ teaspoon table salt

2 tablespoons chopped fresh dill

8 slices pumpernickel sandwich bread

2 Easy-Peel Hard-Cooked Eggs, sliced thin (page 42)

4 leaves Bibb lettuce

1 Combine cucumber, onion, vinegar, and ½ teaspoon salt in bowl; set aside, tossing occasionally.

2 Process ¾ cup chickpeas, mayonnaise, lemon juice, and salt in food processor until smooth, about 30 seconds, scraping down sides of bowl as needed. Add dill and remaining chickpeas to food processor and pulse until coarsely chopped with some larger pieces remaining, about 4 pulses. Season with salt to taste.

3 Drain cucumber mixture. Spread chickpea salad evenly over 4 bread slices. Layer eggs, cucumber mixture, and then lettuce over salad. Top with remaining 4 bread slices. Serve.

Spiced Smashed Chickpea Wraps

Why This Recipe Works We love chickpeas for their hearty bite and earthy flavor, not to mention the versatility and convenience of the canned variety. When we coarsely mashed the chickpeas to lightly break their skins, the dense legumes not only became chunky in texture, but also developed a creamier consistency, which enhanced their ability to soak up spice. Leaning into peppery flavors, we seasoned the chickpeas with warming cumin and zingy Asian chili-garlic sauce. To turn the chickpeas into a handheld meal, we took a cue from Greek gyros by spreading toasted pitas with a generous smear of a creamy sauce before adding the seasoned beans and lavishing them with cooling cucumber, zippy pepperoncini, and bracing red onion. For more heat, serve with extra Asian chili-garlic sauce. We like to spread the pitas with our Tahini-Yogurt sauce, but you can substitute simply seasoned Greek yogurt if you prefer.

- 2 (15-ounce) cans chickpeas, rinsed
- 2 tablespoons Asian chili-garlic sauce
- 2 teaspoons ground cumin
- ½ teaspoon table salt
- 1 cup Tahini-Yogurt Sauce (page 244)
- 4 (8-inch) pitas, lightly toasted
- ½ English cucumber, halved lengthwise and sliced thin on bias
- ½ cup pepperoncini, stemmed and sliced into thin rings
- ¼ cup thinly sliced red onion

1 Using potato masher, mash chickpeas very coarse in bowl. Stir chili-garlic sauce, cumin, and salt into chickpeas.

2 Spread ¼ cup tahini-yogurt sauce evenly over 1 side of each pita. Divide reserved chickpea mixture, cucumber, pepperoncini, and onion evenly among pitas. Fold pitas in half, wrap tightly in parchment paper, and serve.

Parsnip and Chicken Shawarma

Why This Recipe Works Shawarma—arguably one of the most beloved street foods in the Levant—is usually made with spiced, slow-roasted chicken, lamb, or beef. Across the Arab world, restaurants and street vendors cook the meats on slow-rotating vertical spits, then shave off juicy, tender pieces to order. Often, the proteins get wrapped inside lavash for a handheld meal that's perfect for lunch or a late-night snack. To develop a shawarma wrap that's lighter on the meat, we turned to parsnips for their dense texture and penchant for soaking up seasoning. To mimic the shape of shaved chicken, we cut the vegetable into batons and seasoned it with a symphony of shawarma-inspired spices like coriander, turmeric, and cardamom. We seared chicken thighs to render their fat, then used the hot oil to bloom a bevy of spices, creating an aromatic mixture perfect for drenching the parsnips and chicken in spicy flavor. We then cooked the vegetable and meat in the oven simulta-neously before removing the chicken to rest while the parsnips finished cooking. Not only did this streamline the cooking process, but it also allowed the parsnips to take on the rich, savory flavor of the chicken. Spreading Tahini-Garlic Sauce on the lavash lent the wrap nutty flavor and creaminess, while folding kosher dill pickle spears into the wrap added substantial crunch and welcome tang.

- 1 teaspoon ground allspice
- 1 teaspoon ground ginger
- 1 teaspoon garlic powder
- 1 teaspoon ground coriander
- ½ teaspoon pepper
- ½ teaspoon ground turmeric
- ¼ teaspoon ground cinnamon
- ¼ teaspoon ground cardamom
- ¼ teaspoon cayenne pepper
- 2 pounds parsnips, peeled
- 3 (5- to 7-ounce) bone-in chicken thighs, trimmed

- 1 tablespoon extra-virgin olive oil, plus extra if necessary
- 1 teaspoon table salt
- 4 (12 by 9-inch) lavash
- 1 recipe Tahini-Garlic Sauce (page 244)
- 8 kosher dill pickle spears

1 Adjust oven rack to upper-middle position and heat oven to 450 degrees. Combine allspice, ginger, garlic powder, coriander, pepper, turmeric, cinnamon, cardamom, and cayenne in small bowl; set aside. Trim parsnips, then cut each parsnip to separate bulbous end from thinner end. Cut bulbous ends into ¼-inch-thick planks, then cut planks lengthwise into ¼-inch-thick matchsticks. Repeat with thinner ends, halving planks crosswise if necessary, so matchsticks are no longer than 3 inches. Transfer to large bowl.

2 Pat chicken dry with paper towels. Heat oil in 12-inch ovensafe skillet over medium-high heat until just smok-ing. Place chicken skin side down in skillet and cook until skin is golden brown and crispy, 5 to 7 minutes. Flip chicken and cook until second side is golden brown, about 5 minutes. Transfer to bowl with parsnips.

3 Remove skillet from heat and let cool until smoke subsides, about 1 minute. Pour off all but 1 tablespoon fat from skillet (or add oil until it measures 1 table-spoon), then add reserved spice mixture to fat left in skillet and let bubble for 30 seconds (spices will become fragrant and begin to darken). Use silicone spatula to scrape spice mixture out of skillet and over parsnip-chicken mixture in bowl, then add salt and mix until parsnips and chicken are well coated with spice mixture.

4 Return seasoned parsnip-chicken mixture to now-empty skillet. Arrange chicken thighs skin side up on top of parsnips and drizzle any remaining oil in bowl over top. Transfer skillet to oven and roast until chicken registers at least 195 degrees, 25 to 35 minutes.

5 Transfer chicken to cutting board and let rest, uncov-ered, while finishing parsnips. Stir parsnips in skillet, then return to oven and roast for an additional 10 to 15 minutes, until parsnips are very soft and edges are deep golden brown. Transfer parsnips to clean bowl.

6 Remove skin from chicken and chop skin; add to bowl with parsnips. Using your hands to separate meat from bones, shred chicken fine (aim for strips no more than ¼ inch wide) and add to bowl with parsnips, discarding bones. Toss to combine and season with salt to taste.

7 Working with 1 lavash at a time, lay on clean counter with short edge parallel to counter edge. Spread 3 tablespoons tahini-garlic sauce evenly over lavash, leaving ½-inch border around perimeter. Arrange one-quarter parsnip-chicken mixture in even layer over bottom third of lavash, then top with 2 pickle spears. Fold bottom of lavash up and over filling, then fold in sides and roll tightly away from you around filling. Serve.

Ta'ameya

Why This Recipe Works   Across the Mediterranean region, falafel (in ball or patty form) nestled into pitas and adorned with vegetables and tahini sauce is a beloved street food. While many versions are made from chickpeas, falafel in Egypt, known as ta'ameya there, uses sweet, nutty fava beans. Flavored with warm spices and often coated with sesame seeds, the fried patties have a gorgeous green hue, further amplified by fresh herbs and scallions. We used ground pita and an egg as binders, and added baking powder to the mash to make it fluffier. Frozen favas shaved down the cooking time without affecting the end result. No falafel is complete without toppings, so we stuffed the pitas with juicy tomatoes, crisp cucumbers, and zingy onions; drizzled over our creamy Tahini-Yogurt Sauce; and scattered pickled turnips on top, for even more crunch and tang. You can substitute a quarter of an English cucumber for the Persian cucumbers if you prefer. When taking the temperature of the frying oil, carefully tilt the skillet so the oil pools on one side.

¾ cup torn pita, plus 2 (8-inch) pitas, halved

½ teaspoon fennel seeds, toasted and cracked

1⅓ pounds frozen shelled fava beans (4⅓ cups), thawed, sheaths removed

¼ cup chopped fresh cilantro and/or parsley

1 large egg, lightly beaten

2 scallions, sliced thin

2 garlic cloves, minced

½ teaspoon baking powder

½ teaspoon ground coriander

½ teaspoon ground cumin

½ teaspoon table salt

¼ teaspoon pepper

2 teaspoons sesame seeds

½ cup extra-virgin olive oil, for frying

1 tomato, cored and chopped

2 Persian cucumbers, halved lengthwise and sliced thin

½ red onion, sliced thin

½ cup Tahini-Yogurt Sauce (page 244)

1 recipe Pink Pickled Turnips (recipe follows)

1 teaspoon nigella seeds (optional)

1   Process torn pita pieces and fennel seeds in food processor until finely ground, about 15 seconds. Add fava beans, cilantro, egg, scallions, garlic, baking powder, coriander, cumin, salt, and pepper and pulse until fava beans are coarsely chopped and mixture is cohesive, about 15 pulses, scraping down sides of bowl as needed.

2   Working with 2 tablespoons mixture at a time, shape into 2-inch-wide patties and transfer to large plate (you should have 16 patties). Sprinkle sesame seeds evenly over falafel patties and press lightly to adhere.

3   Set wire rack in rimmed baking sheet and line with triple layer of paper towels. Heat oil in 12-inch nonstick skillet over medium heat to 350 degrees. Add half of ta'ameya and fry until deep golden brown, 2 to 3 minutes per side, using 2 spatulas to carefully flip patties. Transfer to prepared rack to drain and repeat with remaining ta'ameya, adjusting heat as needed if ta'ameya begin to brown too quickly.

4   Stuff each pita half with ta'ameya, tomato, cucumbers, and onion and top with tahini-yogurt sauce; pickled turnips; and nigella seeds, if using. Serve.

Pink Pickled Turnips

Makes two 1-pint jars (4 cups)
Total time: 30 minutes, plus 2 days chilling

1¼	cups white wine vinegar
1¼	cups water
2½	tablespoons sugar
1½	tablespoons kosher salt
3	garlic cloves, smashed and peeled
¾	teaspoon whole allspice berries
¾	teaspoon black peppercorns
1	pound turnips, peeled and cut into 2 by ½-inch sticks
1	small beet, trimmed, peeled, and cut into 1-inch pieces

1 Bring vinegar, water, sugar, salt, garlic, allspice, and peppercorns to boil in medium saucepan over medium-high heat. Cover, remove from heat, and let steep for 10 minutes. Strain brine through fine-mesh strainer, then return to saucepan.

2 Place two 1-pint jars under hot running water until heated through, 1 to 2 minutes; shake dry. Pack turnips vertically into hot jars with beet pieces evenly distributed throughout.

3 Return brine to brief boil. Using funnel and ladle, pour hot brine over vegetables to cover. Let jars cool to room temperature, cover with lids, and refrigerate for at least 2 days before serving. (Pickled turnips can be refrigerated for up to 1 month; turnips will soften over time.)

Mumbai Frankie Wraps

Why This Recipe Works In Mumbai, India, handheld street foods like these wraps are hugely popular. Frankies take many forms but tend to consist of a warm, tender chapati or roti (whole-wheat flatbreads) filled with spiced potatoes as well as proteins or vegetables and topped with condiments such as chutneys, sauces, and pickles. We kept our take on the frankie plant-forward, roasting dense, hearty cauliflower and chickpeas which we seasoned with fragrant, earthy garam masala. Next, we mashed Yukon Gold potatoes with shallot, ginger, garlic, turmeric, and coriander; we enriched this mixture with creamy coconut milk, taking care to scrape up the flavor-packed browned bits in the pan. We spread the potato mash over our wrap, sprinkled it with the cauliflower-chickpea mixture, and then topped it all with sweet-spicy pickled onion and a bright herbal chutney before rolling it into a cone shape. We like to prepare these with our homemade Chapati, but you can use store-bought if you prefer. We do not recommend naan or other (thicker) flatbreads. For easiest assembly, we suggest making the pickled onion, chutney, and wraps ahead.

12 ounces cauliflower florets, cut into 1-inch pieces

1 (15-ounce) can chickpeas, rinsed

2 tablespoons vegetable oil, divided

¾ teaspoon garam masala

¾ teaspoon table salt, divided

1 pound Yukon Gold potatoes, peeled and cut into 1-inch pieces

1 shallot, minced

3 garlic cloves, minced

1 tablespoon grated fresh ginger

1 teaspoon ground turmeric

⅛ teaspoon ground coriander

Pinch cayenne pepper

½ cup canned coconut milk

1 recipe Chapati (recipe follows), warmed

½ cup Cilantro-Mint Chutney (page 245)

¼ cup Quick Sweet and Spicy Pickled Red Onion (page 33)

1 Adjust oven rack to lowest position and heat oven to 500 degrees. Line rimmed baking sheet with aluminum foil. Toss cauliflower, chickpeas, 1 tablespoon oil, garam masala, and ¼ teaspoon salt together in bowl. Spread cauliflower mixture in even layer on prepared sheet and roast, stirring halfway through roasting, until cauliflower is spotty brown and tender, about 10 minutes; set aside. (Cauliflower mixture can be refrigerated up to 24 hours; let come to room temperature before serving.)

2 Place potatoes and remaining ½ teaspoon salt in large saucepan, add cold water to cover by 1 inch, and bring to boil over high heat. Reduce heat to medium and simmer until potatoes are tender, about 12 minutes; drain well.

3 Heat remaining 1 tablespoon oil in now-empty saucepan over medium heat until shimmering. Add shallot and cook until softened and lightly browned, 3 to 5 minutes. Stir in garlic, ginger, turmeric, coriander, and cayenne and cook until fragrant, about 30 seconds. Stir in coconut milk, scraping up any browned bits, and bring to simmer. Stir in potatoes, then remove from heat and mash with potato masher until mostly smooth, about 2 minutes. Season with salt to taste; set aside. (Potato mixture can be refrigerated up to 24 hours; heat in microwave, covered, before serving.)

4 Divide potato mixture evenly among whole-wheat wraps, then spread in even layer over half of each wrap. Divide cauliflower mixture evenly over top, then top each with 2 tablespoons chutney and 2 tablespoons pickled onion. Roll into cone shape and serve.

Chapati

Makes 4 wraps
Total time: 40 minutes, plus 30 minutes resting

This recipe can easily be doubled. You can use a 12-inch nonstick skillet in place of the cast-iron skillet if you prefer. In step 5, heat ½ teaspoon oil over medium heat in skillet until shimmering, then wipe out skillet before adding first dough round.

- ¾ cup (4⅛ ounces) whole-wheat flour
- ¾ cup (3¾ ounces) all-purpose flour
- 1 teaspoon table salt
- ½ cup warm water
- 3 tablespoons plus 2 teaspoons vegetable oil, divided

1 Whisk flours and salt together in bowl. Stir in water and 3 tablespoons oil until cohesive dough forms. Transfer dough to lightly floured counter and knead by hand to form smooth ball, 1 minute.

2 Divide dough into 4 pieces and cover with plastic wrap. Form 1 piece of dough into rough ball by stretching dough around your thumb and pinching edges together so that top is smooth (keep remaining pieces covered). Place ball seam side down on clean counter and, using your cupped hand, drag in small circles until dough feels taut and round. Repeat with remaining dough pieces. Place on plate seam side down.

3 Cover dough with plastic wrap and let sit for 30 minutes. (Dough can be refrigerated for up to 3 days.)

4 Line rimmed baking sheet with parchment paper. Roll 1 dough ball into 9-inch circle on lightly floured counter (keep remaining dough balls covered). Transfer to prepared sheet and top with additional sheet of parchment. Repeat with remaining dough balls.

5 Heat 12-inch cast-iron skillet over medium heat for 3 minutes. Add ½ teaspoon oil to skillet, then use paper towels to carefully wipe out skillet, leaving thin film of oil on bottom; skillet should be just smoking. Place 1 dough round in hot skillet and cook until dough is bubbly and bottom is browned in spots, about 2 minutes. Flip dough and press firmly with spatula all over to encourage puffing, cooking until puffed and second side is spotty brown, 1 to 2 minutes. Transfer to clean plate and cover with dish towel to keep warm. Repeat with remaining oil and dough rounds. Serve. (Cooked chapatis can be refrigerated for up to 3 days or frozen for up to 3 months. To freeze, layer wraps between parchment and store in zipper-lock bag. To serve, stack wraps on plate, cover with damp dish towel, and microwave until warm, 60 to 90 seconds.)

Mumbai Frankie Wraps

(page 220)

Black Bean and Cheese Arepas

Why This Recipe Works In Venezuela, arepas—the corn cakes popular in many Latin countries—are served split open and stuffed with anything from meat and cheese to beans, corn, or fish. The arepas come together from a dough made with masarepa (an instant flour made from precooked corn), water, and salt, but getting the consistency right can be tricky. We found that using just a half-cup more water than masarepa produced a dough that was easy to shape, and a small amount of baking powder lightened the texture. We shaped the dough into rounds, browned them in a skillet, and finished them in the oven. For a hearty filling, we combined canned black beans with Monterey Jack cheese; cilantro added fresh-ness, lime juice offered an acidic boost, and chili powder brought a hint of heat. Masarepa is also known as harina precocida and masa al instante. We had best results using P.A.N. precooked white cornmeal. Do not use Goya brand masarepa blanca.

Arepas

- 2 cups (10 ounces) masarepa blanca
- 1 teaspoon table salt
- 1 teaspoon baking powder
- 2½ cups warm water
- ¼ cup vegetable oil, divided

Black Bean Filling

- 1 (15-ounce) can black beans, rinsed
- 4 ounces Monterey Jack cheese, shredded (1 cup)
- 2 tablespoons minced fresh cilantro
- 2 scallions, sliced thin
- 1 tablespoon lime juice
- ¼ teaspoon chili powder

1 For the arepas Adjust oven rack to middle position and heat oven to 400 degrees. Whisk masarepa, salt, and baking powder together in large bowl. Gradually add water, stirring until combined. Using generous ⅓ cup dough for each round, form into eight 3-inch rounds, each about ½ inch thick.

2 Heat 2 tablespoons oil in 12-inch nonstick skillet over medium-high heat until shimmering. Add 4 arepas and cook until golden on both sides, about 4 minutes per side. Transfer arepas to wire rack set in rimmed baking sheet. Wipe out skillet with paper towels and repeat with remaining 2 tablespoons oil and remaining 4 are-pas. (Fried arepas can be refrigerated for up to 3 days or frozen for up to 1 month. Increase baking time as needed; if frozen, do not thaw before baking.) Bake arepas on wire rack until they sound hollow when tapped on bottom, about 10 minutes.

3 For the filling Meanwhile, using potato masher or fork, mash beans in bowl until most are broken. Stir in Monterey Jack, cilantro, scallions, lime juice, and chili powder and season with salt and pepper to taste.

4 Using fork, gently split hot, baked arepas open. Stuff each with 3 heaping tablespoons filling. Serve.

Tofu Summer Rolls with Spicy Almond Butter Sauce

Why This Recipe Works We love how the pleasantly chewy rice paper wrappers in Vietnamese gỏi cuốn, also known as summer rolls, give way to an ensemble of flavors: soft rice noodles, crisp vegetables, and often a marinated protein like shrimp or pork. For a protein-rich meatless version, we swapped in tofu while keeping a similar flavor profile. We marinated strips of the tofu in rice vinegar, soy sauce, and sriracha. We also skipped the noodles in favor of a rainbow of veggies: red cabbage, red bell pepper, cucumber, carrots, and basil. For dipping, we whisked up a sriracha-spiked almond butter sauce, a rich, thick condiment that clung to our rolls. Be sure to make one roll at a time to keep the wrappers moist and pliable. Different brands of rice paper wrappers may vary in the time it takes to soak and become pliable. For the nut butter, you can use a smooth or chunky variety.

Sauce

- 3 tablespoons almond or peanut butter
- 3 tablespoons water
- 1 tablespoon rice vinegar
- 1 tablespoon soy sauce
- 2 teaspoons grated fresh ginger
- 1 teaspoon sriracha
- 1 garlic clove, minced

Rolls

- 6 tablespoons unseasoned rice vinegar
- 1 tablespoon soy sauce
- 2 teaspoons sriracha
- 2 scallions, sliced thin on bias
- 7 ounces extra-firm tofu, cut into 3-inch-long by ½-inch-thick strips
- ½ small head red cabbage, halved, cored, and sliced thin (3½ cups)
- 12 (8-inch) round rice paper wrappers

- 1 cup fresh basil leaves
- 1 red bell pepper, stemmed, seeded, and cut into 2-inch-long matchsticks
- ½ seedless English cucumber, cut into 3-inch matchsticks
- 2 carrots, peeled and shredded

1 For the sauce Whisk all ingredients in bowl until well combined; set aside until ready to serve.

2 For the rolls Whisk 2 tablespoons vinegar, soy sauce, sriracha, and scallions in shallow dish until well combined. Add tofu and let sit for 1 hour. Toss cabbage with remaining ¼ cup vinegar and let sit for 1 hour.

3 Drain cabbage in fine-mesh strainer, pressing gently with back of spatula to remove as much liquid as possible. Transfer to large plate and pat dry with paper towels.

4 Spread clean, damp dish towel on work surface. Fill 9-inch pie plate with 1 inch room-temperature water. Submerge 1 wrapper in water until just pliable, 10 seconds to 2 minutes; lay softened wrapper on towel. Scatter 3 basil leaves over wrapper. Arrange 5 matchsticks each of bell pepper and cucumber horizontally on wrapper, leaving 2-inch border at bottom. Top with 1 tablespoon carrots, then arrange 2 tablespoons cabbage on top of carrots. Place 1 strip tofu horizontally on top of vegetables, being sure to shake off excess marinade.

5 Fold bottom of wrapper over filling, pulling back on it firmly to tighten it around filling, then fold sides of wrapper in and continue to roll tightly into spring roll. Transfer to platter and cover with second damp dish towel.

6 Repeat with remaining wrappers and filling. Serve with reserved almond butter sauce. (Spring rolls are best eaten immediately but can be covered with a clean, damp dish towel and refrigerated for up to 4 hours.)

Red Lentil Kibbeh

Why This Recipe Works Kibbeh is a popular Middle Eastern dish made from bulgur, minced onions, various spices, and (traditionally) ground meat. During Lent, those who observe often prepare this meal with lentils in lieu of meat. To start, we softened onion and bell pepper on the stovetop before seasoning them with two red pastes that enhanced both the color and flavor of the dish: harissa, for smoky heat, and tomato paste, for sweetness and an umami quality. After bringing water to a simmer, we gave the bulgur a head start before adding the quicker-cooking lentils, so the two could finish cooking at the same time. A splash of lemon juice and showering of parsley brightened up the kibbeh. The spoonable mixture can be served on its own with some Bibb lettuce and yogurt, but it also makes a showstopping addition to a larger spread, alongside dips, nuts, pickled radishes, and pita. We like to make this with our homemade Harissa, but you can use store-bought if you prefer.

1 Heat 1 tablespoon oil in large saucepan over medium heat until shimmering. Add onion, bell pepper, and salt and cook until softened, about 5 minutes. Stir in harissa; tomato paste; and cayenne, if using, and cook, stirring frequently, until fragrant, about 1 minute.

2 Stir in water and bulgur and bring to simmer. Reduce heat to low; cover; and simmer gently until bulgur is barely tender, about 8 minutes. Stir in lentils; cover; and continue to cook, stirring occasionally, until lentils and bulgur are tender, 8 to 10 minutes.

3 Off heat, lay clean dish towel underneath lid and let mixture sit for 10 minutes. Stir in parsley, lemon juice, and 1 tablespoon oil and stir vigorously until mixture is cohesive. Season with salt and pepper to taste. Transfer to platter and drizzle with remaining 1 tablespoon oil. Spoon kibbeh into lettuce leaves and drizzle with yogurt. Serve with lemon wedges.

3 tablespoons extra-virgin olive oil, divided

1 onion, chopped fine

1 red bell pepper, stemmed, seeded, and chopped fine

1 teaspoon table salt

2 tablespoons Harissa (page 153)

2 tablespoons tomato paste

½ teaspoon cayenne pepper (optional)

4 cups water

1 cup medium-grind bulgur, rinsed

¾ cup dried red lentils, picked over and rinsed

½ cup chopped fresh parsley

2 tablespoons lemon juice, plus lemon wedges for serving

1 head Bibb lettuce (8 ounces), leaves separated

½ cup plain yogurt

Blackened Chicken and Okra Tacos

Why This Recipe Works When developing a meat-light take on a chicken taco, we asked ourselves what cooking method would make the most of a small amount of meat. We turned to the modern Cajun technique of blackening: liberally coating a protein in a spice blend before searing it at a very high temperature until deeply charred. We opted for quick-cooking chicken breasts, which we pounded thin to shorten their time in the skillet; this ensured that a blast of heat would char (rather than burn) the exterior while fully cooking the inside. Blackening the meat gave us such intense flavor that we welcomed the addition of vegetables to balance it out. Okra made a fantastic foil for the meat's spicy, smoky aroma. We found that quickly sautéing whole pods over medium-high heat minimized the release of their mucilage and maximized their crispness. For brightness, we smeared the tacos with a remoulade-inspired mayo and topped them with lemon-pickled radishes. Okra pods less than 3 inches long will be the most tender; cut any pods longer than 4 inches in half crosswise. A rasp-style grater makes quick work of turning the garlic into a paste.

- 6 radishes, trimmed and sliced thin
- ¼ teaspoon grated lemon zest plus 2½ tablespoons juice, divided
- ⅓ cup mayonnaise
- 2 teaspoons whole-grain mustard
- 1 teaspoon Worcestershire sauce
- ¼ teaspoon garlic, minced to paste
- 1 tablespoon paprika
- 1½ teaspoons garlic powder
- 1½ teaspoons dried thyme
- 1 teaspoon table salt, divided
- ¾ teaspoon pepper
- ¼–½ teaspoon cayenne pepper
- 2 (6- to 8-ounce) boneless, skinless chicken breasts, trimmed
- 2 tablespoons vegetable oil, divided
- 1 pound okra, stemmed
- 12 (6-inch) corn tortillas, warmed

1 Combine radishes and 2 tablespoons lemon juice in small bowl; set aside. Whisk mayonnaise, mustard, Worcestershire, garlic, lemon zest, and remaining 1½ teaspoons lemon juice in separate bowl; set aside. Combine paprika, garlic powder, thyme, ¾ teaspoon salt, pepper, and cayenne in wide, shallow bowl. Wad up paper towel and place within reach of stove.

2 Halve 1 chicken breast crosswise, then cut thick half in half horizontally, creating 3 cutlets of similar thickness. Repeat with remaining breast. Place cutlets between sheets of plastic wrap and gently pound to even ⅓-inch thickness. Working with 1 cutlet at a time, dredge thoroughly in spice mixture, pressing to adhere, then shake off excess. Place cutlets in single layer on rimmed baking sheet.

3 Heat 1 tablespoon oil in 12-inch cast-iron skillet over high heat until just smoking. Add cutlets to skillet in single layer, press on each firmly with spatula, and cook undisturbed for 2 minutes. Flip cutlets, then press cutlets against skillet with spatula and cook for 1 minute. Remove skillet from heat, transfer cutlets to cutting board, tent with aluminum foil, and let rest while cooking okra. Wipe out skillet with paper towels to remove any debris.

4 Heat remaining 1 tablespoon oil in now-empty skillet over medium-high heat until just smoking. Add okra and remaining ¼ teaspoon salt and cook, stirring occasionally, until crisp-tender and well charred on most sides, 5 to 7 minutes (okra may not fit in single layer to start; that is OK). Transfer okra to bowl.

5 Slice chicken thin. Divide reserved sauce evenly among tortillas, then top with chicken, okra, and reserved radishes. Serve.

Cutting Chicken Breasts into Thirds

1 Working with 1 chicken breast at a time, halve crosswise. Then cut thick half in half horizontally, creating 3 cutlets of similar thickness.

2 Place cutlets between sheets of plastic wrap and gently pound to even ⅓-inch thickness.

Chipotle Mushroom and Cauliflower Tacos

Why This Recipe Works   Mushrooms and cauliflower are both excellent flavor absorbers, which makes them a delicious duo in a taco filling. Roasting them in the oven not only deepened their flavors but also gave them a crisp golden-brown exterior, while keeping the insides tender. For added heat and complexity, we mixed in some canned chipotle chiles in adobo sauce for the last few minutes of cooking. Meanwhile, we steeped red onions in a solution of vinegar, sugar, and salt and then popped them in the microwave—an easy way to pickle them—before stirring in cabbage to make a tangy, crunchy topping. The combination of crema and more chipotle in adobo created a quick, luscious sauce. Garnish with fresh cilantro leaves and serve with lime wedges, if desired.

1¼   pounds cremini mushrooms, trimmed and quartered

1¼   pounds cauliflower florets, cut into 1-inch pieces

¼   cup vegetable oil

2   teaspoons table salt, divided

¼   cup minced canned chipotle chile in adobo sauce, divided

½   red onion, sliced thin

½   cup distilled white vinegar

2   tablespoons sugar

⅔   cup Mexican crema

3   cups thinly sliced red cabbage

12   (6-inch) corn tortillas, warmed

1   Adjust oven rack to lowest position and heat oven to 500 degrees. Toss mushrooms, cauliflower, oil, and 1½ teaspoons salt together on rimmed baking sheet. Roast until liquid has mostly evaporated, 23 to 25 minutes. Stir 3 tablespoons chipotle into mushroom mixture and continue to roast until lightly browned, 3 to 5 minutes longer.

2   Meanwhile, combine onion, vinegar, sugar, and remaining ½ teaspoon salt in large bowl. Microwave, covered, until hot, about 2 minutes. Combine crema and remaining 1 tablespoon chipotle in small bowl.

3   Stir cabbage into onion mixture. Divide crema evenly among tortillas, then top with mushroom mixture and cabbage mixture. Serve.

SERVES 4 | TOTAL TIME 50 MINUTES • *vegetarian* • *fiber-ful* • *one-pan* •

Sweet Potato, Poblano, and Black Bean Tacos

Why This Recipe Works When sweet potatoes and poblano chiles unite in a taco, the results are spicy-sweet and wonderfully hearty. We seasoned the two with fragrant garlic, cumin, coriander, and oregano to emphasize their earthy undertones and introduce warm, peppery notes. Roasting the vegetables caramelized the exteriors and drew out their natural sweetness. Black beans boosted the protein and fiber content to make these tacos extra-satiating. For a tangy, spicy finish, we topped them with our Quick Sweet and Spicy Pickled Red Onion. We like to dollop these tacos with our Avocado Crema, but you can use avocado chunks, queso fresco, or sour cream if you prefer.

3 tablespoons extra-virgin olive oil

3 garlic cloves, minced

1½ teaspoons ground cumin

1½ teaspoons ground coriander

1 teaspoon minced fresh oregano or ¼ teaspoon dried

1 teaspoon table salt

½ teaspoon pepper

1 pound sweet potatoes, peeled and cut into ½-inch pieces

4 poblano chiles, stemmed, seeded, and cut into ½-inch-wide strips

1 large onion, halved and sliced ½ inch thick

1 (15-ounce) can black beans, rinsed

¼ cup chopped fresh cilantro

1 recipe Avocado Crema (page 244)

12 (6-inch) corn tortillas, warmed

1 recipe Quick Sweet and Spicy Pickled Red Onion (page 33)

1 Adjust oven racks to upper-middle and lower-middle positions and heat oven to 450 degrees. Whisk oil, garlic, cumin, coriander, oregano, salt, and pepper together in large bowl. Add potatoes, poblanos, and onion to oil mixture and toss to coat.

2 Spread vegetable mixture in even layer over 2 foil-lined rimmed baking sheets. Roast vegetables until tender and golden brown, about 30 minutes, stirring vegetables and switching and rotating sheets halfway through baking.

3 Return vegetables to now-empty bowl, add black beans and cilantro, and gently toss to combine. Divide avocado crema evenly among tortillas, then top with roasted vegetables and pickled onion. Serve.

Nopales and Shrimp Tacos

Why This Recipe Works Nopales, or fresh cactus paddles, are beloved in Mexico, where cooks add them to salads, stews, tacos, and more. They have the tender yet slightly snappy texture of green beans or asparagus, but with a decidedly citrusy flavor reminiscent of sorrel or purslane. Salting the cleaned and cut nopales released some of their mucilage, which we rinsed off before adding the cactus to the other ingredients. To complement the nopales, we seasoned sautéed shrimp with lime zest and garlic, and whipped up a batch of our creamy, cooling Avocado Crema. Look for fresh cactus paddles at Mexican and Latino grocery stores; you might also find them at some well-stocked supermarkets. We prefer untreated shrimp, but if your shrimp are treated with salt or additives such as sodium tripolyphosphate (STPP), do not add the salt in step 4. The nopales will continue to release mucilage if left to sit; add the nopales to the salad last and serve immediately.

- 1   pound nopales (4 to 5 paddles)
- ¼   teaspoon plus ⅛ teaspoon table salt, divided, plus salt for salting vegetables
- 6   ounces grape tomatoes, quartered
- ⅓   cup finely chopped white onion
- ¼   cup fresh chopped cilantro
- 4   teaspoons extra virgin olive oil, divided
- 1   teaspoon grated lime zest plus 2 teaspoons juice, plus lime wedges for serving
- ½   serrano chile, seeded and minced
- 1   pound extra-large shrimp (21 to 25 per pound), peeled, deveined, and tails removed, halved lengthwise
- 1   garlic clove, minced
- 1   recipe Avocado Crema (page 244)
- 12 (6-inch) corn tortillas, warmed

1 Working with 1 cactus paddle at a time, place flat on cutting board, and grasp thick end with tongs or dish towel. Place knife blade parallel to paddle, then slide knife away from you across surface to remove any thorns and small raised bumps. Repeat process on second side. Trim outer ¼ inch of paddle, then trim bottom ½ inch of thick end of paddle; discard trimmings. Rinse paddles well and clean cutting board.

2 Line rimmed baking sheet with dish towel; set aside. Cut paddles into ¼-inch-wide by 3-inch-long matchsticks. Combine nopales and 1 tablespoon salt in bowl, stirring until nopales are well coated and begin to release a viscous liquid, about 1 minute. Let nopales sit for 10 minutes, stirring occasionally. Transfer nopales to colander and rinse under cold running water, agitating vigorously with your hands to remove all viscous liquid. Drain well, then transfer to prepared baking sheet in even layer to dry; set aside.

3 Combine tomatoes, onion, cilantro, 2 teaspoons oil, lime juice, serrano, and ¼ teaspoon salt, in large bowl. Set aside.

4 Heat remaining 2 teaspoons oil in 12-inch nonstick skillet over medium-high heat until shimmering. Pat shrimp dry with paper towels and sprinkle with remaining ⅛ teaspoon salt. Add shrimp to skillet in even layer and cook, stirring frequently, until just opaque, about 2 minutes. Off heat, stir in garlic and lime zest.

5 Add reserved nopales (nopales may not be completely dry) to tomato mixture and toss to combine. Divide avocado crema evenly among tortillas, then top with nopal mixture and shrimp. Serve immediately with lime wedges.

Preparing Nopales

1 Grasp thick end of cactus paddle with tongs or dish towel and slide knife away from you across surface to remove any thorns and small raised bumps. Repeat on second side.

2 Trim outer ¼ inch of paddle, then trim bottom ½ inch of thick end of paddle; discard trimmings.

Salmon Tacos with Super Slaw

Why This Recipe Works California-style fish tacos are usually filled with deep-fried fish, tangy cabbage slaw, and a creamy sauce to bind it all together. We wanted to amp up the nutritiousness of each element for a supercharged take on tacos. Since we were forgoing the frying, we opted for salmon, which is richer than the more typically used white fish. A flavorful spice rub gave the fillets a nice crust without the need for frying batter. For a hearty slaw with plenty of bite, we chose collard greens, which, when thinly sliced, required no precooking. Combined with crunchy radishes, cooling jicama, red onion, cilantro, and lime, they perfectly complemented the fish. Our Avocado Crema—avocado processed with lime juice, yogurt, and cilantro—rounded out each bite with a luxurious creaminess. We chose skin-on salmon fillets because they hold together better during cooking, and the skin helps keep the fish moist. If your salmon is less than 1 inch thick, start checking for doneness early. You can substitute 2 cups thinly sliced purple cabbage for the collards if you prefer.

1 Whisk lime zest and juice and ¼ teaspoon salt together in large bowl. Add collards, jicama, radishes, onion, and cilantro and toss to combine; set aside until ready to serve.

2 Combine chili powder, pepper, and remaining ¾ teaspoon salt in small bowl. Pat salmon dry with paper towels and sprinkle evenly with spice mixture. Heat oil in 12-inch nonstick skillet over medium-high heat until shimmering. Cook salmon, skin side up, until well browned, 3 to 5 minutes. Flip and continue to cook until salmon is still translucent when checked with tip of paring knife and registers 125 degrees (for medium-rare), 3 to 5 minutes. Transfer salmon to plate and let cool slightly, about 2 minutes. Using 2 forks, flake fish into 2-inch pieces, discarding skin.

3 Divide avocado crema evenly among tortillas, then top with salmon and collard slaw and drizzle with hot sauce to taste. Serve.

- ¼ teaspoon grated lime zest plus 2 tablespoons juice
- 1 teaspoon table salt, divided
- 4 ounces collard greens, stemmed and sliced thin (2 cups)
- 4 ounces jicama, peeled and cut into 2-inch-long matchsticks
- 4 radishes, trimmed and cut into 1-inch-long matchsticks
- ½ small red onion, halved and sliced thin
- ¼ cup fresh cilantro leaves
- 1½ teaspoons chili powder
- ¼ teaspoon pepper
- 2 (6- to 8-ounce) skin-on salmon fillets, 1 inch thick
- 1 tablespoon vegetable oil
- 1 recipe Avocado Crema (page 244)
- 12 (6-inch) corn tortillas, warmed
- Hot sauce

Weeknight Ground Beef and Lentil Tacos

Why this recipe works We wanted to develop a delicious taco that was time-efficient and craveable enough for Taco Tuesdays, while upping the ratio of vegetables to meat. Our solution was a combination of lentils and ground beef, which made for an especially hearty, satiating meal that came together in a flash. Cooking the two in one skillet gave the beef a chance to distribute its fat and flavor to the lentils. The legumes also beautifully absorbed the taco seasoning, a blend of warming spices including cumin, coriander, and cayenne. The texture of the lentils also meshed seamlessly with that of the crumbly beef. Choosing canned lentils was a no-brainer for shortening the cook time. To complete the taco experience, we topped each with shredded cheddar, shredded lettuce, and diced tomatoes. Serve with any of your favorite taco toppings; we like diced onion and sour cream.

1 tablespoon vegetable oil

1 small onion, chopped fine

3 garlic cloves, minced

2 tablespoons chili powder

1 teaspoon ground cumin

1 teaspoon ground coriander

½ teaspoon dried oregano

½ teaspoon table salt

¼ teaspoon cayenne pepper

4 ounces 90 percent lean ground beef

1 (15-ounce) can lentils, rinsed

½ cup canned tomato sauce

½ cup chicken broth

1 teaspoon packed brown sugar

1 teaspoon cider vinegar

12 taco shells, warmed

4 ounces cheddar cheese, shredded (1 cup)

2 cups shredded iceberg lettuce

2 small tomatoes, cored and chopped

1 Heat oil in 10-inch skillet over medium heat until shimmering. Add onion and cook, stirring occasionally, until softened, about 5 minutes.

2 Add garlic, chili powder, cumin, coriander, oregano, salt, and cayenne and cook, stirring constantly, until fragrant, about 1 minute. Add ground beef and cook, breaking meat up with wooden spoon and scraping pan bottom to prevent scorching, until beef is no longer pink, 3 to 4 minutes.

3 Add lentils, tomato sauce, broth, sugar, and vinegar and bring to simmer. Reduce heat to medium-low and simmer until thickened, stirring frequently and breaking up meat so that no pieces larger than ¼ inch remain, about 8 minutes. Season with salt and pepper to taste.

4 Spoon filling into center of each taco shell and top with cheddar, lettuce, tomatoes, and more toppings as desired. Serve.

Rajas Poblanas con Crema y Elote

Why This Recipe Works   To make rajas poblanas con crema y elote—the Mexican dish of charred poblano strips cooked with cream and corn—we started by broiling poblanos until they were completely charred and then wrapping them in foil to steam. This imbued the chiles with smoky flavor and made them easy to peel. Next, we gently cooked white onion and garlic in butter to extract the aromatics' sweet, nutty flavors, before tossing in the charred poblanos and corn and stirring in Mexican crema. Crema made the mixture creamy, lightly salty, and tangy, which tempered the mild heat of the poblanos without eclipsing it. Cooking times will vary depending on the broiler, so watch the chiles carefully. If you can't find Mexican crema, substitute heavy cream. Rajas poblanas con crema y elote is a versatile dish that can also be enjoyed alongside grilled meat or fish, rice, or beans, or as a filling for quesadillas.

- 1 pound (3 to 4) poblano chiles, stemmed, halved, and seeded
- 2 tablespoons unsalted butter
- ½ white onion, sliced through root end ¼ inch thick
- 2 garlic cloves, minced
- ¾ cup fresh or frozen corn
- ½ teaspoon table salt
- ¼ teaspoon pepper
- ¾ cup Mexican crema
- 12 (6-inch) corn tortillas, warmed

1   Line rimmed baking sheet with aluminum foil. Arrange poblanos skin side up on prepared sheet and press to flatten. Adjust oven rack 3 to 4 inches from broiler element and heat broiler. Broil until skin is puffed and most of surface is well charred, 5 to 10 minutes, rotating sheet halfway through broiling.

2   Using tongs, pile poblanos in center of foil. Gather foil over poblanos and crimp to form pouch. Let steam for 10 minutes. Open foil packet carefully and spread out poblanos. When cool enough to handle, peel poblanos (it's OK if some bits of skin remain intact) and discard skins. Slice lengthwise into ½-inch-thick strips. (Rajas can be refrigerated for up to 3 days.)

3   Melt butter in 12-inch nonstick skillet over medium heat. Add onion and cook, stirring occasionally until onion has softened and edges are just starting to brown, 6 to 8 minutes. Add garlic and cook until fragrant, about 30 seconds. Add rajas, corn, salt, and pepper and cook until warmed through, about 1 minute. Add crema and cook, stirring gently but frequently, until crema has thickened and clings to vegetables, 2 to 3 minutes. Serve immediately with tortillas.

A dollop of one of these condiments can go a long way in tempering heat, enhancing richness, or boosting flavor. Smear these condiments liberally on sandwiches, burgers, wraps, and tacos, or mix and match them with other recipes in this book.

Sauces and Spreads

Classic Burger Sauce

Makes about 1 cup
Total time: 5 minutes

- ½ cup mayonnaise
- ¼ cup ketchup
- 2 teaspoons sweet pickle relish
- 2 teaspoons distilled white vinegar
- 1 teaspoon pepper

Whisk all ingredients together in bowl. Season with salt and pepper to taste. (Sauce can be refrigerated in airtight container for up to 4 days.)

Avocado Crema

Makes about ⅔ cup
Total time: 10 minutes

- ½ avocado, chopped
- ½ cup fresh chopped cilantro
- ¼ cup sour cream
- ¼ cup water
- ½ serrano chile, seeded and minced
- 1 teaspoon lime juice
- ¼ teaspoon table salt

Process avocado, cilantro, sour cream, water, serrano, lime juice, and salt in food processor until smooth, about 1 minute, scraping down sides of bowl as needed. Season with salt and pepper to taste. (Crema can be refrigerated for up to 3 days.)

Tahini-Yogurt Sauce

Makes 1 cup
Total time: 5 minutes, plus 30 minutes resting

- ⅓ cup tahini
- ⅓ cup plain Greek yogurt
- ¼ cup water
- 3 tablespoons lemon juice
- 1 garlic clove, minced
- ¾ teaspoon table salt

Whisk all ingredients together in bowl. Let sit until flavors meld, about 30 minutes. Season with salt and pepper to taste. (Sauce can be refrigerated for up to 4 days.)

Cilantro-Mint Chutney

Makes about 1 cup
Total time: 10 minutes

2	cups fresh cilantro leaves
1	cup fresh mint leaves
⅓	cup plain yogurt
¼	cup finely chopped onion
1	tablespoon lime juice
1½	teaspoons sugar
½	teaspoon ground cumin
¼	teaspoon table salt

Process all ingredients in food processor until smooth, about 20 seconds, scraping down sides of bowl as needed. Season with salt and pepper to taste. (Chutney can be refrigerated for up to 2 days.)

Easy Barbecue Sauce

Makes about 1¼ cups
Total time: 25 minutes

1	tablespoon vegetable oil
¼	cup grated onion
½	teaspoon garlic powder
½	teaspoon chili powder
⅛	teaspoon cayenne pepper
¾	cup ketchup
2	tablespoons molasses
1½	tablespoons Worcestershire sauce
1½	tablespoons cider vinegar
1	tablespoon Dijon mustard
½	teaspoon hot sauce

1 Heat oil in small saucepan over medium heat until shimmering. Add onion and cook, stirring occasionally, until softened, 3 to 5 minutes. Stir in garlic powder, chili powder, and cayenne and cook until fragrant, about 30 seconds.

2 Stir in ketchup, molasses, Worcestershire, vinegar, mustard, and hot sauce and bring to simmer. Reduce heat to low and cook until flavors meld, about 5 minutes. Let cool completely before serving. (Cooled sauce can be refrigerated for up to 1 week.)

Everyday Dinners

Red Curry Chicken and Sweet Potatoes

Why This Recipe Works We drew inspiration from the aromatic, funky, deeply savory flavors of Thai curries to make this hearty and filling meal that uses just 12 ounces of chicken thighs. To start, we coated the chicken with red curry paste, to make sure our modest amount of meat was thoroughly infused with flavor. Rendering the chicken helped bloom the paste and also gave us a rich base to which we added dense and satiating sweet potatoes. The tubers made a robust partner to the chicken by contributing heft and absorbing the meat's savory flavor. Along with the sweet potatoes, we added coconut milk and water, making sure to scrape up the flavorful browned bits at the bottom of the pot. Thanks to the starch from the tubers, the curry thickened to a lusciously velvety consistency as it cooked. A final sprinkle of cilantro and scallion offered an herbaceous counterpoint to the warm, spicy flavor profile of the dish. Serve with rice.

1 Pat chicken dry with paper towels and toss with curry paste. Heat oil in 12-inch skillet over medium-high heat until shimmering. Add chicken and cook until lightly browned on all sides, 5 to 7 minutes.

2 Stir in sweet potatoes, coconut milk, and water, scraping up any browned bits, and bring to simmer. Reduce heat to medium-low; cover; and cook until sweet potatoes are just tender, about 10 minutes.

3 Uncover and continue to simmer until sweet potatoes are fully tender, 8 to 10 minutes. Off heat, stir in cilantro, season with salt and pepper to taste, sprinkle with scallions, and serve with lime wedges.

12 ounces boneless, skinless chicken thighs, trimmed and cut into ¾-inch pieces

2 tablespoons Thai red curry paste

2 teaspoons vegetable oil

1 pound sweet potatoes, peeled and cut into ½-inch pieces

1 cup canned coconut milk

½ cup water

¼ cup chopped fresh cilantro

4 scallions, sliced thin

Lime wedges

Kare Raisu

Why This Recipe Works Kare raisu, or curry rice, is one of Japan's go-to comfort foods: a bowl filled with fragrant spiced stew (the curry) on one side and a mound of steamed rice on the other. We used just 1 pound of chicken thighs, but ended up with incredible savoriness thanks to the concentrated umami of the curry roux. Cooks typically make the curry by adding a commercial curry-roux "brick" (roux that's seasoned with Japanese curry powder and sometimes umami boosters, and solidified) to the cooking liquid, doctoring the velvety gravy with additional seasonings and bulking it up with vegetables and/or proteins. But it's easy to fully customize the dish by making your own curry roux. The bricks freeze well and are great for pulling out any time you need a fast, hearty, belly-warming meal. In this version, we cooked the roux only until golden brown (not darker, like many commercial versions); this not only enabled the spices to stand out but also heightened the roux's thickening power, since browning the fat-flour paste weakens its ability to thicken liquid. Carefully blending the spices resulted in a warm, delicately sweet-savory curry powder, and starting with commercial ground spices made for a smoother curry than one made from spices ground at home. Adding a little sugar and miso rounded out the flavors of the curry roux, and refrigerating it in a loaf pan molded it into a flat "brick" that could easily be halved and used to make two batches of curry rice. To cook the stew, we sautéed aromatics—onions, garlic, ginger—and chunks of boneless, skinless chicken thighs, which are succulent and easy to prep. We salted the meat prior to cooking to ensure the seasoning sufficiently penetrated each piece. We then added chicken broth, as well as carrots and potatoes, both of which are classic in Japanese curry. We also dropped in our homemade curry-roux brick, plus dashes of soy and Worcestershire sauces for even more umami depth, during the last few minutes of cooking; these seasoned and thickened the stew. Though this recipe only calls for a pound of meat, it's deeply savory from the curry roux, which coats the protein and vegetables in complex layers of savoriness. Fukujinzuke is a traditional mixture of sweet-tart (sometimes vibrantly pink or red) pickled vegetables. Look for it in vacuum-sealed packages in the refrigerated section of your local Japanese or Korean grocery store.

1 pound boneless, skinless chicken thighs, trimmed and cut into 1-inch pieces

1¼ teaspoons kosher salt, divided

1 tablespoon vegetable oil

1 onion, chopped

2½ teaspoons grated fresh ginger

1 garlic clove, minced

1 pound Yukon Gold potatoes, peeled and cut into ¾-inch pieces

2 carrots, peeled and cut into ½-inch pieces (1 cup)

2⅔ cups chicken broth

1 (4-ounce) curry-roux brick (recipe follows)

2 teaspoons soy sauce

1 teaspoon Worcestershire sauce

4 cups cooked short-grain white rice (page 303)

1 scallion, sliced thin on bias

Fukujinzuke or pickled ginger or lemon wedges

1 Toss chicken and 1 teaspoon salt in bowl. Heat oil in medium saucepan over medium heat until shimmering. Add onion and remaining ¼ teaspoon salt and cook, stirring frequently, until onion is browned, about 8 minutes. Add ginger and garlic and cook, stirring constantly, until fragrant, about 30 seconds.

2 Add chicken and cook, stirring frequently, until chicken is no longer pink, about 3 minutes. Stir in potatoes and carrots. Add broth and bring to simmer over high heat. Adjust heat to maintain gentle simmer and cook until potatoes are just tender, about 20 minutes.

3 Add curry-roux brick, soy sauce, and Worcestershire to broth mixture, and let block dissolve, about 1 minute. Stir gently, scraping curry from bottom of pot, and simmer until liquid thickens, about 3 minutes. Season with salt and pepper to taste.

4 Divide rice evenly among 4 shallow bowls, spreading it over half of each bowl. Divide curry evenly among bowls, making sure to ladle curry next to rice. Sprinkle scallion over curry and serve with fukujinzuke.

Japanese Curry-Roux Bricks

Makes two 4-ounce curry-roux bricks | Total time: 25 minutes, plus 30 minutes chilling

We prefer commercially ground spices for this recipe because they are very finely ground. If using whole spices, grind each individually until very fine and sift through a fine-mesh strainer before measuring. You can substitute mustard powder for the ground brown mustard. White miso has a sweeter flavor and a fine texture that we like here; red miso makes a slightly coarse, more robustly savory curry. If using the curry roux immediately in the Kare Raisu, divide the mixture in half at the end of step 2. Use half in the curry rice recipe, transfer the remaining mixture to a loaf pan (the roux will not cover the surface), and proceed with step 3.

1½ teaspoons sugar

1½ teaspoons ground turmeric

1½ teaspoons ground coriander

1½ teaspoons ground ginger

½ teaspoon ground cardamom

½ teaspoon ground cumin

½ teaspoon ground cinnamon

½ teaspoon ground fennel

½ teaspoon ground fenugreek

½ teaspoon garlic powder

¼ teaspoon ground brown mustard

¼ teaspoon pepper

8 tablespoons unsalted butter

⅔ cup all-purpose flour

1 tablespoon white miso

1 Stir sugar, turmeric, coriander, ginger, cardamom, cumin, cinnamon, fennel, fenugreek, garlic powder, mustard, and pepper together in bowl.

2 Melt butter in 10-inch skillet over low heat. Off heat, sprinkle flour over butter and whisk until smooth. Return skillet to medium heat and cook, whisking very frequently, until flour mixture is pale golden brown, 3 to 4 minutes. Remove from heat and immediately whisk in spices. Add miso and whisk until very well combined (mixture will not be totally smooth).

3 Transfer mixture to loaf pan and smooth into even layer. Refrigerate until fully set, about 30 minutes. Run knife around edge of pan to release curry brick. Remove brick from pan and cut into 2 equal pieces. (Bricks can be refrigerated in airtight container for up to 1 week or frozen for up to 3 months.)

Kare Raisu
(page 250)

Green Mole with Chayote and Chicken

Why This Recipe Works Mole verde, an herby green variety of mole, is highly popular in Mexico. Unlike mole poblano (which is perhaps more famous globally and uses an assortment of dried chiles, fruit, and spices), green mole uses fresh chiles and tomatillos, sesame seeds, pepitas, and piles of herbs. For our take, we used a pound of chicken thighs cut into pieces, then bulked up the meat with tender bites of chayote. Though the meat is usually poached first (and the cooking liquid used as broth for the mole), we added the raw meat straight to the sauce to maximize its impact; the protein released its rich juices into the sauce as it cooked. To make the mole sauce, we blended the aromatics and seeds and then cooked the mixture in oil to concentrate the flavors. You can substitute one drained 28-ounce can of tomatillos for fresh. If you can't find chayote, you can substitute 1½ pounds of zucchini, halved lengthwise and then sliced crosswise ¼ inch thick. After searing the zucchini in step 4, transfer it to a bowl, then stir it into the pot with the poblanos in step 6. Serve with rice or warm corn tortillas.

- 3 poblano chiles, stemmed, halved, and seeded
- 1 pound tomatillos, husks and stems removed, rinsed well and dried
- 1 serrano or jalapeño chile, stemmed, halved, and seeded
- 1 onion, chopped coarse
- ½ cup roasted, unsalted pepitas plus extra for serving
- ¼ cup sesame seeds, toasted, plus extra for serving
- 4 garlic cloves, chopped
- 1¼ teaspoons table salt, divided
- 1 teaspoon dried Mexican oregano
- ¾ teaspoon ground cumin
- ½ teaspoon ground allspice
- 1 tablespoon vegetable oil
- 1½ pounds chayote, peeled, cored, and cut into ½-inch pieces
- 1 pound boneless, skinless chicken thighs, trimmed and cut into 1-inch pieces
- 1¾ cups chicken broth, divided, plus extra as needed
- 1 ounce fresh cilantro leaves and tender stems (about 2½ cups)

1 Adjust oven rack 3 to 4 inches from broiler element and heat broiler. Line rimmed baking sheet with aluminum foil. Arrange poblanos skin side up on prepared sheet and press to flatten. Broil until skin is puffed and most of surface is well charred, 5 to 10 minutes, rotating sheet halfway through broiling.

2 Using tongs, pile poblanos in center of foil. Gather foil over poblanos and crimp to form pouch. Let steam for 10 minutes. Open foil packet carefully and spread out poblanos. When cool enough to handle, peel poblanos (it's OK if some bits of skin remain intact) and discard skins. Slice crosswise into ½-inch-thick strips and set aside.

3 Meanwhile, combine tomatillos, serrano, onion, pepitas, sesame seeds, garlic, ¾ teaspoon salt, oregano, cumin, and allspice in blender and process until smooth, about 2 minutes.

4 Heat oil in Dutch oven over medium-high heat until just smoking. Add chayote and ¼ teaspoon salt and cook until well browned, 8 to 10 minutes. Off heat, carefully add sauce (sauce will splatter). Cook over medium heat, stirring frequently, until slightly darkened and thickened, about 5 minutes.

5 Stir chicken, 1¼ cups broth, and remaining ¼ teaspoon salt into pot and bring to simmer. Cover; reduce heat to medium-low; and simmer gently until chicken is cooked through and chayote is tender, about 20 minutes.

6 Combine cilantro and remaining ½ cup broth in clean, dry blender jar and process until just smooth, 30 to 45 seconds (do not overprocess). Stir cilantro mixture and reserved poblanos into mole in pot and bring to simmer. Season with salt and pepper to taste, and thin mole with extra broth as needed. Sprinkle individual portions with extra pepitas and sesame seeds and serve.

Prepping Chayote

1 After peeling chayote, cut in half lengthwise.

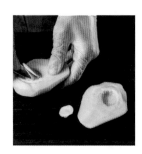

2 Using small spoon or your fingers, scoop out core and discard.

Cast Iron Steak and Vegetable Fajitas

Why This Recipe Works Skirt steak has a strong beefy flavor, so eating even a small amount can feel deeply satisfying—especially when it's in fajitas, paired with a generous portion of vegetables. Because it's such a thin cut, skirt steak also offers ample surface area—all the more opportunity for the seasonings to cling to the meat. To start, we made a flavorful spice mix—which included cumin, chili powder, oregano, and allspice—and sprinkled it over 12 ounces of skirt steak. We then cooked the steak in a cast-iron pan, the high heat of which gave the meat a nice char without overcooking the interior. While the steak rested, we used the same pan to cook poblanos, bell pepper, and onion. The vegetables blistered, softened, and browned quickly as they soaked up the rich, seasoning-laced fat left behind by the meat, distributing the steak's rich flavor throughout the dish. Off the heat, a drizzle of lime juice and a scattering of chopped cilantro gave the vegetables a bright, zesty edge that made an excellent counterbalance to the savoriness they'd absorbed during cooking. Be sure to slice the steak as thin as possible against the grain; otherwise, it will be very chewy. Serve the fajitas with pico de gallo, avocado or guacamole, sour cream, and/or your favorite hot sauce. A nonstick skillet can also be used here; in step 1, add 2 tablespoons of oil to the skillet, swirl to coat, and heat until the oil is just smoking before adding steak.

1 teaspoon kosher salt

½ teaspoon pepper

½ teaspoon ground cumin

½ teaspoon chili powder

½ teaspoon granulated garlic

½ teaspoon dried oregano

Pinch ground allspice

12 ounces skirt steak, trimmed and cut with grain into 3 equal pieces

2 tablespoons vegetable oil, divided

3 poblano chiles, stemmed, seeded, and cut into ¼-inch wide strips

1 yellow, red, or orange bell pepper, stemmed, seeded, and cut into ¼-inch-wide strips

1 onion, halved and sliced ¼ inch thick

2 garlic cloves, minced

¼ cup chopped fresh cilantro

1 tablespoon lime juice, plus lime wedges for serving

12 (6-inch) flour tortillas, warmed

1 Combine salt, pepper, cumin, chili powder, granulated garlic, oregano, and allspice in bowl. Pat steak dry with paper towels and sprinkle with spice mixture. Heat 12-inch cast-iron skillet over medium heat for 3 minutes. Add 1 tablespoon oil to skillet and swirl to coat. Place seasoned steak in skillet and cook until well browned and meat registers 135 degrees (for medium), 2 to 4 minutes per side. Transfer to cutting board, tent with aluminum foil, and let rest while cooking pepper mixture.

2 Add remaining 1 tablespoon oil, poblanos, and bell pepper to now-empty skillet and cook for 3 minutes. Stir in onion and cook until vegetables are just softened, 3 to 5 minutes. Stir in garlic and cook until fragrant, about 30 seconds. Off heat, stir in cilantro and lime juice and season with salt and pepper to taste.

3 Slice steaks thin against grain. Stir any accumulated juices from cutting board into vegetables in skillet. Push vegetables to 1 side of skillet and place beef on empty side. Serve with tortillas and lime wedges.

Stir-Fried Beef and Gai Lan

Why This Recipe Works: For our take on the ever-evolving Chinese American standard of stir-frying beef with a leafy green, we chose gai lan, also known as Chinese broccoli, and filet mignon. The sturdy, absorbent gai lan became infused with wok hei (the smoky, slightly charred flavor that comes from cooking it in a seasoned wok), while the rich, buttery meat's melt-in-your-mouth quality made it luxurious to eat, even in smaller quantities. We found that an 8-ounce portion of meat—coupled with double the weight in gai lan—was all we needed for an appealingly beefy stir-fry (and conveniently, filet mignon is readily available to buy in small portions). For easy slicing, we started by briefly chilling the meat in the freezer to firm up, before coating it in a simple yet savory mixture of soy sauce, Shaoxing wine, and cornstarch. While the meat chilled, we sliced the gai lan stalks thin on the bias and cut the tender leaves into wide ribbons. We started the stir-frying process by cooking the stalks in oil in a hot wok. As they sizzled, the oil smoldered, infusing the dish with smoky wok hei. We then set the stalks aside and stir-fried the leaves with garlic and toasted sesame oil, speeding their cooking with a small but flavorful addition of chicken broth before arranging the leaves on a serving platter. Finally, we stir-fried the beef; returned the stalks to the wok; and stirred in a blend of chicken broth, oyster sauce, soy sauce, Shaoxing wine, toasted sesame oil, and cornstarch, thickening the sauce in no time. We arranged the beef mixture over the leaves, ensuring that each bite was satisfyingly meaty. If gai lan is unavailable, you can use broccolini, substituting the florets for the gai lan leaves. Do not use standard broccoli.

1 (8-ounce) center-cut filet mignon, trimmed

1 pound gai lan, stalks trimmed

5 teaspoons Shaoxing wine, divided

1 tablespoon soy sauce, divided

2 teaspoons cornstarch, divided

¾ cup chicken broth, divided

2 tablespoons oyster sauce

1½ teaspoons toasted sesame oil, divided

2 tablespoons vegetable oil, divided

1½ teaspoons grated fresh ginger

¾ teaspoon minced garlic, divided

1 Cut beef into 4 equal wedges. Transfer to plate and freeze until very firm, 20 to 25 minutes. Meanwhile, remove leaves, small stems, and florets from gai lan stalks; slice leaves crosswise into 1½-inch strips (any florets and stems can go into pile with leaves); and cut stalks on bias into ¼-inch-thick pieces. Set aside. When beef is firm, stand 1 piece on its side and slice against grain ¼ inch thick. Repeat with remaining pieces. Transfer to bowl. Add 1 teaspoon Shaoxing wine, 1 teaspoon soy sauce, and 1 teaspoon cornstarch and toss until beef is evenly coated; set aside.

2 In second bowl, whisk together ½ cup broth, oyster sauce, ½ teaspoon sesame oil, remaining 4 teaspoons Shaoxing wine, remaining 2 teaspoons soy sauce, and remaining 1 teaspoon cornstarch; set aside. In third bowl, combine 4 teaspoons vegetable oil, ginger, and ¼ teaspoon garlic.

3 Heat empty 14-inch flat-bottomed wok or 12-inch carbon-steel skillet over high heat until just beginning to smoke. Drizzle 1 teaspoon vegetable oil around perimeter of wok and heat until just smoking. Add gai lan stalks and cook, stirring slowly but constantly, until spotty brown and crisp-tender, 3 to 4 minutes; transfer to separate bowl.

4 Add remaining 1 teaspoon sesame oil, remaining 1 teaspoon vegetable oil, and remaining ½ teaspoon garlic to now-empty wok and cook, stirring constantly, until garlic is fragrant, about 15 seconds. Add gai lan leaves and cook, stirring frequently, until vibrant green, about 1 minute. Add remaining ¼ cup broth and cook, stirring constantly, until broth evaporates, 2 to 3 minutes. Spread mixture evenly in serving dish.

5 Add ginger-garlic mixture to now-empty wok and cook, stirring constantly, until fragrant, about 30 seconds. Add beef mixture and cook, stirring slowly but constantly, until no longer pink, about 2 minutes. Return stalks to wok and add oyster sauce mixture. Cook, stirring constantly, until sauce thickens, 30 to 60 seconds. Place mixture on top of leaves. Serve.

Cheesy Black Bean and Pork Skillet Bake

Why This Recipe Works This comforting casserole that starts on the stovetop and finishes in the oven makes for a gratifyingly flavorful yet simple weeknight dinner, relying on kitchen staples to create a filling and well-seasoned dish. To start, we browned just 6 ounces of ground pork in an ovensafe skillet before adding onion, red bell pepper, garlic, chili powder, and oregano; as the mixture cooked in the rendered fat, the vegetables softened and took on the savory flavor of the pork, while the spices intensified in fragrance. Black beans and diced tomatoes—both from a can—as well as frozen corn not only bulked up the dish with additional fiber, but also absorbed the porky umami as the mixture simmered. A sprinkle of pepper Jack cheese ensured that each bite had an extra kick of heat and richness; broiling the dish in the oven made the cheesy surface appetizingly gooey and browned in spots. A final sprinkle of sliced scallions offered a fresh, peppery note that made a welcome complement to the hearty richness of the dish. You will need a 10-inch ovensafe skillet for this recipe. This dish is great served on its own, but you could also eat it with tortillas or serve it with rice.

1 Adjust oven rack 6 inches from broiler element and heat broiler. Heat oil in 10-inch ovensafe skillet over medium-high heat until just smoking. Add pork and cook, breaking up meat with wooden spoon, until just beginning to brown, 3 to 5 minutes.

2 Add onion and bell pepper, and cook until softened, about 5 minutes. Stir in chili powder, oregano, and garlic and cook until fragrant, about 1 minute. Stir in beans and their liquid, tomatoes, and corn. Bring to simmer, and cook until mixture has thickened slightly, about 5 minutes. Off heat, season with salt and pepper to taste, then sprinkle evenly with pepper Jack.

3 Transfer skillet to oven and broil until cheese is browned in spots, 3 to 5 minutes. Let cool for 10 minutes, then sprinkle with scallions and serve with lime wedges.

1 tablespoon vegetable oil

6 ounces ground pork

1 onion, chopped fine

1 red bell pepper, stemmed, seeded, and chopped

1 tablespoon chili powder

1 tablespoon minced fresh oregano or 1 teaspoon dried

2 garlic cloves, sliced thin

1 (15-ounce) can black beans, undrained

1 (14.5-ounce) can diced tomatoes, drained

1 cup frozen corn

6 ounces pepper Jack cheese, shredded (1½ cups)

2 scallions, sliced thin

Lime wedges

Squash, Pork, and Tamarind Curry

Why This Recipe Works For this simple yet highly flavorful dish, we took a cue from the curries of Myanmar (also known as Burma), which often rely on a generous amount of shallots, garlic, and ginger; a few choice spices, most commonly turmeric and chile powder; and sometimes fresh herbs, to produce an abundance of flavor in minimal time. Inspired by a tamarind and squash curry recipe in Naomi Duguid's cookbook, *Burma: Rivers of Flavor*, we made those two ingredients the stars of this dish, with ground pork as a supporting character. We browned 8 ounces of ground pork on the stovetop to render it and then cooked our aromatics and spices in this fat so they could sponge up the porky richness. After pouring in water—and taking care to scrape up the browned bits of savory goodness at the bottom of the pot—we added butternut squash, which has a knack for sopping up flavor and seasonings. Fish sauce further amped up the curry's savory depth, while tamarind juice concentrate imbued the dish with a tangy, sweet, and fruity dimension that complemented the umami notes. For additional fiber and textural interest, we incorporated gai lan, also known as Chinese broccoli, a vegetable popular in Myanmar. Gai lan delivers two textures at once—tender, quick-cooking leaves and snappy, crunchy stalks—both of which contrasted deliciously with the soft, dense squash. A sprinkle of Thai basil leaves finished the curry with a dose of licorice-scented pepperiness. Look for Thai/Indonesian-style tamarind concentrate labeled "nuoc me chua"; do not use Indian-style tamarind concentrates (see page 15 for more information). You can substitute kabocha squash for butternut or acorn, but you will need to extend the cook time in step 3 to about 20 minutes. If you can't find gai lan, you can substitute broccolini, using the florets in place of the gai lan leaves. Serve with rice.

8 ounces gai lan, stalks trimmed
8 ounces ground pork
4–6 large shallots, chopped (1½ cups)
5 garlic cloves, minced
4 teaspoons grated fresh ginger
2 teaspoons paprika
1 teaspoon ground turmeric
¼ teaspoon cayenne pepper
2 cinnamon sticks
2¾ cups water
1 pound butternut or acorn squash, peeled and cut into 1-inch pieces
¼ cup tamarind juice concentrate
2 tablespoons fish sauce
½ cup fresh Thai basil leaves, torn if large

1 Remove leaves, small stems, and florets from gai lan stalks; slice leaves crosswise into 1½-inch strips (any florets and stems can go into pile with leaves); and cut stalks into ½-inch-thick pieces. Set aside.

2 Cook pork in Dutch oven over medium heat, breaking up large pieces, until golden-brown fond begins to form on bottom of pot, 5 to 8 minutes. Add shallots and cook until very soft, about 3 minutes.

3 Stir in garlic, ginger, paprika, turmeric, cayenne, and cinnamon sticks and cook until fragrant, about 30 seconds. Stir in water, scraping up any browned bits, then add squash, tamarind juice concentrate, fish sauce, and gai lan stalks. Bring to simmer, then reduce heat to medium-low; cover; and simmer until squash is tender, about 10 minutes.

4 Stir in gai lan leaves, and cook, uncovered, until leaves wilt but are still bright green, 1 to 2 minutes. Discard cinnamon sticks, sprinkle with basil, and serve.

'Nduja with Beans and Greens

Why This Recipe Works Some meats pack a remarkable punch without much doctoring up needed, and spicy Italian 'nduja is one of them. The soft, spreadable cured sausage that hails from Calabria boasts heat, acidity, and funk, even in small amounts. For this weeknight-friendly dish, we sautéed just 6 ounces of 'nduja, which practically melted into the pan as we rendered its spice-infused fat. We then stirred in quick-cooking, fortifying canned cannellini beans and kale, which sopped up the 'nduja's spicy umami flavor while the mixture simmered. Off the heat, we stirred in Parmesan cheese, which endowed the dish with nutty richness and amped up its savoriness. For a buttery boost that also added a dose of protein, we fried up a few eggs; their crisp, lacy edges and creamy yolks brought even more textural contrast to this satisfying meal.

6 ounces 'nduja, casings removed

2 (15-ounce) cans cannellini beans (1 can drained and rinsed, 1 can undrained)

1 pound kale, stemmed and chopped

½ teaspoon pepper, divided

1 ounce Parmesan cheese, grated (½ cup), divided

1 tablespoon extra-virgin olive oil, plus extra for drizzling

4 large eggs

¼ teaspoon salt

1 Cook 'nduja in Dutch oven over medium-high heat, breaking up meat with wooden spoon, until meat darkens in color and fat is rendered, 3 to 5 minutes. Stir in beans and their liquid, kale, and ¼ teaspoon pepper and bring to simmer. Reduce heat to medium-low; cover; and cook, stirring occasionally, until kale is tender and sauce has thickened slightly, 5 to 7 minutes. Off heat, stir in ¼ cup Parmesan.

2 Meanwhile, heat oil in 12-inch nonstick skillet over medium-high heat until shimmering. Crack 2 eggs into small bowl. Repeat with remaining 2 eggs and second small bowl. Sprinkle eggs with salt and remaining ¼ teaspoon pepper. Working quickly, pour 1 bowl of eggs into 1 side of pan and second bowl of eggs into other side. Cover and cook for 1 minute. Remove skillet from heat and let sit, covered, 15 to 45 seconds for runny yolks (white around edge of yolk will be barely opaque), 45 to 60 seconds for soft but set yolks, and about 2 minutes for medium-set yolks. Serve beans and kale with fried eggs, sprinkling individual portions with remaining ¼ cup Parmesan and drizzling with extra oil.

SERVES 4 | TOTAL TIME 55 MINUTES • *fiber-ful* • *one-pan* •

Roasted Radicchio, Fennel, and Root Vegetables with Sausage and Herbs

Why This Recipe Works A medley of robust vegetables—bitter-earthy radicchio, peppery fennel, creamy potatoes, and aromatic shallots—creates an intriguing balance of flavors and textures in this hearty oven-roasted dinner. To ensure that the vegetables roasted evenly, we cut them into comparably sized pieces. We started by seasoning our vegetables with garlic, rosemary, and sugar; the sugar helped encourage flavorful browning. We roasted the fennel, potatoes, and shallots first to give them a head start, as they take longer to soften; we added the radicchio and sausage partway through. Arranging the radicchio in the center of the baking sheet with the other vegetables around the perimeter kept the more delicate radicchio from charring. Placing herby Italian sausages on top of the vegetables allowed the meat's flavorful juices to drip down and enrich the vegetables. Once all the vegetables were caramelized, we drizzled the whole shebang with a lemony dressing that we enhanced by smashing the garlic from our sheet pan; the oven time gave the garlic, and hence our dressing, a nutty complexity. When coring the radicchio, leave just enough core to hold each wedge together.

2 fennel bulbs, halved, cored, and sliced into ½-inch wedges

1 pound red potatoes, unpeeled, cut into ¾-inch pieces

1 head radicchio (10 ounces), halved, cored, and cut into 2-inch wedges

8 shallots, peeled and halved

¼ cup extra-virgin olive oil, divided

6 garlic cloves, peeled

1 teaspoon minced fresh rosemary or ¼ teaspoon dried

1 teaspoon sugar

¾ teaspoon table salt

¼ teaspoon pepper

1 pound sweet or hot Italian sausage

¼ cup chopped fresh basil

¼ cup minced fresh chives

3 tablespoons lemon juice

1 tablespoon water

1 Adjust oven rack to middle position and heat oven to 450 degrees. Toss fennel, potatoes, radicchio, shallots, 1 tablespoon oil, garlic, rosemary, sugar, salt, and pepper together in bowl. Spray rimmed baking sheet with vegetable oil spray.

2 Spread vegetables, excluding radicchio, into single layer on prepared sheet. Roast for 10 minutes. Push vegetables to sides of sheet and arrange radicchio wedges, cut side down, in center. Place sausages on top of vegetables and roast for 10 minutes. Rotate sheet; flip sausages; and continue to roast until sausages register 160 degrees and vegetables are tender and golden brown, about 10 minutes longer.

3 Transfer sausages to cutting board and cut into 1-inch pieces; return to sheet. Transfer garlic cloves to cutting board and smash into paste using flat side of chef's knife. Whisk basil, chives, lemon juice, water, garlic paste, and remaining 3 tablespoons oil in bowl until combined. Drizzle half of dressing over vegetables and sausages on sheet. Serve, seasoning with salt and pepper to taste, and passing remaining dressing separately.

Everyday Dinners 267

Sausage-Stuffed Portobello Mushrooms with Cabbage Salad

Why This Recipe Works Portobello mushrooms have a particularly meaty chew that makes them ultrasatisfying—and they also happen to make perfect pockets for any number of stuffings. When we asked ourselves what filling would stand up to the mushrooms' dense bite, we found that hearty kale or spinach—enriched with flavorful hot Italian sausage—was an excellent choice. To start, we salted and par-roasted portobello caps to remove excess moisture and concentrate their umami. For the filling, we cooked the sausage and kale together in a skillet, along with more (chopped) portobello mushrooms. Though we only used 6 ounces of meat, sautéing the spicy sausage released plenty of juice—enough to greatly enrich the mushrooms and greens. We then added shredded cheddar, which not only made an effective binder but also injected the mixture with nutty depth. To serve alongside, we made a simply seasoned cabbage salad, a perfectly tangy, crunchy complement to the earthy stuffed mushrooms. Combining the salad components during the mushrooms' initial roast allowed enough time for the cabbage to sit and soften. Thinly sliced cabbage is key to the vinegar and salt softening the cabbage— use a mandoline or the slicing disk on a food processor.

- 10 portobello mushrooms (4 to 5 inches in diameter), stems removed and reserved
- ½ teaspoon table salt, divided
- ½ head green cabbage, halved, cored, and sliced thin (6 cups)
- 4 teaspoons extra-virgin olive oil, divided
- 1 tablespoon white wine vinegar
- 1½ teaspoons minced fresh thyme or ½ teaspoon dried, divided
- 1 teaspoon pepper, divided
- 6 ounces hot Italian sausage, casings removed
- 12 ounces frozen chopped kale or spinach, thawed and squeezed dry
- 3 garlic cloves, minced
- 3 ounces extra-sharp cheddar cheese, shredded (¾ cup)

1 Adjust oven rack to upper-middle position and heat oven to 500 degrees. Set wire rack in rimmed baking sheet lined with aluminum foil and spray rack with vegetable oil spray. Place 8 portobellos gill side up on rack and sprinkle evenly with ⅛ teaspoon salt. Flip and sprinkle tops evenly with ⅛ teaspoon salt. Transfer to oven and roast until tender, about 20 minutes.

2 Meanwhile, combine cabbage, 1 tablespoon oil, vinegar, ½ teaspoon thyme, ½ teaspoon pepper, and ⅛ teaspoon salt; season with salt and pepper to taste and set aside until ready to serve. Chop remaining 2 portobellos, then pulse with reserved stems in food processor until finely chopped, 10 to 14 pulses.

3 Heat remaining 1 teaspoon oil in 12-inch nonstick skillet over medium heat until shimmering. Add pulsed mushrooms and remaining ⅛ teaspoon salt; cover; and cook until mushrooms have released their liquid, 3 to 5 minutes. Add sausage and kale to skillet, breaking up meat into small pieces with wooden spoon, and cook until mushrooms and sausage are starting to brown, about 5 minutes. Stir in garlic, remaining 1 teaspoon thyme, and remaining ½ teaspoon pepper and cook until fragrant, about 30 seconds. Off heat, stir in cheddar.

4 Flip mushrooms gill side up, then divide mushroom-sausage mixture among mushrooms, spreading into even layer. Bake until filling is spotty brown, about 5 minutes. Transfer to platter and serve with cabbage salad.

Okonomiyaki

Why This Recipe Works Okonomiyaki is a savory filled pancake that's beloved in Japan as both a street food and a home-cooked staple. Though it has many delectable variations, it usually features flour, eggs, cabbage, and a bit of pork, but the translation of okonomiyaki, "grilled as you'd like," means that it can certainly be adapted to personal taste and different ingredients. Our recipe—a mostly meatless take made with 6 ounces of pork belly—aims to represent the popular Osaka-style okonomiyaki, in which ingredients are mixed into the batter (as opposed to Hiroshima-style, in which the ingredients and batter are cooked in distinct layers). A defining characteristic of okonomiyaki is its soft, slightly custardy interior, which it gets from adding grated yamaimo, Japanese mountain yam; as you grate the yam, it forms a viscous, slippery paste that makes the batter very creamy. We combined the grated yamaimo with flour and eggs, seasoning the mixture with instant dashi powder for an easy but powerful jolt of umami. To this batter, we added thinly sliced pork belly (cut into pieces for better flavor distribution) and bulked up the mixture with plenty of cabbage for bite and fiber. Traditionally prepared on a teppan, a Japanese iron griddle, okonomiyaki lends itself to cooking in a cast-iron skillet, which crisps the outside of the pancake while maintaining the interior's signature tenderness. As the mixture sizzled, the fat in the pork belly melted and enriched the dish. Delicious as it is, okonomiyaki is only complete with the traditional toppings: Homemade okonomiyaki sauce provides sweet tang, Kewpie mayo adds savory richness, and katsuobushi (smoked bonito flakes) and aonori (dried and powdered green seaweed) bring umami and slight saltiness. Yamaimo can also be labeled nagaimo, or Chinese yam. When peeling and grating, use disposable kitchen gloves, as the yamaimo will produce a slippery, liquid-y paste that may cause skin irritation when handled raw. If unavailable, substitute 3 tablespoons potato starch. Thinly sliced uncured pork belly can often be found in the freezer section of a Japanese or Chinese grocery store; if using frozen pork belly, be sure to thaw it completely before using. Thinly sliced hickory bacon is a suitable alternative. You will need a 12-inch cast-iron, carbon-steel, or nonstick skillet with a tight-fitting lid for this recipe. If using a nonstick skillet, add the oil to the skillet in step 3 before heating and do not reduce the heat. Okonomiyaki is typically served whole on a communal platter; provide a thin spatula or pie server to help separate portions.

Okonomiyaki Sauce

- 2 tablespoons ketchup
- 1 tablespoon Worcestershire sauce
- 1 tablespoon soy sauce
- 1 tablespoon sugar

Okonomiyaki

- ¾ cup boiling water
- ¾ teaspoon instant dashi powder, such as Hondashi
- 1 cup (5 ounces) all-purpose flour
- 2 large eggs
- 3 tablespoons finely grated yamaimo
- ¾ teaspoon table salt
- 2½ cups ½-inch-pieces green cabbage
- 6 ounces thinly sliced pork belly, cut into 1-inch pieces
- 2 scallions, sliced thin
- 2 tablespoons beni-shoga (red pickled ginger), drained, plus extra for serving
- 1 tablespoon vegetable oil
- Kewpie mayonnaise
- Katsuobushi
- Aonori

1 For the okonomiyaki sauce Combine all ingredients in bowl; set aside for serving.

2 For the okonomiyaki Combine boiling water and instant dashi powder in small bowl; let cool slightly. Whisk dashi, flour, eggs, yamaimo, and salt in large bowl until combined. Gently fold in cabbage, pork belly, scallions, and beni-shoga until just combined.

3 Heat skillet over medium heat for 3 minutes. Reduce heat to medium-low. Add oil to skillet, swirling to coat bottom, and heat until shimmering. Add cabbage mixture and spread into even 10-inch round, about 1 inch thick. Cover and cook until okonomiyaki is lightly golden on bottom, 10 to 12 minutes, rotating skillet halfway through cooking and adjusting heat if bottom begins to brown too quickly.

4   Slide okonomiyaki onto large plate, then invert onto second large plate. Slide okonomiyaki back into skillet browned side up and cook, uncovered, until golden brown on bottom, about 10 minutes, rotating skillet halfway through cooking and adjusting heat if bottom begins to brown too quickly.

5   Off heat, spread sauce evenly over top of okonomiyaki. Drizzle generously with Kewpie mayonnaise, sprinkle with katsuobushi and aonori, and top with extra beni-shoga. Serve.

Variation

Shrimp Okonomiyaki

Substitute 8 ounces peeled and deveined shrimp, cut into ½-inch pieces, for pork belly.

Warm White Beans with Tuna, Fennel, and Radishes

Why This Recipe Works A single jar of oil-packed tuna can greatly enhance the savoriness of a vegetable-forward dish. Compared to water-packed tuna, the oil-bathed version can feel like a revelation, a rich and meaty ingredient on its own with little adornment needed. For a weeknight dinner centered around this pantry staple, we warmed white beans (a classic Mediterranean pairing with tuna), flavoring the legumes with lemon zest and a sprinkle of chile flakes. While the beans cooked, we made a light, crunchy salad of fresh fennel, peppery radish, and fistfuls of dill and coated the mixture in a lemon–olive oil dressing—a bright, tangy contrast to the creamy, earthy beans and briny fish. Paired with toasted bread smeared with garlicky, citrusy aioli, this meal was as vibrant and elegant as it was quick to whip up. We like watermelon radish in this dish for its striking color, but you can substitute another type of radish if you prefer. Tuna jar sizes vary brand to brand; we prefer a 6½-ounce jar (which yields about 4 ounces when drained). You can substitute another type of tinned fish if desired. A rasp-style grater makes quick work of turning the garlic into a paste.

- 1 shallot, sliced thin
- 2 teaspoons grated lemon zest, divided, plus 3 tablespoons plus 1 teaspoon lemon juice, divided, plus lemon wedges for serving (2 lemons)
- ¼ cup mayonnaise
- ¼ teaspoon garlic, minced to paste
- 3 tablespoons extra-virgin olive oil, divided, plus extra for drizzling
- ¼ teaspoon red pepper flakes
- 2 (15-ounce) cans cannellini beans, 2 tablespoons canning liquid reserved, beans rinsed
- ¼ teaspoon plus ⅛ teaspoon table salt, divided
- ¼ teaspoon pepper, divided
- 2 tablespoons capers, rinsed
- 1 (8-inch) piece baguette, cut on bias into 8 slices
- ¼ teaspoon Dijon mustard
- ½ fennel bulb, stalks discarded, bulb cored and sliced thin
- 1 watermelon radish, trimmed, halved and sliced thin (1½ cups)
- ½ cup chopped fresh dill and/or parsley
- 1 (6½ ounce) jar olive oil-packed tuna, drained and broken into 1½-inch pieces

1 Combine shallot and 2 tablespoons lemon juice in small bowl; set aside, tossing shallot occasionally. Whisk mayonnaise, garlic, and ½ teaspoon lemon zest and 1 teaspoon lemon juice together in small bowl. Season with salt and pepper to taste; set aside until ready to serve.

2 Heat 2 tablespoons oil in medium saucepan over medium heat until shimmering. Add pepper flakes and remaining 1½ teaspoons lemon zest and cook until fragrant, about 30 seconds. Add beans, reserved bean liquid, ¼ teaspoon salt, and ⅛ teaspoon pepper and cook until warmed through, about 3 minutes, stirring occasionally. Off heat, stir in capers and remaining 1 tablespoon lemon juice and let sit until flavors meld, about 15 minutes.

3 Meanwhile, adjust oven rack 4 inches from broiler element and heat broiler. Place bread on rimmed baking sheet and broil until golden, 1 to 2 minutes per side.

4 Drain reserved shallots in fine-mesh strainer set over medium bowl. Pour off all but 2 teaspoons lemon juice from bowl, then add mustard, remaining 1 tablespoon oil, remaining ⅛ teaspoon salt, and remaining ⅛ teaspoon pepper and whisk to combine. Add drained shallot, fennel, radish, and dill and toss to combine.

5 Spread garlic mayonnaise over toasted bread slices. Arrange beans on serving platter, then top with fennel mixture and tuna and drizzle with extra oil. Serve with lemon wedges, scooping up beans with bread slices.

Spiced Mahi-Mahi with Mashed Plantains and Pickled Onion

Why This Recipe Works   Savory mashed plantains perfectly complement jerk-seasoned mahi-mahi in this quick, flavorful meal. To start, we simmered plantains until a knife could be easily slipped in and out of them, reserving some of the cooking liquid for mashing the plantains into a smooth, starchy consistency. Enriching the plantains with butter gave the mash an extra-rich, satisfying mouthfeel. Coating mahi-mahi fillets with jerk seasoning before searing not only ingrained the fish with warm, spicy savoriness, but also helped create a crisp crust and lock in the moisture of the interior. Before serving, we topped the mashed plantains with our Quick Sweet and Spicy Pickled Red Onion, as well as a shower of cilantro leaves, for a fresh, zesty dimension that complemented the rich plantains and buttery fish. We call for green (unripe) plantains here. If your plantains have started to yellow, they will be on the sweeter side. You may find it easier to source one 1- to 1½-pound mahi-mahi fillet than four individual fillets. if you can't find mahi-mahi, you can substitute cod or haddock.

3   green plantains, peeled, halved lengthwise, and cut into 1-inch pieces

1½   teaspoons table salt, divided, plus salt for cooking plantains

3   tablespoons unsalted butter

4   (4- to 6-ounce) skinless mahi-mahi fillets, 1 to 1½ inches thick

2   tablespoons jerk seasoning

½   teaspoon pepper

2   tablespoons vegetable oil

1   recipe Quick Sweet and Spicy Pickled Red Onion (page 33)

¼   cup fresh cilantro leaves

1   Place plantains and 2 teaspoons salt in large saucepan, add water to cover by 1 inch, and bring to boil over high heat. Reduce heat to medium and simmer until paring knife can be easily slipped in and out of plantains, 18 to 22 minutes. Reserve 1 cup cooking liquid, drain plantains, and return to pot. Using potato masher, mash plantains until smooth and no lumps remain. Stir in butter, ¾ teaspoon salt, and ¾ cup reserved cooking liquid until fully combined. Cover and keep warm. (Adjust plantain consistency with remaining ¼ cup cooking liquid as necessary before serving.)

2   Meanwhile, pat mahi-mahi dry with paper towels and sprinkle with jerk seasoning, pepper, and remaining ¾ teaspoon salt. Heat oil in 12-inch nonstick skillet over medium-high heat until just smoking. Add mahi-mahi and cook until well browned on both sides and registers 140 degrees, 6 to 7 minutes per side.

3   Serve, topping fish and mashed plantains with pickled onion and cilantro.

Roasted Salmon with White Beans, Fennel, and Tomatoes

Why This Recipe Works The vibrant abundance of vegetables and impressive amount of protein packed into this one-pan meal—crisp-tender salmon served alongside earthy, subtly tangy beans; crisp fennel; and sweet-tart tomatoes—belie its simplicity. To ensure all the ingredients were perfectly cooked, we staggered their addition to a single sheet pan—starting with sliced fennel, which needs some solo oven time to soften and develop tasty browning. While the fennel roasted, we tossed cherry tomatoes and two cans of creamy, hearty cannellini beans with wine and garlic, imbuing the tomatoes and beans with aromatic depth. We then spread salmon fillets with a lemon-thyme compound butter to give the fish a citrusy, earthy boost. We stirred the bean mixture into the fennel and arranged the salmon on top of the vegetables before returning the sheet pan to the oven. As the dish continued roasting, the acidity and subtle sweetness of the wine helped caramelize and soften the vegetables, while the butter distributed its herby richness into the fish. The cherry tomatoes released so much flavorful juice that we had to make the most of it: We stirred extra compound butter and some lemon juice into the bean mixture before serving, producing a velvety sauce. To ensure uniform pieces of salmon that cook at the same rate, buy a whole 1½–pound center-cut fillet and cut it into four equal pieces

2 (1-pound) fennel bulbs, stalks discarded, bulbs halved, cored, and sliced ¼ inch thick

2 tablespoons extra-virgin olive oil, divided

1¼ teaspoons table salt, divided

¾ teaspoon pepper, divided

2 (15-ounce) cans cannellini beans, rinsed

10 ounces cherry tomatoes, halved

¼ cup dry white wine

3 garlic cloves (2 sliced thin, 1 minced)

4 tablespoons unsalted butter, softened

1 teaspoon minced fresh thyme

1 teaspoon grated lemon zest plus 1 tablespoon juice

4 (4- to 6-ounce) skinless center-cut salmon fillets, 1 to 1½ inches thick

2 tablespoons chopped fresh parsley

1 Adjust oven rack to middle position and heat oven to 450 degrees. Toss fennel, 1 tablespoon oil, ¼ teaspoon salt, and ¼ teaspoon pepper together on rimmed baking sheet. Spread fennel into even layer and roast until beginning to brown around edges, about 15 minutes.

2 Meanwhile, toss beans, tomatoes, wine, sliced garlic, ½ teaspoon salt, ¼ teaspoon pepper, and remaining 1 tablespoon oil together in bowl. Combine butter, thyme, lemon zest, and minced garlic in small bowl, mashing with fork until homogenous. Pat salmon dry with paper towels and sprinkle with remaining ½ teaspoon salt and remaining ¼ teaspoon pepper. Spread half of butter mixture evenly over fillets.

3 Remove sheet from oven. Add bean mixture to sheet with fennel, stir to combine, and spread into even layer. Arrange salmon on top of bean mixture, butter side up. Roast until centers of fillets register 125 degrees (for medium-rare), 12 to 18 minutes.

4 Transfer salmon to serving platter. Stir lemon juice and remaining half of butter mixture into bean mixture until butter is melted. Transfer to serving platter with salmon and sprinkle with parsley. Serve.

Crispy Tempeh with Sambal Sauce

Why This Recipe Works Sambals are hugely popular throughout Indonesia. These condiment sauces, which can be served cooked or raw, are typically made from chiles, aromatics such as onion, fresh herbs, and spices. Shrimp paste is also frequently included for its funky, umami depth. Here, a mouth-warming but not exceedingly hot sambal makes an intensely flavorful sauce for coating cubes of tempeh—slabs of fermented soybeans beloved in Indonesia for their nutty, earthy flavor and dense, chewy bite. We started by using a food processor to quickly combine all the sambal ingredients, stopping when the mixture reached a pleasingly coarse texture. We then fried tempeh until it was golden brown and slightly crispy on the outside but still meaty-textured on the inside. Tempeh is often deep-fried for this preparation, but we found that a shallow fry in a cup of oil gave us similar results. We used a small portion of the remaining oil from frying the tempeh to cook the sambal, which partially tamed the fruity heat of the Fresno chiles and rendered the onion and garlic tender and sweet. Then, it was just a matter of tossing the crispy tempeh in the sambal sauce and stirring in plenty of fresh basil. Lemon basil is traditional in Indonesia, but Thai and Italian basil are both excellent substitutes. If you can't find kecap manis, you can substitute a combination of 1½ tablespoons dark brown sugar and 1 teaspoon soy sauce. To make this fully meatless, you can omit the shrimp paste. Serve with rice.

1 Process chiles, onion, garlic, shrimp paste, if using, and salt in food processor until finely chopped, about 30 seconds, scraping down sides of bowl as needed; transfer to bowl.

2 Adjust oven rack to middle position and heat oven to 200 degrees. Set wire rack in rimmed baking sheet and line rack with triple layer of paper towels. Heat oil in 14-inch flat-bottomed wok or 12-inch nonstick skillet over medium-high heat to 375 degrees. Carefully add half of tempeh to hot oil and increase heat to high. Cook, turning as needed, until golden brown, 3 to 5 minutes. Adjust burner, if necessary, to maintain oil temperature between 350 and 375 degrees. Off heat, using slotted spoon, transfer tempeh to prepared rack and keep warm in oven. Return oil to 375 degrees over medium-high heat and repeat with remaining tempeh; transfer to rack.

3 Carefully pour off all but 2 tablespoons oil from wok. Add chile mixture to oil left in wok and cook over medium-high heat, tossing slowly but constantly, until darkened in color and completely dry, 7 to 10 minutes. Off heat, stir in water and kecap manis until combined. Add tempeh and basil and toss until well coated. Serve.

12 ounces Fresno chiles, stemmed, seeded, and chopped coarse

 1 small onion, chopped coarse

 5 garlic cloves, peeled

 2 teaspoons shrimp paste (optional)

¼ teaspoon table salt

 1 cup vegetable oil for frying

 1 pound tempeh, cut into ½-inch pieces

½ cup water

 2 tablespoons kecap manis

1½ cups fresh Thai basil leaves

Loaded Sweet Potato Wedges with Tempeh

Why This Recipe Works Sturdy, caramelized wedges of sweet potatoes make a satisfyingly starchy base for a filling meal. To further amp up the satiation factor, we paired the hearty root vegetable with crisp crumbles of equally hearty tempeh. While the sweet potatoes roasted in the oven, we browned ground tempeh on the stovetop, seasoning it with a quartet of spices: cumin, coriander, paprika, and cinnamon. After topping the potato wedges with the tempeh mixture, we loaded them with vegetables—sweet cherry tomatoes, crisp radishes, spicy jalapeño, and fresh cilantro—amping up the fiber, flavor, and color of the dish. To complement the earthy flavors with a bright, cooling dimension, we whisked up a quick avocado-yogurt sauce, flavored with warm cumin and zesty lime juice. This dish is great as is, but we also like it served with Quick Sweet and Spicy Pickled Red Onion (page 33). You can substitute sour cream for the yogurt when serving if you prefer.

1 ripe avocado, halved, pitted, and cut into ½-inch pieces

¼ cup plain yogurt, plus extra for serving

1 teaspoon lime juice, plus wedges for serving

1½ teaspoons ground cumin, divided

⅛ teaspoon plus ¾ teaspoon table salt, divided

⅛ teaspoon pepper

2 pounds sweet potatoes, unpeeled, cut lengthwise into 2-inch-wide wedges

5 tablespoons extra-virgin olive oil, divided

8 ounces tempeh, crumbled into pea-size pieces

1 teaspoon ground coriander

1 teaspoon smoked paprika

⅛ teaspoon ground cinnamon

4 ounces cherry tomatoes, halved

4 radishes, trimmed, halved, and sliced thin

1 jalapeño, stemmed and sliced into thin rings

¾ cup chopped fresh cilantro

3 scallions, sliced thin

1 Using sturdy whisk, mash and stir avocado, yogurt, lime juice, ½ teaspoon cumin, ⅛ teaspoon salt, and pepper together in bowl until as smooth as possible. Season with salt and pepper to taste and set aside until ready to serve.

2 Adjust oven rack to middle position and heat oven to 450 degrees. Line rimmed baking sheet with aluminum foil and spray with vegetable oil spray. Toss potatoes with 1 tablespoon oil and ½ teaspoon salt in bowl, then arrange potato wedges, cut sides down, in single layer on prepared sheet. Roast until tender and sides in contact with sheet are well browned, about 30 minutes.

3 Meanwhile, heat remaining ¼ cup oil in 12-inch skillet over medium heat until shimmering. Add tempeh, coriander, paprika, cinnamon, remaining 1 teaspoon cumin, and remaining ¼ teaspoon salt and cook until well browned, 8 to 12 minutes, stirring often; set aside until ready to serve.

4 Transfer sweet potatoes to platter or individual serving plates and top with crispy tempeh, cherry tomatoes, radishes, jalapeño, cilantro, and scallions. Serve with reserved avocado sauce, extra yogurt, and lime wedges.

Sweet and Spicy Glazed Tofu with Coconut-Braised Mustard Greens and Winter Squash

Why This Recipe Works We wanted to develop a hearty tofu dish that echoed some of the flavors found in two popular Caribbean dishes: jerk chicken and callaloo. Jerk cooking involves coating meat in a Scotch bonnet–allspice marinade, so we used both spices to season our tofu. We tore the tofu into chunks to create craggy edges—and textural variation when crisped up in a skillet. We coated the tofu in a sweet-tangy mixture of brown sugar and vinegar, as well as soy sauce for its umami. As this mixture reduced in the skillet, it clung appetizingly to the uneven surfaces of the tofu. To complement this boldly flavored protein, we paired it with mustard greens and butternut squash braised in creamy coconut milk—a nod to the beloved leafy-green dish callaloo.

14 ounces firm or extra-firm tofu, drained

2 tablespoons plus 1 teaspoon vegetable oil, divided

4 scallions, white and green parts separated and sliced thin

1 Scotch bonnet or habanero chile, stemmed, seeded, and minced, divided

5 garlic cloves, minced

2 teaspoons minced fresh thyme, divided

2 cups water

2 pounds butternut squash, peeled, seeded, and cut into ½-inch pieces (5 cups)

¾ teaspoon table salt, divided

1 pound mustard greens, stemmed and cut into 1-inch pieces

2 tablespoons soy sauce

1 tablespoon packed brown sugar

1 tablespoon cider vinegar

½ teaspoon ground allspice

¼ teaspoon ground ginger

¾ cup coconut milk

Lime wedges

1 Line rimmed baking sheet with triple layer of paper towels. Tear tofu into rough ¾-inch pieces and transfer to prepared sheet. Top tofu with second layer of paper towels and set aside to drain.

2 Heat 1 tablespoon oil in Dutch oven over medium heat until shimmering. Add scallion whites, half of chile, garlic, and 1 teaspoon thyme and cook until fragrant, about 1 minute. Add water, squash, and ½ teaspoon salt and bring to boil. Stir in mustard greens (mustard greens will not be fully submerged); reduce heat to medium-low; and simmer, covered, stirring occasionally until vegetables are just tender, 12 to 15 minutes.

3 Meanwhile, combine soy sauce, sugar, and vinegar in bowl. Combine 1 teaspoon oil, allspice, ginger, remaining half of chile, and remaining 1 teaspoon thyme in second bowl. Press tofu dry with paper towels.

4 Heat remaining 1 tablespoon oil in 12-inch nonstick skillet over medium-high heat until shimmering. Add tofu and cook until golden brown, 8 to 10 minutes, turning as needed. Clear space in skillet and add allspice mixture. Cook, stirring frequently, until fragrant, about 30 seconds. Stir in soy sauce mixture and cook, stirring frequently, until sauce is reduced and tofu is coated, 2 to 4 minutes. Set aside off heat until ready to serve.

5 Stir coconut milk and remaining ¼ teaspoon salt into squash mixture and bring to brief boil. Simmer, uncovered, until thickened slightly, 3 to 5 minutes. Season with salt and pepper to taste. Serve with tofu and lime wedges, sprinkling individual portions with scallion greens.

Mapo Tofu

Why This Recipe Works A famous culinary export of China's Sichuan Province, mapo tofu is named for an old widow whose face was scarred by smallpox. The legend goes that people traveled far and wide to visit her restaurant near Chengdu and sample this dish, which was so beloved that it gained the name "pockmarked old woman tofu." A thrilling hallmark of the Sichuan canon, the dish is a fiery showcase for tofu as well as spices that are prominent in Sichuan. The dish uses ground pork more as a seasoning than a primary protein source, so 8 ounces was enough for lots of porky flavor; we rendered its fat to cook the bold seasonings in our sauce base. Ginger, garlic, and four Sichuan powerhouses—doubanjiang (broad bean chile paste, also called toban djan), douchi (fermented black beans), Sichuan chili flakes, and Sichuan peppercorns—made for an immensely vibrant sauce. Microwaving soft tofu in chicken broth with scallions imbued the cubes with savoriness and helped them stay intact during the braise. Stirring in cornstarch at the end created velvety thickness. If you can't find Sichuan chili flakes, you can substitute gochugaru. We developed this recipe in a 14-inch wok, but you can use a large saucepan instead. Serve with rice.

1 Place tofu, broth, and scallions in large bowl and microwave, covered, until steaming, 5 to 7 minutes. Let stand while preparing remaining ingredients.

2 Cook pork and vegetable oil in 14-inch flat-bottomed wok over medium heat, breaking up meat with wooden spoon, until meat just begins to brown, 5 to 7 minutes. Using slotted spoon, transfer pork to separate bowl. Pour off all but ¼ cup fat from wok. (If necessary, add vegetable oil to equal ¼ cup.)

3 Add garlic, doubanjiang, ginger, douchi, chili flakes, and peppercorns to fat left in wok and cook over medium heat until spices darken and oil begins to separate from paste, 2 to 3 minutes.

4 Gently pour tofu with broth into wok, followed by hoisin, sesame oil, and cooked pork. Cook, stirring gently and frequently, until simmering, 2 to 3 minutes. Whisk water and cornstarch together in small bowl. Add cornstarch mixture to wok and continue to cook, stirring frequently, until sauce has thickened, about 3 minutes. Serve.

28 ounces soft tofu, cut into ½-inch cubes

1 cup chicken broth

6 scallions, sliced thin

8 ounces ground pork

1 teaspoon vegetable oil, plus extra as needed

9 garlic cloves, minced

⅓ cup doubanjiang (broad bean chile paste)

1 tablespoon grated fresh ginger

1 tablespoon douchi (fermented black beans)

1 tablespoon Sichuan chili flakes

1 tablespoon Sichuan peppercorns, toasted and ground coarse

2 tablespoons hoisin sauce

2 teaspoons toasted sesame oil

2 tablespoons water

1 tablespoon cornstarch

• *fast* • *vegetarian* • *fiber-ful* • *one-pan* •

Stir-Fried Portobellos with Soy-Maple Sauce

Why This Recipe Works Spongy, hefty portobello mushrooms, in conjunction with snappy snow peas and crunchy carrots, make for a delectable stir-fry that requires no meat to be hearty and filling. Cooking the mushrooms in two batches kept them from steaming in their own juices, guaranteeing even cooking and plenty of flavorful browning. Adding a quick salty-sweet glaze of maple syrup, mirin, and soy sauce at the end gave the mushrooms an umami boost that complemented their natural earthy notes. We then stir-fried snow peas and carrots in the same wok until crisp-tender, before adding garlic and ginger and cooking until these aromatics were fragrant. The snow peas and carrots stayed snappy and crunchy while taking on the pleasant scent of the aromatics. Finally, we stirred in the mushrooms and sauce—a savory, fragrant concoction of chicken (or vegetable) broth, soy sauce, mirin, rice vinegar, and toasted sesame oil, thickened with a little cornstarch—to coat everything with glossy, savory goodness. To remove the gills, use a spoon to gently scrape them from the underside of each portobello cap. Serve with rice.

Glaze

- 3 tablespoons maple syrup
- 2 tablespoons mirin
- 1 tablespoon soy sauce

Sauce

- ½ cup chicken or vegetable broth
- 2 tablespoons soy sauce
- 1½ tablespoons mirin
- 2 teaspoons rice vinegar
- 2 teaspoons cornstarch
- 2 teaspoons toasted sesame oil

Vegetables

- 3 tablespoons vegetable oil, divided
- 2 pounds portobello mushroom caps, gills removed, cut into 2-inch wedges
- 8 ounces snow peas, strings removed, sliced ¼ inch thick on bias
- 2 carrots, peeled and cut into 2-inch-long matchsticks
- 2 garlic cloves, minced
- 2 teaspoons grated fresh ginger
- ¼ teaspoon red pepper flakes

1 **For the glaze** Whisk maple syrup, mirin, and soy sauce together in bowl.

2 **For the sauce** Whisk all ingredients together in bowl.

3 **For the vegetables** Heat 1 tablespoon oil in 14-inch flat-bottomed wok or 12-inch nonstick skillet over high heat until shimmering. Add half of mushrooms and cook, tossing slowly but constantly, until browned on 1 side, 2 to 3 minutes. Flip mushrooms; reduce heat to medium; and cook until second side is browned and mushrooms are tender, about 5 minutes. Transfer to second bowl. Repeat with 1 tablespoon oil and remaining mushrooms.

4 Return all mushrooms to wok, add glaze, and cook over medium-high heat, tossing slowly but constantly, until glaze is thickened and mushrooms are coated, 1 to 2 minutes. Return to bowl.

5 Wipe now-empty wok clean with paper towels. Heat 2 teaspoons oil in clean wok over high heat until shimmering. Add snow peas and carrots and cook, tossing slowly but constantly, until vegetables are crisp-tender, about 5 minutes. Push vegetables to 1 side of wok, add remaining 1 teaspoon oil, garlic, ginger, and pepper flakes to clearing. Cook, mashing garlic mixture into wok, until fragrant, about 30 seconds. Stir garlic mixture into vegetables.

6 Return mushrooms to wok. Whisk sauce to recombine, then add to wok. Cook, tossing gently, until sauce has thickened, 1 to 2 minutes. Serve.

Charred Sichuan-Style Okra

Why This Recipe Works   Since okra stands up so well to heat and bold seasonings (think Creole cuisine), it made sense that it would also pair well with a spicy Sichuan-style flavor profile. Okra also has an especially hearty, robust chew—perfect for starring in a vegetarian stir-fry. We started by making a concentrated chile oil spiked with tingle-inducing Sichuan peppercorns. The addition of doubanjiang, or broad bean chili paste, gave the sauce heat and the distinct umami of fermented beans, while hoisin sauce and rice wine brought sweetness, acidity, and body. Charring the okra pods whole before cloaking them with the sauce ensured that their exteriors were beautifully seared while the insides remained tender. We then added Shaoxing wine and water before reducing the liquid to concentrate its flavor. A sprinkle of cilantro introduced a fresh, herbaceous note that contrasted nicely with the spicy, earthy flavors of this stir-fry. If you can't find dried bird chiles (Thai red chiles), you can substitute ground red pepper flakes. Use a spice grinder to grind the bird chiles and Sichuan peppercorns. Okra pods less than 3 inches long will be the most tender; do not substitute frozen okra here. Serve with rice.

1   Combine ⅓ cup oil, garlic, ginger, ground chiles, ground Sichuan peppercorns, and star anise in small saucepan and cook over medium-high heat until sizzling, 1 to 2 minutes. Reduce heat to low and gently simmer until garlic and ginger are softened but not browned, about 5 minutes. Let cool off heat for 5 minutes, then stir in 2 tablespoons Shaoxing wine, hoisin, and doubanjiang until combined; set aside.

2   Heat remaining 2 tablespoons oil in 14-inch flat-bottomed wok or 12-inch nonstick skillet over medium-high heat until just smoking. Add okra and cook, tossing occasionally, until okra is crisp-tender and well browned on most sides, 5 to 7 minutes.

3   Stir remaining ¼ cup Shaoxing wine, water, and scallion whites and greens into wok with okra; reduce heat to medium; and cook until liquid is reduced by half and scallion greens are just wilted, about 30 seconds. Off heat, stir in garlic-hoisin mixture until combined. Discard star anise and sprinkle with cilantro. Serve immediately.

⅓   cup plus 2 tablespoons vegetable oil, divided

2   garlic cloves, sliced thin

1   (½-inch) piece fresh ginger, peeled and sliced into thin rounds

5   dried bird chiles, ground fine (1½ teaspoons)

1   teaspoon Sichuan peppercorns, ground fine (½ teaspoon)

1   star anise pod

6   tablespoons Shaoxing wine, divided

¼   cup hoisin sauce

3   tablespoons doubanjiang (broad bean chile paste)

1   pound okra, stemmed

¼   cup water

6   scallions, white parts sliced thin on bias, green parts cut into 1-inch pieces

12   sprigs fresh cilantro, chopped coarse

Madras Okra Curry

Why This Recipe Works The vivid heat and earthy depth of Madras curry powder makes the spice mix a great ingredient to keep on hand for quick, flavorful dinners. The warmth of the seasoning blend (which typically includes spices like coriander, turmeric, and mustard seeds) can give vibrancy and complexity to all sorts of vegetables—including okra, which has a long history in Indian cuisine. We wanted our Madras-style curry to have a hefty amount of rich sauce, with a sturdy vegetable that retained some of its pleasurably snappy, meaty bite. We started by browning our okra until crisp-tender; searing the pods whole, rather than letting them stew in the sauce, maintained their slight crunch. We then made a flavor-packed sauce using onion, ginger, garlic, curry powder, and vegetable or chicken broth. To thicken the mixture to a velvety consistency that would cling to our okra, we stirred in a mixture of coconut milk, honey, and cornstarch. Fresh cilantro sprigs and bright lime wedges balanced out our rich curry. We prefer the spicier flavor of Madras curry powder here, but you can substitute regular curry powder. Okra pods less than 3 inches long will be the most tender; do not substitute frozen okra here. Serve with rice.

1 Heat 2 tablespoons oil in 12-inch skillet over medium-high heat until just smoking. Add half of okra to skillet and cook, stirring occasionally, until crisp-tender and well browned on most sides, 5 to 7 minutes; transfer to bowl. Repeat with 2 tablespoons oil and remaining okra; transfer to bowl. Let skillet cool slightly.

2 Heat remaining 2 tablespoons oil in now-empty skillet over medium heat until shimmering. Add onion and cook until softened, about 5 minutes. Stir in garlic, ginger, and curry powder and cook until fragrant, about 1 minute. Stir in broth, scraping up any browned bits, and bring to simmer. Cook, stirring occasionally, until reduced to 1¼ cups, 15 to 20 minutes.

3 Whisk coconut milk, honey, and cornstarch in bowl to dissolve cornstarch, then whisk mixture into skillet. Bring to simmer and cook until slightly thickened, about 30 seconds. Stir in okra and any accumulated juices and salt and return to brief simmer to warm through. Season with salt and pepper to taste. Sprinkle with cilantro and serve with lime wedges.

6   tablespoons vegetable oil, divided

1½ pounds okra, stemmed, divided

1   small onion, chopped fine

3   garlic cloves, minced

1   tablespoon grated fresh ginger

1   tablespoon Madras curry powder

2½ cups vegetable or chicken broth

1   cup canned coconut milk

2   teaspoons honey

1   teaspoon cornstarch

¼   teaspoon table salt

10 sprigs fresh cilantro, chopped coarse

    Lime wedges

Aloo Gobi

Why This Recipe Works   Aloo gobi, or "potato cauliflower," is an Indian mainstay that combines two dense, hearty vegetables to spectacular effect. To tenderize both while retaining some bite, we first shallow-fried them to crisp their exteriors before removing from the pot. Then, we bloomed spices (including asafetida for its savory oniony character, and amchoor for its citrusy fragrance) and aromatics in oil. The veggies went back in, along with water to steam them through. As the water reduced, the potatoes and cauliflower became coated in a flavorful paste. If you are sensitive to spice, seed the serrano chile before using. Look for asafetida, Kashmiri chile powder, and amchoor (also known as aamchur or amchur) at South Asian grocery stores; you might also find them at some well-stocked supermarkets. If you can't find asafetida, you can omit it. If you can't find Kashmiri chile powder, substitute ½ teaspoon paprika plus a pinch of cayenne. If you can't find amchoor, stir 1½ teaspoons lemon juice into the dish at the end of cooking. Serve with roti, basmati rice, or our Chapati (page 221).

1   Heat oil in Dutch oven over medium heat until shimmering. Add potatoes and cook, stirring frequently (potatoes may stick to pot), until golden brown in spots, 4 to 5 minutes. Transfer to bowl.

2   Add cauliflower to now-empty pot and cook, gently stirring occasionally, until golden brown in spots, 4 to 5 minutes. Transfer cauliflower to bowl with potatoes.

3   Add cumin seeds and asafetida to now-empty pot and cook, stirring constantly, until fragrant and sizzling, 30 to 60 seconds. Add onion and salt and cook, stirring frequently, until onion is golden brown, 3 to 4 minutes. Add serrano, garlic, ginger, coriander, amchoor, turmeric, and chile powder and cook, stirring frequently, until fragrant, about 1 minute.

4   Return potatoes and cauliflower to pot, along with any excess oil from bowl. Stir in water, scraping up any browned bits. Bring to simmer. Adjust heat to medium-low; cover; and simmer, gently stirring occasionally, until vegetables have absorbed water, 15 to 18 minutes. Transfer to shallow bowl, sprinkle with cilantro, and serve.

- 6   tablespoons vegetable oil
- 1   pound Yukon Gold potatoes, peeled and cut into 1-inch pieces
- 1   pound cauliflower florets, cut into 1-inch pieces
- 1¼   teaspoons cumin seeds
- ¼   teaspoon ground asafetida
- 1   cup finely chopped onion
- 1¼   teaspoons table salt
- 1   serrano chile, halved lengthwise but left intact at stem end
- 1   tablespoon minced garlic
- 1   tablespoon minced fresh ginger
- 1   teaspoon ground coriander
- 1   teaspoon amchoor
- ½   teaspoon ground turmeric
- ½   teaspoon Kashmiri chile powder
- ¾   cup water
- 1   tablespoon chopped fresh cilantro

Jackfruit and Chickpea Makhani

Why This Recipe Works Makhani, meaning butter, refers to a North Indian preparation that involves blanketing a protein—often chicken, paneer, or legumes—in a velvety spiced sauce. For a hearty, satiating vegetarian riff that channels this preparation's luscious richness and tomatoey tang, we turned to jackfruit and chickpeas. Young jackfruit, when cooked and shredded, has a tender, stringy, remarkably meaty texture, which played well with dense, creamy chickpeas. To give our dish a flavorful base, we cooked our aromatics and spices until they were fragrant and then deglazed the pan with chickpea liquid to scrape up the flavor-packed browned bits at the bottom. We then blitzed this mixture with yogurt, butter, and sugar to produce a luscious, subtly sweet sauce. Coating the jackfruit in yogurt before charring it in the oven made the fruit crisp while locking in the interior tenderness. Be sure to use young (unripe) jackfruit packed in brine or water; do not use mature jackfruit packed in syrup. Jackfruit seeds are tender and edible; there is no need to remove them. Serve with rice and/or warm naan.

- 2 tablespoons vegetable oil
- 1 onion, chopped fine
- 5 garlic cloves, minced
- 4 teaspoons grated fresh ginger
- 1 serrano chile, stemmed, seeded, and minced
- 1/3 cup tomato paste
- 1 tablespoon garam masala
- 1 teaspoon ground coriander
- 1/2 teaspoon ground cumin
- 1/2 teaspoon pepper
- 2 (15-ounce) cans chickpeas, drained with liquid reserved
- 1 cup plain Greek yogurt, divided
- 2 tablespoons unsalted butter
- 1 tablespoon sugar
- 1 (20-ounce) can young green jackfruit packed in brine or water, drained and cut into 3/4-inch pieces (2 cups)
- 1/2 teaspoon table salt, divided
- 3 tablespoons chopped fresh cilantro, divided

1 Heat oil in large saucepan over medium heat until shimmering. Add onion, garlic, ginger, and serrano and cook, stirring frequently, until onion is softened and lightly browned, 6 to 8 minutes. Add tomato paste, garam masala, coriander, cumin, and pepper and cook, stirring frequently, until fragrant and tomato paste begins to brown, about 2 minutes. Stir in chickpea canning liquid, scraping up any browned bits.

2 Transfer mixture to blender. Add 1/2 cup yogurt, butter, and sugar and process until smooth, about 30 seconds, scraping down sides of blender jar as needed. Return sauce to now-empty saucepan and bring to brief simmer over medium heat. Remove from heat, season with salt and pepper to taste, and cover to keep warm.

3 Adjust oven rack 6 inches from broiler element and heat broiler. Line rimmed baking sheet with aluminum foil and spray with vegetable oil spray. Pat jackfruit dry with paper towels, then toss with remaining 1/2 cup yogurt and salt until well coated. Spread jackfruit evenly over prepared sheet and broil until lightly charred, 10 to 12 minutes, flipping jackfruit halfway through broiling.

4 Stir jackfruit and chickpeas into saucepan and bring to simmer over medium heat. Cover; reduce heat to low; and cook, stirring and scraping bottom of saucepan occasionally, until chickpeas are softened, about 15 minutes. Stir in 2 tablespoons cilantro and season with salt to taste. Transfer to platter and sprinkle with remaining 1 tablespoon cilantro. Serve.

Chana Masala

Why This Recipe Works Chana masala, a spiced chickpea dish, is arguably one of North India's best-known vegetarian creations—a hearty dish of chickpeas simmered until tender in a tangy, spiced tomato-ginger sauce. To form the savory base, we started by processing our aromatics—onion, cilantro, ginger, garlic, and serranos—in a food processor before softening the mixture on the stovetop. We seasoned this mixture with paprika, cumin, turmeric, and fennel seeds to give it earthy warmth before adding the chickpeas. We opted for canned chickpeas, as their flavor and texture were nearly indistinguishable from cooked dried chickpeas. We also skipped draining them; the canning liquid contributed necessary body and depth of flavor. Since canned chickpeas are great at absorbing flavor, we blitzed canned tomatoes and added the sauce to the saucepan along with the legumes; as the chickpeas softened, they drank up the tomatoes' savory brightness. Sweet, delicate garam masala went in toward the end, to preserve its complex aroma. Serve with rice and/or warm naan.

  1 small red onion, quartered, divided
 10 sprigs fresh cilantro, stems and leaves separated
  1 (1½-inch) piece ginger, peeled and chopped coarse
  2 garlic cloves, chopped coarse
  2 serrano chiles, stemmed, halved, seeded, and sliced thin crosswise, divided
  3 tablespoons vegetable oil
  1 (14.5-ounce) can whole peeled tomatoes
  1 teaspoon paprika
  1 teaspoon ground cumin
  ½ teaspoon ground turmeric
  ½ teaspoon fennel seeds
  2 (15-ounce) cans chickpeas, undrained
1½ teaspoons garam masala
  ½ teaspoon table salt
     Lime wedges

1 Chop three-quarters of onion coarse; reserve remaining quarter for garnish. Cut cilantro stems into 1-inch lengths. Process chopped onion, cilantro stems, ginger, garlic, and half of serranos in food processor until finely chopped, scraping down sides of bowl as needed, about 20 seconds. Cook oil and onion mixture in large saucepan over medium-high heat, stirring frequently, until onion is fully softened and beginning to stick to saucepan, 5 to 7 minutes.

2 While onion mixture cooks, process tomatoes and their juice in now-empty food processor until smooth, about 30 seconds. Add paprika, cumin, turmeric, and fennel seeds to onion mixture and cook, stirring constantly, until fragrant, about 1 minute. Stir in chickpeas and their liquid and processed tomatoes and bring to boil. Adjust heat to maintain simmer, then cover and simmer for 15 minutes. While mixture cooks, chop reserved onion quarter fine.

3 Stir garam masala and salt into chickpea mixture and continue to cook, uncovered and stirring occasionally, until chickpeas are softened and sauce is thickened, 8 to 12 minutes. Season with salt to taste. Transfer to wide, shallow serving bowl. Sprinkle with finely chopped onion, cilantro leaves, and remaining serranos and serve, passing lime wedges separately.

Cheesy Bean and Tomato Bake

Why This Recipe Works This cheesy, comforting casserole of hearty cannellini beans, sweet-tangy tomatoes, and gooey mozzarella is one kids and adults alike will ask for and crave. It's also a snap to whip up, relying on pantry-friendly staples and coming together in a single skillet that starts on the stovetop and finishes in the oven. For a savory foundation to our dish, we softened onion in the skillet and seasoned it with garlic, oregano, and red pepper flakes. We then introduced the savory tang of canned tomatoes, which we seasoned with a pinch of sugar to enhance the tomatoes' natural sweetness. After stirring in creamy canned cannellini beans, mozzarella, and Parmesan, we topped this ultrasatisfying casserole with more mozzarella to maximize the ooziness (who can resist a cheese pull?). We finished the dish with a mixture of panko bread crumbs and oil, for a topping that browned nicely in the oven into a crisp crust.

 3 tablespoons extra-virgin olive oil, divided

 1 small onion, chopped fine

 ¾ teaspoon table salt

 3 garlic cloves, minced

 1 teaspoon dried oregano

    Pinch red pepper flakes (optional)

 1 (28-ounce) can crushed tomatoes

 ⅓ cup water

    Pinch sugar

 2 (15-ounce) cans cannellini beans, rinsed

 4 ounces mozzarella cheese, shredded (1 cup), divided

 ½ ounce Parmesan cheese, grated (¼ cup)

 ½ cup panko bread crumbs

1 Adjust oven rack to middle position and heat oven to 475 degrees. Heat 1 tablespoon oil in 12-inch skillet over medium heat until shimmering. Add onion and salt and cook until softened, about 5 minutes. Stir in garlic; oregano; and pepper flakes, if using, and cook until fragrant, about 30 seconds.

2 Stir in tomatoes, water, and sugar and bring to boil. Reduce heat to medium-low and simmer, stirring occasionally, until slightly thickened, about 10 minutes.

3 Stir in beans and cook until warmed through, about 5 minutes. Remove skillet from heat. Stir in half of mozzarella and Parmesan, then spread beans into even layer. Sprinkle remaining mozzarella evenly over top. Combine panko and remaining 2 tablespoons oil in bowl, then sprinkle evenly over top of cheese in skillet.

4 Bake until cheese is melted and panko is well browned, 5 to 8 minutes. Remove skillet from oven and let cool for 5 minutes. Serve.

Stuffed Delicata Squash

Why This Recipe Works Delicata squash offers earthy, autumnal sweetness similar to the flavor of acorn or butternut squash, but with none of the elbow grease required to prepare those varieties. Delicata's narrow shape and smaller size ensures you won't have to hack through and peel away layers of tough outer skin—its tender skin is thin and perfectly edible. Here, we halved the squash to create boats—ideal for holding a hearty stuffing. To start, we simply seasoned the squash halves and microwaved them until the flesh was tender and the skin was softened—no shell removal required. We then stuffed the squash halves with a savory, nutty filling: We cooked mushrooms, onion, and spinach in butter to imbue the vegetables with milky richness, then stirred in bulgur, toasted pecans, and shredded cheddar for a mixture with plenty of bite and savory flavor. Before broiling the squash, we brushed the surfaces of the filling with melted butter to add a bit more richness and to encourage flavorful browning.

2   delicata squashes (about 1 pound each), halved lengthwise and seeded

1¾   teaspoons table salt, divided, plus salt for cooking bulgur

½   teaspoon pepper

1   cup medium-grind bulgur

4   tablespoons unsalted butter, plus 2 tablespoons melted

10   ounces cremini mushrooms, trimmed and chopped

1   onion, chopped

5   ounces (5 cups) baby spinach, chopped coarse

1   teaspoon minced fresh thyme

½   cup chopped toasted pecans

2   ounces sharp cheddar cheese, shredded (½ cup)

1   Sprinkle cut sides of squash with 1 teaspoon salt and pepper. Microwave in large covered bowl until tender, 12 to 15 minutes. Bring 2 quarts water to boil in large saucepan. Add bulgur and 1 teaspoon salt. Reduce heat to medium-low and simmer until tender, 5 to 8 minutes. Drain.

2   Meanwhile, melt 4 tablespoons butter in 12-inch nonstick skillet over medium-high heat. Add mushrooms, onion, and remaining ¾ teaspoon salt and cook, stirring occasionally, until vegetables are browned, about 10 minutes. Stir in spinach and thyme and cook until wilted, about 3 minutes. Off heat, stir in bulgur, pecans, and cheddar.

3   Adjust oven rack 8 inches from broiler element and heat broiler. Transfer squash, cut side up, to rimmed baking sheet. Tightly pack bulgur mixture into squash halves, mounding bulgur mixture up over squash rims. Brush filling with remaining 2 tablespoons melted butter. Broil until lightly browned, 4 to 5 minutes. Serve.

Kimchi Bokkeumbap

Why This Recipe Works Like most forms of fried rice, kimchi bokkeumbap is comfort in a bowl. The unfussy, unscripted nature of this Korean home-cooking staple is rooted in the spirit of making do with what you have. At its core is leftover cooked rice stir-fried with the gently spicy fermented napa cabbage that most Korean cooks keep on hand. But from there, the permutations are endless—since that rib-sticking, umami-charged base is just the thing to capture odds and ends. In any given kitchen, you'll find the rice bulked up with ham, Spam, or seafood; seasoned with gochujang, plum extract, or oyster sauce; dolloped with mayonnaise; topped with crumbled gim (dried seaweed); or teeming with gooey cheese. For our riff, we chose to use two slices of deli ham—smoky, widely available, and flavorful even in small amounts. We also fried up a few eggs, which gave our fried rice a buttery, tender component that delectably complemented the toothsome grains and crisp kimchi. This recipe works best with day-old rice; alternatively, cook your rice 2 hours ahead, spread it on a rimmed baking sheet, and let it cool completely before chilling it for 30 minutes. Plain pre-toasted seaweed snacks can be substituted for the gim; omit the toasting in step 1. You'll need at least a 16-ounce jar of kimchi; if it doesn't yield ¼ cup of juice, make up the difference with water. If using soft, well-aged kimchi, omit the water and reduce the cooking time at the end of step 2 to 2 minutes.

- 1 (8-inch square) sheet gim
- 2 tablespoons plus 2 teaspoons vegetable oil, divided
- 2 (¼-inch-thick) slices deli ham, cut into ¼-inch pieces (about 4 ounces)
- 1 large onion, chopped
- 6 scallions, white and green parts separated and sliced
- 1¼ cups cabbage kimchi, drained with ¼ cup juice reserved, cut into ¼-inch strips
- ¼ cup water
- 4 teaspoons soy sauce
- 4 teaspoons gochujang
- ½ teaspoon plus ⅛ teaspoon pepper, divided
- 3 cups cooked short-grain white rice (recipe follows)
- 4 teaspoons toasted sesame oil
- 4 large eggs
- ⅛ teaspoon table salt
- 1 tablespoon sesame seeds, toasted

1 Grip gim with tongs and hold 2 inches above low flame on gas burner. Toast gim, turning every 3 to 5 seconds, until gim is aromatic and shrinks slightly, about 20 seconds. (If you do not have a gas stove, toast gim on rimmed baking sheet in 275-degree oven until gim is aromatic and shrinks slightly, 20 to 25 minutes, flipping gim halfway through toasting.) Using kitchen shears, cut gim into four 2-inch-wide strips. Stack strips and cut crosswise into thin strips.

2 Heat 1 tablespoon vegetable oil in 14-inch flat-bottomed wok or 12-inch nonstick skillet over medium-high heat until shimmering. Add ham, onion, and scallion whites and cook, stirring frequently, until onion is softened and ham is beginning to brown at edges, 6 to 8 minutes. Stir in kimchi and reserved juice, water, soy sauce, gochujang, and ½ teaspoon pepper. Cook, stirring occasionally, until kimchi turns soft and translucent, 4 to 6 minutes.

3 Add rice; reduce heat to medium-low; and cook, tossing slowly but constantly until mixture is evenly coated, about 3 minutes. Stir in sesame oil and 1 tablespoon vegetable oil. Increase heat to medium-high and cook, stirring occasionally, until mixture begins to stick to wok, about 4 minutes. Transfer to serving bowl.

4 Heat remaining 2 teaspoons oil in now-empty wok over medium-high heat until shimmering. Meanwhile, crack 2 eggs into small bowl. Repeat with remaining 2 eggs and second small bowl. Sprinkle eggs with salt and remaining ⅛ teaspoon pepper. Working quickly, pour 1 bowl of eggs into 1 side of wok and second bowl of eggs into other side. Cover and cook for 1 minute. Remove wok from heat and let sit, covered, 15 to 45 seconds for runny yolks (white around edge of yolk will be barely opaque), 45 to 60 seconds for soft but set yolks, and about 2 minutes for medium-set yolks. Sprinkle rice with sesame seeds, scallion greens, and gim and serve with fried eggs.

Steamed Short-Grain White Rice

Makes 4 cups | Total time: 35 minutes

You can use any short-grain white rice in this recipe.

   1 cup short-grain white rice

Place rice in fine-mesh strainer and rinse under running water, stirring occasionally, until water runs clear, about 1½ minutes. Drain rice well and transfer to small saucepan. Stir in 1¼ cups of water. Bring rice to boil over high heat. Adjust heat to maintain bare simmer. Cover and cook until water is absorbed, about 20 minutes. Remove from heat and let stand, covered, for 10 minutes to finish cooking. (Rice can be refrigerated for up to 3 days.)

Joloff-Inspired Fonio

Why This Recipe Works   Jollof rice is a beloved West African specialty, the foundational ingredients of which are rice, tomatoes, onions, and spices, though many variations exist throughout the region. We wanted to apply joloff's signature bright, savory flavors to fonio, an ancient variety of millet that also hails from West Africa. We began by blitzing canned tomatoes and an assortment of aromatics in a blender to create a smooth, flavorful cooking liquid for the fonio. As the grains simmered, the fonio took on a rouge color, characteristic of joloff rice, and drank up the tomatoes' savory brightness. We enriched this concoction with butter, and topped it with sweet, soft caramelized onions and fresh parsley. Hearty, comforting, and deeply flavorful, this dish works equally well as a hearty side or a meal on its own.

    3   cups vegetable or chicken broth, divided
    1   (14.5-ounce) can whole peeled tomatoes
    1   red onion (½ onion quartered, ½ onion sliced thin)
    4   garlic cloves, peeled
    1   teaspoon table salt
    1   teaspoon packed brown sugar
  ½   teaspoon red pepper flakes
  ¼   cup vegetable oil, divided
    1   cup fonio
    2   bay leaves
    2   tablespoons unsalted butter
    2   tablespoons chopped fresh parsley

1 Process 1 cup broth, tomatoes and their juice, quartered onion, garlic, salt, sugar, and pepper flakes in blender on high speed until smooth, 1 to 2 minutes.

2 Heat 2 tablespoons oil in 12-inch nonstick skillet over medium heat until shimmering. Add tomato mixture and cook, stirring occasionally, until slightly thickened, 5 to 7 minutes.

3 Add fonio, bay leaves, and remaining 2 cups broth and stir well. Cook, stirring occasionally, until most liquid has been absorbed, 3 to 4 minutes. Stir in butter, remove from heat, and cover. Let stand until all liquid has been absorbed, 10 to 15 minutes.

4 While fonio stands, heat remaining 2 tablespoons vegetable oil in 10-inch nonstick skillet over medium heat until shimmering. Add sliced onion and cook, stirring occasionally, until it begins to brown at edges, 2 to 3 minutes. Reduce heat to low and continue to cook, stirring occasionally, until onion is soft and deeply brown, 15 to 20 minutes.

5 Fluff fonio and top with caramelized onion and parsley. Serve.

Fregula with Chickpeas, Tomatoes, and Fennel

Why This Recipe Works Fregola sarda, or fregula, is a sun-dried and toasted spherical pasta hand-rolled from semolina, similar to pearl couscous. Its dense, tender chew makes for hearty and satisfying meals. Here, we paired the fregula with chickpeas to echo the tooth-someness of the pasta. We cooked them together with the chickpea liquid, as well as grape tomatoes. The tomatoes contributed bursts of sweet acidity, while their juices, coupled with the chickpea liquid, thickened to a risotto-like texture. Licorice-scented fennel (a fresh bulb for sweetness, and seeds for more intense flavor) and piney rosemary—typical Sardinian aromatics—gave the dish earthy underpinnings. A final sprinkling of Pecorino Romano (try Pecorino Sardo, made from the typical sheep's milk of Sardinia, if you can find it) added just the right amount of richness and salt to finish the dish on a savory, nutty note. A final dash of lemon juice gave our pasta a tart dimension that complemented the dish's nutty flavor profile beautifully.

1 Heat oil in Dutch oven over medium heat until shimmering. Add sliced fennel and onion and cook until vegetables are softened, 5 to 7 minutes. Stir in garlic, rosemary, fennel seeds, salt, pepper, and pepper flakes and cook until fragrant, about 30 seconds.

2 Stir in water, chickpeas and their liquid, tomatoes, and fregula and bring to boil. Reduce heat to medium-low and simmer until fregula is tender, about 25 minutes, stirring occasionally. Stir in lemon juice and fennel fronds and season with salt and pepper to taste. Serve, drizzling individual portions with extra oil and passing Pecorino separately.

- 3 tablespoons extra-virgin olive oil, plus extra for drizzling
- 1 fennel bulb, ¼ cup fronds minced, stalks discarded, bulb halved, cored, and sliced thin
- 1 onion, chopped fine
- 3 garlic cloves, minced
- 2 teaspoons minced fresh rosemary or ¾ teaspoon dried
- 1 teaspoon fennel seeds
- ½ teaspoon table salt
- ½ teaspoon pepper
- ¼ teaspoon red pepper flakes
- 4 cups water
- 2 (15-ounce) cans chickpeas, undrained
- 10 ounces grape tomatoes
- 8 ounces fregula
- 1 tablespoon lemon juice

  Grated Pecorino Romano cheese

Orecchiette with Navy Beans, Brussels Sprouts, and Bacon

Why This Recipe Works   Pasta and beans have something powerful in common: full-bodied cooking liquid. Helped by a bit of sour cream for extra body and richness, the two liquids form the base of this pasta's glossy sauce. We deliberately cooked the pasta in a small volume of water to concentrate its starch—ideal for building a creamy sauce. (The water also boiled quickly, which had the bonus effect of shortening the overall cooking time.) Two slices of bacon—chopped fine to maximize surface area and browning potential—provided a savory foundation for cooking the brussels sprouts. Added to the rendered bacon fat, the sliced sprouts became both soft and crisp-edged as they soaked up the smoky flavor. We then stirred in navy beans along with their starchy liquid, plus some of the pasta cooking water, which thickened the sauce as it bubbled. The dense orecchiette was deliciously chewy, its concave shape perfect for delivering bits of chunky sauce. We finished our pasta with a dusting of spicy, mustard-scented bread crumbs, which we cooked in a skillet to a toasty golden brown.

 2   teaspoons vegetable oil

 ¼   cup panko bread crumbs

 2   teaspoons Dijon mustard

 ⅛   teaspoon plus ½ teaspoon table salt, divided, plus salt for cooking pasta

     Pinch cayenne pepper

 8   ounces orecchiette

 2   slices bacon, chopped fine

 10 ounces brussels sprouts, trimmed, halved, and sliced thin

 1   (15-ounce) can navy beans, undrained

 1   tablespoon cider vinegar

 ½   teaspoon pepper

 ⅓   cup sour cream

1 Bring 2 quarts water to boil in large saucepan. While water is coming to boil, combine oil, panko, mustard, ⅛ teaspoon salt, and cayenne in 12-inch nonstick skillet. Cook over medium-high heat, stirring frequently, until panko is golden brown, about 5 minutes. Transfer to small bowl and let cool completely (do not wash skillet).

2 Add pasta and 1½ teaspoons salt to boiling water and cook, stirring often, until al dente. Reserve 1 cup cooking water and drain pasta. Return pasta to pot and cover to keep warm.

3 While pasta is cooking, cook bacon in now-empty skillet over medium-high heat, stirring frequently, until crispy, 4 to 5 minutes. Using slotted spoon, transfer bacon to paper towel to drain, leaving fat in skillet. Add brussels sprouts, 1 tablespoon water, and remaining ½ teaspoon salt and stir to coat. Cover and cook, stirring occasionally, until sprouts are crisp-tender and bright green, about 4 minutes. Stir in beans and their liquid, ¼ cup reserved pasta cooking water, vinegar, and pepper and cook until bubbling.

4 Add brussels sprout mixture and sour cream to pasta and stir until all ingredients are combined. Adjust consistency with remaining reserved cooking water as needed. Season with salt and pepper to taste. Divide among 4 shallow bowls. Sprinkle bread crumbs and bacon over pasta. Serve.

Pea and Pistachio Pesto Pasta

Why This Recipe Works   When we set out to develop a cool, creamy alternative to popular basil-based pestos, we quickly found that pistachios and green peas—enlivened with refreshing mint—made a perfectly light yet nutty and buttery combination. After cooking the pasta until just al dente, we added fiber-rich Swiss chard leaves to blanch briefly in the same pot before we drained the pasta and greens together. The greens studded our pasta with some leafy chew, while also upping the satiation factor. Similar to classic pesto preparations, we simply processed the peas, pistachios, and mint leaves with Pecorino or Parmesan cheese, lemon zest, garlic, and olive oil. We opted not to toast the pistachios before blitzing them, as we found that doing so significantly reduced their nutty flavor and vibrant green color. Adding reserved pasta water to the pesto gave it starchiness, which helped the sauce evenly coat the noodles and Swiss chard.

1   Bring 4 quarts water to boil in large pot. Add pasta and 1 tablespoon salt and cook, stirring often. One minute before pasta is finished cooking, add chard to pot, stirring to submerge. Reserve ¾ cup cooking water, then drain pasta and chard and return them to pot.

2   While pasta cooks, process peas, pistachios, oil, cheese, mint, lemon zest, garlic, pepper, and salt until smooth, about 1 minute, scraping down sides of processor bowl as needed.

3   Add pesto and ¼ cup reserved cooking water to pasta–chard mixture in pot and toss to combine. Adjust consistency with remaining reserved cooking water as needed and season with salt to taste. Serve with extra Pecorino.

- 1   pound penne, fusilli, or campanelle
- 1½   teaspoons table salt, plus salt for cooking pasta
- 1   pound Swiss chard, stemmed and chopped
- 1   cup frozen peas, thawed
- ⅔   cup shelled pistachios
- ½   cup extra–virgin olive oil
- 1   ounce grated Pecorino Romano or Parmesan cheese (½ cup), plus extra for serving
- ¼   cup fresh mint leaves
- 2   teaspoons grated lemon zest
- 1   garlic clove, chopped
- ¼   teaspoon pepper

Swiss Chard Macaroni and Cheese

Why This Recipe Works Macaroni and cheese is comfort in a bowl, and this version delivers all the decadence and satisfaction of the American favorite with a dose of vegetables and fiber. Swiss chard, cooked until wilted and tender, bulked up the creamy pasta dish with bites of earthy, mildly bitter greens. The decision to use whole-wheat pasta and panko bread crumbs was an easy one, as they were more fiber-rich—and thus filling—than their more refined counterparts. Bold, umami-rich Gruyère, which becomes luxuriously smooth when melted, gave our mac and cheese a velvety texture and pleasant caramel notes, while cream cheese added extra creaminess and tangy complexity. We toasted the panko to crisp it up before combining it with Parmesan, to make a crunchy, savory topping. We love the nutty flavor of Gruyère in this recipe, but if you prefer a milder cheese sauce, you can substitute sharp cheddar. The whole-wheat pasta and panko bread crumbs work well with the Gruyère, but you can use traditional white flour pasta and panko bread crumbs if you prefer.

¼ cup whole-wheat panko bread crumbs

2 tablespoons vegetable oil, divided

⅛ teaspoon cayenne pepper, divided

2 tablespoons grated Parmesan cheese

12 ounces Swiss chard, stemmed and cut into 1-inch pieces

8 ounces whole-wheat or regular elbow macaroni

¼ teaspoon table salt, plus salt for cooking pasta

1 tablespoon all-purpose flour

¾ teaspoon dry mustard

2 cups milk

4 ounces Gruyère cheese, shredded (1 cup)

2 ounces cream cheese, softened

1 Stir panko, 1 teaspoon oil, and pinch cayenne in 8-inch nonstick skillet until combined. Cook over medium heat, stirring frequently, until fragrant and crisp, about 3 minutes. Off heat, transfer to bowl and stir in Parmesan.

2 Heat 2 teaspoons oil in large saucepan over medium heat until shimmering. Add Swiss chard and cook until wilted, about 4 minutes; transfer to bowl. Bring 2 quarts water to boil in now-empty saucepan. Add macaroni and 1½ teaspoons salt and cook, stirring often, until al dente; drain macaroni and wipe pot dry with paper towels.

3 Heat remaining 1 tablespoon oil in now-empty saucepan over medium-high heat until shimmering. Add flour, mustard, remaining pinch cayenne, and salt and cook, whisking constantly, until fragrant and mixture darkens slightly, about 1 minute. Gradually whisk in milk. Bring mixture to boil, whisking constantly. Reduce heat to medium and simmer vigorously, whisking occasionally, until thickened to consistency of heavy cream, about 6 minutes.

4 Off heat, gradually whisk in Gruyère and cream cheese until completely melted and smooth. Stir in macaroni and wilted Swiss chard and cook over medium-low heat until warmed through, about 2 minutes. Season with salt and pepper to taste, and sprinkle with panko mixture. Serve.

Cashew e Pepe e Funghi

Why This Recipe Works   This oh-so-creamy and comforting dish is a marriage of the best hallmarks of pasta carbonara and pasta cacio e pepe—studded with meaty bites of savory oyster mushrooms. We knew that soaked cashews would blitz into a richly thick and creamy (but not heavy) sauce base because of their uniquely low fiber and high starch content. We discovered that by breaking the cashews up in a blender (to increase their surface area), we could soak them for just 15 minutes. We processed the nuts with nutritional yeast and miso, two powerful umami boosters. Though we usually use raw cashews for their more neutral flavor in creamy sauces, we opted for roasted nuts here. Since we only used ½ cup, we wanted them to make an impact, and roasted cashews gave the dish lovely, nuanced warmth without imparting a nutty taste. Plenty of coarsely ground pepper brought subtle heat. Oyster mushrooms went a long way in maximizing heartiness; because they contain very little moisture relative to other mushrooms, they quickly cooked into chewy, golden, almost bacon-like nuggets that infused every bite of pasta with irresistibly savory character. Some parsley and a splash of lemon juice provided freshness and acidity. You can substitute portobello mushrooms for the oyster mushrooms, but the mushroom "bacon" won't be nearly as crisp.

½ cup roasted cashews

¼ cup nutritional yeast

2 tablespoons white miso

½ teaspoon table salt, plus salt for cooking pasta

¼ cup extra-virgin olive oil

6 ounces oyster mushrooms, trimmed and chopped

5 garlic cloves, sliced thin

1 teaspoon coarsely ground pepper

1 pound spaghetti

2 tablespoons chopped fresh parsley

1 teaspoon lemon juice

1   Process cashews in blender on low speed to consistency of fine gravel mixed with sand, 10 to 15 seconds. Add 1½ cups water, nutritional yeast, miso, and salt and process on low speed until combined, about 5 seconds. Scrape down sides of blender jar and let mixture sit for 15 minutes.

2   Process on low speed until all ingredients are well blended, about 1 minute. Scrape down sides of blender jar, then process on high speed until sauce is completely smooth, 3 to 4 minutes.

3   Heat oil in 12-inch skillet over medium-high heat until shimmering. Add mushrooms and cook until deep golden brown and crisp, 7 to 10 minutes. Off heat, stir in garlic and pepper and cook using residual heat of skillet until fragrant, about 1 minute.

4   Meanwhile, bring 4 quarts water to boil in large pot. Add pasta and 1 tablespoon salt and cook, stirring often, until al dente. Reserve ½ cup cooking water, then drain pasta and return it to pot.

5   Add sauce, mushroom mixture, parsley, and lemon juice to pasta and toss until sauce is thickened slightly and pasta is well coated, about 1 minute. Before serving, adjust consistency with reserved cooking water as needed and season with salt and pepper to taste.

Rigatoni with Quick Mushroom Bolognese

Why This Recipe Works Once we decided to develop a pasta sauce reminiscent of Bolognese without using meat, our tests quickly confirmed that cremini mushrooms, pulsed to small bits, did an excellent job of mimicking ground beef. The fungus's spongy texture, absorbent quality, and high glutamate content (the amino acid that gives meat its umami) helped the ingredient fulfill the role meat ordinarily plays in a classic Bolognese. We cooked the mushrooms in a skillet with onion, carrot, and tomato paste so the cremini could soak; to make use of the flavor-packed fond that developed, we deglazed the skillet with wine, stirring until the alcohol cooked off. We then added pasta cooking water, which contributed enough starchiness to turn our mushroom mixture into a decadently velvety sauce. Rigatoni was an easy choice: The tubes perfectly capture and hold on to chunky sauces like this mushroom Bolognese. We tossed our rigatoni with the meaty, umami-rich sauce and then stirred in Pecorino Romano for additional savory oomph and nuttiness. Garnish with chopped chives and red pepper flakes if desired.

1 pound rigatoni

¾ teaspoon table salt, plus salt for cooking pasta

1 pound cremini mushrooms, trimmed and quartered

3 tablespoons extra-virgin olive oil

1 small onion, chopped fine

1 carrot, peeled and chopped fine

¼ cup tomato paste

3 garlic cloves, minced

¼ cup dry white wine

¼ cup grated Pecorino Romano cheese, plus extra for serving

1 Bring 4 quarts water to boil in Dutch oven. Add pasta and 1 tablespoon salt and cook, stirring occasionally, until al dente. Reserve 1 cup cooking water, then drain pasta and return it to pot.

2 Meanwhile, pulse mushrooms in food processor until finely chopped, about 10 pulses. Heat oil in 12-inch skillet over medium-high heat until just smoking. Add mushrooms, onion, carrot, and salt and cook until mushrooms appear dry and begin to stick to bottom of skillet, about 14 minutes.

3 Stir in tomato paste and garlic and cook until fond forms on bottom of skillet, about 1 minute. Stir in wine, scraping up any browned bits, and cook until evaporated, about 2 minutes. Stir in reserved cooking water and bring to boil. Add sauce and Pecorino to pasta in pot and stir to combine. Serve with extra Pecorino.

Sesame Noodles with Pan-Seared Salmon

Why This Recipe Works A delectable staple of Chinese restaurants and home kitchens, chilled sesame noodles can make a tasty partner for any number of proteins. Here, we opted for salmon fillets; not only did their fattiness echo the richness of the noodles' fragrant sesame dressing, but their firm, flaky texture also punctuated the meal with bites of meatiness. To start, we cooked wheat noodles at a very gentle simmer until they were almost tender, tossed them with toasted sesame oil, and spread them onto a baking sheet to chill in the refrigerator. Simmering the noodles over low heat, slightly undercooking them, and skipping rinsing kept them free from gummy starch while ensuring that they retained a satisfying chew; cooling the noodles in the fridge also helped them firm up, further bolstering their appealing resiliency. We coated the chilled noodles with a savory sauce, the linchpin of which was Chinese sesame paste, a condiment made by roasting and milling unhulled sesame seeds. We loosened the paste with toasted sesame oil and chili oil and then emulsified it with a bit of mayonnaise, which made for a slicker, richer dressing. Soy sauce, vinegar, sugar, ginger, and garlic made for a complex, deeply layered sauce, which clung to our noodles. Searing salmon in a skillet rendered its fat while crisping up its surfaces. Flaking the fish distributed its buttery richness and chewy mouthfeel, allowing us to use just two 6- to 8-ounce fillets. A finishing scattering of red bell pepper and cucumber made refreshing counterpoints to the strong flavors in this dish. Look for sesame paste that is dark and smooth; stir before using. If Chinese sesame paste is unavailable, use unsalted, unsweetened natural peanut butter. We prefer the chewy texture of fresh noodles that are about ⅛ inch thick, but if they are unavailable, substitute 8 ounces of dried Chinese wheat noodles or spaghetti and increase the cooking time to 6 to 10 minutes. If you can't find Persian cucumber, use one-third of an English cucumber.

1 pound fresh Chinese wheat noodles

2 teaspoons toasted sesame oil, divided

2 (6- to 8-ounce) skin-on salmon fillets, 1 to 1½ inches thick

¼ cup Chinese sesame paste

1 tablespoon mayonnaise

2 teaspoons chili oil, plus extra for seasoning

3 tablespoons soy sauce

5 teaspoons Chinese black vinegar

4 teaspoons sugar

1 garlic clove, minced, plus extra for seasoning

1 teaspoon grated fresh ginger

1 red bell pepper, stemmed, seeded, and sliced thin

1 Persian cucumber, cut into 3-inch-long matchsticks

¼ cup fresh cilantro leaves

Toasted sesame seeds (optional)

1 Bring 4 quarts water to boil in large pot. Add noodles; reduce heat to maintain very gentle simmer; and cook, stirring occasionally, until almost tender (center of noodles should be firm with slightly opaque dot), 1 minute less than package instructions.

2 Drain noodles very well in colander. Transfer noodles to bowl and toss with 1 teaspoon sesame oil until lightly coated. Transfer noodles to rimmed baking sheet and spread into even layer. Refrigerate until cold, about 20 minutes. (Do not wash bowl.)

3 Meanwhile, pat salmon dry with paper towels. Place salmon skin side down in 12-inch nonstick skillet and cook over medium-high heat until fat is rendered and skin is crispy, about 7 minutes. Flip salmon and continue to cook until center is still translucent when checked with tip of paring knife and registers 125 degrees, about 7 minutes. Transfer salmon to plate and flake into large pieces with fork; set aside.

4 Whisk sesame paste, mayonnaise, chili oil, and remaining 1 teaspoon sesame oil together in now-empty bowl. Add soy sauce, vinegar, 4 teaspoons water, sugar, garlic, and ginger and whisk until smooth. Season dressing with extra chili oil and extra minced garlic to taste. Add chilled noodles and toss until well combined. Divide noodles evenly among serving bowls and top with reserved flaked salmon; bell pepper; cucumber; cilantro; and sesame seeds, if using. Serve immediately.

Yaki Udon

Why This Recipe Works   Yaki udon, the stir-fried
noodle dish from southern Japan, is a harmonious medley
of flavors and textures: chewy udon noodles, crisp-tender
vegetables, and a bit of meat or seafood, all slicked with
a glossy, salty-sweet sauce. A relative to yakisoba (a
similar dish made with thin wheat noodles), yaki udon
comes together quickly and is easily customizable based
on what vegetables or meat you have on hand—fantastic
for a busy weeknight. Our version builds upon the dish's
usual suspects—cabbage, carrot, and onion—by adding
shiitake mushrooms, bean sprouts, and scallions to amp
up the fiber and introduce more textural interest. In place
of the more commonly used pork belly, we cooked a few
slices of bacon; their concentrated smoky richness not
only allowed us to utilize minimal meat, but also complemented the subtle sweetness of the vegetables. While
several sauces can be used in yaki udon, we concocted a
sweet-savory one using pantry staples such as ketchup
and soy sauce; instant dashi powder was the key, enriching
our sauce with a jolt of extra umami. You can substitute
thinly sliced pork belly for the bacon if you prefer. We
developed this recipe in a 14-inch wok. You can use a
12-inch nonstick skillet, but you will need to transfer the
cabbage mixture to a large bowl before adding the
noodles and sauce to the skillet. Once the noodles are
heated through, transfer them to the bowl and toss to
combine with the cabbage mixture. Garnish with drained
beni-shoga (red pickled ginger) and katsuobushi (smoked
bonito flakes) if desired.

2 tablespoons ketchup

1 tablespoon soy sauce

1 tablespoon Worcestershire sauce

1 tablespoon sugar

2 garlic cloves, minced

½ teaspoon instant dashi powder, such as Hondashi

½ teaspoon table salt

1 pound fresh or frozen udon noodles

1 tablespoon vegetable oil

1 small onion, sliced thin

4 slices bacon, cut into 1-inch pieces

4 ounces shiitake mushrooms, stemmed and sliced thin

1 carrot, peeled, halved lengthwise, and sliced thin on bias

½ head green cabbage, halved, cored, and sliced thin (6 cups)

4 ounces (2 cups) bean sprouts

3 scallions, cut into 2-inch lengths, white parts halved lengthwise

1   Whisk ¼ cup water, ketchup, soy sauce, Worcestershire, sugar, garlic, dashi powder, and salt together in small bowl; set aside.

2   Bring 2 quarts water to boil in large saucepan. Add noodles and cook, stirring often, until almost tender (center should still be firm with slightly opaque dot), 2 to 4 minutes (cooking times will vary). Drain noodles and rinse under cold running water until water runs clear. Drain well and set aside.

3   Heat oil in 14-inch flat-bottomed wok over medium-high heat until just smoking. Add onion and bacon and cook, stirring slowly and constantly until starting to brown, about 3 minutes. Add mushrooms and carrot and cook until carrot is crisp-tender, about 2 minutes. Reduce heat to medium; add cabbage and bean sprouts; and cook, stirring occasionally, until cabbage has wilted, about 3 minutes. Add udon, sauce, and scallions and toss to combine. Cook until noodles are warmed through, 2 to 3 minutes. Serve immediately.

Vegetable Lo Mein

Why This Recipe Works Tender and bouncy tangles of fresh Chinese noodles are traditionally the star of lo mein, which may get its name from the Cantonese "lou minh," meaning "stirred noodles." Though variations of this comforting dish spread around the world in the 20th century, it actually dates back thousands of years in China. After being boiled, the egg (or wheat) noodles are stir-fried with a savory sauce and tossed with stir-fried meat and/or vegetables. Part of the fun of lo mein is that it's endlessly customizable with mix-ins. For this vegetable rendition, we chose ingredients with plenty of bite—shiitake mushrooms, snow peas, bell pepper, and carrot. We coated the whole concoction in soy, oyster, and hoisin sauces for a salty, sweet, spicy dish dripping with umami. You can substitute 8 ounces dried lo mein noodles for the fresh noodles.

- 10 scallions, white parts sliced thin, green parts cut into 1-inch pieces
- 2 tablespoons vegetable oil, divided
- 2 garlic cloves, minced
- 2 teaspoons grated fresh ginger
- ½ cup vegetable or chicken broth
- 3 tablespoons soy sauce
- 2 tablespoons Shaoxing wine
- 2 tablespoons oyster sauce or vegan oyster sauce
- 2 tablespoons hoisin sauce
- 1 tablespoon toasted sesame oil
- 1 teaspoon cornstarch
- ⅛ teaspoon five-spice powder
- 8 ounces shiitake mushrooms, stemmed and halved if small or quartered if large
- 8 ounces snow peas, strings removed
- 1 red bell pepper, stemmed, seeded, and cut into 2-inch-long matchsticks
- 1 carrot, peeled and sliced on bias ⅛ inch thick
- 12 ounces fresh lo mein noodles

1 Combine scallion whites, 1 tablespoon vegetable oil, garlic, and ginger in small bowl; set aside. Whisk broth, soy sauce, Shaoxing wine, oyster sauce, hoisin, sesame oil, cornstarch, and five-spice powder together in second small bowl; set aside.

2 Heat remaining 1 tablespoon vegetable oil in 14-inch flat-bottomed wok or 12-inch nonstick skillet over medium-high heat until just smoking. Add mushrooms, snow peas, bell pepper, and carrot and increase heat to high. Cook, tossing vegetables slowly but constantly, until crisp-tender, 4 to 6 minutes. Add scallion greens and cook until tender, about 1 minute; transfer to large bowl.

3 Meanwhile, bring 4 quarts water to boil in large pot. Add noodles and cook, stirring often, until almost tender (center should still be firm, with slightly opaque dot). Drain noodles in colander and rinse under cold running water, tossing with tongs, until cool to touch, about 1 minute. Drain noodles very well.

4 Whisk broth mixture to recombine. Return now-empty wok to medium heat. Add scallion white mixture and cook, mashing mixture into pan, until fragrant, about 30 seconds. Add broth mixture and noodles and increase heat to high. Cook, tossing slowly but constantly, until noodles are warmed through, about 2 minutes. Transfer to bowl with vegetables and toss to combine. Serve.

Soba Noodles with Roasted Eggplant and Sesame

Why This Recipe Works We love the nutty flavor of buckwheat soba noodles and wanted to make them the base of a maximally hearty dinner. Pairing the noodles with eggplant made sense; with its absorbent flesh and mild flavor, eggplant is an excellent vehicle for sauces and seasonings. It also cooks up tender and creamy, providing a nice textural contrast to the springy noodles. To start, we seasoned the eggplant with soy sauce before roasting it in the oven until it was nicely browned and tender. While waiting for the oven to go off, we made a deeply savory sauce using a medley of pantry condiments, including soy sauce, sesame oil, and chili-garlic sauce, with some sake for extra complexity. Fish sauce, coupled with some brown sugar, brought just the right degree of briny sweetness. As we tossed the roasted eggplant and noodles with this umami-rich mixture, the sauce coated them with delectable savoriness. Garnishing with cilantro and sesame seeds kept the finishing touches simple while adding freshness, complementary nutty flavor, and visual appeal. We prefer this dish made with sake, but an equal amount of vermouth can be substituted. For a fully meatless version, make our Vegan Fish Sauce (page 14).

¼ cup vegetable oil, divided

2 pounds eggplant, cut into 1-inch pieces

¼ cup soy sauce, divided

3 tablespoons packed brown sugar

2 tablespoons toasted sesame oil

4 teaspoons sake or dry vermouth

1 tablespoon chili-garlic sauce

1 tablespoon fish sauce or vegan fish sauce

8 ounces dried soba noodles

¾ cup fresh cilantro leaves

2 teaspoons sesame seeds, toasted

1 Adjust oven rack to middle position and heat oven to 450 degrees. Line rimmed baking sheet with aluminum foil and brush with 1 tablespoon vegetable oil. Toss eggplant with remaining 3 tablespoons vegetable oil and 1 tablespoon soy sauce, then spread onto prepared sheet. Roast until well browned and tender, 25 to 30 minutes, stirring halfway through roasting.

2 Whisk remaining 3 tablespoons soy sauce, sugar, sesame oil, sake, chili-garlic sauce, and fish sauce together in small saucepan. Cook over medium heat until sugar has dissolved, about 1 minute; cover and set aside.

3 Meanwhile, bring 2 quarts water to boil in large pot. Add noodles and cook, stirring often, until tender. Reserve ½ cup cooking water, then drain noodles and return them to pot. Add sauce and roasted eggplant and toss to combine, adjusting consistency with reserved cooking water as needed. Sprinkle individual portions with cilantro and sesame seeds and serve.

A scoop of starches can make the perfect bed for a ladle of curry, soak up a saucy stir-fry, or complement a plate of roasted vegetables and meat. Whether you decide on hung kao mun gati (Thai coconut rice) or a creamy polenta, these versatile grains will take your meal to satisfying heights.

Round It Out

Hung Kao Mun Gati

Serves 4 to 6
Total time: 45 minutes

Many brands of coconut milk separate during storage; stir yours until it's smooth before measuring it.

- 1½ cups jasmine rice or long-grain white rice
- 1 cup canned coconut milk
- 1 tablespoon sugar
- ¾ teaspoon table salt

1 Place rice in fine-mesh strainer and rinse under running water, swishing with your hands, until water runs clear. Drain thoroughly. Stir rice, 1½ cups water, coconut milk, sugar, and salt together in large saucepan. Bring to boil over high heat. Reduce heat to maintain bare simmer. Cover and cook until all liquid is absorbed, 18 to 20 minutes.

2 Remove saucepan from heat and let sit, covered, for 10 minutes. Mix rice gently but thoroughly with silicone spatula. (Rice can be refrigerated for up to 3 days.)

Simple Brown Rice

Serves 4 to 6
Total time: 40 minutes

You can substitute long-grain white rice; start checking for doneness after 10 minutes.

- 1½ cups long-grain brown rice
  Table salt for cooking rice
- 2½ teaspoons sesame oil (optional)

Bring 4 quarts water to boil over high heat in large saucepan. Add rice and 2½ teaspoons salt and return to boil. Reduce heat to medium and simmer until rice is tender, 25 to 30 minutes. Drain rice well and return to saucepan. Toss with sesame oil, if using. (Rice can be refrigerated for up to 3 days.)

Brown Rice Pilaf

Serves 4 to 6
Total time: 1 hour 40 minutes

- 3 tablespoons unsalted butter
- 1 onion, chopped fine
- 2 bay leaves
- 2 sprigs fresh thyme
- 2 cups long-grain brown rice, rinsed
- 4½ cups chicken or vegetable broth
- ½ cup water
- 1 teaspoon table salt

1 Adjust oven rack to middle position and heat oven to 375 degrees. Melt butter in Dutch oven over medium heat. Add onion, bay leaves, and thyme, and cook until onion is softened but not browned, about 5 minutes.

2 Stir in rice and cook, stirring occasionally, until half of rice grains begin to brown at edges, 10 to 15 minutes. Stir in broth and water, cover, and bring to boil. Transfer covered pot to oven and bake until liquid is absorbed and rice is tender, about 1 hour.

3 Remove pot from oven and let sit covered for 10 minutes. Discard bay leaves and thyme and fluff with fork. (Rice can be refrigerated for up to 3 days.)

Spiced Basmati Rice

Serves 4 to 6
Total time: 50 minutes

For basmati rice with a bright yellow color, add ¼ teaspoon of ground turmeric and a pinch of saffron threads with the water in step 2. Alternatively, skip the spices altogether for an unadorned white rice pilaf.

- 1½ cups basmati rice
- 3 tablespoons unsalted butter
- 1 teaspoon cumin seeds
- 3 green cardamom pods, lightly crushed
- 3 whole cloves
- 2¼ cups water
- 1 cinnamon stick
- 1 bay leaf
- 1 teaspoon table salt

1 Place rice in fine-mesh strainer and rinse under cold running water until water runs clear. Place strainer over bowl and set aside. Melt butter in medium saucepan over medium heat. Add cumin, cardamom, and cloves and cook, stirring constantly, until fragrant, about 1 minute. Add rice and cook, stirring constantly, until fragrant, about 1 minute.

2 Add water, cinnamon stick, bay leaf, and salt and bring to boil. Reduce heat to low; cover; and simmer until all water is absorbed, about 17 minutes. Let stand, covered, off heat for at least 10 minutes. Discard cardamom, cloves, cinnamon stick, and bay leaf. Fluff rice with fork. (Rice can be refrigerated for up to 3 days.)

Creamy Parmesan Polenta

Serves 4
Total time: 45 minutes

We developed this recipe with Bob's Red Mill yellow corn polenta. Coarse-ground grits also work well. Avoid quick-cooking or instant polenta or cornmeal.

- 4½ cups water
- 1 cup coarse-ground polenta
- 1 teaspoon table salt
  Pinch baking soda
- 1 ounce Parmesan cheese, grated (½ cup)
- 1 tablespoon unsalted butter

1 Bring water to boil in medium saucepan over high heat. Whisk in polenta, salt, and baking soda. Bring mixture to boil, stirring frequently. Reduce heat to lowest possible setting, cover, and cook for 5 minutes. Whisk until smooth; cover; and continue to cook until grains are tender but slightly al dente, about 25 minutes longer. (Polenta should be loose and barely hold its shape when drizzled from whisk; it will continue to thicken as it cools.)

2 Remove from heat, whisk in Parmesan and butter, and season with salt and pepper to taste. (Polenta can be refrigerated for up to 3 days.)

Sunday Suppers

Herby Roasted Cauliflower and Chicken with Quinoa Pilaf

Why This Recipe Works Roast chicken's crispy skin and juicy meat make the dish beloved comfort food. To capture these qualities while paring down the quantity of meat, we turned to bone-in chicken thighs—the ultimate rich, tender cut. First, we seared the chicken in a skillet to render some of its fat, which was perfect for cooking our cauliflower; the vegetable absorbed the savory juices and browned beautifully. Returning the chicken to the pan before transferring to a hot oven ensured that the meat and vegetables would finish cooking at the same time. Keeping the skillet uncovered during cooking allowed the skin to shed even more moisture, making it extra-crispy; this had the added benefit of basting the cauliflower, further imbuing it with umami. Lining some sweet grape tomatoes along the skillet's rim caused them to shrivel slightly and brown as their sugars caramelized. To make this a complete meal, we paired it with an easy quinoa pilaf and served it all with an herbaceous tarragon-parsley sauce spiked with garlic and lemon. We like the convenience of prewashed quinoa here; the rinsing removes the quinoa's bitter protective coating. If you buy unwashed quinoa, rinse it and then spread it out on a clean dish towel to dry for 15 minutes.

3 tablespoons extra-virgin olive oil, divided

3 tablespoons minced fresh parsley, divided

2 tablespoon minced fresh tarragon, divided

¼ teaspoon garlic, minced to paste

¼ teaspoon grated lemon zest plus 1 tablespoon juice, divided, plus lemon wedges for serving

⅛ teaspoon plus ¾ teaspoon table salt, divided

1 onion, chopped fine

1½ cups water

1 cup prewashed red or white quinoa

4 (5- to 7-ounce) bone-in chicken thighs, trimmed

1 head cauliflower (2 pounds), cored and cut into 1- to 2-inch florets

½ cup chicken broth

8 ounces grape or cherry tomatoes

1 Adjust oven rack to upper-middle position and heat oven to 450 degrees. Combine 2 tablespoons oil, 2 tablespoons parsley, 1 tablespoon tarragon, garlic, lemon zest, 1 teaspoon lemon juice, and ⅛ teaspoon salt in small bowl; set aside.

2 Heat 2 teaspoons oil in medium saucepan over medium heat until shimmering. Add onion and ¼ teaspoon salt and cook until softened, 5 to 7 minutes. Increase heat to medium-high, stir in water and quinoa, and bring to simmer. Cover, reduce heat to low, and simmer until grains are just tender and liquid has been fully absorbed, 18 to 20 minutes, stirring once halfway through cooking. Remove saucepan from heat and let sit, covered, while cooking chicken and vegetables.

3 Meanwhile, pat chicken dry with paper towels and sprinkle with ¼ teaspoon salt. Heat remaining 1 teaspoon oil in 12-inch skillet over medium-high heat until just smoking. Add chicken and cook until well browned, about 5 minutes per side. Transfer to plate.

4 Add cauliflower florets and remaining ¼ teaspoon salt to fat left in skillet. Cook until browned on 1 side, 4 to 5 minutes. Off heat, flip florets and add broth. Nestle chicken, skin side up, and any accumulated juices into skillet. Arrange tomatoes around perimeter of skillet and transfer to oven. Cook until chicken registers at least 175 degrees, 20 to 25 minutes.

5 Fluff quinoa with fork; stir in remaining 1 tablespoon parsley, 1 tablespoon tarragon, and 2 teaspoons lemon juice; and season with salt and pepper to taste. Serve with roast chicken, vegetables, herb sauce, and lemon wedges.

Cannellini Beans with Chicken, Kale, and Mustard

Why This Recipe Works This hearty bean dish that leans on pantry staples gets a hearty dose of fiber from kale; full-flavored brightness and tang from whole-grain mustard; and rich savoriness from chicken. To make the most of four thighs, we seared the meat—opting for bone-in for maximum flavor—and then used the flavorful and unctuous rendered fat to cook our onion, garlic, and fennel seeds. Deglazing the pot with white wine gave us a deeply flavorful base, which proved exceptional at imbuing cannellini beans and kale with ample richness. The subtle sweetness of the fennel seeds enhanced the mild and nutty flavor of the beans. Slicing the kale into thin ribbons and adding it to the pot a handful at a time ensured that the greens wilted evenly. We also made good use of the bean canning liquid; adding it to the pot not only doubled down on the flavor of the legumes but also gave the dish more viscosity. We nestled the chicken back into the pot and cooked it slowly in the oven, where the meat further distributed its rich juices throughout the entire dish. Stirring in whole-grain mustard at the end brightened up the meal and gave it a spicy kick. Toast the fennel in a dry skillet over medium heat until fragrant (about 1 minute), and then remove the skillet from the heat so the fennel won't scorch. You can substitute Swiss chard for the kale, if you prefer.

4 (5- to 7-ounce) bone-in chicken thighs, trimmed

½ teaspoon table salt

¼ teaspoon pepper

¼ cup extra-virgin olive oil, plus extra for drizzling

1 small onion, halved and sliced thin

4 garlic cloves, minced

2 teaspoons fennel seeds, toasted and cracked

¼ cup dry white wine

1 pound kale, stemmed and sliced thin crosswise

2 (15-ounce) cans cannellini beans, undrained

¼ cup whole-grain mustard

1 Adjust oven rack to lower-middle position and heat oven to 350 degrees. Pat chicken dry with paper towels and sprinkle with salt and pepper. Heat oil in Dutch oven over medium-high heat until just smoking. Add chicken and cook until well browned, about 5 minutes per side. Transfer to plate.

2 Add onion to oil left in pot, and cook until softened, 2 to 3 minutes. Add garlic and fennel seeds and cook until fragrant, about 30 seconds. Add wine and cook, scraping up any browned bits, until liquid is reduced to glaze, about 30 seconds.

3 Stir in kale, 1 handful at a time, and cook until wilted, about 3 minutes. Stir in beans and their liquid and bring to simmer. Return chicken and any accumulated juices to Dutch oven, skin side up (skin will be above surface of liquid). Cover pot, transfer to oven, and cook until kale is tender and chicken registers at least 185 degrees, 25 to 30 minutes.

4 Transfer chicken to platter, tent with aluminum foil, and let rest while finishing dish. Stir in mustard, bring to simmer, and cook over medium heat until flavors meld, about 1 minute.

5 Divide kale mixture among individual serving plates and top with chicken. Drizzle with extra oil and season with salt and pepper to taste. Serve.

Peruvian Arroz con Pollo

Why This Recipe Works It's easy to see why hearty, comforting arroz con pollo, or rice with chicken, is so beloved in Peru. The aromatic, stick-to-your-ribs dish has complex layers of seasonings, so we found we only needed a pound of chicken thighs to produce the savory flavor profile the dish is known for. We also cooked the rice in an herbaceous cooking liquid that infused every grain with maximum flavor. To start, we created our aderezo (Spanish for seasoning), the dish's aromatic base. This typically includes seasonings like ají amarillo (Peru's fruity, moderately hot yellow chile) paste, cumin, and oregano, which we bloomed in a skillet alongside onion and bell pepper to invigorate the spices' aroma and coat the vegetables with flavor. We then deglazed the pan with beer to amplify the impact of all the flavor-rich browned bits on the bottom of the pot. Using a food processor, we blitzed our aderezo with cilantro and spinach into a green cooking liquid for the rice. Toasting the grains in the skillet before cooking enriched them with a nutty edge. Cooking the rice and chicken together allowed the grains to sponge up the flavorful juices released by the meat. Any browned rice at the bottom of the pot adds to the overall experience of the dish, so be sure to include it when serving. For the beer, look for a brown ale or mild lager. Do not substitute other hot pepper pastes for ají amarillo. You will need a 12-inch nonstick skillet with a tight-fitting lid for this recipe. We like to serve this with Sarza Criolla (page 361).

1 tablespoon vegetable oil, divided

1 red onion, halved and sliced into ½-inch-wide strips

1 red bell pepper, stemmed, seeded, and cut into ½-inch-wide strips, divided

1½ teaspoons table salt, divided

3 garlic cloves, smashed and peeled

1 tablespoon ají amarillo paste

1 teaspoon ground cumin

1 teaspoon dried oregano

½ teaspoon pepper, divided

1 cup beer

1½ cups fresh cilantro leaves and tender stems

1 cup baby spinach

¾ cup chicken broth, plus extra as needed

1½ cups long-grain white rice, rinsed

2 carrots, peeled, halved lengthwise, and sliced crosswise ½ inch thick

1 pound boneless, skinless chicken thighs, trimmed and cut into 1-inch strips

½ cup frozen peas

1 Heat 2 teaspoons oil in 12-inch nonstick skillet over medium-high heat until shimmering. Add onion, half of bell pepper, and 1 teaspoon salt and cook over medium heat until softened and lightly browned, about 5 minutes. Stir in garlic, ají amarillo paste, cumin, oregano, and ¼ teaspoon pepper and cook until fragrant, about 30 seconds. Stir in beer, scraping up any browned bits, and cook until liquid has reduced slightly, about 3 minutes.

2 Transfer vegetable mixture to blender. Add cilantro, spinach, broth, remaining ½ teaspoon salt, and remaining ¼ teaspoon pepper and process until smooth, about 1 minute, scraping down sides of blender jar as needed. Transfer mixture to 4-cup liquid measuring cup. (You should have 3½ cups; if necessary, spoon off excess or add extra broth so that volume equals 3½ cups.)

3 Heat remaining 1 teaspoon oil in now-empty skillet over medium-high heat until shimmering. Add rice and carrots and cook until rice is lightly toasted and fragrant, about 2 minutes. Stir in pureed vegetable mixture and chicken and bring to simmer. Arrange remaining bell pepper strips attractively over top. Reduce heat to medium-low; cover; and cook until rice is tender, 25 to 30 minutes.

4 Off heat, scatter peas over top; cover; and let sit until heated through, about 10 minutes. Season with salt and pepper to taste and serve.

Chicken and Spiced Freekeh with Cilantro and Preserved Lemon

Why This Recipe Works We wanted to celebrate the dynamic duo that is freekeh and chicken, which appear together often in Middle Eastern cuisines, especially in Lebanon. We turned to bone-in chicken thighs, as the cut stays exceptionally juicy and tender while readily distributing richness to surrounding ingredients. To start, we browned the meat in a Dutch oven; we then removed it and used the rendered fat to cook onion and garlic and bloom our spices: smoked paprika, cardamom, and red pepper flakes. We deglazed the pan with chicken broth, which echoed and amplified the flavor of the meat, and used this richly seasoned liquid to cook the freekeh. We also nestled the chicken in with the grains so that the meat's flavor could deeply penetrate the freekeh. Prior to serving, we shredded the thighs into bite-size pieces, which gave us pleasingly textured edges and dispersed the meat throughout the dish. Freshly chopped cilantro and toasted pistachios offered grassy notes along with a satisfying crunch, while preserved lemon brought tangy complexity. If you can't find preserved lemon, you can substitute 1 tablespoon lemon zest. Do not substitute whole freekeh for the cracked freekeh in this recipe.

4 (5- to 7-ounce) bone-in chicken thighs, trimmed

½ teaspoon table salt

¼ teaspoon pepper

1 tablespoon extra-virgin olive oil, plus extra for drizzling

1 onion, chopped fine

4 garlic cloves, minced

1½ teaspoons smoked paprika

¼ teaspoon ground cardamom

¼ teaspoon red pepper flakes

2¼ cups chicken broth

1½ cups cracked freekeh, rinsed

6 tablespoons chopped fresh cilantro, divided

½ cup shelled pistachios, toasted and chopped

2 tablespoons rinsed and minced preserved lemon

1 Adjust oven rack to lower-middle position and heat oven to 350 degrees. Pat chicken dry with paper towels and sprinkle with salt and pepper. Heat oil in Dutch oven over medium-high heat until just smoking. Add chicken and cook until well browned, about 5 minutes per side. Transfer to plate.

2 Add onion to fat left in pot and cook over medium heat until softened, about 5 minutes. Stir in garlic, paprika, cardamom, and pepper flakes and cook until fragrant, about 30 seconds. Stir in broth, scraping up any browned bits, then stir in freekeh.

3 Nestle chicken, skin side up, into freekeh mixture along with any accumulated juices. Cover, transfer pot to oven, and cook until freekeh is tender and chicken registers 195 degrees, 35 to 40 minutes.

4 Remove pot from oven. Transfer chicken to cutting board, let cool slightly, then chop chicken skin and shred meat into bite-size pieces using 2 forks; discard bones.

5 Meanwhile, gently fluff freekeh with fork. Lay clean dish towel over pot, replace lid, and let sit for 5 minutes. Stir in chicken and chicken skin, ¼ cup cilantro, pistachios, and preserved lemon. Season with salt and pepper to taste. Sprinkle with remaining 2 tablespoons cilantro and drizzle with extra oil. Serve.

Turkey Shepherd's Pie

Why This Recipe Works We love how shepherd's pie features a meaty base bulked up by an assortment of vegetables. For a different take, we swapped in cauliflower for potato and used turkey as a leaner option. Keeping the meat tender required us to refrain from browning it; instead, we browned mushrooms and onion first, which gave us savory fond that we enhanced with tomato paste and garlic. Carrots, thyme, and Worcestershire evoked the flavors we know and love in shepherd's pie. We simmered all this with chicken broth, making sure to scrape up the browned bits in the skillet. Only then did we add the meat, which we tenderized with baking soda. Pinching off pieces of turkey by hand before incorporating them ensured craggy edges, which maximized the surface area through which it could absorb flavor. Cauliflower, cooked and then pureed to a creamy consistency, made a highly satisfying topping. Be sure to use 93 percent lean ground turkey, not 99 percent fat-free ground turkey breast, or the filling will be tough. You will need a 10-inch broiler-safe skillet for this recipe.

3 tablespoons extra-virgin olive oil, divided

1 large head cauliflower (3 pounds), cored and cut into ½-inch pieces

½ cup plus 2 tablespoons water, divided

1 teaspoon table salt, divided

1 large egg, lightly beaten

3 tablespoons minced fresh chives

1 pound 93 percent lean ground turkey

¼ teaspoon pepper

¼ teaspoon baking soda

8 ounces cremini mushrooms, trimmed and chopped

1 onion, chopped

1 tablespoon tomato paste

2 garlic cloves, minced

¾ cup chicken broth

2 carrots, peeled and chopped

2 sprigs fresh thyme

1 tablespoon Worcestershire sauce

1 tablespoon cornstarch

1 Heat 2 tablespoons oil in Dutch oven over medium-low heat until shimmering. Add cauliflower and cook, stirring occasionally, until softened and beginning to brown, 10 to 12 minutes. Stir in ½ cup water and ¾ teaspoon salt; cover; and cook until cauliflower falls apart easily when poked with fork, about 10 minutes.

2 Transfer cauliflower and any remaining liquid to food processor and let cool for 5 minutes. Process until smooth, about 45 seconds. Transfer to large bowl and stir in beaten egg and chives; set aside.

3 Meanwhile, toss turkey, pepper, baking soda, 1 tablespoon water, and remaining ¼ teaspoon salt in bowl until thoroughly combined. Set aside for 20 minutes.

4 Heat remaining 1 tablespoon oil in broiler-safe 10-inch skillet over medium heat until shimmering. Add mushrooms and onion and cook, stirring occasionally, until liquid has evaporated and fond begins to form on bottom of skillet, 10 to 12 minutes. Stir in tomato paste and garlic and cook until bottom of skillet is dark brown, about 2 minutes.

5 Add broth, carrots, thyme, and Worcestershire and bring to simmer, scraping up any browned bits. Reduce heat to medium-low, pinch off turkey in ½-inch pieces and add to skillet, and bring to gentle simmer. Cover and cook until turkey is cooked through, 8 to 10 minutes, stirring and breaking up meat halfway through cooking.

6 Whisk cornstarch and remaining 1 tablespoon water together in small bowl, then stir mixture into filling and continue to simmer until thickened, about 1 minute. Discard thyme sprigs and season with salt and pepper to taste.

7 Adjust oven rack 5 inches from broiler element and heat broiler. Transfer cauliflower mixture to large zipper-lock bag. Using scissors, snip 1 inch off filled corner. Squeezing bag, pipe mixture in even layer over filling, making sure to cover entire surface. Smooth mixture with back of spoon, then use tines of fork to make ridges over surface. Place skillet on aluminum foil–lined rimmed baking sheet and broil until topping is golden brown and crusty and filling is bubbly, 10 to 15 minutes. Let cool for 10 minutes before serving.

Pork Tenderloin with White Beans and Mustard Greens

Why This Recipe Works The south of France is known for its rich stews that combine creamy white beans, fresh greens, and tender pork. We set out to re-create the rustic appeal of these dishes, but with less meat and in less time, so we turned to moist, quick-cooking pork tenderloin. To maximize the meaty flavor from our pound of pork, we browned it and used the juices it released to build a flavorful base with onion, thyme, garlic, and wine. Next, we stirred in fiber-rich, mildly spicy mustard greens and bulked up the dish with navy beans. Resting the pork on top of the greens and beans lifted the lean cut out of the braising liquid; this helped surround the meat with steam so it could cook gently and stay tender, while simultaneously allowing the pork's flavor to seep into the vegetables below. While the dish baked, we whipped up some lemon-scented bread crumbs for a bright, crisp garnish. Crumbles of tangy goat cheese made a rich, pleasantly funky finish.

3 tablespoons extra-virgin olive oil, divided

1 (1-pound) pork tenderloin, trimmed and halved crosswise

½ teaspoon table salt

¼ teaspoon pepper

1 onion, chopped fine

1 tablespoon minced fresh thyme or 1 teaspoon dried

2 garlic cloves, minced

¾ cup chicken broth

¼ cup dry white wine

1 pound mustard greens, stemmed and cut into 2-inch pieces

2 (15-ounce) cans navy beans, rinsed

½ cup panko bread crumbs

2 tablespoons chopped fresh parsley

½ teaspoon grated lemon zest plus 1 teaspoon juice

4 ounces goat cheese, crumbled (1 cup)

1 Adjust oven rack to middle position and heat oven to 450 degrees. Heat 2 tablespoons oil in Dutch oven over medium-high heat until just smoking. Pat pork dry with paper towels and sprinkle with salt and pepper. Brown pork on all sides, 5 to 7 minutes; transfer to plate.

2 Add onion to fat left in pot and cook over medium heat until softened, about 5 minutes. Stir in thyme and garlic and cook until fragrant, about 30 seconds. Stir in broth and wine, scraping up any browned bits. Add mustard greens, 1 handful at a time, and cook, stirring constantly, until beginning to wilt, 2 to 3 minutes.

3 Stir in beans. Nestle pork on top of mustard greens mixture. Transfer pot to oven and cook until pork registers 135 degrees and greens are tender, about 15 minutes.

4 Meanwhile, toss panko with remaining 1 tablespoon oil in bowl until evenly coated. Microwave, stirring every 30 seconds, until light golden brown, 2 to 5 minutes. Let cool slightly, then stir in parsley and lemon zest.

5 Remove pot from oven. Transfer pork to cutting board, tent with aluminum foil, and let rest for 5 minutes. Stir lemon juice into mustard greens mixture and season with salt and pepper to taste. Slice pork ½ inch thick and serve with mustard greens mixture, sprinkling individual portions with bread crumbs and goat cheese.

Bún Chả

Why This Recipe Works

Vietnamese bún chả is a vibrant meal of grilled pork patties, crisp salad, and chewy rice vermicelli, all united with a light, bright, deeply flavorful sauce. Because the dish teems with vegetables and noodles, we needed just a pound of ground pork for plenty of savory satisfaction. We started by boiling dried rice vermicelli, after which we rinsed the noodles well and spread them on a platter to dry, to ensure the delicate strands didn't overcook. We then mixed Thai chile, garlic, fish sauce, and lime juice into the spicy, zesty sauce known as nuoc cham; adding some sugar helped us grind the solid ingredients into a fine, well-blended paste. Seasoning our pork with shallot, fish sauce, and sugar heightened the meat's inherent savoriness. For extra-juicy patties, we mixed baking soda into the meat to raise its pH, which retained the meat's moisture while also helping it brown. Though the patties are traditionally griddled, we opted for the ease of cooking them in a 12-inch cast-iron skillet, which gave us plenty of char while keeping the interior succulent and tender. Briefly soaking the patties in the nuoc cham after cooking infused the meat with tangy-savory flavor. We plated all the components separately so diners could combine them according to their tastes. A stainless-steel skillet can be used in place of cast iron if you prefer; add the oil to the skillet and heat over medium-high heat until just smoking before adding the patties.

Noodles and Salad

- 8 ounces rice vermicelli
- 1 head Boston lettuce (8 ounces), torn into bite-size pieces
- 1 English cucumber, peeled, quartered lengthwise, seeded, and sliced thin on bias
- 1 cup fresh cilantro leaves and stems
- 1 cup fresh mint leaves, torn if large
- 2 carrots, peeled and shredded
- 1 cup bean sprouts
- ½ cup cherry tomatoes, halved

Sauce

- 1 small Thai chile, stemmed and minced
- 3 tablespoons sugar, divided
- 1 garlic clove, minced
- ⅔ cup hot water
- 3 tablespoons fish sauce
- ¼ cup lime juice (2 limes)

Pork Patties

- 1 large shallot, minced
- 1½ teaspoons sugar
- 1 teaspoon fish sauce
- ½ teaspoon baking soda
- ½ teaspoon pepper
- 1 pound ground pork
- 2 teaspoons vegetable oil

1 For the noodles and salad Bring 4 quarts water to boil in large pot. Stir in noodles and cook until tender but not mushy, 4 to 12 minutes. Drain noodles and rinse under cold running water until cool. Drain noodles very well, spread on large plate, and let stand at room temperature to dry. Arrange lettuce, cucumber, cilantro, mint, carrots, bean sprouts, and tomatoes separately on large platter and refrigerate until needed.

2 For the sauce Using mortar and pestle (or on cutting board using flat side of chef's knife), mash Thai chile, 1 tablespoon sugar, and garlic to fine paste. Transfer to medium bowl and add hot water and remaining 2 tablespoons sugar. Stir until sugar is dissolved. Stir in fish sauce and lime juice and set aside.

3 For the pork patties Combine shallot, sugar, fish sauce, baking soda, and pepper in medium bowl. Add pork and mix until well combined. Shape pork mixture into seventeen 1-ounce patties.

4 Heat empty cast–iron skillet over medium heat for 3 minutes. Add oil, increase heat to medium–high, and heat until oil is just smoking. Transfer patties to skillet and cook until well browned on first side, about 2½ minutes. Flip patties and continue to cook until browned on second side.

5 Transfer patties to bowl with sauce and gently toss to coat. Let stand for 5 minutes, then transfer patties to plate. Serve, passing noodles, salad, and remaining sauce separately.

Spiced Stuffed Peppers

Why This Recipe Works   Stuffed peppers are always a crowd-pleaser, and the filling in our version is inspired by kibbeh, a hearty, well-seasoned Middle Eastern dish made from bulgur, beef or lamb, onions, and spices. We used just 12 ounces of ground beef, which turned into a generous portion once we added the bulgur and a medley of flavor-packed mix-ins. We browned the beef and shallots before adding spices—dried mint, sumac, fenugreek, cumin, and mustard seeds—to the pan, where the heat bloomed their flavors. After adding water and scraping up the flavorful bits at the bottom of the pan, we had a savory base for imbuing the bulgur with flavor. Earthy lentils and sweet dried apricots gave our filling more textural diversity, not to mention a well-rounded flavor profile. We charred the peppers before stuffing; the broiler deepened their sweet, vegetal flavor. A topping of fried shallots echoed the dish's oniony flavor and added crispy contrast, while a drizzle of yogurt tied the whole meal together with a cool, creamy element. Look for bell peppers that weigh at least 8 ounces each. We prefer to make this with our Crispy Shallots, but you can substitute store-bought; use extra-virgin olive oil in place of the reserved shallot oil.

4   red bell peppers, halved lengthwise through stem and seeded

1   recipe Crispy Shallots, plus 2 tablespoons shallot oil (page 85)

1   teaspoon table salt, divided

12   ounces 90 percent lean ground beef

3   shallots, chopped

3   tablespoons dried mint, divided

1½   tablespoons ground sumac, plus extra for sprinkling

4   garlic cloves, minced

1   tablespoon ground fenugreek

2   teaspoons ground cumin

2   teaspoons mustard seeds

3   cups water

¾   cup medium-grind bulgur, rinsed

1   (15-ounce) can lentils, rinsed

½   cup dried apricots, chopped

½   cup plain yogurt

1   Adjust oven rack 6 inches from broiler element and heat broiler. Line rimmed baking sheet with aluminum foil and place bell peppers on sheet. Drizzle bell peppers with shallot oil and sprinkle with ½ teaspoon salt, then rub all over to coat. Arrange bell peppers skin side up and broil until spotty brown, 9 to 11 minutes. Set aside to cool while making filling.

2   Heat oven to 350 degrees. Cook beef and chopped shallots in large saucepan over medium-high heat, breaking up meat with wooden spoon, until beef is cooked through and shallots are softened and beginning to brown, 8 to 10 minutes. Stir in 1½ tablespoons mint, sumac, garlic, fenugreek, cumin, mustard seeds, and remaining ½ teaspoon salt and cook until fragrant, about 1 minute.

3   Stir in water and bulgur, scraping up any browned bits, and bring to simmer. Reduce heat to low, cover, and simmer gently until bulgur is just tender and no liquid remains, about 10 minutes. Off heat, stir in lentils and apricots, lay clean dish towel underneath lid, and let mixture sit for 10 minutes. Season with salt and pepper to taste.

4   Turn cooled bell pepper halves cut side up on sheet and divide beef-bulgur mixture evenly among halves, packing mixture and mounding as needed. Bake until warmed through, 20 to 25 minutes. Transfer to serving platter, drizzle with yogurt, and sprinkle with fried shallots, remaining 1½ tablespoons mint, and extra sumac. Serve.

Hashweh Stuffed Swiss Chard

Why This Recipe Works These stuffed Swiss chard leaves bathed in a delicate ginger broth make a hearty and impressive dinner. They're filled with hashweh, which is Arabic for "stuffing" and refers to a rice-and-meat mixture that's redolent with warm spices and often used as a filling. To make ours, we used just 8 ounces of ground lamb, which infused the dish with the meat's distinctly earthy flavor. We cooked the meat with lightly caramelized onion and aromatic spices, including allspice and cardamom, to create a savory foundation for the hashweh. We then added jasmine rice (which we first soaked in boiling water to shorten the cooking time) along with fruity raisins and crunchy toasted almonds. To turn Swiss chard into tender wrappers, we covered the leaves in boiling water, which made them sufficiently pliable without causing them to fall apart. After stuffing the leaves with hashweh, we steamed the pouches in a small amount of water, which not only helped the leaves stay intact, but also preserved their minerality and bitter edge. A splash of fresh lemon juice before serving injected the dish with a burst of brightness that balanced the warmth of the spiced filling. Seasoning chicken broth simply with ginger and dried shiitake mushrooms made for a clean yet savory broth that was perfect for serving the vibrantly flavored stuffed Swiss chard. Look for large Swiss chard leaves that are about 7 inches long and 5 inches wide. You can use smaller leaves, though you'll need more Swiss chard leaves in order to use up the filling. If any leaves rip, patch them up with another small piece of leaf. Serve with plain whole-milk yogurt.

1 cup jasmine rice

12 large Swiss chard leaves

2 tablespoons extra-virgin olive oil

1 onion, chopped fine

2 teaspoons ground allspice

1½ teaspoons ground cinnamon

1 teaspoon ground cardamom

½ teaspoon pepper

8 ounces ground lamb

⅓ cup golden raisins

2 tablespoons slivered almonds, toasted

1¼ teaspoons table salt

2 tablespoons lemon juice

1 cup chicken broth

3 garlic cloves, lightly crushed and peeled

½ ounce dried shiitake mushrooms, rinsed and minced

1 tablespoon grated fresh ginger

1 Cover rice with boiling water and let sit for 30 minutes; drain in fine-mesh strainer and set aside. Meanwhile, trim any chard stems that extend beyond leaves and chop fine; set aside. Place chard leaves in bowl and cover with boiling water. Let sit for 1 minute, then drain leaves and set aside.

2 Heat oil in 12-inch skillet over medium heat until shimmering. Add onion and cook, stirring occasionally, until softened and just beginning to brown, 5 to 7 minutes. Stir in finely chopped chard stems and cook for 1 minute. Stir in allspice, cinnamon, cardamom, and pepper and cook until fragrant, about 30 seconds. Stir in lamb and cook, breaking up meat with wooden spoon and scraping up fond from bottom of skillet, until lamb is mostly cooked through, 3 to 5 minutes. Stir in raisins, almonds, salt, and drained rice, then transfer to bowl. Wipe skillet clean with paper towels.

3 Place 1 chard leaf flat on counter with long side parallel to counter edge. Place 3 to 4 tablespoons rice mixture in center of leaf, then fold right side of leaf over filling followed by left side, tucking any excess leaf underneath. Fold bottom of leaf up over pouch, followed by top of leaf, tucking any excess leaf underneath (you should end up with a roughly square-shaped pouch). Repeat with remaining chard leaves and remaining rice mixture.

4 Arrange stuffed chard pouches seam side down in clean, dry skillet, stacking chard pouches if needed. Add 1¼ cups water to skillet; bring to simmer; cover; and cook over medium-low heat until rice is cooked through, 35 to 40 minutes (to test rice doneness, cut small slice in 1 pouch and extract rice). If skillet looks dry at any point during steaming, add extra water, 2 tablespoons at a time. Off heat, sprinkle lemon juice over chard pouches in skillet.

5 Meanwhile, combine broth, ¼ cup water, garlic, mushrooms, and ginger in small saucepan. Bring to simmer, cover, and simmer over low heat for 15 minutes. Season with salt to taste, and remove from heat. Let sit, covered to keep warm, until ready to serve.

6 Spoon seasoned broth into individual bowls, add chard pouches, and serve.

Swiss Chard Enchiladas

Why This Recipe Works
Traditional enchiladas consist of fried tortillas filled with meat, cheese, and more, all topped with sauce and more cheese. We wanted to put a vegetable-forward spin on the filling, but with equally hearty and irresistible results. So we turned to chewy Swiss chard, snappy bell peppers, and creamy pinto beans—plants with robust, meaty texture. To wilt the leafy greens and soften the peppers, we cooked them in a skillet with garlic and onions, which infused the vegetables with nutty depth. To add creamy cohesiveness and a protein boost, we mashed half a can of pinto beans and mixed it into the filling; the rest of the beans went in whole, for textural contrast. Like any enchiladas, ours needed a robust sauce; simmering canned tomato sauce with aromatics and spices gave us a quick, flavorful concoction to spread all over our enchiladas. Instead of frying the tortillas, we found that brushing them with oil and microwaving worked just as well—and without the mess. To finish, we scattered shredded Monterey Jack over the top; the cheese melted to a decadently gooey consistency in the oven. Cilantro leaves made the perfect refreshing garnish.

¼ cup vegetable oil, divided

2 onions, chopped fine, divided

3 tablespoons chili powder

6 garlic cloves, minced, divided

2 teaspoons ground cumin

2 teaspoons sugar

2 (8-ounce) cans tomato sauce

½ cup water

1 pound Swiss chard, stemmed and sliced into ½-inch-wide strips

2 green bell peppers, stemmed, seeded, and cut into ½-inch pieces

1 (15-ounce) can pinto beans, rinsed, divided

12 (6-inch) corn tortillas, warmed

4 ounces Monterey Jack cheese, shredded (1 cup)

¼ cup fresh cilantro leaves

Lime wedges

1 Adjust oven rack to middle position and heat oven to 450 degrees. Heat 1 tablespoon oil in large saucepan over medium heat until shimmering. Add half of onions and cook until softened, about 5 minutes. Stir in chili powder, half of garlic, cumin, and sugar and cook until fragrant, about 30 seconds. Stir in tomato sauce and water, bring to simmer, and cook until slightly thickened, about 7 minutes. Season with salt and pepper to taste; set sauce aside.

2 Meanwhile, heat 1 tablespoon oil in Dutch oven over medium heat until shimmering. Add remaining onions and cook until softened and just beginning to brown, 5 to 7 minutes. Add remaining garlic and cook until fragrant, about 30 seconds. Add chard and bell peppers, cover, and cook until chard is tender, 6 to 8 minutes. Using potato masher, coarsely mash half of beans in large bowl. Stir in chard-pepper mixture, ¼ cup sauce, and remaining whole beans. Season filling with salt and pepper to taste.

3 Spread ½ cup sauce over bottom of 13 by 9-inch baking dish. Brush both sides of tortillas with remaining 2 tablespoons oil. Stack tortillas, wrap in damp dish towel, and place on plate; microwave until warm and pliable, about 1 minute. Working with 1 warm tortilla at a time, spread ¼ cup chard filling across center. Roll tortilla tightly around filling and place seam side down in baking dish; arrange enchiladas in 2 columns across width of dish. Cover completely with remaining sauce and sprinkle evenly with Monterey Jack.

4 Cover dish tightly with greased aluminum foil and bake until enchiladas are heated through and cheese is melted, 15 to 20 minutes. Let enchiladas cool for 10 minutes. Sprinkle with cilantro and serve with lime wedges.

Brothy Savoy Cabbage with Pancetta, Rye Bread, and Fontina

Why This Recipe Works This decadent combination of beef broth, cabbage, rye bread, pancetta, and fontina cheese is an homage to Italian ski country, high in the Alps, where savoy cabbage is a regional favorite. To season and tenderize the cabbage, we braised it with a small amount of pancetta. Rendering the pancetta's fat before adding the cabbage went a long way in imbuing the vegetable with plenty of richness. We deepened the flavors further by adding onion, garlic, bay leaf, and beef broth and simmering everything until the cabbage turned tender. The subtly sweet flavor and chewy bite of the vegetable paired beautifully with earthy, chewy rye bread croutons, which added a welcome crunchy, starchy component to the dish. We baked the cabbage mixture with the croutons scattered on top, along with a sprinkling of shredded fontina that turned bubbly and appetizingly crisp under the broiler. Any type of hearty rye bread will work well here; if you can't find an unsliced loaf, substitute 6 ounces sliced rye bread. You will need a broiler-safe 13 by 9-inch baking dish for this recipe.

1 Adjust oven rack to upper-middle position and heat oven to 375 degrees. Spread bread in even layer in 13 by 9-inch broiler-safe baking dish and bake, stirring occasionally, until dried and crisp throughout, 15 to 17 minutes; transfer croutons to bowl and let cool completely. Do not wash baking dish.

2 Meanwhile, heat oil and butter in Dutch oven over medium heat until butter is melted. Add pancetta and cook until browned and fat is rendered, about 8 minutes. Stir in onion and cook until softened and lightly browned, 5 to 7 minutes. Stir in garlic and cook until fragrant, about 30 seconds. Stir in cabbage, broth, and bay leaf and bring to boil. Reduce heat to low; cover; and simmer until cabbage is tender, about 40 minutes.

3 Heat broiler. Discard bay leaf. Arrange cabbage mixture in even layer in now-empty baking dish, then sprinkle with croutons and fontina. Broil until cheese is melted and croutons are browned, 2 to 4 minutes. Sprinkle with parsley and serve.

6 ounces rye bread, cut into 1-inch pieces

1½ tablespoons extra-virgin olive oil

2 teaspoons unsalted butter

3 ounces pancetta, chopped fine

1 small onion, halved and sliced thin

2 garlic cloves, minced

1 head savoy cabbage (1½ pounds), cored and cut into 1-inch pieces (16 cups)

3 cups beef broth

1 bay leaf

3 ounces fontina cheese, shredded (¾ cup)

1 tablespoon chopped fresh parsley

Cabbage, Kohlrabi, and Lamb Tagine with Prunes

Why This Recipe Works Most North African tagines are generously spiced, assertively flavored stews made from a medley of meats, vegetables, and/or fruits and slow-cooked in earthenware vessels of the same name. For a vegetable-forward take on this hearty category, we drew inspiration from a popular sweet dish eaten throughout Algeria during Ramadan known as lham lahlou—Arabic for "sweet meat"—an unctuous, syrupy tagine of tender lamb simmered with sweet fruits. Taking cues from this complex flavor profile while adapting it to lean less sweet and reducing the amount of meat, we turned to sturdy red cabbage, kohlrabi, and potatoes—satiating ingredients with appealing bite. To make the most of a pound of bone-in lamb shoulder chops, we browned them in a skillet to render their fat and then used the rendered fat to brown our onions and bloom an assortment of spices: cumin, ginger, cinnamon, and cayenne. After adding water and loosening up the flavorful browned bits at the bottom of the pot, we added the vegetables and nestled the lamb among them so the meat could imbue the vegetables with earthy, meaty flavor as they cooked. Prunes injected pops of sweetness into our tagine. After cooking, we shredded the lamb into bite-size pieces to further distribute its richness and satisfying chew throughout the dish. A splash of orange blossom water finished the dish with a delicate floral note, while sliced almonds brought a satisfying crunch. Serve with rice, steamed couscous, or barley.

1 pound bone-in lamb shoulder chops, trimmed

1¼ teaspoons table salt, divided

¼ teaspoon pepper

3 tablespoons extra-virgin olive oil, divided

2 onions, chopped

4 garlic cloves, minced

1 teaspoon ground cumin

½ teaspoon ground ginger

½ teaspoon ground cinnamon

¼ teaspoon cayenne pepper

1½ cups water

½ head (1 pound) red cabbage, halved, cored, and cut into 2-inch pieces (6 cups)

1 pound Yukon gold potatoes, peeled and cut into 1-inch pieces

1 pound kohlrabi, peeled, halved, and cut into 1-inch-thick wedges

2 tablespoons honey

¾ cup prunes

½ teaspoon orange blossom water (optional)

2 tablespoons sliced almonds, toasted

1 Adjust oven rack to lower-middle position and heat oven to 325 degrees. Pat lamb dry with paper towels and sprinkle with ¼ teaspoon salt and pepper. Heat 1 tablespoon oil in Dutch oven over medium-high heat until just smoking. Brown lamb on both sides, 7 to 10 minutes; transfer to plate.

2 Heat remaining 2 tablespoons oil in now-empty Dutch oven over medium heat until shimmering. Add onions and ½ teaspoon salt and cook until onions are softened and browned, 8 to 10 minutes. Stir in garlic, cumin, ginger, cinnamon, and cayenne and cook until fragrant, about 30 seconds.

3 Stir in water, scraping up any browned bits. Stir in cabbage, potatoes, kohlrabi, honey, and remaining ½ teaspoon salt. Nestle browned lamb along with any accumulated juices into pot and bring to simmer. Cover pot, transfer to oven, and cook for 1 hour.

4 Stir in prunes and continue to cook, covered, until lamb and vegetables are tender, about 1 hour.

5 Remove pot from oven. Transfer lamb to cutting board, let cool slightly, then shred into bite-size pieces using 2 forks; discard fat and bones. Stir lamb and orange blossom water, if using, into vegetables in pot. Season with salt and pepper to taste. Sprinkle with almonds. Serve.

Baharat Cauliflower and Eggplant with Chickpeas

Why This Recipe Works Mild cauliflower and egg-plant make exceptional canvases for bold spices—such as baharat, an aromatic seasoning blend popular across the Middle East that includes cinnamon, cumin, cloves, and cardamom. The two vegetables are also dense and sturdy, which not only makes them satisfying to eat, but also ensures that they stand up well to roasting. We roasted them together in one sheet pan, incorporating chickpeas into the mix for a satiating, protein-rich addition. The baharat imparted irresistible nuttiness and subtle sweetness, while the legumes studded the dish with their appealingly dense, creamy mouthfeel. A sprin-kle of cilantro, a dash of lemon juice, and a shower of pickled red onion complemented this earthy meal with welcome brightness and tang. A lemony, garlicky tahini sauce—sweetened with honey and spiced with cayenne—gave each bite a rich, creamy dimension that further enlivened this assertively spiced dish.

1½ pounds eggplant, cut into 1½-inch pieces

1 teaspoon table salt, divided

⅓ cup tahini

3 tablespoons water

5 tablespoons lemon juice (2 lemons), divided, plus lemon wedges for serving

1 small garlic clove, grated

½ teaspoon honey

⅛ teaspoon cayenne (optional)

1 small head cauliflower (1½ pounds), cored and cut into 1½-inch florets

1 (15-ounce) can chickpeas, rinsed and patted dry

¼ cup extra-virgin olive oil

1 tablespoon Baharat (recipe follows)

¾ cup chopped fresh cilantro, divided

1 recipe Quick Sweet and Spicy Pickled Red Onion (page 33)

Plain yogurt

Pita bread, warmed

1 Adjust oven rack to lower-middle position and heat oven to 450 degrees. Line rimmed baking sheet with aluminum foil and spray with vegetable oil spray. Toss eggplant with ½ teaspoon salt in colander and let drain for 30 minutes, tossing occasionally. Whisk together tahini; water; 3 tablespoons lemon juice; garlic; honey; and cayenne, if using, until smooth. Season with salt and pepper to taste, and set aside until ready to serve. (If needed, add more water 1 teaspoon at a time until sauce is thick but pourable.)

2 Pat eggplant dry with paper towels, then toss with cauliflower florets, chickpeas, oil, baharat, and remain-ing ½ teaspoon salt in large bowl. Spread in even layer on prepared sheet and roast until vegetables are very tender and beginning to brown in spots, 30 to 40 min-utes, stirring occasionally.

3 Gently toss roasted vegetables with ½ cup cilantro and remaining 2 tablespoons lemon juice and season with salt and pepper to taste. Sprinkle with remaining ¼ cup cilantro and serve with tahini sauce, pickled red onion, yogurt, pita, and lemon wedges.

Baharat

Makes about ½ cup | Total time: 10 minutes

---

    3 (3-inch) cinnamon sticks, broken into pieces

4¾ teaspoons cumin seeds

1½ tablespoons coriander seeds

    1 tablespoon black peppercorns

    2 teaspoons whole cloves

    1 tablespoon ground cardamom

    2 teaspoons ground nutmeg

Process cinnamon sticks in spice grinder until finely ground, about 30 seconds. Add cumin seeds, coriander seeds, peppercorns, and cloves and process until finely ground, about 30 seconds. Transfer to bowl and stir in cardamom and nutmeg. (Baharat can be stored in airtight container at room temperature for up to 1 month.)

Seared Tofu with Panch Phoron, Green Beans, and Pickled Shallot

Why This Recipe Works   Firm tofu's neutral flavor makes it an excellent vehicle for seasoning, while its dense bite goes a long way in making a dish more filling and hearty. In this flavorful take, we hand-tore tofu to create craggy edges—all the more surface area for each chunk to absorb flavor. As we seared the tofu in a skillet, the edges turned pleasingly crisp. For a hearty vegetable to pair with the tofu, we chose green beans, cooking them with a little water to help them steam-cook; when the water evaporated, we seared them to encourage flavorful browning. We tossed everything with panch phoron, an aromatic spice blend of whole fenugreek, mustard, cumin, fennel, and nigella seeds. To bolster the spices' impact, we adopted the Indian method of tadka—meaning tempering or blooming—a technique for releasing maximum flavor from spices. Tossed in the skillet with the beans and tofu, the fragrant seeds infused the dish with exceptional aroma. For a pretty presentation, we spread a serving plate with cilantro- and lime-spiked yogurt and topped it with the tofu and beans, leaving the rim of the yogurt visible. To add a pop of piquancy, we sprinkled the whole thing with quick-pickled shallot slices, which were a snap to make in the microwave. You will need a 12-inch nonstick skillet with a tight-fitting lid for this recipe.

⅓   cup red wine vinegar

2   tablespoons sugar

1⅛   teaspoons table salt, divided

1   large shallot, sliced thin

1   cup plain whole-milk yogurt

¾   cup minced fresh cilantro

1   teaspoon grated lime zest plus 1 tablespoon juice

2   garlic cloves, minced

28   ounces extra-firm or firm tofu, drained

1   pound green beans, trimmed and halved

2   tablespoons water

¼   cup vegetable oil, divided

¾   teaspoon ground turmeric

4   teaspoons Panch Phoron (recipe follows)

1   Microwave vinegar, sugar, and ⅛ teaspoon salt in medium bowl until steaming, about 2 minutes. Add shallot and stir until submerged. Let sit for 10 minutes, stirring occasionally. Drain shallot and set aside for serving.

2   Meanwhile, combine yogurt, cilantro, lime zest and juice, and garlic in separate bowl and season with salt to taste; set sauce aside for serving.

3   Line rimmed baking sheet with triple layer of paper towels. Tear tofu into rough 1½-inch pieces and transfer to prepared sheet. Top tofu with second layer of paper towels and let drain for 10 minutes.

4   Combine green beans, water, 1 tablespoon oil, and ¼ teaspoon salt in 12-inch nonstick skillet. Cover and cook over medium-high heat, tossing occasionally, until beans are nearly tender, 6 to 8 minutes. Uncover and continue to cook until water has evaporated and beans are just beginning to brown in spots, 2 to 4 minutes; transfer to large bowl.

5   Sprinkle tofu with turmeric and remaining ¾ teaspoon salt. Heat 1 tablespoon oil in now-empty skillet over medium-high heat until shimmering. Add tofu and cook until golden brown, 8 to 10 minutes, turning as needed and adding 1 tablespoon oil halfway through cooking. Transfer tofu to bowl with green beans.

6   Add panch phoron and remaining 1 tablespoon oil to again-empty skillet and cook over medium-high heat until fragrant and seeds start to pop, about 1 minute. Off heat, immediately add green beans and tofu and toss gently to combine.

7   Spread reserved yogurt sauce over surface of serving platter. Arrange tofu and green bean mixture attractively on top, sprinkle with pickled shallot, and serve.

Panch Phoron

Makes about ¼ cup | Total time: 5 minutes

1 tablespoon cumin seeds

1 tablespoon fennel seeds

1 tablespoon mustard seeds

1 tablespoon nigella seeds

1½ teaspoons fenugreek seeds

Combine all ingredients in bowl. (Panch phoron can be stored in airtight container for up to 1 month.)

Saag Tofu

Why This Recipe Works A spicy sauce of pureed stewed spinach studded with pieces of fresh cheese and often finished with cream or butter, saag paneer is a revered—and superbly comforting—Indian dish. The dense, mild paneer reminded us of firm tofu, so we thought using tofu would make for a fun and delicious rendition with no shortage of protein and heartiness. We built layers of flavor by frying an assortment of spices and caramelizing onion, jalapeño, garlic, ginger, and tomatoes, ensuring a well-seasoned base. We blitzed half of this mixture in a food processor—along with milk and cashews, for buttery richness—until smooth, which gave our dish an appealing chunky consistency. Mustard greens, which are often used in this dish in northern India, added extra fiber and mildly spicy pungency; we pureed half and chopped half for a good balance of smoothness and bite. All we needed to do with the tofu cubes was heat them in the flavorful sauce. We prefer firm tofu here, but you can substitute extra-firm tofu; do not use soft tofu, as it will disintegrate. For a spicier dish, include the ribs and seeds from the jalapeño. Serve over rice.

14 ounces firm or extra-firm tofu, cut into ½-inch pieces

⅛ teaspoon plus ¾ teaspoon table salt, divided

    Pinch pepper

12 ounces curly-leaf spinach, stemmed

12 ounces mustard greens, stemmed

3 tablespoons vegetable oil

1 teaspoon cumin seeds

1 teaspoon ground coriander

1 teaspoon paprika

½ teaspoon ground cardamom

¼ teaspoon ground cinnamon

1 onion, chopped fine

1 jalapeño chile, stemmed, seeded, and minced

3 garlic cloves, minced

1 tablespoon grated fresh ginger

1 (14.5-ounce) can diced tomatoes, drained and chopped

1½ cups milk, divided

½ cup roasted cashews, chopped, divided

1 teaspoon sugar

1½ tablespoons lemon juice

3 tablespoons minced fresh cilantro

1 Spread tofu on paper towel–lined baking sheet and let drain for 20 minutes. Press dry with paper towels and sprinkle with ⅛ teaspoon salt and pepper.

2 Meanwhile, microwave spinach in covered bowl until wilted, about 3 minutes; transfer ½ cup spinach to blender. Chop remaining spinach; set aside. Microwave mustard greens in now-empty covered bowl until wilted, about 4 minutes; transfer ½ cup to blender with spinach. Chop remaining mustard greens; set aside.

3 Heat oil in 12-inch skillet over medium-high heat until shimmering. Add cumin seeds, coriander, paprika, cardamom, and cinnamon and cook until fragrant, about 30 seconds. Add onion and remaining ¾ teaspoon salt and cook, stirring frequently, until softened, about 3 minutes. Stir in jalapeño, garlic, and ginger and cook until lightly browned and just beginning to stick to pan, about 3 minutes. Stir in tomatoes, scraping up any browned bits, and cook until pan is dry and tomatoes are beginning to brown, about 4 minutes.

4 Transfer half of onion-tomato mixture, ¾ cup milk, ¼ cup cashews, and sugar to blender with greens and process until smooth, about 1 minute. Add pureed greens mixture, chopped greens, lemon juice, and remaining ¾ cup milk to skillet with remaining onion-tomato mixture and bring to simmer over medium-high heat. Reduce heat to low and season with salt and pepper to taste. Stir in tofu and cook until warmed through, about 2 minutes. Sprinkle with cilantro and remaining ¼ cup cashews and serve.

Tacu Tacu

Why This Recipe Works Tacu tacu is a wonderfully hearty, earthy Peruvian rice-and-bean cake that's fried to crisp perfection and usually accompanied by sarza criolla, a zesty onion salsa. The bean of choice is the canary bean, a creamy variety with a mild flavor. Following the traditional preparation method, we simmered the beans until tender and blended a portion in a food processor, which gave our beans a pleasingly chunky consistency. We combined the beans with cooked rice before seasoning the mixture with ají amarillo paste, a fruity, spicy yellow chili pepper paste that is a staple in Peruvian kitchens. Next, we used a skillet to sear the bean-rice mixture—shaping them into large oval disks on the stovetop—until they were delectably golden brown on the outside yet tender on the inside. For even more protein and heartiness, we paired the tacu tacu with fried eggs, which lent the meal a rich, jammy quality. If you can't find canary beans, you can substitute cannellini beans. This is a great way to use up leftover rice; omit step 4 and add 2 cups day-old cooked rice in step 5. Serve with Sarza Criolla (recipe follows).

1½ tablespoons table salt for brining

8 ounces (1 cup) dried canary or cannellini beans, picked over and rinsed

¾ teaspoon plus ⅛ teaspoon table salt, divided, plus salt for cooking beans

1 cup long-grain white rice, rinsed

6 tablespoons extra-virgin olive oil, divided

½ red onion, chopped fine

2 tablespoons ají amarillo paste

3 garlic cloves, minced to paste

1 teaspoon ground cumin

¾ teaspoon dried oregano

¼ teaspoon pepper, divided

1 cup chicken or vegetable broth

3 tablespoons chopped fresh cilantro

4 large eggs

Lime wedges

1 Dissolve 1½ tablespoons salt in 2 quarts cold water in large container. Add beans and soak at room temperature for at least 8 hours or up to 24 hours. Drain and rinse well. (If you're pressed for time, see page 69 for information on quick-brining your beans.)

2 Bring soaked beans and 7 cups water to simmer in large saucepan. Simmer, partially covered, over medium-low heat until beans are tender, 30 to 40 minutes. Remove from heat, stir in 1½ teaspoons salt, cover, and let sit until completely tender, about 15 minutes.

3 Drain beans and transfer to large bowl. Process 1 cup cooked beans in food processor until smooth, about 30 seconds, scraping sides of processor as needed. Transfer to bowl with remaining cooked beans, stirring and mashing as needed to combine; set aside.

4 Meanwhile, bring rice, 1½ cups water, and ¼ teaspoon salt to simmer in medium saucepan over medium-high heat. Reduce heat to medium-low, cover and simmer gently until rice is tender and all liquid has been absorbed, 11 to 13 minutes. Remove from heat and let sit, covered, for 10 minutes. Fluff rice with fork and set aside.

5 Adjust oven racks to upper-middle and lower-middle positions and heat oven to 200 degrees. Heat 1 tablespoon oil in 12-inch nonstick skillet over medium heat until shimmering. Add onion and cook, stirring occasionally, until softened and just beginning to brown, 5 to 7 minutes. Stir in ají amarillo paste, garlic, cumin, oregano, ⅛ teaspoon pepper, and ½ teaspoon salt and cook until fragrant, about 1 minute. Off heat, add reserved bean mixture and reserved rice and stir to combine. Return skillet to medium heat, stir in broth, and bring to simmer. Cook until liquid is absorbed and rice mixture thickens, 3 to 5 minutes, stirring frequently; mixture should be sticky. Transfer to bowl, stir in cilantro, and let sit for 10 minutes.

6 In clean, dry skillet, heat 1½ teaspoons oil over medium heat until shimmering. Add one-quarter rice and bean mixture and, using rubber spatula, press mixture against 1 side of skillet while tilting skillet towards tacu tacu (tilting makes it easier to pack rice and bean mixture firmly). Firmly press mixture until it is a rough oval and measures about 8 inches in length. Cook until golden brown along edges, 2 to 4 minutes.

7 Place skillet flat on stovetop and, using 2 spatulas, carefully flip tacu tacu. (If it breaks, firmly press into side of skillet matching shape of tacu tacu to bring back together.) Add 1½ teaspoons oil to skillet and nestle tacu tacu into side of skillet that matches its shape. Repeat firmly pressing tacu tacu into side of skillet while tilting skillet slightly. Cook until golden brown along edges, 2 to 4 minutes. Carefully slide tacu tacu onto serving plate and transfer to oven to keep warm. Repeat with 3 tablespoons oil and remaining rice and bean mixture.

8 Heat remaining 1 tablespoon oil in clean, dry skillet over medium heat until shimmering. Meanwhile, crack 2 eggs into small bowl. Repeat with remaining 2 eggs and second small bowl. Sprinkle eggs with remaining ⅛ teaspoon salt and remaining ⅛ teaspoon pepper. Working quickly, pour 1 bowl of eggs into 1 side of pan and second bowl of eggs into other side. Cover and cook for 1 minute. Remove skillet from heat and let sit, covered, for 15 to 45 seconds for runny yolks (white around edge of yolk will be barely opaque), 45 to 60 seconds for soft but set yolks, or about 2 minutes for medium-set yolks. Top each tacu tacu with 1 egg and serve with lime wedges.

Sarza Criolla

Makes ½ cup
Total time: 15 minutes, plus 30 minutes chilling

This recipe can be easily doubled.

- ½ red onion, sliced thin
- 1 tablespoon lime juice
- ¼ teaspoons table salt
  Pinch pepper
- 2 tablespoons chopped fresh cilantro

Soak onion in ice water for 10 minutes. Drain well and pat dry with paper towels. Combine onion, lime juice, salt, and pepper in bowl. Cover with plastic wrap and refrigerate for at least 30 minutes or up to 2 days. Stir in cilantro just before serving.

Gigantes Plaki

Why This Recipe Works Gigantes plaki is a popular dish often found at tavernas and on family dining tables throughout Greece. It derives its name from the type of bean (gigantes) and the method of cooking it in the oven (plaki). The large, meaty legumes are exceptionally hearty and dense, and make this dish particularly satisfying to eat. After simmering our beans, we cooked a strongly flavored base for the dish by browning onion, celery, and carrots and enhancing them with tomato paste, garlic, oregano, and cinnamon. After deglazing the pot with canned tomatoes and their juice, we stirred the beans into this concoction. We transferred everything to a baking dish so the legumes could cook further in the oven, where they became luxuriously creamy while developing crisp, caramelized edges. Refreshing dill and grassy olive oil were just the finishing touches to complete this comforting dish. If you can't find gigante beans, substitute large dried lima beans. Gigantes plaki can be eaten warm or at room temperature, as a hearty side dish or delicious main, with a hunk of bread to sop up the sauce.

1½ tablespoons table salt for brining

1 pound (2½ cups) dried gigante beans, picked over and rinsed

¼ cup extra-virgin olive oil, plus extra for drizzling

1 onion, chopped

2 carrots, peeled and chopped

2 celery ribs, chopped

1 teaspoon table salt

2 tablespoons tomato paste

4 garlic cloves, minced

1 tablespoon chopped fresh oregano or 1 teaspoon dried

¼ teaspoon ground cinnamon

1 (14.5-ounce) can whole peeled tomatoes, drained with juice reserved, chopped

1 tablespoon honey

2 bay leaves

2 tablespoons chopped fresh dill

1 Dissolve 1½ tablespoons salt in 2 quarts cold water in large container. Add beans and soak at room temperature for at least 8 hours or up to 24 hours. Drain and rinse well. (If you're pressed for time, see page 69 for information on quick-brining your beans.)

2 Bring soaked beans and 3 quarts water to boil in Dutch oven. Reduce heat and simmer, stirring occasionally, until beans are tender, 1 to 1½ hours. (Skim any loose bean skins or foam from surface of liquid as beans cook.) Drain beans and set aside. Wipe out pot with paper towels.

3 Adjust oven rack to middle position and heat oven to 400 degrees. Heat oil in now-empty pot over medium heat until shimmering. Add onion, carrots, celery, and salt and cook until softened and beginning to brown, 7 to 10 minutes. Stir in tomato paste, garlic, oregano, and cinnamon and cook until fragrant, about 30 seconds. Add tomatoes and their juice and 1¼ cups water, scraping up any browned bits. Stir in beans, honey, and bay leaves and bring to simmer. Season with salt and pepper to taste.

4 Transfer bean mixture to 13 by 9-inch baking dish, smoothing top with silicone spatula. Transfer dish to oven and bake until beans are cooked through and edges are golden brown and bubbling, 30 to 45 minutes. Let cool for 15 minutes, then sprinkle with dill and drizzle with extra oil. Serve.

Red Beans and Rice with Okra and Tomatoes

Why This Recipe Works

Red beans and rice is a comfortingly stick-to-your-ribs New Orleans favorite. We boosted the flavor and heartiness by adding okra and tomatoes for juiciness and fiber. To make the dish using widely available ingredients, we made some simple substitutions: We swapped out Camellia-brand dried red beans for small red beans, and replaced tasso ham with similarly smoky bacon; four slices of bacon were just enough to give us plenty of savory flavor. We crisped it up in a Dutch oven before using the rendered fat to enrich onion, bell pepper, and celery and bloom an assortment of spices. We then added chicken broth and the beans to simmer in this flavorful concoction. To ensure the okra kept some of its crunchy bite, we tossed the whole pods in salt and let them sit for an hour before rinsing, cutting, and adding them to the beans for the final half hour of cooking. To cook the rice, we simmered it with a bit of butter, giving us fluffy grains with a subtle richness. This large batch is ideal for feeding a crowd—or reheat it to enjoy the leftovers just as much the next day. While we prefer the flavor and texture of fresh okra in this recipe, you can substitute frozen cut okra, thawed and thoroughly patted dry. If using frozen, skip step 2.

Red Beans

- 1½ tablespoons table salt for brining
- 1 pound (2 cups) small red beans, picked over and rinsed
- 1 pound okra, stemmed
  Table salt for salting okra
- 4 slices bacon, chopped fine
- 1 onion, chopped fine
- 1 green bell pepper, stemmed, seeded, and chopped fine
- 1 celery rib, minced
- 3 garlic cloves, minced
- 1 teaspoon minced fresh thyme or ¼ teaspoon dried
- 1 teaspoon paprika
- 2 bay leaves
- ¼ teaspoon cayenne pepper
- ¼ teaspoon pepper
- 3 cups chicken broth
- 2 (14.5-ounce) cans diced tomatoes, drained
- 1 tablespoon red wine vinegar, plus extra for seasoning
- 3 scallions, sliced thin
  Hot sauce

Rice

- 1 tablespoon unsalted butter
- 2 cups long-grain white rice, rinsed
- 3 cups water
- 1 teaspoon table salt

1 For the red beans Dissolve 1½ tablespoons salt in 2 quarts cold water in large container. Add beans and soak at room temperature for at least 8 hours or up to 24 hours. Drain and rinse well. (If you're pressed for time, see page 69 for information on quick-brining your beans.)

2 Toss okra with 1 teaspoon salt, and let sit for 1 hour, stirring halfway through. Rinse well, then cut into 1-inch pieces; set aside.

3 Cook bacon in Dutch oven over medium heat, stirring occasionally, until crispy, 5 to 7 minutes. Add onion, bell pepper, and celery and cook until vegetables are softened, 5 to 7 minutes. Stir in garlic, thyme, paprika, bay leaves, cayenne, and pepper and cook until fragrant, about 30 seconds.

4 Stir in beans, 5 cups water, and broth and bring to boil over high heat. Reduce to vigorous simmer and cook, stirring occasionally, until beans are just softened and liquid begins to thicken, 45 minutes to 1 hour.

5 Stir in okra, tomatoes, and vinegar and cook until liquid is thickened and beans are fully tender and creamy, about 30 minutes.

6 For the rice Meanwhile, melt butter in large saucepan over medium heat. Add rice and cook, stirring often,
until edges begin to turn translucent, about 2 minutes.
Stir in water and salt and bring to boil. Cover; reduce
heat to low; and simmer until liquid is absorbed and rice
is tender, about 20 minutes. Remove pot from heat, lay
clean folded dish towel underneath lid, and let rice sit
for 10 minutes. Fluff rice with fork.

7 Discard bay leaves from beans. Season with salt,
pepper, and extra vinegar to taste. Top individual
portions of rice with beans and sprinkle with scallions.
Serve with hot sauce.

Cuban-Style Black Beans and Rice

Why This Recipe Works Beans and rice is a familiar combination the world over, but the Cuban take on the pairing is special in that the rice is cooked in the concentrated liquid left over from cooking the beans, rendering the grains particularly earthy. For even more depth of flavor, we used 6 ounces of salt pork, which brings potent smokiness to many Cuban dishes. Rendering it gave us a savory base for lightly browning a portion of sofrito—a traditional mix of aromatics that includes garlic, bell pepper, and onion—which we blitzed into a puree in a food processor. To this mixture, we added black beans (which we first simmered with more sofrito, to infuse the legumes with vegetable flavor) and uncooked rice, both of which absorbed the aroma of the pork and aromatics as the concoction simmered. Finishing the dish in the oven eliminated the crusty bottom that forms when it's cooked on the stovetop. This large batch is ideal for feeding a crowd—or reheat it to enjoy the leftovers just as much the next day. It is important to use lean—not fatty—salt pork. If you can't find it, substitute six slices of bacon. If using bacon, decrease the cooking time in step 4 to 8 minutes.

1½ tablespoons table salt for brining

1 cup dried black beans, picked over and rinsed

2 cups chicken broth

2 large green bell peppers, halved, stemmed, and seeded, divided

1 large onion, halved crosswise and peeled, root end left intact, divided

1 head garlic (5 cloves minced, remaining head halved crosswise with skin left intact)

2 bay leaves

1½ teaspoons table salt, divided

2 tablespoons extra-virgin olive oil, divided

6 ounces salt pork, cut into ¼-inch pieces

4 teaspoons ground cumin

1 tablespoon minced fresh oregano

1½ cups long-grain white rice, rinsed

2 tablespoons red wine vinegar

2 scallions, sliced thin

Lime wedges

1 Dissolve 1½ tablespoons salt in 2 quarts cold water in large container. Add beans and soak at room temperature for at least 8 hours or up to 24 hours. Drain and rinse well. (If you're pressed for time, see page 69 for information on quick-brining your beans.)

2 Combine soaked beans, broth, 2 cups water, 1 bell pepper half, 1 onion half (with root end), halved garlic head, bay leaves, and 1 teaspoon salt in Dutch oven. Bring to simmer over medium-high heat, cover, and reduce heat to low. Cook until beans are just soft, 30 to 40 minutes. Discard bell pepper, onion, garlic, and bay leaves, then drain beans in colander set over large bowl, reserving 2½ cups bean cooking liquid. (If you don't have enough bean cooking liquid, add water to equal 2½ cups.) Do not wash out Dutch oven.

3 Adjust oven rack to middle position and heat oven to 350 degrees. Cut remaining bell peppers and onion into 2-inch pieces and process in food processor until broken into rough ¼-inch pieces, about 8 pulses, scraping down sides of bowl as necessary; set vegetables aside.

4 In now-empty Dutch oven, cook 1 tablespoon oil and salt pork over medium-low heat, stirring frequently, until lightly browned and rendered, 15 to 20 minutes. Add remaining 1 tablespoon oil, processed vegetables, cumin, and oregano. Increase heat to medium and cook, stirring frequently, until vegetables are softened and beginning to brown, 10 to 15 minutes. Add minced garlic and cook, stirring constantly, until fragrant, about 1 minute. Add rice and stir to coat, about 30 seconds.

5 Stir in beans, reserved bean cooking liquid, vinegar, and remaining ½ teaspoon salt. Increase heat to medium-high and bring to simmer. Cover and transfer to oven. Bake until liquid is absorbed and rice is tender, about 30 minutes. Fluff with fork and let rest, uncovered, for 5 minutes. Serve, passing scallions and lime wedges separately.

Cauliflower Biryani

Why This Recipe Works Biryani places fragrant long-grain basmati center stage, enriching it with saffron and a variety of fresh herbs and pungent spices for a hearty dish that brims with flavor. However, traditional recipes often take a long time to develop deep flavor, steeping whole spices and cooking each component on its own before marrying them. We decided to deconstruct this dish to make it easier and faster, while staying true to its hearty warmth and home-style appeal. We chose to pair our rice with sweet, earthy roasted cauliflower, a dense vegetable with meaty chew and excellent flavor-absorbing abilities. We cut the cauliflower into small florets to speed up roasting and tossed them with warm spices for vibrant flavor. While the cauliflower roasted, we sautéed onion, jalapeño, garlic, and more spices; we then added rice to this spicy, flavor-packed mixture and simmered it until tender. Once the rice finished cooking, we let the residual heat plump a handful of currants and bloom the saffron. Finally, we stirred in lots of bright mint and cilantro and folded in our roasted cauliflower. Biryani is traditionally served with a cooling yogurt sauce; we made it before starting the biryani to allow the flavors in the sauce time to meld. You can substitute long-grain white, jasmine, or Texmati rice for the basmati, if you prefer.

1 cup plain whole-milk yogurt

1 teaspoon grated lemon zest plus 2 tablespoons juice

¼ cup minced fresh cilantro, divided

¼ cup minced fresh mint, divided

5 garlic cloves, minced, divided

1 head cauliflower (2 pounds), cored and cut into ½-inch florets

¼ cup extra-virgin olive oil, divided

1 teaspoon table salt, divided

¼ teaspoon pepper

¼ teaspoon ground cardamom, divided

¼ teaspoon ground cumin, divided

1 onion, sliced thin

1 jalapeño chile, stemmed, seeded, and minced

⅛ teaspoon ground cinnamon

⅛ teaspoon ground ginger

1½ cups basmati rice, rinsed

2¼ cups water

¼ cup dried currants or raisins

½ teaspoon saffron threads, lightly crumbled

1 Adjust oven rack to middle position and heat oven to 425 degrees. Whisk yogurt, lemon zest and juice, 2 tablespoons cilantro, 2 tablespoons mint, and 1 teaspoon garlic together in bowl. Cover and refrigerate while cooking biryani, or at least 30 minutes.

2 Toss cauliflower florets, 2 tablespoons oil, ½ teaspoon salt, pepper, ⅛ teaspoon cardamom, and ⅛ teaspoon cumin together in bowl. Spread florets onto rimmed baking sheet and roast until tender, 15 to 20 minutes.

3 Meanwhile, heat remaining 2 tablespoons oil in large saucepan over medium-high heat until shimmering. Add onion and cook, stirring often, until soft and dark brown around edges, 10 to 12 minutes.

4 Stir in jalapeño, cinnamon, ginger, remaining garlic, remaining ⅛ teaspoon cardamom, and remaining ⅛ teaspoon cumin and cook until fragrant, about 1 minute. Stir in rice and cook until well coated, about 1 minute. Add water and remaining ½ teaspoon salt and bring to simmer. Reduce heat to low; cover; and simmer until all liquid is absorbed, 16 to 18 minutes.

5 Remove pot from heat and sprinkle currants and saffron over rice. Cover, laying clean folded dish towel underneath lid, and let sit for 10 minutes. Fold in remaining 2 tablespoons cilantro, remaining 2 tablespoons mint, and roasted cauliflower. Season with salt and pepper to taste, and serve with yogurt sauce.

Mushroom Tea Rice with Chicken and Caramel-Braised Shallots

Why This Recipe Works The umami-rich liquid left over from soaking dried mushrooms is an ultraflavorful byproduct—and it's perfect for cooking rice, imbuing each grain with savoriness. Dishes such as Haitian djon djon rice and Japanese kinoko gohan employ this technique to delicious effect; these dishes gave us the idea for this recipe that makes the most of mushroom "tea" to create a rice dish brimming with umami. We seasoned jasmine rice with a generous amount of garlic, star anise, and cinnamon before cooking the grains with a pair of chicken thighs in a mixture of chicken broth and reserved mushroom tea. Just two thighs were enough to disseminate plenty of rich savoriness into the grains as the dish cooked, while the sweet warmth of the spices counterbalanced the savory notes. For a deeply flavorful topping, we coated shallots and ginger in sugar and braised them—a technique inspired by kho, a Vietnamese and Cambodian cooking technique in which proteins are cooked in a caramel sauce; coconut water and fish sauce amped up the complexity. We garnished the dish with cilantro and mint for freshness and Thai chiles for heat. For perfectly tender shallots, we recommend using shallots that measure 1½ to 2 inches long and 1½ inches in diameter for this recipe. Halve larger shallots through the root end so that the root keeps each half intact.

Caramel-Braised Shallots

- 1 pound small shallots, peeled
- 1 tablespoon grated fresh ginger
- ¼ cup sugar
- 1½ cups unsweetened coconut water
- 1 tablespoon fish sauce
- ½ tablespoon unsalted butter

Mushroom Tea Rice

- 2 cups water
- 1 ounce dried shiitake mushrooms, rinsed
- 2 (5- to 7-ounce) bone-in chicken thighs, trimmed
- 2 tablespoons vegetable oil
- 5 garlic cloves, sliced thin
- 3 star anise pods
- 1 cinnamon stick
- 2 cups jasmine rice, rinsed
- 1 cup chicken broth
- 1½ teaspoons table salt
- ¼ teaspoon pepper
- 2 Thai chiles, stemmed, seeded, and sliced thin
- ¼ cup fresh cilantro and/or mint leaves

1 For the caramel-braised shallots Toss shallots with ginger in small bowl. Add sugar to medium saucepan and shake saucepan gently to spread sugar into even layer. Cook, without stirring, over medium-high heat until sugar begins to change color, 2 to 4 minutes. Stir sugar, then continue to cook, stirring occasionally, until sugar is color of honey, 15 to 30 seconds. Reduce heat to low and continue to cook, stirring occasionally, until sugar is dark amber, 3 to 6 minutes.

2 Immediately add shallot-ginger mixture and increase heat to medium-high (caramel may begin to smoke, which is okay). Add coconut water and fish sauce and bring to boil. Reduce heat to low and simmer gently, stirring occasionally, until shallots are tender and caramel is dark, flipping shallots halfway through, 45 to 55 minutes. Remove saucepan from heat, stir in butter until melted, and set aside.

3 For the mushroom tea rice Meanwhile, microwave water and mushrooms in covered bowl for 3 minutes. Let sit until softened, about 15 minutes. Drain mushrooms in fine-mesh strainer, reserving soaking liquid. Discard mushroom stems and halve mushrooms; set mushrooms and soaking liquid aside.

4 Pat chicken dry with paper towels. Heat oil in large saucepan over medium-high heat until just smoking. Place chicken, skin side down, in saucepan and cook until skin is golden brown and crispy, 5 to 7 minutes. Flip chicken and cook until second side is golden brown, about 3 minutes. Transfer chicken to plate.

5 Let saucepan cool off heat for 1 minute, then add garlic, star anise, and cinnamon to oil left in saucepan and cook, stirring frequently, over medium-low heat until fragrant, about 30 seconds. Add rice and toast, stirring occasionally, for 2 minutes. Stir in broth, salt, pepper, mushrooms, and mushroom soaking liquid. Nestle chicken, skin side up, and any accumulated juices into saucepan and bring to simmer. Cover and cook until rice is tender and chicken registers at least 175 degrees, about 15 minutes.

6 Remove saucepan from heat. Transfer chicken to cutting board and discard star anise pods and cinnamon stick. Let rice stand, covered, for 10 minutes, and let chicken rest until cool enough to handle.

7 Remove skin from chicken and chop; set aside. Using your hands to separate meat from bones, chop chicken into bite-size pieces and discard bones. Gently stir chopped chicken and crispy skin into rice and season with salt to taste. Top with caramel-braised shallots, Thai chiles, and cilantro and/or mint.

Beet Barley Risotto

Why This Recipe Works

Hearty pearl barley holds its own against the sweet earthiness of beets and sturdy beet greens in this hearty, comforting risotto. Pearl barley has had its outer husk removed, exposing the starchy interior. Here, the starch helped the barley cooking liquid thicken into an irresistibly velvety sauce as it simmered. Simmering the barley just until the grains were still somewhat firm in the center helped them retain some of their satisfying bite. Cooking the grains with white wine and vegetable (or chicken) broth imbued the barley with complex flavor and savoriness. We stirred raw grated beets into the barley in two parts—half at the beginning for a base of flavor, and half at the end for freshness, color, and pleasant chew—which gave each bite textural interest. Parmesan, folded into the risotto at the end, gave the dish a rich, buttery aroma. A scattering of parsley made the perfect fresh garnish. Do not substitute hulled, hull-less, quick-cooking, or presteamed barley for the pearl barley. You can use the large holes of a box grater or a food processor fitted with a shredding disk to shred the beets. If you can't find beets with their greens attached, you can replace the greens with 2 cups stemmed and chopped Swiss chard.

- 3   cups vegetable or chicken broth
- 3   cups water
- 2   tablespoons extra-virgin olive oil
- 1   pound beets with greens attached, beets trimmed, peeled, and shredded, divided, greens stemmed and cut into 1-inch pieces (2 cups)
- 1   onion, chopped
- ½   teaspoon table salt
- 1½   cups pearl barley, rinsed
- 4   garlic cloves, minced
- 1   teaspoon minced fresh thyme or ¼ teaspoon dried
- 1   cup dry white wine
- 1   ounce Parmesan cheese, grated (½ cup)
- 2   tablespoons chopped fresh parsley

1   Bring broth and water to simmer in medium saucepan. Reduce heat to lowest setting and cover to keep warm.

2   Heat oil in large saucepan over medium heat until shimmering. Add half of shredded beets, onion, and salt and cook until vegetables are softened, 5 to 7 minutes. Stir in barley and cook, stirring often, until fragrant, about 4 minutes. Stir in garlic and thyme and cook until fragrant, about 30 seconds. Stir in wine and cook until fully absorbed, about 2 minutes.

3   Stir in 3 cups warm broth mixture. Simmer, stirring occasionally, until liquid is absorbed and bottom of pan is dry, 22 to 25 minutes. Stir in 2 cups warm broth mixture and simmer, stirring occasionally, until liquid is absorbed and bottom of pan is dry, 15 to 18 minutes.

4   Add beet greens and continue to cook, stirring often and adding remaining broth as needed to prevent bottom of pan from becoming dry, until greens are softened and barley is cooked through but still somewhat firm in center, 5 to 10 minutes. Off heat, stir in remaining shredded beets and Parmesan. Season with salt and pepper to taste, and sprinkle with parsley. Serve.

SERVES 4 TO 6 | TOTAL TIME 1¼ HOURS   • *vegetarian* • *fiber-ful* •

Farro and Broccoli Rabe Gratin

Why This Recipe Works This comforting vegetable gratin proves casseroles can be light, vibrant, and fresh—far from heavy or stodgy. This one leans on creamy white beans, robust broccoli rabe, and chewy farro—sturdy ingredients with lots of fiber and plenty of pleasing chew. Toasting the farro in a medley of aromatics heightened its special nutty quality. To inject the grains with savory notes, we cooked them with vegetable or chicken broth, adding a dollop of white miso for a potent dose of umami that deepened the flavor of the farro. As the grains cooked, they turned tender while the remaining liquid thickened into a sauce. To flavor the broccoli rabe, we cooked it in a skillet with garlic and pepper flakes, giving the vegetable an exceptionally nutty, spicy edge. White beans contributed a great deal of protein, and their starchiness further amped up the casserole's creaminess—no milk or cream needed. Sun-dried tomatoes punctuated the casserole with welcome acidity. For an appealing finish, we sprinkled the whole dish with a mixture of panko bread crumbs and grated Parmesan and then broiled it until we had a browned, appetizingly crisp topping. Do not substitute pearl, quick-cooking, or presteamed farro for the whole farro in this recipe. You will need a broiler-safe 3-quart gratin dish or a broiler-safe 13 by 9-inch baking dish for this recipe.

3 tablespoons extra-virgin olive oil, divided

1 onion, chopped fine

¼ teaspoon table salt, plus salt for cooking broccoli rabe

1½ cups whole farro

2 cups vegetable or chicken broth

2 tablespoons white miso

½ cup panko bread crumbs

¼ cup grated Parmesan cheese

1 pound broccoli rabe, trimmed and cut into 2-inch pieces

6 garlic cloves, minced

⅛ teaspoon red pepper flakes

1 (15-ounce) can small white beans or navy beans, rinsed

¾ cup oil-packed sun-dried tomatoes, chopped

1 Heat 1 tablespoon oil in large saucepan over medium heat until shimmering. Add onion and salt and cook until softened and lightly browned, 5 to 7 minutes. Stir in farro and cook, stirring occasionally, until lightly toasted, about 2 minutes. Stir in 2½ cups water, broth, and miso. Bring to simmer and cook, stirring often, until farro is just tender and remaining liquid has thickened into creamy sauce, 25 to 35 minutes.

2 Meanwhile, toss panko with 1 tablespoon oil in bowl and microwave, stirring occasionally, until golden brown, 1 to 2 minutes. Stir in Parmesan and set aside.

3 Bring 4 quarts water to boil in Dutch oven. Add broccoli rabe and 1 tablespoon salt and cook until just tender, about 2 minutes. Drain broccoli rabe and set aside. Combine remaining 1 tablespoon oil, garlic, and pepper flakes in now-empty pot and cook over medium heat until fragrant and sizzling, 1 to 2 minutes. Stir in broccoli rabe and cook until hot and well coated, about 2 minutes. Off heat, stir in beans, tomatoes, and farro mixture. Season with salt and pepper to taste.

4 Adjust oven rack 10 inches from broiler element and heat broiler. Transfer bean-farro mixture to broiler-safe 3-quart gratin dish (or broiler-safe 13 by 9-inch baking dish) and sprinkle with reserved panko mixture. Broil until lightly browned and hot, 1 to 2 minutes. Serve.

Spinach and Ricotta Gnudi with Tomato-Butter Sauce

Why This Recipe Works Pillowy, verdant, milky-rich gnudi are Italian dumplings cobbled together from ricotta and greens (usually fresh spinach or chard), delicately seasoned, and bound with egg and flour and/or bread crumbs. The trick to making this comforting dish well is water management: Both the cheese and the greens are loaded with moisture, much of which needs to be either removed or bound up—otherwise, the dough can be too difficult to handle or require so much binder that the dumplings are leaden instead of light. We found that "towel-drying" the ricotta on a paper towel–lined rimmed baking sheet efficiently drained the cheese in just 10 minutes. Instead of blanching fresh spinach to break down its cells and release its water, we used frozen spinach, which readily gives up its water when it thaws; all we had to do was squeeze it dry. A combination of protein-rich egg whites, flour, and panko bread crumbs bound the mixture into a light, tender dough that we scooped and rolled into rounds and then gently poached in salted water. Taking inspiration from two traditional sauces—bright tomato sugo and rich browned butter—we made a hybrid accompaniment by toasting garlic in browning butter and adding halved fresh cherry tomatoes, which collapsed and spilled their bright juices into the rich backdrop. Squeezing the spinach should remove ½ to ⅔ cup of liquid; you should have ⅔ cup of finely chopped spinach.

Gnudi

- 12 ounces (1½ cups) whole-milk ricotta cheese
- ½ cup all-purpose flour
- 1 ounce Parmesan cheese, grated (½ cup), plus extra for garnishing
- 1 tablespoon panko bread crumbs
- ¾ teaspoon table salt, plus salt for cooking gnudi
- ½ teaspoon pepper
- ¼ teaspoon grated lemon zest
- 10 ounces frozen whole-leaf spinach, thawed and squeezed dry
- 2 large egg whites, lightly beaten

Sauce

- 4 tablespoons unsalted butter
- 3 garlic cloves, sliced thin
- 12 ounces cherry or grape tomatoes, halved
- 2 teaspoons cider vinegar
- ¼ teaspoon table salt
- ¼ teaspoon pepper
- 2 tablespoons shredded fresh basil

1 For the gnudi Line rimmed baking sheet with double layer of paper towels. Spread ricotta in even layer over towels; set aside and let sit for 10 minutes. Place flour, Parmesan, panko, salt, pepper, and lemon zest in large bowl and stir to combine. Process spinach in food processor until finely chopped, about 30 seconds, scraping down sides of bowl as needed. Transfer spinach to bowl with flour mixture. Grasp paper towels and fold ricotta in half; peel back towels. Rotate sheet 90 degrees and repeat folding and peeling 2 more times to consolidate ricotta into smaller mass. Using paper towels as sling, transfer ricotta to bowl with spinach mixture. Discard paper towels but do not wash sheet. Add egg whites to bowl and mix gently until well combined.

2 Transfer heaping teaspoons of dough to now-empty sheet (you should have 45 to 50 portions). Using your dry hands, gently roll each portion into 1-inch ball.

3 For the sauce Melt butter in small saucepan over medium heat. Add garlic and cook, swirling saucepan occasionally, until butter is very foamy and garlic is pale golden brown, 2 to 3 minutes. Off heat, add tomatoes and vinegar; cover and set aside.

4 Bring 1 quart water to boil in Dutch oven. Add 1½ teaspoons salt. Using spider skimmer or slotted spoon, transfer all gnudi to water. Return water to gentle simmer. Cook, adjusting heat to maintain gentle simmer, for 5 minutes, starting timer once water has returned to simmer (to confirm doneness, cut 1 dumpling in half; center should be firm).

5 While gnudi simmer, add salt and pepper to sauce and cook over medium–high heat, stirring occasionally, until tomatoes are warmed through and slightly softened, about 2 minutes. Divide sauce evenly among 4 bowls. Using spider skimmer or slotted spoon, remove gnudi from pot, drain well, and transfer to bowls with sauce. Garnish with basil and extra Parmesan. Serve immediately.

Mostly Meatless Meatballs and Marinara

Why This Recipe Works We set out to create a meatball that contained a lower ratio of meat to vegetables, but was so succulent, tender, and flavorful that no one would miss the swapped-out beef. Mushrooms are a superb source of savory glutamates, making them perfect for blending with beef and accentuating the meat's own distinct umami; mushrooms also have a spongy chew that incorporated seamlessly into the beef. Taking cues from an innovative approach originally developed for our Mushroom-Beef Blended Burgers (page 186), we blitzed mushrooms and canned chickpeas (the neutral-flavored legumes lent bulk and didn't eclipse the beef) in a food processor; we then added the meat as well as other binders. Processing the beef in the food processor developed the meat's myosin—a protein that gives meat "bounciness"—which we needed to give structure to our mushroom-heavy meatballs. Panko bread crumbs lightened and tenderized the meatballs' texture, making them easy to cut with the side of a fork. Finally, we incorporated sautéed onions and garlic, as well as a few other traditional meatball seasonings, like Parmesan and oregano. The result was a meatball that was only 40 percent beef, but—paired with a quick and flavorful tomato sauce and a tangle of spaghetti—100 percent satisfaction. This recipe makes enough meatballs and sauce to serve with 12 ounces of pasta; reserve ½ cup of pasta cooking water to adjust the consistency of the sauce as needed. Alternatively, serve the meatballs and sauce in sub rolls or with our Creamy Parmesan Polenta (page 327).

2 tablespoons extra-virgin olive oil

2 onions, chopped fine (2 cups)

5 garlic cloves, minced

2 teaspoons dried oregano

¼ teaspoon red pepper flakes

¼ cup dry red wine

1 (28-ounce) can crushed tomatoes

½ cup water

1½ ounces Parmesan cheese, grated (¾ cup), divided, plus extra for serving

3 tablespoons chopped fresh basil

1 teaspoon table salt, divided

¼ teaspoon sugar

12 ounces white mushrooms, trimmed

¾ cup canned chickpeas, rinsed

12 ounces 85 percent lean ground beef, broken into rough 1½-inch pieces

6 tablespoons panko bread crumbs

½ teaspoon pepper

1 Heat oil in large saucepan over medium heat until shimmering. Cook onions, stirring occasionally, until golden around edges, about 10 minutes. Stir in garlic, oregano, and pepper flakes and cook until fragrant, about 30 seconds. Transfer half of onion mixture to medium bowl and set aside.

2 Add wine to onions in pot and cook over medium heat until mostly evaporated, 30 to 60 seconds. Stir in tomatoes and water and bring to simmer. Reduce heat to low and cook, covered, stirring occasionally, for 15 minutes. Off heat, stir in ¼ cup Parmesan, basil, ¼ teaspoon salt, and sugar; cover to keep warm.

3 Adjust oven rack to upper-middle position and heat oven to 475 degrees. Line rimmed baking sheet with aluminum foil and place wire rack on sheet. Spray rack with vegetable oil spray. While sauce simmers, process mushrooms and chickpeas in food processor until smooth paste forms (paste will resemble thick oatmeal), scraping down sides of bowl as needed, about 1 minute. Transfer to second bowl and cover. (Do not wash out processor bowl.)

4   Microwave mushroom–chickpea mixture until liquid released begins to boil, 3 to 5 minutes, stirring halfway through microwaving. Transfer mixture to large fine-mesh strainer set over large liquid measuring cup. Using spatula, press on mixture to extract ½ cup liquid (if more than ½ cup is removed, stir extra liquid back into mushroom mixture). Discard liquid and add mushroom mixture to bowl with reserved onion mixture. Refrigerate to cool slightly, about 10 minutes.

5   Return mushroom–onion mixture to food processor bowl. Add beef and remaining ¾ teaspoon salt and process until mixture is uniform and begins to pull away from sides of processor bowl, 15 to 20 seconds; transfer to now-empty bowl. Add panko, pepper, and remaining ½ cup Parmesan, and knead mixture with your hands until well combined. Divide mixture into 12 scant ⅓-cup portions, then roll into balls. (Meatballs can be refrigerated for up to 24 hours before cooking.) Place on prepared rack, spacing meatballs evenly apart, and roast until golden brown on top, about 20 minutes.

6   Serve meatballs with sauce and extra Parmesan.

Pittsburgh-Style Haluski

Why This Recipe Works This rendition of haluski—a buttery combination of tender cabbage, onions, and egg noodles—draws inspiration from the Hungarian interpretation served at the now-closed Józsa Corner in Pittsburgh. Though this recipe features no meat, it brims with savoriness and is supremely comforting and hearty. To start, we slowly cooked the cabbage and onions in butter until deeply golden brown, which imbued the vegetables with richness. Adding a hefty amount of salt helped draw out moisture from the vegetables and concentrate their flavors, while a cup of water created steam that, when the skillet was covered, enabled the vegetables to soften efficiently. Frequent stirring incorporated the browning vegetables back into the mix and kept the sugars from burning. After tossing the cabbage mixture with egg noodles, as well as more butter for an extra dose of richness, we showered it all with fresh dill for an herbaceous note and served it with cooling sour cream. Use a sharp knife or a food processor fitted with a slicing blade to slice the cabbage. You will need a 12-inch non-stick skillet with a tight-fitting lid for this recipe.

1 Melt 4 tablespoons butter in 12-inch nonstick skillet over medium-high heat. Add cabbage, onions, water, garlic, and salt. Cover and cook, stirring occasionally, until cabbage is softened, about 15 minutes. (Pan will be very full and lid may not fit at first; vegetables will decrease in volume as they cook.)

2 Remove lid and continue to cook, stirring often, until vegetables are deep golden brown and sticky, about 25 minutes longer.

3 Meanwhile, bring 4 quarts water to boil in large pot. Add noodles and 1 tablespoon salt and cook, stirring often, until tender. Drain noodles and return to pot.

4 Off heat, add 1 tablespoon dill, cooked cabbage mixture, and remaining 4 tablespoons butter to noodles and toss until butter is melted and vegetables and noodles are evenly combined. Season with salt and pepper to taste. Transfer to platter and sprinkle with remaining 1 tablespoon dill. Serve, dolloping individual portions with sour cream.

  8 tablespoons unsalted butter, cut into 1-tablespoon pieces, divided

  1 head green cabbage (2 pounds), cored and sliced thin

  2 onions, halved and sliced thin

  1 cup water

  2 garlic cloves, minced

1¼ teaspoons table salt, plus more for cooking noodles

12 ounces (6 cups) wide egg noodles

  2 tablespoons minced fresh dill, divided

    Sour cream

Vegetable Lasagna

Why This Recipe Works Lasagna is a classic comfort food, so we wanted to develop an extremely hearty version starring vegetables. Eggplant and mushroom made excellent choices: Not only do they have pleasingly chewy texture, but they're also wonderful at taking on seasonings. Microwaving the eggplant and sautéing the mushrooms eliminated excess moisture—ensuring a sturdy and not watery lasagna—and deepened their flavors. Swapping white lasagna noodles for whole-wheat was an easy choice; it gave our dish a dose of added fiber, making for a heartier lasagna. To keep our sauce simple, we pureed canned tomatoes with basil, olive oil, and garlic. For the cheesy layers, we blitzed part-skim ricotta with spinach and basil in a food processor, which gave us a bright green filling that was rich and milky, yet so ethereally airy it was reminiscent of soufflé. A mix of mozzarella and Parmesan made the perfect topping, crisping up in the oven to a delectable golden brown. You will need a 12-inch nonstick skillet with a tight-fitting lid and a 13 by 9-inch baking dish for this recipe.

Tomato Sauce

- 1 (28-ounce) can crushed tomatoes
- 1 (14.5-ounce) can diced tomatoes, drained
- ¼ cup fresh basil leaves
- 1 tablespoon extra-virgin olive oil
- 2 garlic cloves, minced
- ½ teaspoon table salt

Lasagna

- 12 ounces whole-wheat lasagna noodles
- 1¼ teaspoons table salt, divided, plus salt for cooking noodles
- 8 ounces (8 cups) baby spinach
- ⅓ cup fresh basil leaves, plus 2 tablespoons chopped
- 2 tablespoons extra-virgin olive oil, divided
- 8 ounces (1 cup) part-skim ricotta cheese
- 1 large egg
- 1 ounce Parmesan cheese, grated (½ cup), divided
- ¼ teaspoon pepper
- 2 pounds eggplant, peeled and cut into ½-inch pieces
- 1½ pounds cremini mushrooms, trimmed and sliced thin
- 4 garlic cloves, minced
- 4 ounces whole-milk mozzarella cheese, shredded (1 cup)

1 For the tomato sauce Process all ingredients in food processor until smooth, about 30 seconds. Transfer to bowl and set aside.

2 For the lasagna Bring 4 quarts water to boil in large pot. Add lasagna noodles and 1 tablespoon salt and cook, stirring often, until just tender. Drain noodles and set aside. Pulse spinach, whole basil leaves, and 1 tablespoon oil in clean, dry food processor bowl until finely chopped, scraping down sides of bowl as needed, about 6 pulses. Add ricotta, egg, ¼ cup Parmesan, pepper, and ½ teaspoon salt and pulse until just combined, about 6 pulses; transfer to bowl and set aside.

3 Adjust oven rack to middle position and heat oven to 375 degrees. Line large plate with double layer of coffee filters and spray with vegetable oil spray. Toss eggplant with ½ teaspoon salt and spread evenly over coffee filters. Microwave eggplant, uncovered, until dry to touch and slightly shriveled, 10 to 12 minutes, stirring once halfway through microwaving.

4 Heat remaining 1 tablespoon oil in 12-inch nonstick skillet over medium-high heat until shimmering. Add mushrooms and remaining ¼ teaspoon salt and cook, covered, until mushrooms release their liquid, 6 to 8 minutes. Uncover, increase heat to high, stir in eggplant, and cook until vegetables are lightly browned, 8 to 10 minutes. Stir in garlic and cook until fragrant, about 30 seconds; remove skillet from heat.

5 Spread 1½ cups tomato sauce evenly over bottom of 13 by 9-inch baking dish. Arrange 4 noodles on top of sauce (noodles will overlap). Spread half of ricotta mixture over noodles in even layer. Spread half of eggplant mixture over ricotta. Repeat layering with 1 cup sauce, 4 noodles, remaining half of ricotta and remaining half of eggplant mixture. For final layer, arrange remaining 4 noodles on top and cover completely with remaining 1½ cups tomato sauce. Sprinkle with mozzarella and remaining ¼ cup Parmesan.

6 Cover dish tightly with greased aluminum foil and bake until edges are just bubbling, about 35 minutes, rotating dish halfway through baking. Remove foil from lasagna, return to oven, and continue to bake until top is lightly browned, 10 to 15 minutes longer. Let lasagna cool for 20 minutes, then sprinkle with remaining 2 tablespoons basil. Serve.

Dan Dan Mian with Shiitake Mushrooms

Why This Recipe Works A popular dish in China's Sichuan province, dan dan mian consists of chewy noodles bathed in a spicy, fragrant chili sauce and topped with deeply savory pork and juicy bok choy. We wanted a version that was light on meat without sacrificing the big flavors that make this dish iconic, so we opted for just 4 ounces of pork bulked up with minced shiitakes. The mushrooms lent umami, while their chewy, spongy texture helped them blend seamlessly with the pork. Gently heating Sichuan chili powder, ground Sichuan peppercorns, and cinnamon in vegetable oil for 10 minutes yielded a flavorful chili-oil base for the sauce. Whisking in soy sauce, Chinese black vinegar, sweet wheat paste, and Chinese sesame paste added earthy, faintly sweet depth and appropriately thickened the mixture. We spread the ground pork into a thin layer across the wok with a spatula, jabbed at it with the tool's edge to break the meat into bits, and then seared them to produce ultracrispy pieces that clung to the noodles. Blanched baby bok choy punctuated the dish with its bright color and provided a palate-cleansing element. Saving the blanching water to boil the noodles was efficient; we rinsed the noodles after cooking to wash away any surface starch that would have caused them to stick together. Ya cai, Sichuan preserved mustard greens, gave these noodles a funky boost; look for it online or at a Chinese grocery store. If you can't find it, omit and increase soy sauce in step 2 to 2 teaspoons. Look for sesame paste that is dark and smooth; stir before using. If you can't find it, you can substitute unsalted, unsweetened natural peanut butter. You can substitute gochugaru (Korean chili flakes) for the Sichuan chili powder, and 8 ounces of dried Chinese wheat noodles or lo mein noodles for the fresh Chinese wheat noodles.

Sauce

- ¼ cup vegetable oil
- 1 tablespoon Sichuan chili powder
- 2 teaspoons Sichuan peppercorns, ground fine
- ¼ teaspoon ground cinnamon
- 2 tablespoons soy sauce
- 2 teaspoons Chinese black vinegar
- 2 teaspoons sweet wheat paste or hoisin sauce
- 1½ teaspoons Chinese sesame paste

Noodles

- 4 ounces ground pork
- 2 teaspoons Shaoxing wine
- 1 teaspoon soy sauce
- 1 tablespoon vegetable oil, divided
- 8 ounces shiitake mushrooms, minced
- 3 garlic cloves, minced
- 2 teaspoons grated fresh ginger
- 2 small heads baby bok choy (about 3 ounces each), trimmed, halved lengthwise, and rinsed
- 1 pound fresh Chinese wheat noodles
- ⅓ cup ya cai
- 2 scallions, sliced thin

1 For the sauce Heat oil, chili powder, peppercorns, and cinnamon in 14-inch flat-bottomed wok or 12-inch nonstick skillet over low heat for 10 minutes. Using silicone spatula, scrape oil mixture into small bowl (do not wash wok). Whisk soy sauce, vinegar, wheat paste, and sesame paste into oil mixture. Divide evenly among 4 shallow bowls.

2 For the noodles Bring 4 quarts water to boil in large pot. While water comes to boil, combine pork, Shaoxing wine, and soy sauce in medium bowl and toss with your hands until well combined; set aside.

3 Heat 2 teaspoons oil in now-empty wok over medium-high heat until shimmering. Add mushrooms and cook until mushroom liquid is evaporated, about 3 minutes. Add reserved pork mixture and use silicone spatula to smear into thin layer across surface of wok. Break up meat mixture into ¼-inch chunks with edge of spatula and cook, stirring frequently, until pork is firm and well browned, about 5 minutes. Push pork mixture to far side of wok and add garlic, ginger, and remaining 1 teaspoon oil to cleared space. Cook, stirring constantly, until garlic mixture begins to brown, about 1 minute. Stir to combine pork and mushroom mixture with garlic mixture. Remove wok from heat.

4 Add bok choy to boiling water and cook until leaves are vibrant green and stems are crisp-tender, about 1 minute. Using slotted spoon or spider skimmer, transfer bok choy to plate; set aside. Add noodles to boiling water and cook, stirring often, until almost tender (center should still be firm with slightly opaque dot). Drain noodles. Rinse under hot running water, tossing with tongs, for 1 minute. Drain well.

5 Divide noodles evenly among prepared bowls. Return wok with pork mixture to medium heat. Add ya cai and cook, stirring frequently, until warmed through, about 2 minutes. Spoon pork mixture evenly over noodles. Divide bok choy evenly among bowls, shaking to remove excess moisture as you portion. Top with scallions and serve, leaving each diner to stir components together before eating.

Mì Xào Giòn

Why This Recipe Works This mouthwatering Vietnamese favorite features a delicate tangle of golden noodles that are dropped into hot oil in a wok, fried until crisp, and topped with a stir-fry of proteins and vegetables in a glossy, umami-rich sauce. The delicately fried noodles should transform after they take on the sauce from the stir-fry—they might be tender, chewy, or crunchy, depending on when and where you take a bite. Because the dish has so many vegetables, we didn't need more than one small boneless pork loin chop, which is readily available in 8-ounce portions. We sliced it thin, tossed it in a solution of water and baking soda—to raise the meat's pH, helping it retain its moisture—and seasoned it with soy sauce and Shaoxing wine. We then blanched shiitakes, leaving the shiitake juices in place so they could penetrate the gai lan, bell pepper, and noodles that we boiled in the water next. Briefly cooking gai lan and bell pepper softened them slightly while retaining their crisp bite. Frying the noodles into a crisp disk gave us crunchy edges while the center stayed springy and pliable. After flavoring some oil with scallion and ginger, we quickly stir-fried our marinated pork slivers and used the juices left behind to stir-fry the shiitakes. We also stirred in umami powerhouses: oyster, soy, and fish sauces and chicken broth. Adding a cornstarch slurry thickened the whole mixture so that it was perfect for spooning over and clinging to our crisp noodles. For serving, kitchen shears or a large spoon work well for cutting through the softer noodles near the center.

1 (8-ounce) boneless pork chop, ¾ to 1 inch thick, trimmed of all visible fat

6 ounces gai lan, stalks trimmed

¼ teaspoon baking soda

4 teaspoons Shaoxing wine, divided

1 tablespoon soy sauce, divided

2½ tablespoons cornstarch

2 tablespoons oyster sauce

1½ tablespoons fish sauce

1 tablespoon sugar

1 teaspoon toasted sesame oil

¼ teaspoon white pepper

6 ounces shiitake mushrooms, stemmed and sliced ½ inch thick

1 red bell pepper, stemmed, seeded, and cut into ¾-inch pieces

6 ounces fresh or thawed frozen Hong Kong–style noodles

2½ cups vegetable oil, for frying

2 scallions, cut into 1½-inch pieces

2 teaspoons grated fresh ginger

1⅔ cups chicken broth

1 Place pork chop on plate and freeze until very firm, about 20 minutes. While pork freezes, prepare gai lan. Remove leaves, small stems, and florets from stalks; slice leaves crosswise into 1½-inch strips (any florets and stems can go into pile with leaves); and cut stalks on bias into ¼-inch-thick pieces. Set aside.

2 Stir 1 tablespoon water and baking soda together in medium bowl. When pork is firm, use sharp knife to shave pork crosswise as thin as possible. (Slices needn't be perfectly intact.) Transfer to bowl with baking soda mixture and toss until well coated. Add 1 teaspoon Shaoxing wine and 2 teaspoons soy sauce and toss to combine. Set aside.

3 Bring 4 quarts water to boil in large pot. While water heats, stir cornstarch and ¼ cup water together in small bowl. Stir oyster sauce, fish sauce, sugar, sesame oil, white pepper, and remaining 1 teaspoon soy sauce together in separate bowl.

4 Add mushrooms to boiling water and cook until tender and pliant, about 30 seconds. Using spider skimmer or slotted spoon, transfer mushrooms to bowl. Return water to boil. Add bell pepper and cook until crisp-tender, about 30 seconds. Using spider skimmer, transfer bell pepper to second bowl. Return water to boil. Add gai lan and cook until stems are crisp-tender, about 1 minute. Using spider skimmer, transfer gai lan to bowl with bell pepper.

5   Return water to boil. Add noodles and cook, stirring often, until almost tender (center of noodles should be firm with slight opaque dot), 45 to 90 seconds. Drain noodles in colander and rinse under cold running water, tossing with tongs, until cool to touch, about 1 minute. Drain noodles very well.

6   Line large serving plate with triple layer of paper towels. Add oil to 14-inch flat-bottomed wok or 12-inch cast-iron skillet until it measures about ¾ inch deep and heat over medium-high heat to 350 degrees. Carefully lower noodles into oil (oil will bubble vigorously; do not use colander to tip noodles into oil). Using spatula, spread noodles into even layer. Fry until outer 2 inches of noodle disk are crisp and lightly browned, 3 to 5 minutes, occasionally rotating disk for even crisping. Using 2 thin spatulas, transfer noodle disk to prepared plate. Carefully pour off oil from wok into bowl. Reserve 1 tablespoon oil (reserve remaining oil for other use) and wipe out wok. Leaving noodle disk on plate, remove and discard paper towels. Pour off any excess water from cooked bell pepper and gai lan.

7   Heat now-empty wok over medium heat until smoking. Add 1½ teaspoons reserved oil, scallions, and ginger and cook, stirring constantly, until fragrant, about 15 seconds. Increase heat to high and add pork. Cook, stirring constantly, until pork is no longer pink, 1 to 2 minutes. Transfer to bowl with bell pepper and gai lan.

8   Add remaining 1½ teaspoons reserved oil and mushrooms to now-empty wok and cook, stirring constantly, until mushrooms have shrunken slightly, about 2 minutes. Add remaining 1 tablespoon Shaoxing wine and cook, stirring constantly, until no liquid remains in wok, about 15 seconds. Add oyster sauce mixture and cook, stirring constantly, until bubbling, about 15 seconds.

9   Add broth, pork, and vegetables and bring to simmer. Stir cornstarch mixture to recombine; add to wok; and cook, stirring constantly, until sauce is thick and translucent, about 1 minute. Spoon pork and vegetables over noodles and serve immediately. Use large spoon to cut through noodles at table; scoop noodles and stir-fry onto individual serving plates.

SERVES 4 TO 6 | TOTAL TIME 2 HOURS, PLUS 1½ HOURS CHILLING • *vegetarian* •

Celery Root Galette with Blue Cheese and Walnuts

Why This Recipe Works When we set out to develop a showstopping savory vegetarian galette worthy of a dinner party, we wanted the filling to showcase a vegetable that was sturdy and flavorful, ensuring pleasing bite and maximum heartiness. Celery root, with its herbaceous aroma and firm texture, proved to be just the ticket; we softened it in a skillet for flavorful browning. Tossing the vegetable in a glaze of orange juice, honey, vinegar, and thyme injected it with sweet, tangy, and earthy notes. For the dough, we used a mix of all-purpose and whole-wheat flours for a heartier chew and extra nuttiness. To assemble the galette, we layered on a fragrant mixture of browned leeks and wilted spinach. We also added blue cheese; its pungence and funk complemented the herbaceous character of the vegetables. For a finishing gremolata, we combined parsley, orange zest, and garlic, which gave the dish a refreshing component that tied all the flavors together. You will need a 12-inch ovensafe skillet with a tight-fitting lid for this recipe. If you don't have a bowl large enough to accommodate the entire amount of spinach, microwave it in a smaller bowl in 2 batches; reduce the water to 2 tablespoons per batch and microwave the spinach for about 1½ minutes.

Dough

- 1 cup (5 ounces) all-purpose flour
- ½ cup (2¾ ounces) whole-wheat or rye flour
- ½ cup chopped walnuts
- 1 tablespoon sugar
- ¾ teaspoon table salt
- 10 tablespoons unsalted butter, cut into ½-inch pieces and chilled
- 7 tablespoons ice water
- 1 teaspoon distilled white vinegar

Filling

- 3 tablespoons plus 1 teaspoon extra-virgin olive oil, divided
- 1½ pounds celery root, peeled and cut into ¾-inch pieces
- 1 teaspoon kosher salt, divided
- ⅛ teaspoon pepper
- 6 ounces (6 cups) baby spinach
- 1½ pounds leeks, white and light green parts only, sliced ½ inch thick and washed thoroughly (4½ cups)
- 3 sprigs fresh thyme, plus ½ teaspoon minced
- 2 tablespoons crème fraîche
- 1 tablespoon Dijon mustard
- 3 tablespoons orange juice
- 2 tablespoons honey
- 2 teaspoons distilled white vinegar
- 3 ounces blue cheese, crumbled (¾ cup), divided
- 1 large egg, lightly beaten

Gremolata

- 2 tablespoons minced fresh parsley
- 1 teaspoon grated orange zest
- 1 garlic clove, minced

1 For the dough Pulse all-purpose flour, whole-wheat flour, walnuts, sugar, and salt in food processor until walnuts are finely ground, 8 to 10 pulses. Add butter and pulse until butter is cut into pea-size pieces, about 10 pulses. Transfer mixture to medium bowl and sprinkle water and vinegar over top. Using silicone spatula, fold mixture until loose, shaggy mass forms with some dry flour remaining (do not overwork). Transfer mixture to center of large sheet of plastic wrap, press gently into rough 4-inch square, and wrap tightly. Refrigerate for 45 minutes.

2 Transfer dough to lightly floured counter. Roll into 11 by 8-inch rectangle with short side parallel to counter edge. Starting at bottom of dough, fold into thirds like business letter to make 8 by 4-inch rectangle. Turn dough 90 degrees counterclockwise. Roll out lengthwise again into 11 by 8-inch rectangle and fold into thirds. Turn dough 90 degrees counterclockwise and repeat rolling and folding dough into thirds, then fold dough in half to create 4-inch square. Press top of dough gently to seal. Wrap tightly in plastic wrap and refrigerate for at least 45 minutes or up to 2 days (or freeze for up to 1 month).

3 **For the filling** Adjust oven rack to lower-middle position, place baking stone on rack, and heat oven to 425 degrees. Heat 1 tablespoon oil in 12-inch skillet over medium heat until shimmering. Add celery root, ½ teaspoon salt, and pepper and cook, stirring occasionally, until softened and lightly browned, 5 to 7 minutes. Place skillet on baking stone and roast until deep golden brown and tender, 8 to 16 minutes, stirring halfway through roasting. Being careful of hot skillet handle, transfer celery root to plate; set aside. Wipe skillet clean with paper towels.

4 Meanwhile, microwave spinach and ¼ cup water in large covered bowl until spinach is wilted and decreased in volume by half, 3 to 4 minutes. Remove bowl from microwave and keep covered for 1 minute. Carefully transfer spinach to colander and, using back of silicone spatula, gently press spinach against colander to release excess liquid. Transfer spinach to cutting board and chop. Return spinach to colander and press again with spatula.

5 Heat 1 tablespoon oil in now-empty skillet over medium heat until shimmering. Add leeks and minced thyme; cover; and cook, stirring occasionally, until leeks are tender and beginning to brown, 5 to 7 minutes. Transfer leek mixture to medium bowl; add spinach, crème fraîche, and mustard; and gently stir to combine. Season with salt and pepper to taste; set aside. Wipe skillet clean with paper towels.

6 Bring 3 tablespoons water, orange juice, honey, vinegar, and thyme sprigs to simmer in again-empty skillet over medium-high heat. Cook, stirring constantly, until reduced to syrup consistency, about 2 minutes. Off heat, discard thyme springs. Add celery root to skillet and toss gently to coat with glaze.

7 Remove dough from refrigerator and let sit at room temperature for 15 minutes. Roll dough into 14-inch circle on generously floured counter. Trim edges as needed to form uniform circle. Transfer dough to parchment paper–lined rimmed baking sheet (dough will hang over edges of sheet). With plastic drinking straw or tip of paring knife, cut five ¼-inch circles in dough (one at center and four evenly spaced midway from center to edge of dough). Brush top of dough with 2 teaspoons oil.

8 Spread half of leek and spinach filling evenly over dough, leaving 2-inch border around edge. Sprinkle with 6 tablespoons blue cheese and top with remaining leek and spinach filling. Evenly distribute celery root over filling. Sprinkle with remaining 6 tablespoons blue cheese and drizzle with remaining 2 teaspoons oil. Carefully grasp 1 edge of dough and fold up outer 2 inches over filling. Repeat around circumference of tart, overlapping dough every 2 to 3 inches; gently pinch pleated dough to secure, but do not press dough into filling. Brush dough with egg and sprinkle with remaining ½ teaspoon salt.

9 Reduce oven temperature to 375 degrees, then immediately place sheet on baking stone and bake galette until crust is deep golden brown and filling is beginning to brown, 35 to 45 minutes. Transfer galette, still on sheet, to wire rack and let cool for 10 minutes.

10 **For the gremolata** Combine all ingredients in bowl. Using wide metal spatula, loosen galette from parchment and carefully slide it off parchment onto cutting board. Sprinkle with gremolata, cut into wedges, and serve.

Celery Root Galette with Blue Cheese and Walnuts

(page 388)

Whole-Wheat Pizza with Kale and Sunflower Seed Pesto

Why This Recipe Works When we set out to develop a vegetarian recipe that would scratch any pizza itch while packing plenty of nutrients, we knew that a rich, very flavorful sauce would be our linchpin. We started by toasting garlic in a skillet until it was brown in spots and then toasting sunflower seeds to intensify their aroma. We then processed the two with kale and basil to make a wonderfully nutty pesto; some Parmesan added buttery funk. To give the pizza dough a fiber boost, we replaced over half of the bread flour with whole-wheat flour, which required making an extra-wet dough to ensure optimal chew. For toppings, we strewed the dough with more kale and sweet-tart cherry tomatoes; as the pizza baked, the greens turned wonderfully crisp, while the tomatoes oozed sweet-tart juices, complementing the earthy pesto underneath. A drizzle of olive oil and a few shavings of Parmesan before serving rounded out each bite with just the right amount of richness. The pizza dough needs to proof for at least 18 hours before baking. If you do not have a baking stone, you can use a preheated rimless (or inverted rimmed) baking sheet; however, the crust will be less crisp. Shape the second dough ball while the first pizza bakes, but don't top the second pizza until right before you bake it. You can use store-bought pizza dough if you prefer; just be sure to bring it to room temperature before shaping.

   2 garlic cloves, unpeeled

 ½ cup raw sunflower seeds

9½ ounces curly kale, stemmed and cut into 1½-inch pieces (5½ cups), divided

   1 cup fresh basil leaves

   1 teaspoon red pepper flakes (optional)

 ½ cup plus 1 tablespoon extra-virgin olive oil, divided, plus extra for drizzling

2½ ounces Parmesan cheese, 1½ ounces grated (¾ cup) and 1 ounce shaved (⅓ cup), divided

 ¼ teaspoon table salt

   1 recipe Whole-Wheat Pizza Dough (recipe follows)

   6 ounces cherry tomatoes, quartered, divided

1 Adjust oven rack to middle position, set baking stone on rack, and heat oven to 500 degrees. Toast garlic in 8-inch skillet over medium heat, shaking skillet occasionally, until softened and spotty brown, about 8 minutes. When garlic is cool enough to handle, remove and discard skins and chop coarse. Meanwhile, toast sunflower seeds in now-empty skillet over medium heat, stirring often, until golden and fragrant, 4 to 5 minutes.

2 Place 2 cups kale and basil in 1-gallon zipper-lock bag. Pound bag with flat side of meat pounder or with rolling pin until all leaves are bruised. Process garlic; sunflower seeds; bruised kale-basil mixture; and pepper flakes, if using, in food processor until finely chopped, about 1 minute, scraping down sides of bowl as needed. With processor running, slowly add ½ cup oil until incorporated. Transfer pesto to bowl, stir in grated Parmesan, and season with salt and pepper to taste. (Pesto can be refrigerated for up to 3 days or frozen for up to 3 months. To prevent browning, press plastic wrap flush to surface or top with thin layer of olive oil. Bring to room temperature before using.)

3 Combine salt, remaining 3½ cups kale, and remaining 1 tablespoon oil in bowl and massage lightly to coat leaves evenly; set aside. Heat broiler for 10 minutes. Press, stretch, and roll 1 dough ball into 12-inch round on lightly floured counter. Transfer dough to well-floured pizza peel and stretch into 13-inch round.

4 Spread half of pesto over surface of dough, leaving ½-inch border around edge. Scatter half of tomatoes and half of reserved kale mixture over pizza. Slide pizza carefully onto stone, return oven to 500 degrees, and bake until crust is well browned and edges of kale leaves are crisp and brown, 8 to 10 minutes. Remove pizza, place on wire rack, and let pizza rest for 5 minutes. Drizzle with extra oil and sprinkle with half of shaved Parmesan. Slice and serve.

5 Heat broiler for 10 minutes. Repeat process of stretching, topping, and baking with remaining dough ball and toppings, returning oven to 500 degrees when pizza is placed on stone.

Whole-Wheat Pizza Dough

Makes enough for two 13-inch pizzas | Total time: 25 minutes, plus 19 hours resting

1½ cups (8¼ ounces) whole-wheat flour

 1 cup (5½ ounces) bread flour

 2 teaspoons sugar

¾ teaspoon instant or rapid-rise yeast

1¼ cups ice water

 2 tablespoons extra-virgin olive oil

1¾ teaspoons table salt

1 Process whole-wheat flour, bread flour, sugar, and yeast in food processor until combined, about 2 seconds. With processor running, slowly add ice water and process until dough is just combined and no dry flour remains, about 10 seconds. Let dough rest for 10 minutes.

2 Add oil and salt to dough and process until dough forms satiny, sticky ball that clears sides of bowl, 45 to 60 seconds. Transfer dough to lightly oiled counter and knead by hand to form smooth, round ball, about 1 minute. Place dough seam side down in lightly greased large bowl, cover tightly with plastic wrap, and refrigerate for at least 18 hours or up to 2 days.

3 Remove dough from refrigerator and divide in half. Shape each half into smooth, tight ball. Space dough balls 3 inches apart on lightly oiled rimmed baking sheet, cover loosely with greased plastic wrap, and let rest for 1 hour.

Similar to the main dishes in this book, these sides make splendid use of umami-enhancing ingredients to jazz up vegetables. You can easily bulk up dinner with delicious plants, whether they're in the form of refreshing pai huang gua (Sichuan smashed cucumbers) or crisp-tender brussels sprouts.

More Veggies, Please

Braised Savoy Cabbage with Pancetta

Serves 4 to 6
Total time: 1 hour 10 minutes

Rendering pancetta on the stovetop enhanced our cabbage with intense umami and richness.

- 2 tablespoons unsalted butter
- 4 ounces pancetta, chopped fine
- 1 onion, halved and sliced thin
- 4 garlic cloves, sliced thin
- 1 head savoy cabbage (1½ pounds), cored and sliced thin
- 2 cups chicken broth
- 1 bay leaf
- 2 tablespoons minced fresh parsley

1 Melt butter in Dutch oven over medium heat. Add pancetta and cook until browned and fat is rendered, 5 to 7 minutes. Add onion and cook until softened and lightly browned, 5 to 7 minutes. Stir in garlic and cook until fragrant, about 30 seconds.

2 Stir in cabbage, broth, and bay leaf and bring to boil. Reduce heat to medium-low. Simmer, partially covered, until cabbage is tender and no broth remains, about 45 minutes. Discard bay leaf. Stir in parsley and season with salt and pepper to taste. Serve.

Pai Huang Gua

Serves 4
Total time: 30 minutes

Chinese black vinegar, soy sauce, and toasted sesame oil give this simple cucumber dish earthy, fragrant depth. A rasp-style grater makes quick work of turning the garlic into a paste.

- 2 English cucumbers
- 1½ teaspoons kosher salt
- 4 teaspoons Chinese black vinegar
- 1 teaspoon garlic, minced to paste
- 1 tablespoon soy sauce
- 2 teaspoons toasted sesame oil
- 1 teaspoon sugar
- 1 teaspoon sesame seeds, toasted

1 Trim and discard ends from cucumbers. Cut each cucumber crosswise into 3 equal lengths. Place pieces in large zipper-lock bag and seal bag. Using small skillet or rolling pin, firmly but gently smash cucumbers until flattened and split lengthwise into 3 or 4 spears each. Tear spears into rough 1- to 1½-inch pieces and transfer to colander set in large bowl. Toss cucumbers with salt and let stand for at least 15 minutes or up to 30 minutes.

2 While cucumbers sit, whisk vinegar and garlic together in small bowl; let stand for at least 5 minutes or up to 15 minutes.

3 Whisk soy sauce, oil, and sugar into vinegar mixture until sugar has dissolved. Transfer cucumbers to medium bowl, discarding any extracted liquid. Add dressing and sesame seeds to cucumbers and toss to combine. Serve immediately.

Skillet-Roasted Brussels Sprouts with Lemon and Pecorino Romano

Serves 4
Total time: 15 minutes

Nutty Pecorino Romano enriches brussels sprouts with funky flavor. Look for brussels sprouts that are similar in size, with small, tight heads that are no more than 1½ inches in diameter, as they're likely to be sweeter and more tender than larger sprouts.

- 1 pound small (1 to 1½ inches in diameter) brussels sprouts, trimmed and halved
- 5 tablespoons extra-virgin olive oil
- 1 tablespoon lemon juice
- ¼ teaspoon table salt
- ¼ cup shredded Pecorino Romano cheese

1 Arrange brussels sprouts in single layer, cut sides down, in 12-inch nonstick skillet. Drizzle oil evenly over sprouts. Cover skillet, place over medium-high heat, and cook until sprouts are bright green and cut sides have started to brown, about 5 minutes.

2 Uncover and continue to cook until cut sides of sprouts are deeply and evenly browned and paring knife slides in with little to no resistance, 2 to 3 minutes longer, adjusting heat and moving sprouts as necessary to prevent them from overbrowning. While brussels sprouts cook, combine lemon juice and salt in small bowl.

3 Off heat, add lemon juice mixture to skillet and stir to evenly coat brussels sprouts. Season with salt and pepper to taste. Transfer sprouts to large plate, sprinkle with Pecorino, and serve.

Pan-Steamed Kale with Garlic

Serves 4
Total time: 25 minutes

Steaming kale in chicken broth infuses the fiber-rich leaves with meaty savoriness.

- 1 cup chicken or vegetable broth
- 3 tablespoons extra-virgin olive oil, divided
- 1¼ pounds curly kale, stemmed and cut into 2-inch pieces (14 cups)
- 2 garlic cloves, sliced thin
- ⅛ teaspoon red pepper flakes
- 1 teaspoon lemon juice, plus extra for seasoning

1 Bring broth and 2 tablespoons oil to boil in Dutch oven over high heat. Add kale, cover, and reduce heat to medium-high. Cook until kale is tender with some resilience, about 7 minutes, stirring halfway through cooking. While kale cooks, combine garlic, pepper flakes, and remaining 1 tablespoon oil in small bowl.

2 Uncover, increase heat to high, and cook, stirring frequently, until liquid has evaporated and kale starts to sizzle, 2 to 3 minutes. Push kale to 1 side of pot, add garlic mixture to empty side, and cook until garlic is fragrant, about 1 minute. Stir garlic mixture into kale. Off heat, stir in lemon juice. Season with salt and extra lemon juice to taste. Serve.

Nutritional Information for Our Recipes

To calculate the nutritional values of our recipes per serving, we used The Food Processor SQL by ESHA Research. When using this program, we entered all the ingredients, using weights for important ingredients such as most vegetables. We also used our preferred brands in these analyses. When the recipe called for seasoning with an unspecified amount of salt and pepper, we added ½ teaspoon of salt and ¼ teaspoon of pepper to the analysis. We did not include additional salt or pepper for food that's "seasoned to taste." If there is a range in the serving size, we used the highest number of servings to calculate the nutritional values.

	Cal	Total Fat (g)	Sat Fat (g)	Chol (mg)	Sodium (mg)	Total Carbs (g)	Dietary Fiber (g)	Total Sugars (g)	Added Sugar (g)	Protein (g)
A Guide to Mostly Meatless Eating										
Fish Sauce Substitute (1 tbsp)	0	0	0	0	420	0	0	0	0	0
1 Breakfast All Day										
Fried Egg Sandwiches with Hummus and Sprouts	340	15	5	200	710	32	7	6	0	19
Breakfast Wraps with Sweet Potatoes and Broccolini	480	19	5	195	470	56	3	6	0	19
Kale and Black Bean Breakfast Burritos	310	14	3	185	780	31	5	3	0	13
Avocado and Bean Toast	250	13	2	0	690	26	8	3	0	8
Quick Sweet and Spicy Pickled Red Onion	10	0	0	0	10	2	0	2	1	0
Savory Oatmeal with Pancetta, Mushrooms, and Shaved Parmesan	410	20	5	25	800	43	7	4	0	18
Breakfast Fried Rice with Spinach and Shiitakes	540	28	6	150	670	57	8	6	3	16
Gochujang Maple Sauce	70	4	1	0	30	7	0	4	3	2
Mangú	440	23	8	40	970	51	4	25	2	12
Huevos Rancheros with Beans	230	9	2	185	1000	25	8	9	2	12
Ful Medames	340	13	1.5	0	810	45	9	1	0	15
Easy-Peel Hard-Cooked Eggs	70	5	1.5	185	70	0	0	0	0	6
Chilaquiles Verdes with Sheet-Pan Fried Eggs	570	37	8	200	790	48	7	7	0	17
Gallo Pinto	370	12	2.5	185	730	50	7	6	0	15
Ratatouille with Poached Eggs	290	20	3.5	185	570	21	7	12	0	11
Smoked Trout Hash with Eggs	300	14	3	210	420	25	5	3	0	19

	Cal	Total Fat (g)	Sat Fat (g)	Chol (mg)	Sodium (mg)	Total Carbs (g)	Dietary Fiber (g)	Total Sugars (g)	Added Sugar (g)	Protein (g)
2 Soups, Stews, and Chilis										
Spiced Chicken Soup with Squash and Navy Beans	220	5	1	55	990	28	6	3	0	18
Garlic–Chicken and Wild Rice Soup	240	9	1	30	280	25	4	3	0	17
Carrot Ribbon, Chicken, and Coconut Curry Soup	440	29	14	100	850	23	4	11	3	25
Tortilla Soup with Black Beans and Spinach	270	11	1	55	920	27	3	3	0	17
Chickpea Noodle Soup	200	7	0	0	820	27	5	5	0	8
Creamy White Bean Soup with Chorizo Oil and Garlicky Bread Crumbs	430	26	7	20	960	33	7	3	0	15
Black Bean Soup with Chipotle Chiles	400	9	1.5	10	1320	58	9	11	0	21
Soupe au Pistou	270	13	2.5	5	620	28	7	4	0	11
Lentil and Escarole Soup	260	10	1.5	0	890	34	9	4	0	10
Turkish Bulgur and Lentil Soup	330	9	1.5	0	740	49	9	3	0	16
Chorba Frik	270	13	2.5	40	850	25	7	3	0	13
Creamy Butternut Squash Soup with Sausage Crumbles and Apple	290	9	2.5	15	1130	45	7	13	0	13
Hot and Sour Soup	170	8	2	50	517	10	1	3	0	13
Miso Dashi Soup with Udon and Halibut	410	6	0.5	35	1010	66	8	4	0	28
Shiitake, Tofu, and Mustard Greens Soup	140	6	0.5	0	770	12	2	3	0	9
Laksa Soup	670	24	11	120	1260	89	5	44	4	28
Crispy Shallots	15	1	0	0	0	1	0	1	0	0
Madzoon ov Kofte	410	22	10	90	1290	34	5	4	0	19
Almost Beefless Beef Stew	350	12	2	45	820	36	5	10	0	20
Bean Bourguignon	330	11	1.5	0	890	39	10	10	0	14
Beans Marbella	480	11	2.5	15	1540	78	17	24	7	22
Green Gumbo	220	15	1	0	810	20	5	3	0	5
Caldo Verde	360	24	7	35	1190	22	2	1	0	14
Kimchi Jjigae	230	13	2	20	1290	10	2	4	1	19
Misir Wot	290	12	1.5	0	660	37	10	5	0	12
Palak Dal	260	9	4.5	20	620	33	9	1	0	15
Sancocho	430	14	4.5	45	1120	63	5	15	0	17
Hot Ukrainian Borscht	240	11	2	40	750	22	5	7	0	15
Simple Beef Chili with Kidney Beans	490	24	7	75	1260	43	11	16	0	31
Vegetarian Chili	400	12	1.5	0	1700	59	14	7	0	15

	Cal	Total Fat (g)	Sat Fat (g)	Chol (mg)	Sodium (mg)	Total Carbs (g)	Dietary Fiber (g)	Total Sugars (g)	Added Sugar (g)	Protein (g)
2 Soups, Stews, and Chilis Continued										
Classic Croutons	60	4	0.5	0	60	5	0	1	0	1
Umami Croutons	50	3	0	0	80	5	0	0	0	1
Herbed Croutons	70	2	1	5	75	11	0	2	0	2
Pita Crumble	40	2.5	0	0	75	4	0	0	0	1
Crispy Leeks	25	2	0	0	0	2	0	1	0	0
Chili Oil	90	10	1.5	0	50	1	1	0	0	0
3 Salads and Bowls										
Charred Broccoli Salad with Avocado, Grapefruit, and Ginger–Lime Dressing	350	22	2.5	0	510	39	14	19	4	9
Chicken and Arugula Salad with Figs and Warm Spices	390	23	3	55	340	26	6	14	1	23
Neorm Sach Moan	230	6	1	30	1300	28	5	18	13	17
Pinto Bean, Ancho, and Beef Salad with Pickled Poblanos	570	27	10	85	1260	47	14	9	5	37
Bitter Greens and Chickpea Salad with Warm Vinaigrette	410	21	4	10	630	46	9	26	0	10
Shrimp and White Bean Salad	370	19	2.5	105	940	29	8	5	0	21
Chopped Salad with Spiced Skillet–Roasted Chickpeas	260	13	3.5	15	790	27	8	6	3	11
Charred Cabbage Salad with Torn Tofu and Plantain Chips	450	31	5	0	1040	37	6	20	4	14
Beet and Carrot Noodle Salad with Chicken	420	21	3.5	60	930	35	8	20	5	28
Salmon, Avocado, Grapefruit, and Watercress Salad	360	26	4.5	40	370	15	7	7	0	18
Shaved Salad with Pan–Seared Scallops	470	25	4	40	860	38	8	19	4	25
Zucchini Noodle Salad with Tahini–Ginger Dressing	250	17	2.5	0	820	19	5	9	3	10
Farro and Kale Salad with Fennel, Olives, and Pecorino	270	11	2	5	380	36	5	2	0	10
Bulgur Salad with Spinach, Chickpeas, and Apples	580	29	3.5	0	530	72	14	15	4	14
Quinoa Taco Salad	280	14	2.5	5	470	30	9	3	0	9
Sweet Potato and Lentil Salad with Crispy Shallots	440	19	6	15	580	52	13	5	0	20
Roasted Vegetable and Black Chickpea Salad	320	16	5	10	220	44	4	12	0	13
Harissa	110	11	1.5	0	150	2	1	0	0	1
Gado Gado	700	43	11	185	610	49	7	15	7	25
Indian–Spiced Carrot and Coconut Salad with Tilapia	400	19	3.5	35	870	39	8	17	9	22
Green Goodness Bowl	520	26	6	135	460	18	8	5	0	54
Spinach Pesto Pasta Bowl	350	10	2.5	10	740	53	5	5	0	18

	Cal	Total Fat (g)	Sat Fat (g)	Chol (mg)	Sodium (mg)	Total Carbs (g)	Dietary Fiber (g)	Total Sugars (g)	Added Sugar (g)	Protein (g)
3 Salads and Bowls Continued										
Saffron Bulgur with Fennel and Sausage Bowl	620	26	8	95	1050	65	12	18	0	33
Smoked Salmon Niçoise Bowl	450	19	6	295	410	25	4	5	0	45
Spiced Vegetable Couscous Bowl	350	15	2	0	700	45	6	5	0	10
Ras el Hanout	30	1	0	0	0	5	3	0	0	1
Quinoa, Black Bean, and Mango Bowl	450	27	3.5	0	540	45	8	3	0	9
Spring Halloumi and Freekeh Bowl	760	32	12	45	1120	90	22	11	0	32
Tahini–Garlic Sauce	45	3.5	0.5	0	100	3	0	1	0	1
California Barley Bowls with Avocado, Snow Peas, and Lemon–Mint Yogurt Sauce	550	34	5	5	750	55	14	6	0	13
Beet Poke Bowl	670	28	3.5	0	1130	93	10	13	0	22
Herby Grain Bowl with Fried Eggs and Pickled Edamame	510	22	4.5	185	970	59	8	3	0	18
Laksa Cauliflower Rice Bowl with Shrimp	270	11	4	75	760	26	8	12	3	14
Crispy Tempeh	200	12	1	0	130	13	1	0	0	10
Chipotle Shrimp	80	3	0	95	210	1	0	0	0	10
Lemony Shrimp	70	3	0	95	210	1	0	0	0	10
Gochujang Meatballs	330	21	6	115	850	16	1	7	6	20
Savory Seed Brittle	80	5	1	0	135	6	1	2	2	3
4 Burgers, Sandwiches, Tacos, and More										
Mushroom–Beef Blended Burgers	520	31	12	95	870	27	1	6	0	29
Bacon and Cheese Black Bean Burgers	520	29	7	95	1200	46	5	7	2	18
Black Bean Mole Burgers	330	11	2	45	1070	46	5	7	0	13
Turkey–Zucchini Burgers with Cranberry Relish	400	9	3.5	55	1120	44	3	21	13	37
Turkey–Zucchini Burgers with Smashed Ranch Avocado	510	28	8	105	1020	31	5	6	0	33
Crispy Chickpea Cakes with Zucchini Ribbon Salad	410	27	5	35	1150	32	8	4	0	13
Curried Millet Burgers with Peach–Ginger Chutney	440	19	2.5	50	750	60	8	16	7	11
Pulled Jackfruit and Chicken Sandwiches	450	15	3.5	90	1080	53	7	22	0	25
Philly–Style Sausage and Broccoli Rabe Subs with Portobello	550	27	9	50	1160	48	6	9	0	30
Tofu Katsu Sandwich	470	23	4	95	1130	47	2	9	4	18
Bánh Xèo	370	16	4.5	70	700	45	3	14	9	14
Đồ Chua	70	0	0	0	320	18	2	15	13	1
Creamy Mushroom and Pink Pickled Cabbage Sandwiches	240	9	2.5	10	600	35	5	8	1	8

	Cal	Total Fat (g)	Sat Fat (g)	Chol (mg)	Sodium (mg)	Total Carbs (g)	Dietary Fiber (g)	Total Sugars (g)	Added Sugar (g)	Protein (g)
4 Burgers, Sandwiches, Tacos, and More Continued										
Mushroom, Lettuce, and Tomato Sandwiches	450	13	2	0	1190	56	9	9	0	16
Chickpea Salad Sandwiches with Quick Pickles	490	27	4.5	105	1240	47	10	2	0	16
Spiced Smashed Chickpea Wraps	380	16	3.5	5	1470	46	9	3	0	15
Parsnip and Chicken Shawarma	740	30	6	90	1090	87	13	14	0	30
Ta'ameya	420	17	3.5	50	910	50	9	11	0	18
Pink Pickled Turnips	15	0	0	0	130	3	1	2	1	0
Mumbai Frankie Wraps	630	29	7	0	1150	82	11	5	2	16
Chapati	310	14	1	0	580	41	4	0	0	7
Black Bean and Cheese Arepas	530	23	7	25	1110	66	3	0	0	15
Tofu Summer Rolls with Spicy Almond Butter Sauce	290	10	1	0	670	38	5	9	0	15
Red Lentil Kibbeh	450	19	3	5	760	60	13	6	0	16
Blackened Chicken and Okra Tacos	530	26	3	70	840	51	10	6	0	25
Chipotle Mushroom and Cauliflower Tacos	470	22	4.5	20	960	60	9	15	6	12
Sweet Potato, Poblano, and Black Bean Tacos	540	20	4	10	1050	81	15	13	0	11
Nopales and Shrimp Tacos	370	14	3	115	550	44	10	4	0	18
Salmon Tacos with Super Slaw	470	24	5	55	850	42	8	2	0	23
Weeknight Ground Beef and Lentil Tacos	400	20	9	50	1080	35	10	7	1	22
Rajas Poblanas con Crema y Elote	380	19	10	50	310	47	6	5	0	6
Classic Burger Sauce	100	10	1.5	5	180	3	0	2	2	0
Avocado Crema	70	6	2.5	10	170	3	2	1	0	1
Tahini–Yogurt Sauce	40	3	1	0	115	2	0	0	0	1
Cilantro–Mint Chutney	10	0	0	0	35	1	0	1	0	0
Easy Barbecue Sauce	25	0.5	0	0	135	5	0	4	1	0
5 Everyday Dinners										
Red Curry Chicken and Sweet Potatoes	590	18	12	80	770	80	6	7	0	25
Kare Raisu	580	20	9	135	1100	66	5	5	1	31
Japanese Curry-Roux Bricks	150	11	7	30	60	10	1	1	1	1
Green Mole with Chayote and Chicken	360	17	3	105	1100	24	8	10	0	31
Cast Iron Steak and Vegetable Fajitas	560	25	8	55	1220	56	5	6	0	28
Stir-Fried Beef and Gai Lan	200	13	2.5	35	700	7	3	1	0	14
Cheesy Black Bean and Pork Skillet Bake	480	27	12	70	930	37	8	6	0	26
Squash, Pork, and Tamarind Curry	280	13	4.5	40	760	32	8	7	0	13

	Cal	Total Fat (g)	Sat Fat (g)	Chol (mg)	Sodium (mg)	Total Carbs (g)	Dietary Fiber (g)	Total Sugars (g)	Added Sugar (g)	Protein (g)
'Nduja with Beans and Greens	420	17	5	215	1190	38	12	6	0	33
Roasted Radicchio, Fennel, and Root Vegetables with Sausage and Herbs	480	24	6	35	1190	44	8	12	1	25
Sausage-Stuffed Portobello Mushrooms with Cabbage Salad	400	25	9	45	800	23	8	12	1	21
Okonomiyaki	480	34	10	125	960	31	2	7	3	12
Shrimp Okonomiyaki	300	12	2	165	1030	32	2	7	3	15
Warm White Beans with Tuna, Fennel, and Radishes	520	24	3.5	10	1180	54	10	6	0	23
Spiced Mahi-Mahi with Mashed Plantains and Pickled Onion	430	17	6	105	1160	51	4	26	5	23
Roasted Salmon with White Beans, Fennel, and Tomatoes	620	34	12	90	1290	43	15	13	0	36
Crispy Tempeh with Sambal Sauce	310	12	1.5	0	1240	33	3	9	5	17
Loaded Sweet Potato Wedges with Tempeh	520	27	4.5	0	710	55	10	15	0	13
Sweet and Spicy Glazed Tofu with Coconut-Braised Mustard Greens and Winter Squash	380	22	9	0	960	37	9	9	3	17
Mapo Tofu	310	21	4	25	930	9	1	2	0	18
Stir-Fried Portobellos with Soy-Maple Sauce	290	14	1.5	0	810	33	6	23	9	9
Charred Sichuan-Style Okra	360	28	2	0	770	18	4	6	0	3
Madras Okra Curry	260	22	8	0	320	14	4	4	2	5
Aloo Gobi	330	22	1.5	0	770	31	5	4	0	6
Jackfruit and Chickpea Makhani	410	17	4.5	20	1220	48	11	9	3	18
Chana Masala	210	10	1	0	740	24	8	2	0	8
Cheesy Bean and Tomato Bake	280	12	4	15	970	32	7	9	0	14
Stuffed Delicata Squash	500	26	11	45	1150	60	11	8	0	14
Kimchi Bokkeumbap	280	15	2.5	135	810	26	3	3	0	12
Steamed Short-Grain White Rice	130	0	0	0	0	29	1	0	0	2
Joloff-Inspired Fonio	290	14	3	10	970	38	2	4	1	4
Fregula with Chickpeas, Tomatoes, and Fennel	360	10	1.5	0	620	59	10	4	0	13
Orecchiette with Navy Beans, Brussels Sprouts, and Bacon	450	10	4	15	1060	74	10	3	0	20
Pea and Pistachio Pesto Pasta	580	27	4.5	5	890	67	6	5	0	17
Swiss Chard Macaroni and Cheese	530	25	10	55	730	57	7	9	0	25
Cashew e Pepe e Funghi	680	25	3.5	0	670	96	7	5	0	21
Rigatoni with Quick Mushroom Bolognese	380	9	1.5	0	510	63	4	5	0	13
Sesame Noodles with Pan-Seared Salmon	680	27	4.5	55	1360	75	4	14	4	34

	Cal	Total Fat (g)	Sat Fat (g)	Chol (mg)	Sodium (mg)	Total Carbs (g)	Dietary Fiber (g)	Total Sugars (g)	Added Sugar (g)	Protein (g)
5 Everyday Dinners Continued										
Yaki Udon	460	12	3.5	25	1200	67	6	10	2	20
Vegetable Lo Mein	460	11	1	5	1630	74	7	16	0	15
Soba Noodles with Roasted Eggplant and Sesame	510	23	3	0	1180	69	9	20	10	11
Hung Kao Mun Gati	240	9	7	0	300	39	1	2	2	4
Simple Brown Rice	170	1.5	0	0	100	35	2	0	0	3
Brown Rice Pilaf	290	8	4	15	430	49	3	2	0	6
Spiced Basmati Rice	200	6	3.5	15	390	33	1	0	0	3
Creamy Parmesan Polenta	190	5	3	15	730	27	2	0	0	6
6 Sunday Suppers										
Herby Roasted Cauliflower and Chicken with Quinoa Pilaf	570	34	7	120	710	37	6	6	0	29
Cannellini Beans with Chicken, Kale, and Mustard	510	20	3	80	1260	44	14	6	0	34
Peruvian Arroz con Pollo	330	6	1	70	790	45	2	3	0	21
Chicken and Spiced Freekeh with Cilantro and Preserved Lemon	330	11	1.5	55	1020	39	9	2	0	20
Turkey Shepherd's Pie	250	10	3	60	700	19	6	8	0	26
Pork Tenderloin with White Beans and Mustard Greens	560	22	8	90	1100	43	11	4	0	45
Bún Chả	630	28	9	80	1260	69	5	17	11	27
Spiced Stuffed Peppers	490	26	5	40	510	45	10	16	0	20
Hashweh Stuffed Swiss Chard	450	16	4	35	1290	59	5	11	0	19
Swiss Chard Enchiladas	400	18	4.5	15	1010	49	10	8	1	14
Brothy Savoy Cabbage with Pancetta, Rye Bread, and Fontina	390	21	9	45	1310	32	7	7	0	19
Cabbage, Kohlrabi, and Lamb Tagine with Prunes	440	21	7	45	610	47	7	21	5	17
Baharat Cauliflower and Eggplant with Chickpeas	570	26	4	0	1170	71	13	14	5	16
Baharat	20	1	0	0	0	5	2	0	0	1
Seared Tofu with Panch Phoron, Green Beans, and Pickled Shallot	410	27	4.5	10	710	23	6	8	0	24
Panch Phoron	40	2.5	0	0	5	4	2	0	0	2
Saag Tofu	280	18	3	5	570	19	6	7	1	13
Tacu Tacu	550	23	4	185	1410	65	16	1	0	19
Sarza Criolla	5	0	0	0	150	2	0	1	0	0
Gigantes Plaki	390	10	1.5	0	710	60	17	14	3	18
Red Beans and Rice with Okra and Tomatoes	480	7	3	15	910	81	12	5	0	22
Cuban-Style Black Beans and Rice	410	21	7	20	1190	46	3	4	0	10

	Cal	Total Fat (g)	Sat Fat (g)	Chol (mg)	Sodium (mg)	Total Carbs (g)	Dietary Fiber (g)	Total Sugars (g)	Added Sugar (g)	Protein (g)
6 Sunday Suppers Continued										
Cauliflower Biryani	320	12	2.5	5	450	49	5	9	0	8
Mushroom Tea Rice with Chicken and Caramel–Braised Shallots	730	21	5	75	1280	111	4.23	24	13	22
Beet Barley Risotto	480	11	2	5	960	73	16	7	0	16
Farro and Broccoli Rabe Gratin	410	13	2	5	840	61	10	5	0	17
Spinach and Ricotta Gnudi with Tomato–Butter Sauce	380	23	14	70	1080	19	5	3	0	21
Mostly Meatless Meatballs and Marinara	510	24	7	80	1320	38	7	15	0	35
Pittsburgh–Style Haluski	430	19	11	105	650	53	6	9	0	11
Vegetable Lasagna	400	14	5	45	1050	53	11	11	0	20
Dan Dan Mian with Shiitake Mushrooms	580	21	4.5	25	1240	75	5	11	0	21
Mì Xào Giòn	490	27	4	35	1340	42	4	9	3	20
Celery Root Galette with Blue Cheese and Walnuts	620	40	18	100	850	55	6	12	7	13
Whole–Wheat Pizza with Kale and Sunflower Seed Pesto	600	36	6	10	1000	56	8	3	1	18
Whole–Wheat Pizza Dough	280	6	1	0	680	49	5	2	1	9
Braised Savoy Cabbage with Pancetta	140	9	4.5	25	580	8	3	3	0	7
Pai Huang Gua	50	2.5	0	0	650	4	2	3	1	2
Skillet–Roasted Brussels Sprouts with Lemon and Pecorino Romano	240	20	3.5	5	300	10	4	3	0	7
Pan–Steamed Kale with Garlic	150	12	1.5	0	180	10	4	3	0	5

Conversions and Equivalents

Some say cooking is a science and an art. We would say that geography has a hand in it, too. Flour milled in the United Kingdom and elsewhere will feel and taste differ-ent from flour milled in the United States. So, while we cannot promise that the loaf of bread you bake in Canada or England will taste the same as a loaf baked in the States, we can offer guidelines for converting weights and measures. We also recommend that you rely on your instincts when making our recipes. Refer to the visual cues provided. If the dough hasn't "come together in a ball," as described, you may need to add more flour—even if the recipe doesn't tell you so. You be the judge.

The recipes in this book were developed using standard U.S. measures following U.S. government guidelines. The charts below offer equivalents for U.S. and metric measures. All conversions are approximate and have been rounded up or down to the nearest whole number.

Examples:

1 teaspoon = 4.929 milliliters, rounded up to 5 milliliters
1 ounce = 28.349 grams, rounded down to 28 grams

Volume Conversions

U.S.	Metric
1 teaspoon	5 milliliters
2 teaspoons	10 milliliters
1 tablespoon	15 milliliters
2 tablespoons	30 milliliters
¼ cup	59 milliliters
⅓ cup	79 milliliters
½ cup	118 milliliters
¾ cup	177 milliliters
1 cup	237 milliliters
1¼ cups	296 milliliters
1½ cups	355 milliliters
2 cups (1 pint)	473 milliliters
2½ cups	591 milliliters
3 cups	710 milliliters
4 cups (1 quart)	0.946 liter
1.06 quarts	1 liter
4 quarts (1 gallon)	3.8 liters

Weight Conversions

Ounces	Grams
½	14
¾	21
1	28
1½	43
2	57
2½	71
3	85
3½	99
4	113
4½	128
5	142
6	170
7	198
8	227
9	255
10	283
12	340
16 (1 pound)	454

Conversions for Common Baking Ingredients

Because measuring by weight is far more accurate than measuring by volume, and thus more likely to achieve reliable results, in our recipes we provide ounce measures in addition to cup measures for many ingredients. Refer to the chart below to convert these measures into grams.

Ingredient	Ounces	Grams
Flour		
1 cup all-purpose flour*	5	142
1 cup cake flour	4	113
1 cup whole-wheat flour	5½	156
Sugar		
1 cup granulated (white) sugar	7	198
1 cup packed brown sugar (light or dark)	7	198
1 cup confectioners' sugar	4	113
Cocoa Powder		
1 cup cocoa powder	3	85
Butter†		
4 tablespoons (½ stick, or ¼ cup)	2	57
8 tablespoons (1 stick, or ½ cup)	4	113
16 tablespoons (2 sticks, or 1 cup)	8	227

* U.S. all-purpose flour, the most frequently used flour in this book, does not contain leaveners, as some European flours do. These leavened flours are called self-rising or self-raising. If you are using self-rising flour, take this into consideration before adding leavening to a recipe.

† In the United States, butter is sold both salted and unsalted. We generally recommend unsalted butter. If you are using salted butter, take this into consideration before adding salt to a recipe.

Oven Temperature

Fahrenheit	Celsius	Gas Mark
225	105	¼
250	120	½
275	135	1
300	150	2
325	165	3
350	180	4
375	190	5
400	200	6
425	220	7
450	230	8
475	245	9

Converting Temperatures from an Instant-Read Thermometer

We include doneness temperatures in many of the recipes in this book. We recommend an instant-read thermometer for the job. Refer to the table above to convert Fahrenheit degrees to Celsius. Or, for temperatures not represented in the chart, use this simple formula:

Subtract 32 degrees from the Fahrenheit reading, then divide the result by 1.8 to find the Celsius reading.

Examples:
"Roast chicken until thighs register 175 degrees."

To convert:
175°F − 32 = 143°
143° ÷ 1.8 = 79.44°C, rounded down to 79°C

Index

Note: Page references in *italics* indicate photographs.

L

M